SPAIN
A HISTORY

SPAIN

A HISTORY

EDITED BY

RAYMOND CARR

946 S7335

Spain

OXFORD
UNIVERSITY PRESS

OXFORD
UNIVERSITY PRESS

Great Clarendon Street, Oxford OX2 6DP

Oxford University Press is a department of the University of Oxford.
It furthers the University's objective of excellence in research, scholarship,
and education by publishing worldwide in

Oxford New York

Athens Auckland Bangkok Bogotá Buenos Aires Calcutta
Cape Town Chennai Dar es Salaam Delhi Florence Hong Kong Istanbul
Karachi Kuala Lumpur Madrid Melbourne Mexico City Mumbai
Nairobi Paris São Paulo Singapore Taipei Tokyo Toronto Warsaw

and associated companies in Berlin Ibadan

Oxford is a registered trade mark of Oxford University Press
in the UK and certain other countries

Published in the United States
by Oxford University Press Inc., New York

British Library Cataloguing in Publication Data

Data available

Library of Congress Cataloging in Publication Data

Spain : a history / edited by Raymond Carr.
    Includes bibliographical references and index.
    I. Spain—History. I. Carr, Raymond.
    DP66.S63 2000 946—dc21 99-42639

ISBN 0-19-820619-4

10 9 8 7 6 5 4 3 2 1

Typeset by Best-set Typesetter Ltd., Hong Kong
Printed in Great Britain
on acid-free paper by
Biddles Ltd. *www.biddles.co.uk*

CONTENTS

List of Colour Plates   vii

List of Maps   viii

List of Contributors   ix

Introduction   1
RAYMOND CARR

1. Prehistoric and Roman Spain   11
A. T. FEAR

2. Visigothic Spain, 409–711   39
ROGER COLLINS

3. The Early Middle Ages, 700–1250   63
RICHARD FLETCHER

4. The Late Middle Ages, 1250–1500   90
ANGUS MACKAY

5. The Improbable Empire   116
FELIPE FERNÁNDEZ-ARMESTO

6. Vicissitudes of a World Power, 1500–1700   152
HENRY KAMEN

7. Flow and Ebb, 1700–1833   173
RICHARD HERR

8. Liberalism and Reaction, 1833–1931   205
RAYMOND CARR

9. Spain from 1931 to the Present   243
SEBASTIAN BALFOUR

Further Reading 283

Chronology 287

Illustration Sources 299

Index 301

LIST OF COLOUR PLATES

facing page

Mosaic from the tomb of Optimus (third century)
Museu Nacional Arqueòlogic de Tarragona 54

Votive crown of King Reccesuinth (seventh century)
Museo Arqueológico Nacional, Madrid 55

The Great Mosque of Córdoba (eighth century)
Oronoz 86

La Virgen de los Reyes Catolicos (Virgin of the Catholic Sovereigns)
Painting on wood, Anon (Escuela Hispano-Flamenca), 1490
Rights Reserved © Museo Nacional del Prado, Madrid 87

A hunt in honour of Charles V at the castle of Torgau, 1544,
by Lucas Cranach
Rights Reserved © Museo Nacional del Prado, Madrid 182

The Crockery Vendor, by Francisco Goya, 1778
Rights Reserved © Museo Nacional del Prado, Madrid 183

Poster celebrating the proclamation of the Second Republic, 1931
Postermil 214

Casa Batlló, Barcelona (1904–6), architect Antoni Gaudí
Paul Raftery/Arcaid 215

LIST OF MAPS

1. Prehistoric and Roman Spain   22
2. Visigothic Spain   40
3. Medieval Spain   90
4. Modern Spain   244

LIST OF CONTRIBUTORS

SEBASTIAN BALFOUR Reader and Assistant Director of the Canada Blanch Centre for Contemporary Spanish Studies at the London School of Economics and Political Science

RAYMOND CARR Former Warden of St Antony's College, Oxford

ROGER COLLINS University of Edinburgh

A. T. FEAR Lecturer in Classics, University of Manchester

FELIPE FERNÁNDEZ-ARMESTO Member of the Modern History Faculty, University of Oxford, and Union Pacific Visiting Professor at the University of Minnesota

RICHARD FLETCHER Professor of History, University of York

RICHARD HERR Professor of History Emeritus at the University of California at Berkeley

HENRY KAMEN Professor, Council for Higher Scientific Research, Barcelona

ANGUS MACKAY University of Edinburgh

Introduction

RAYMOND CARR

I

T the hands of a generation of scholars, particularly of Spanish scholars, now freed from the intellectual constraints of Francoism, the history of Spain has undergone a process of revisionism. This process can be seen as a rejection of any treatment of Spain as an exceptional case. It should be studied as one would study the history of any other major European country.

That Spain should have been held to be an exceptional case is not surprising. Alone among the nations of Western Europe large areas of its territory had been occupied by non-European, non-Christian Islamic rulers since the eighth century. The Christian Reconquest (*Reconquista*) was a long process ending only in 1492 when the last Moorish kingdom of Granada fell. For Richard Ford, who published his great *Handbook for Travellers in Spain* in 1844 after travelling himself some 2,000 miles over the country, the Moorish occupation had left an abiding legacy, especially in Andalusia. Andalusians hovered between 'the hat and the turban', and were to be judged by 'oriental' standards. Important as the Reconquest is as the foundation myth of conservative nationalism, the Moorish legacy can no longer serve as a satisfactory explanation for the problem that had begun to obsess both Spaniards and outside observers from the seventeenth century onwards. How had a once great nation, with a vast overseas empire and a flourishing cultural life, come to be considered by the diplomats and statesmen who gathered in Paris in 1814, as *un cour secondaire*, a second-class nation?

To Protestants and liberals alike the answer was clear: they were the heirs of the Black Legend. Invented as a piece of war propaganda in the sixteenth century, it presented Spain as a bastion of intolerance, ignorance, and bigotry. To explain the 'backwardness' of Spain, and the gap which had opened between its wretched poverty and the prospering nations of northern Europe, there was no need to look beyond the

Inquisition which had cut Spain off from the intellectual and scientific achievements which were the basis of the advanced nations' prosperity and progress. Once the eighteenth-century Enlightenment prised open the windows to Europe, reactionaries created a countervailing White Legend: Spain had declined because the men of the Enlightenment, as the heirs of Luther and the disciples of Voltaire and Rousseau, had poisoned Spain's Catholic essence which constituted its sign of identity and the foundation of its greatness. In its battle against liberalism this White Legend became part of the intellectual baggage of the early propagandists of Francoism. Spain was seen as an ideological battleground between the liberal heirs of the Enlightenment and those who sought to preserve the Catholic essence of traditional Spain. To revisionist historians this Manichean vision of 'Two Spains' is a metaphysical construct manipulated by both liberals and reactionaries for political ends. For modern economic historians the two Spains of ideology have become the Spain of relative prosperity and the Spain of rural poverty and stagnation in what has been called 'a dual economy'.

Revisionism does not mean that historians deny the overwhelming social and intellectual influence of a powerful Catholic church nor that, until at least recently, the notion of the 'Two Spains' entered into the collective consciousness and has determined how people have acted. Nor does revisionism mean that Spanish history becomes empty of controversy. The social and cultural consequences of the presence of a large population of Moors and a significant minority of Jews and the consequences of their expulsion are still matters of debate. More recently, economic historians have quarrelled about the relative roles of protectionism and free trade as recipes for growth in what in the nineteenth and twentieth centuries would be regarded as an underdeveloped economy. What modern historians reject *in toto* is the Romantics' vision of an exceptional Spain that had deliberately turned its back on progress, in order to preserve the human, and—according to the German poet Rilke—the spiritual values that bourgeois societies had lost in the race for material prosperity. For the Romantics of the 1830s and many of their successors the emblematic hero was Don Quixote; for them Spain's history was to be explained, not in terms of objective factors, but by some special insight into the Spanish psyche. Modern historians would approve of the novelist Pío Baroja's verdict that half the idiocies about the Spanish soul have been invented by foreigners, the other half by Spaniards themselves.

What revisionism leaves intact is the view that a key to Spanish history is diversity. It is the aim of this introduction to map this diversity, and to examine its political, social, and economic causes and consequences.

II

Until the twentieth century the majority of Spaniards lived and worked on the land. The conditions in which they laboured were determined by the interaction of soil and climate, and by the tenures on which they held their land, which were the legacy of history. By the eighteenth century the diversity of agricultural patterns and techniques impressed all English observers, who came from a country where climatic conditions and the patterns of landholding were more uniform.

First there is the sharp division between wet and dry Spain. 'The north western provinces', observed Richard Ford in the 1830s, 'are more rainy than Devonshire, whilst the centre plains are more calcined than those of the deserts of Arabia.' Galicia, in the north-west, where peasants still carry umbrellas to work, might expect eighty inches of rain to their plots; the central *meseta* receives less than ten inches and Almería sometimes none at all. Dry farming in the central *meseta* of Castile, devoted almost exclusively to the cultivation of cereals, meant extensive fallows to rest the exhausted soils. Yields were amongst the lowest in Europe. To subsistence farmers a bad year, late frosts, or a hailstorm brought near starvation and a descent into debt. In the *huertas*—garden farms—of Murcia and Valencia, irrigation meant that a farmer could hope for three or four crops a year. The owner of ten acres was a rich man. Yet if Valencia contained favoured regions, with the highest agricultural production in Europe, its mountain backlands were almost barren.

Climate and soil were not the only factors determining the diversity of agricultural patterns. Much depended on how land had been settled in the Middle Ages. Areas of precarious subsistence peasant farmers in much of Old Castile contrast with the stable family farms of the Basque Provinces and Catalonia, where the solidly built *masía* dominates the landscape. In Galicia, the church in the Middle Ages had granted long leases to encourage settlers. In the eighteenth century a rise in population led to a process of subdivision which produced, as in Ireland, handkerchief plots of an acre or so. But the most dramatic contrast of all was between such poor holdings and those of the Castilian peasantry and the latifundia of Andalusia and Estremadura, a contrast only paralleled by that between the poverty-stricken Italian *mezzogiorno* and the prosperous north. The military aristocracy who led the Reconquest from the Moors had been granted vast estates, later to be increased by the land sales of church and common land of the nineteenth century. The Spanish aristocracy, unlike the British, were usually absentee, urban landlords. Their estates were worked by *braceros*, gangs of seasonal labourers hired daily in the town square, who starved in the off-seasons.

Diversity was reflected in the landscape and the architecture of rural Spain. In the olive monocultures of Jaén, in Andalusia and on the large ranch estates of Estremadura, the labourers lived in agro towns so that the surrounding countryside appeared a desert in the dry season, where 'the great landowner seems to reign', a French traveller wrote in 1793 'like a lion in his forest, driving away by his roars all who seek to approach his presence'. In the Basque Provinces, Galicia, and Asturias the countryside was dotted with hamlets and farmsteads. Diversity conditions social conflict. Areas of stable family farms tended to be Catholic and conservative. The Carlist armies, in the wars against the liberals of the nineteenth century, were recruited from the Basque Provinces, the most intensely religious region of Spain. The *yunteros* of Estremadura, whose teams of mules ploughed the large owners' cultivable land, and the *braceros* of Andalusia fought a long and sullen struggle against their employers. Andalusia was to become the stronghold of rural anarchism in the nineteenth century with its demand for a *reparto*, the confiscation and division of the great estates.

These patterns established in the Middle Ages suffered changes in the nineteenth century when industrialization began to draw poor peasants to the new factories. But on the whole they held until the 1950s. It was mechanization that destroyed them. Modern tractors and combine harvesters replaced the gangs of *braceros*. The small plots of subsistence farmers could not be mechanized and were consolidated in the hands of the more prosperous farmers. Sons of poor peasants saw no future on the land in this new, capitalist world. The result was the mass rural exodus of the 1960s to new industrial cities.

If geography helps to explain the diversity of agriculture and the struggles of subsistence farmers against inhospitable conditions, it also put obstacles in the way of the development of a national market, its absence indicated by sharp variations in regional prices. Spain long remained a patchwork of local markets separated by mountain barriers and poor roads. The Sierra Morena, once the haunt of brigands, cuts Andalusia off from Castile. The Cantabrian chain isolates Asturias and Galicia.

Spain is a large, square country where the central meseta rises 2,000 feet above the coast. Facing some of the steepest gradients in Europe, roads and railways are costly to construct. Before the coming of the railways in the 1860s, easy access to the sea and the relative cheapness of coastal shipping compared to land transport by mule trains gave the periphery a comparative advantage over the centre. Once the dynamic sector of a wool economy with its great fair of Medina del Campo, Castile became a backwater. By the eighteenth century it was living on its past grandeur: 'skeletons of towns once populous and crammed with factories, workshops and stalls were now full of churches, convents and hospitals... destitute of commerce and supported by the church.' Population prosperity and progress was increasingly shifting to the periphery. Catalonia, after a period of decline, prospered by the export of brandy and textiles to Spanish America to become, in the eighteenth century, the biggest textile centre outside of Lancashire, drawing labour from the impoverished mountain regions. The coastal towns of Valencia Ford described as 'opulent' in comparison with the barren backlands of the country; Malaga prospered in exports of fruit to Northern Europe, Jerez on the sherry trade. Both became home to a prosperous foreign community. 'In the undoubted progress realized in the eighteenth century', writes Pierre Vilar, 'was implicit a relationship between the various regions of the peninsula quite distinct from that of the *Siglo de Oro*. Demographically and economically the centre of Spain loses its dominating position. There is a return to the balance of antiquity where peripheral Spain—especially Mediterranean Spain—attracted to itself population, activity and production.' There was another return to the balance of antiquity. Spain, from Roman times, had attracted investment in its rich mineral resources. Only cheap coal of good quality, the essential ingredient of an industrial revolution, was in short supply. In the 1830s it looked as if Marbella, now the playground of oil sheikhs and European golfers, might become the centre of a flourishing iron industry. But lack of cheap coal moved this to the north. By the 1870s the iron mines around Bilbao made Spain the biggest exporter of iron ore in Europe. The profits and the cheap Welsh coal that came in return enabled it to become the greatest centre of Spain's heavy industry, drawing a flood of poor rural immigrants from Castile.

III

Richard Ford, in a much-quoted phrase, described Spain as 'a bundle of local units tied together by a rope of sand'. A hundred years later Gerald Brenan wrote, in the preface to his influential *The Spanish Labyrinth*:

In what we may call its normal condition Spain is a collection of small, mutually hostile or indifferent republics held together in a loose federation. At certain great periods (the Caliphate, the Reconquista, the Siglo de Oro) these small centres have been infected by a common feeling or idea and have moved in unison: then when the impetus given by this idea declined, they have fallen apart and resumed their separate and egoistic existence.

To single out diversity and political fragmentation as unique characteristics came naturally to English observers, who had long enjoyed a common legal system. But the fact did not escape Spaniards themselves. To Olavide, an enlightened eighteenth-century civil servant, Spain was:

a body composed of other smaller bodies separated, and in opposition to one another, which oppress and despise each other and are in a continuous state of civil war. Each province, each religious house, each profession, is separated from the rest of the nation and concentrated in itself... Modern Spain can be considered as a body without energy... a monstrous Republic formed of little republics which confront each other because the particular interest of each is in contradiction with the general interest.

The imposition of Roman rule over most of Spain created the notion of Hispania as a single political entity. The Visigothic kings, in theory at least, were the legatees of Rome, ruling over a single kingdom. More important, their bishops gave it a single religion with the triumph of Roman Catholicism over the Arian heresy. For Spanish nationalists Roman Catholicism was to become 'consubstantial' with the nation itself. 'Spain', Admiral Carrero Blanco, Franco's *eminence grise*, wrote in the 1970s 'is Catholic or it is nothing.'

The Moorish invasion shatters this unity. Spain was now divided between two political and social systems, two civilizations: the Moorish south and the Christian north—even if, as recent historians have emphasized, the cultural frontier between them was permeable, sometimes allowing flourishing cultural exchanges. But neither the Christian kings nor the Moors triumphed over forces of centripetal localism. The Cordobate of Córdoba fragmented into the *taifa* mini states. Christian Spain, in spite of the 'imperial' mission of Castile, remained in a state of endemic civil war. The Catholic Kings, Ferdinand and Isabella, did not create, as we used to learn at school, a modern nation state. The union of the crowns of Castile and Aragon was a personal union created by their marriage in 1469; the Spain of the Catholic Kings was a federal monarchy in which obedience was conditional on the personal prestige of the monarchs and their respect for the *fueros*, the local constitutions which gave the constituent parts of the federation, in particular the Basque Provinces and the lands of the crown of Aragon which included Catalonia and Valencia, a quasi-independent status with their own Cortes or local parliaments. Protestant propagandists presented Philip II as an absolute monarch. That is not how he saw himself as he journeyed across his kingdoms to extract taxes from the Cortes of Aragon.

To strike a satisfactory balance between the necessities for an efficient, centralized government from Madrid and the strength of local traditions was the task of the Bourbon monarchy as it was of the Second Republic of 1931–6 and the constitutional monarchy after 1975. Too much pressure from the centre set off revolt in the periphery. The overtaxed Castilian subjects of Philip II complained that a disproportionate burden of the costs of empire, which the fiscal privileges of their *fueros* allowed the Aragonese and Catalans to escape, fell on their shoulders. Olivares (1587–1645), the great minister of Philip IV, sought to spread the burden by subjecting Catalonia to the 'customs of Castile'. He was met by the Catalan revolt of 1640. The Habsburg monarchy caved in. The Bourbons after 1714 renewed the attack, abolishing the *fueros* of Catalonia and Valencia. That their success was incomplete Olavide recognized. The most resolute centralizers were the nineteenth-century liberals, 'Jacobins' who divided the historic regions of Spain into provinces on the French pattern, subject to a single uniform constitution for all Spaniards. In the Basque Provinces and Catalonia defence of lost local liberties came to take the form of modern nationalist movements based on the defence of their non-Castilian language and demanding home rule. Granted autonomy statutes by the Second Republic of 1931–6, it is one of the paradoxes of history that General Franco inherited the radical centralizing policies of the nineteenth-century liberals, resulting in the abolition of the autonomy statutes in the name of national unity and the repression of the language and culture of the Basques and Catalans, which in turn was to create in Basque and Catalan nationalism an irresistible force. On Franco's death the new democracy recognized their strengths in the constitution of 1978. The most decentralized constitution in Europe, the 'State of the Autonomies' granted Home Rule to Euzkadi, as the three Basque Provinces had been christened, and to Catalonia. Generous Home Rule struck a balance between the central government and local liberties, as far as Catalonia was concerned, leaving separatism as a minor protest movement. Unhappily Home Rule does not satisfy the more substantial minority of Basque radical nationalists, who have resorted to the terrorism of ETA in order to impose, on Spain and their compatriots, their vision of an independent Euzkadi.

IV

If the establishment of a balance between the demands of the central government in Madrid and a resistant provincialism helps to map the course of Spanish history, the social texture of Spain was long explained in terms of a pervasive localism. To Gerald Brenan, a Spaniard's first loyalty was to his *patria chica*, his 'little country'. 'Every village, every town is the centre of an intense social and political life.' The *pueblo*, the small, inward-looking community, was seen by Brenan, as it was by nineteenth-century Romantics, as a moral universe which preserved the human values that bourgeois capitalist society had lost. It was intensively studied by Anglo-Saxon anthropologists as an enclosed society to which their techniques, evolved in the study of preliterate societies, could be successfully applied.

This idealized pueblo survived in remote districts until the 1960s. In the 1920s Brenan found such survivals in the mountain villages of the Alpujarras, but even he lamented the decline of village life and the adoption of 'modern' lifestyles during and after the Civil War of 1936–9. In the 1940s the novelist Camilo José Cela discovered inns, unchanged since the eighteenth century, in the hill villages of New Castile. Twenty years later John Betjeman's wife found them equipped with plastic tablecloths and blaring radios.

Over much of Spain intrusive elements had always been present, eroding localism: French monks in the Middle Ages; French immigrant workers in the sixteenth and seventeenth centuries. Galicians complained to George Borrow in the 1830s that a flood of Catalan immigrants was ruining their livelihood. Every village had its conscript who had served outside his *pueblo*; one seventeenth-century picaresque tale is the fictional autobiography of a rogue who has served in armies all over Europe. Small villages were under the jurisdiction of large municipalities, however much this subjection was resented. British mining engineers, Protestant missionaries, were a notable presence in southern Spain, as were smugglers from Gibraltar.

Whatever its power as a centre of attraction in the past, the car-borne Spaniard is no longer tied to his *patria chica*. The rapid economic growth of the 1960s that, from a low base, came to exceed that of other industrialized nations, Japan excepted, has transformed Spanish society, making it ever more similar to the urbanized consumer societies that surround it. Those Spaniards who have emigrated to the cities and industrial areas may return to their native pueblos to participate in their local fiestas, but they show no inclination to abandon the amenities of city life for the emotional comforts of ruralism. The abandoned villages, so eloquently described in the novels of Miguel Delibes, are testimony of this.

Traditional institutions which were the core of local life have been eroded. The *tertulia*, the gathering of like-minded friends round a café table, has been replaced by interminable late-night radio chat-shows listened to at home. While the television stations of the autonomous regions, particularly in Catalonia, Galicia, and Euzkadi, have fostered local patriotism, evident in an outpouring of regional histories, TV has homogenized the culture of localism, taking over the role of the cinema in the 1950s, when Spain had the highest number of cinema seats per capita in Europe. Imported films, like mass tourism in the 1960s, brought acquaintance with, and envy of, the consumer societies of Europe and America.

The old Francoist tourist slogan 'Spain is different' hardly serves anymore to describe an increasingly urbanized, industrialized, democratic society, no longer threatened by a military takeover bid as in July 1936, or by the Civil War which followed it. Edmund Burke described eighteenth-century Spain as 'a great whale stranded on the shores of Europe', and the duke of Wellington, in the 1820s, called it 'a country whose manners and habits are so little congenial with those of other nations of Europe'. For them Spain was outside Europe, whilst obsession with decline from Great Power status, dramatically exposed in the loss of the last remnants of her colonial empire in 1898 condemned her to be one of Europe's losers. This concealed her modest steps—brutally interrupted as these were by invasion and civil war—towards modernity since the eighteenth century. Today Spain, as a fully functioning democracy, is an active and enthusiastic member of the European Community, and 'its manners and habits' are those of a Western consumer society.

1 Prehistoric and Roman Spain

A. T. FEAR

ICHARD Ford's statement that Spain is not one country but several, while now almost a cliché, bears repeating. The geography of the Iberian peninsula, like that of what is now modern Greece, breaks the area into distinct and separate regions. It is unsurprising therefore that ancient Spain presents us with a mosaic of diverse cultures. Language reflects this diversity perfectly: no fewer than five languages were spoken in the region. Unfortunately these continue to defy efforts at translation and hence our information comes solely from classical sources. These often have strong presuppositions—plain-dwellers are, for example, seen as necessarily more civilized than mountain-dwellers. We have no further material with which to interpret our archaeological data, and though these sources are thus invaluable, it is also important to remember that with them we see ancient Iberia through a glass darkly.

Human history began early in the peninsula. The bones of one of man's earliest ancestors, *Homo antecessor*, who lived 800,000 years ago, have been unearthed near Burgos, and Neanderthal Man (*c*.60,000 BC) might have been more justly christened Gibraltar Woman, as the Rock was the site of the first Neanderthal finds. In the Upper Palaeolithic (Late Old Stone Age), Cantabria and Asturias formed part of the Magdalenian Culture (*c*.16,000 BC) which has left spectacular cave paintings. The best-known of these are to be found at Altamira near Santander. The paintings are realistic depictions of food animals. Not only are they painted in colour, but the relief of the rock face has been used to create a three-dimensional effect. Similar paintings are found in the Levant, but most rock art there dates from the Middle Stone Age (*c*.10,000 BC). The Levantine paintings, centred on the province of Castellón, are more schematic than their northern ancestors and place a much stronger emphasis on the human figure. As well as hunting scenes, we find depictions of war, dancing groups of men and women, and even of an execution, suggesting the emergence of organized societies.

From c.3,800 BC much of the peninsula participated in the wave of megalithic building which spread through Northern Europe. Iberian megaliths are distributed in a horseshoe pattern running along the Atlantic and southern coasts, but are absent from the Levant and the Meseta. The vast majority are tombs, the most spectacular being those at Antequera in Andalusia, whose sophistication led to theories that they were built by Mycenaean colonists from Greece rather than the native in-habitants of the region. In fact radio-carbon dating shows that the tombs substantially pre-date the Mycenaean world.

In c.2,600 BC copper-using cultures came into being at Los Millares in Almería and the Tagus valley in Portugal. Despite their sophistication (Los Millares has a rock-cut water supply and is defended by three Cyclopean walls, complete with bastions), they seem to have faded away around 1,800 BC, making little impact on later developments. The same is true of the later Agaric Culture of Almería (c.1,700–1,400 BC), which was based on mining and created a population density in the Agar valley not to be rivalled until the nineteenth century, and the Motilla Culture of La Mancha (c.1,600–1,300 BC), centred around small fortified towers. It was interaction with foreign peoples that led to the emergence of a long-lasting Iberian culture. This interaction began early. Mycenaean pottery sherds dating from c.1,200 BC have been found in the peninsula, though it remains a mystery how many hands they had passed through after leaving their place of manufacture, and how regular their arrival was.

The most advanced people to be found in the peninsula in the his-torical period were given the name Iberians in classical antiquity and were found along the Mediterranean and southern Atlantic coasts. The Iberians' ancestry is unclear. They may have been related to the Berbers and hence immigrants from North Africa, but the prevalent view today is that they were natives of the peninsula. Whatever their origins, the Iberi-ans appear to have spoken two related, though distinct, languages, which are not of Indo-European origin and remain undeciphered. The north and west of the peninsula were the preserve of Celtic peoples, though en-claves of Celts were also to be found as far south as the Algarve and An-dalusia. The western Pyrenees are an exception as they were already occupied by the Basques. Basque, like Iberian, is a non-Indo-European language, but attempts to decipher Iberian as a form of proto-Basque and hence to see the Basques as an 'Iberian fringe' have foundered.

Between the Celts and Iberians on the meseta plains are to be found the

Celtiberians who, like the Celts, spoke an Indo-European language and whose most famous son is the Latin poet Martial, a native of Bilbilis, modern Calatayud. Our classical sources unfortunately do not use ethnonyms with precision, but it seems reasonable to see the Celtiberians as a mixture of the Celtic and Iberian populations.

The classical Greeks also took an interest in Spain. The Greek city of Marseilles, itself a colony of Phocaea, established a settlement as a trading post in Catalonia, appropriately named Emporion, the Greek for market-place, around 575 BC. Emporion, modern-day Ampurias, prospered and was one of the main sources of Greek pottery reaching the peninsula. It was soon followed by a further colony nearby, Rhode, modern Rosas. These settlements, however, mark the limit of the Greek presence in the peninsula. Other alleged Greek sites have turned out to be in reality Phoenician settlements or simply landmarks for sailors. The naval Battle of Alalia off Sicily in c.535 BC, when the Phocaeans were defeated by a combined Punic and Etruscan force, effectively brought a halt to Greek expansion in the area.

Greek artefacts did circulate in the peninsula, and Emporion played a key role in this trade. A sixth-century inscription shows dealings between a Greek merchant from the town and an Iberian dealer from Saguntum, modern Sagunto. However, the majority of Greek items reached their final destination via Phoenician middlemen, as can be seen from the Punic graffiti which are frequently found on Greek pottery in Spain. An eloquent attestation of the balance of influence is that in c.290 BC the Greeks of Emporion changed their system of weights and measures to a Punic standard.

Among foreign peoples it was the Phoenicians who had the largest impact on Iberian culture. Their arrival pre-dated that of the Greeks and was more extensive in its scope. Cadiz, whose name derives from the Phoenician word for fortified place, claimed a pedigree extending back to 1,100 BC, though archaeological remains only take the town's history back to the ninth century BC. Cadiz set the pattern for early Punic settlement in Spain. Its location, situated on an island, now joined to the mainland, at the mouth of the Rio Guadalete, was typical of the sites favoured by the Phoenicians. Further settlement along the southern Mediterranean coast soon followed. Like Cadiz, the new foundations were positioned on promontories at river-mouths or on offshore islands. Importantly, such sites did not encroach on the territory of the native peoples. While such locations were previously thought to indicate that Punic communities were mere trading posts, more recent archaeological work has revealed

that they were permanent settlements. The depth of Phoenician influence in this region of Spain can been seen from the remarks of Emperor Augustus' general Agrippa, who, when compiling a map of the area at the end of the first century BC, commented that this coastline was entirely Punic in its outlook.

Punic interaction with the local population, which seems to have been wholly friendly, probably because the Phoenician settlements had no territorial ambitions, produced a vigorous cross-fertilization of oriental and Iberian cultures, engendering the so-called Tartessian culture. Tartessos owes its name and appearance in history to Herodotus, who tells of an accidental landfall in c.640 BC of the Phocaean Colaeus in a fabulously wealthy kingdom ruled over by an equally miraculously long-lived king named Arganthonius (the name, significantly perhaps of Celtic derivation, means 'Man of the Silver Mountain'). Tartessos came to signify for the ancient Greeks an El Dorado in the west, and while Herodotus' tale is in some respects true, its detail needs to be treated with caution. Searches for a town Tartessos have been fruitless: while more than 300 'Tartessian' settlements have been located, none fits the description of a royal capital, and now 'Tartessos' is seen as merely a useful description of a particular culture centred around an axis running from Huelva in the lower Rio Tinto valley to Seville in the Guadalquivir valley. However, in its heyday Tartessian influence spread not only further up the Guadalquivir, a natural line of communication, but also into Estremadura across the Sierra Morena, as can be seen from the golden grave goods from the cemetery of Aliseda in the province of Cáceres. (References in the Old Testament to 'Tarshish', Jonah's intended destination, and its ships have sometimes been seen as applying to Tartessos, but it seems much more likely that they refer to Tarsus or even, as was thought in late antiquity, India.)

Arganthonius' name, whatever his own historical status, marks the commodity most sought after by foreign settlers—silver. In exchange the Phoenicians offered the Tartessians oil and wine. Phoenician amphorae for these commodities are a common find on their sites, as are luxury goods made of precious metals and ivory. The interaction between the

This stone coffin found at Cadiz was possibly imported from Sidon and dates from the fifth century BC. It is parallelled from the Near East and other areas of Phoenician settlement. The majority of these coffins are, like this one, female, though a male example has also been found at Cadiz. Punic religious practices remained strong throughout the Roman period at Cadiz and centred on the Temple of Hercules, who was here a syncretized version of the Phoenician god, Melqart. The temple was famous throughout the Empire and survived until the suppression of paganism.

two cultures (often known as the 'orientalizing period' of Spanish pre-history) was not merely commercial: religious ideas also passed from one side to the other. In Seville a small bronze idol of Astarte, dedicated by the Phoenician brothers Baalyaton and Abdibaal, dates to the eighth century BC. Phoenician religious practices were heavily to influence Iberian religion. The spectacular funerary statues, the Dama de Baza and the Dama de Elche, which date from the high period of Iberian culture in the fourth century BC, have their ancestors in depictions of the Punic goddess Tanit, an example of which is seen in an alabaster enthroned image carved in the seventh century, but buried in an Iberian grave at Galera in the province of Granada around 530 BC. Many Iberian votive offerings found at hilltop shrines, such as those from the Sierra Morena, are modelled on the Punic war gods Hadad and Reshef. The tomb of Pozo Moro in the province of Albacete, dating from c.500 BC, with its complex mythological reliefs, also shows strong Punic influence. The shape of the tomb mirrors the tower tombs of the Syrian Near East, and many of the features of the reliefs such as the 'Lord of Animals' and the 'Tree of Life' also have Near Eastern parallels. The snarling lions or wolves which guard its base were to become a common feature of Iberian sculpture.

The finds at the Tartessian burial site of El Carambolo on the outskirts of Seville illustrate another important Phoenician legacy: that of skilled metalworking. The hoard found here included twenty-one items of twenty-four-carat gold jewelry. These pieces are not simply crude lumps of metal: their fine craftsmanship shows that the Tartessians had learnt the techniques of granulation and filigree work from their neighbours. Further examples of this skill can be seen in the finds from graves located further up the Gaudalquivir valley and in the province of Huelva. Equally sophisticated jewelry is found on the fringes of Tartessian influence in the province of Alicante.

The Phoenicians also brought literacy. A semi-syllabic 'Tartessian' script based on the Phoenician alphabet makes its appearance at this time. Strangely, however, most of the surviving inscriptions of this as-yet un-deciphered script appear not in the Tartessian heartland, but further to the south-west in the Algarve. The majority are to be found on decorated grave stelae, where they frame depictions of warriors who are normally displayed with their weapons of war, including chariots. At the very edge of the distribution of the known stelae, at Luna in the province of Saragossa, one stone also displays a lyre whose closest parallels are with Phoenician instruments. The Greek geographer Strabo speaks of the Turdetanians of Andalusia having oral traditions going back 6,000 years, and while this is clearly an exaggeration perhaps this depiction shows that there is some truth at the back of this claim.

The legend of Argathonius has led to a general belief that the Tartessian culture had a single ruler. Apart from Herodotus' account, fragments of what seem to be genuine Iberian myths preserved by the late-Roman historian Justin about the kings Gargoris, Habis, and Geryon have reinforced this belief. We cannot be sure that this was the case, but the later Iberian tradition of monarchy makes the hypothesis highly plausible. Towards the end of the sixth century BC the Tartessian culture waned. The reason for its eclipse remains a mystery, but the main result appears to have been the diffusion of political power into much smaller political units.

The collapse of 'Tartessos' appears to have had a powerful effect on the Phoenician colonies with whom she had enjoyed a mutually beneficial existence. These diminished in number, but those which survived grew in size. The survivors also fell increasingly within the ambit of the western Mediterranean's most important Phoenician settlement, Carthage. A tradition preserved in the late-Roman authors Macrobius and Justin records that in c.550 BC a native attempt, perhaps itself a sign of Tartessian decay, to storm Cadiz under a king named Theron ('beast-man') was beaten off with the assistance of Carthage.

Iberian culture survived the collapse of 'Tartessos' and indeed flourished, but does not seem to have achieved political unity. Instead, there is a proliferation of small hilltop towns. Most dense in the south-east of the peninsula, these are spread along the entire Mediterranean coast of Spain and even extend into what is now France. The best-known example is that of Ullastret in Catalonia. The towns were built in defensive positions, often heavily fortified with 'cyclopean' masonry, but, while orderly in plan with streets of rectangular houses, appear to have contained no significant public buildings. The forms of political control varied. In general, power appears to have been in the hands of petty kings or *reguli*, as our Latin sources refer to them. But, as among the Celts of Gaul, kings had given way to ruling aristocratic elites in some areas. Livy describes such an oligarchic council as existing among the Volciani in 218 BC.

Political unity should not, however, be confused with cultural advance, and this period saw the high period of Iberian culture, the most striking aspect of which is its sculpture. The most spectacular pieces, the Dama de Baza and the Dama de Elche, dating from the fourth century BC, are funerary in character, both statues having a niche in the back to receive a cinerary urn. At Baza the entire burial was uncovered, showing it to be of a warrior. The sculptures, therefore, must be of a goddess, perhaps related to the Punic Tanit (the Dama de Baza holds a dove, Tanit's emblem). Fragmentary remains from the province of Jaén, of a similar date and probably from a major tomb, depict a variety of mythological scenes, many including warriors wearing complex armour which concurs with literary descriptions of Lusitanian weaponry. While there is some Greek influence in these sculptures, it is minimal. Diffusionist theories of a Phocaean mastercraftsman working in the area can be refuted simply by looking at the pieces, for their aesthetic is almost entirely Iberian. Some Punic influence is also present: one of the fragmentary warriors fights a griffin, a Near Eastern beast, and another has a sword pommel based on a Syrian design.

Most Iberian sculpture, however, consists of small dedicatory pieces found at shrines which appear, like Greek sanctuaries, to have been intertribal. Animals, warriors, and women are all depicted. The female statues, such as the Gran Dama Oferente, have complex dresses, like those of the two Damas mentioned above.

The end of Iberian independence was signalled by Carthage's defeat by Rome in the First Punic War, in 241 BC. The Carthaginians, thwarted in their Sicilian designs, turned their attention to Spain. The driving force behind this policy was Hamilcar Barca. Hamilcar started his campaign from Cadiz, but soon established a new centre of operations at 'the white citadel', perhaps modern Alicante. After Hamilcar came to a violent end in 229 BC, drowning after being defeated outside Elice (probably modern Elche), his place was taken by Hasdrubal, his son-in-law. Hasdrubal continued the policy of expansion and established what was to be the permanent capital of Carthaginian Spain at Qart Hadasht, normally known by its Roman name of New Carthage, modern Cartagena. However, he also seems to have tried to ingratiate himself with the local aristocracy by marrying into the Iberian nobility. According to Diodorus Siculus, he was hailed as king by the local Iberian tribes, but this apparent popularity did not stop him being assassinated by an Iberian slave in 221 BC.

It was the aggressive nature of the Barcids' policy in Spain, a strategy possibly carried out with little reference to Carthage herself, that brought the area to the notice of Rome. In fact, Rome initially seemed indifferent to Hasdrubal's activity. A Roman mission sent to the region in 231 BC re-

The *Dama de Elche* represents the high-point of Iberian sculpture and dates from the fourth century BC. Originally a full-length piece, only this upper section survives. The statue has a niche at the rear to hold a cinerary urn and depicts a funerary goddess, possibly related to the Punic goddess Tanit. The complex head-dress parallels those described by the Greek geographer Strabo.

turned feeling that the Barcids' actions posed no threat. But Rome's ally, Marseilles, on whom she depended for support against the Celts of Gaul, was more concerned because of her Catalonian colonies. It was probably pressure from this quarter that led Rome to make a treaty with Carthage in 225 BC which delineated the river 'Iber', most likely the Ebro, as the *non plus ultra* of Carthaginian arms in the peninsula.

After Hasdrubal's death command of Carthaginian forces in Iberia fell to Hamilcar's son, Hannibal, who had also married a native princess, Imilce of Castulo. By 218 BC Hannibal had pushed across the meseta as far as Salamanca and possibly reached the Ebro valley. The Carthaginians did not merely conquer, they also settled. Cartagena rapidly grew to hold 30,000 inhabitants, many of whom came from a new wave of Punic-speakers, the Blastophoenicians, who arrived from North Africa in the wake of the Barcid conquests. Unfortunately no traces of Barcid Cartagena remain, but the Puerta de Sevilla in the town wall of Carmona in Andalusia dates from this period. The Barcids were also responsible for the development of large-scale mining in Spain. An extensive account of their operations is given by Diodorus Siculus. One mine alone, that of Baebelo, is said to have supplied Hannibal with 300 pounds of silver daily. Carthaginian rule was said to be harsh—Hamilcar is alleged to have tortured, blinded, and then crucified one native ruler, Indortes. On the other hand, given that some Iberian towns remained loyal to the Barcids to the bitter end and that our classical sources do not approach this subject with impartiality, we should be careful in assuming that Punic rule was necessarily worse than what was to follow.

Despite Hasdrubal's treaty, it was impossible for peaceful coexistence between Rome and Carthage to last. The *casus belli* of the Second Punic War was to be the Spanish town of Saguntum. After factional fighting within the town, Hannibal intervened to support those who backed Carthage there. Rome's immediate reply was to claim a long-standing alliance with Saguntum and order Hannibal to desist from interference on the pain of war. If the 'Iber' of Hasdrubal's treaty was the Ebro, as is likely, Saguntum was some 90 miles to its south. Hannibal was placed in an impossible position: he was faced with choosing war with Rome or allowing a precedent which would enable any number of other Iberian towns to claim an auld alliance with Rome and see his power in Spain whittled away piecemeal. He chose war.

While Hannibal advanced across France and the Alps to wage war in Italy, Spain still remained a vital theatre of operations. In 218 BC Gnaeus Cornelius Scipio landed at Ampurias with a force of two legions and

15,000 allied troops, establishing a Roman presence in the peninsula which was to last for over six centuries. He rapidly constructed a base at Tarraco, modern Tarragona, where the walls of his fortress, built with Iberian labour and Iberian techniques, can still be seen. Scipio was soon joined by his brother Publius. Under their command fighting between Roman and Carthaginian forces ebbed and flowed across the peninsula

This tutelary goddess is built into the Torre de Sant Magí, part of the Roman walls of Tarragona built during the Second Punic War. The goddess, Minerva, is classical, but her shield sports not its usual *aegis*, but an Iberian wolf showing the intermingling of Roman and native customs which was to characterize the peninsula in the Roman period. Inside the tower is a dedication to Minerva by Marcus Vibius, one of the oldest pieces of Latin found in the peninsula.

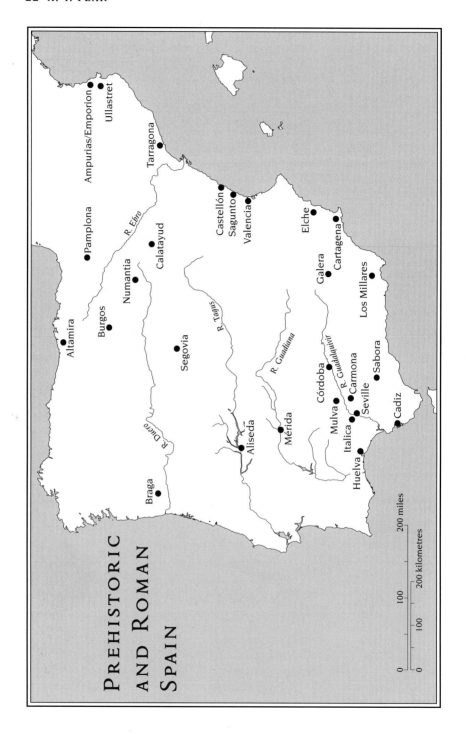

PREHISTORIC
AND ROMAN
SPAIN

for the first six years of the war and possibly reached as far south as the Guadalquivir valley. The native population was to be found fighting on both sides. In our classical sources the war is portrayed as one of a clash between two superpowers, but it must be remembered that the Iberians may well have seen things differently and that accusations of Spanish treachery are simply inappropriate. What the Iberians wanted was for both sides to leave, or perhaps more simply to recruit these foreign armies in the pursuit of local quarrels.

The war in Spain took a significant turn after the death of the two Scipiones in 211 BC and the subsequent appointment to the Spanish command of their brilliant young kinsman, Publius Cornelius Scipio, known to history as Scipio Africanus. Instead of campaigning into the Iberian interior, Scipio launched an all-out attack on Cartagena. On its rapid capture, Punic resistance in Spain began to crumble, and by 206 BC the Carthaginians had been chased out of the peninsula. Punic power in Spain was at an end, but Punic culture remained a feature of the region until the end of the Roman occupation some 600 years later.

Prior to the final rout of Carthaginian arms from Spain, Scipio himself faced a mutiny. One of its consequences was the establishment of the town of Italica, near Seville, for Italian veterans from his army. The foundation of Italica marks the beginning of Roman settlement in the peninsula. It is important, however, not to overestimate its impact. As the Italians were allies of Rome rather than Roman citizens, the town possessed no Roman legal status and lacked imposing buildings. A three-roomed structure once thought to be a temple to the Capitoline Triad of Rome has now been shown to be a warehouse. Nor was Roman culture predominant. A mistress-of-animals terracotta plaque more at home in a Semitic than a Roman religious ambiance has been found in the early levels of the town.

At the end of the Second Punic War the possibility existed for Rome to abandon Spain altogether. In strategic terms there was no need to occupy the peninsula and no threat could spring from it. But this was not to be. In 197 BC two *provinciae* or 'theatres' (the term had not yet acquired a predominantly territorial meaning) were declared in the region. These were Hispania Citerior (the area controlled by Rome from the Pyrenees to the Sierra Morena) and Hispania Ulterior (the eastern half of the Guadalquivir valley). One reason for continuing interest was economic. According to the Greek historian Polybius, by the mid-second century BC the mines of Cartagena alone yielded 10,800 pounds of silver per annum for Rome. The establishment of the provinces marked the beginning of a protracted war of conquest—the peninsula was not fully pacified until Agrippa's subjugation of the Cantabrians in 19 BC. This period of time is remarkable when compared with Rome's much more rapid acquisition of territory to her east or Caesar's later conquest of Gaul, and did not go unnoticed in antiquity.

It is clear that Rome's presence was not welcomed by the inhabitants of Spain, many of whom had assumed that Rome would leave at the end of her war with Carthage. The declaration of the *provinciae* brought about an immediate rebellion by the Turdetani in Ulterior under their kings (significantly allies of Rome in the war against the Carthaginians) against Roman rule. Rebellion spread to Citerior and Rome's grip weakened until the arrival of the Elder Cato who, with a series of sharp campaigns in 195 BC, stabilized the situation. After this, Rome's involvement with Spain can be likened in part to the US experience in Vietnam, a long-protracted campaign against an inferior but determined enemy, and in part to British involvement on the North-West Frontier of India, where there was little danger posed to British rule, but a good theatre in which to obtain military glory and exercise troops. Rome's Spanish wars were not only notably protracted, but also extremely sanguinary. Such behaviour is typical of 'colonial' warfare, and it has been suggested with plausibility that Rome felt fewer scruples about dealing brutally with western barbarians than she did with groups felt to be more akin to herself and hence 'civilized', to be found to the East. One military legacy of the wars was changes to Roman arms and armour. The typical Roman military sword or *gladius* is modelled on a Spanish weapon, and the other standard arm of the Roman legionary, the *pilum*, a javelin designed to bend on impact, may also have a Spanish pedigree.

The history of the Iberian peninsula in the Republican period is one of a gradual expansion of Roman rule from the Mediterranean coast to the north and west. This expansion had no guiding principles (as had, for example, Caesar's conquest of Gaul), and was chiefly a product of 'peripheral imperialism', where a commander on the spot used his office to seek wealth and glory to further his later career at Rome. As the normal period of office was only one year, the temptation to make war was often irresistible, especially as sanctions at home were weak. The Roman state, such as it was, was forced to accept these campaigns as *faits accomplis* to protect the all-important prestige of Rome. One example of this process is Lucullus' attack on the Vaccaei in 151 BC, an act of naked aggression performed simply in pursuit of material gain. Such campaigning also caused massive political instability amongst its victims: offers of land resettlement become a standard feature of Rome's dealings with her native opponents. Such instability made attacks on Roman territory all the more likely, producing an ideal *casus belli* for ambitious governors, hence creating a vicious circle of violence. It also prevented the emergence of a secure ruling group among the native tribes with whom Rome could do business. Given these phenomena and the multiplicity of political units and fortified sites with which Rome had to deal, the length of the conquest of the peninsula becomes more comprehensible.

After Cato's campaigns war remained, for the reasons outlined above, endemic in Spain. A lull occurred after the governorship of Tiberius Gracchus in 180 BC. Gracchus was responsible for the first attempt to create political stability in the region, establishing treaty arrangements with the local tribes and allocating a fixed tribute to be levied in the form of cash and troops. He also reorganized native politics to some degree, establishing a town which took his name, Gracchuris, in the upper Ebro valley and perhaps another, Iliturgi, in the Guadalquivir valley. Gracchus' work marks a shift from the Spanish provinces being seen merely as theatres of operation towards them being conceived of as territorial units.

War broke out again in earnest in the 150s BC, when Rome was challenged in both of her Spanish provinces. In 154 BC the Lusitani of Portugal invaded Hispania Ulterior, defeating the Roman forces there and inflicting some 9,000 casualties. In Citerior trouble began soon afterwards among the confederation centred on the Celtiberian Belli and the town of Segeda. Roman imperialism often produced the dangerous side-effect of forcing her enemies to combine into larger units which would be more able to oppose her. Rome's solution was to enforce a policy of divide and rule. In 189 BC the governor of Ulterior, Aemilius Paullus, 'freed' a small settlement in Andalusia, the Tower of Lascuta, from the rule of its neighbour, Hasta Regia. This was not done for love, but simply to prevent the growth of a potential source of opposition to Roman rule. The Belli's attempt to absorb their neighbours and expand and fortify their main town, Segeda, posed a similar threat. When ordered to destroy these fortifications and pay tribute as agreed under Tiberius Gracchus, they quickly found a technicality under which to refuse.

The Roman response was swift and striking. The province was given to a consul, the highest-ranking Roman magistrate, for the first time since Cato's campaigns, and the beginning of the year was shifted from March to January. This change was to remain permanent and persists to the present day. Opinions differ about the need for such action. At first sight, it suggests that Rome was faced with serious danger and a war on two fronts. Others, however, have seen the Segedan incident as a Roman provocation to provide a 'splendid little war' for political ends. The truth may well lie somewhere between the two.

The consul, Quintus Fulvius Nobilior, if he had expected easy glory, soon found it was not to be had. He lost 10,000 men within a month. The Belli formed an alliance with their neighbours and based their operations on the town of Numantia, near modern Soria. Numantia was no mean city, occupying fifty-five acres in which lay 1,500 houses built on a regular street grid encircled by a curtain wall twenty feet thick. Peace of a sort was finally made in 151 BC. This allowed the two provincial governors to combine forces to deal with the Lusitani to the south. The Lusitani sued for peace and Galba, the governor of Ulterior, summoned them to a meeting, offering as bait a new distribution of land. On their arrival the Lusitanians were summarily massacred. Galba was prosecuted but not condemned for his action, which produced the reverse of his intentions. A Lusitanian who had escaped the massacre, Viriathus, rallied his people and continued the fight. Operating from the 'Hill of Venus', possibly near Talavera, Viriathus was so successful that by 143 BC he had roused the Celtiberi to rebellion once more, sparking off a second siege at Numantia, and managed to surround and force the surrender of an entire Roman army in 141 BC. Now it was the Romans who offered peace. Viriathus was foolish enough to accept. Having obtained a breathing space, Rome renewed the hostilities, but remained unable to defeat the Lusitanian leader militarily. Subterfuge provided a useful alternative, and Viriathus perished at the hands of three paid assassins in 139 BC.

The death of Viriathus brought the Lusitani's challenge to Roman rule to an end, though they were by no means entirely subjugated. The Celtiberi at Numantia, however, continued the fight until 133 BC when, after a siege of nine years' duration, starvation finally forced their surrender. Of the 4,000 survivors, many killed themselves to avoid capture. Scipio Aemilianus, the triumphant commander and usually hailed as a 'progressive' Roman, retained fifty Numantines to display in his triumph, sold the remainder into slavery, and levelled the site of the city. The historian Appian shows the depth of emotion felt about this campaign at Rome when he speaks of the end of Numantia in the same breath as the fall of Carthage, making them events of equal importance. The Belli's allies fared no better; 20,000 were slaughtered by Titus Didius in 98 BC, and this was not the last massacre these tribes were to suffer at Rome's hands. Significantly, Didius took care to avenge the councillors of Belgida, a town in the Jalón valley, who had been burnt alive by their own people when they urged obedience to Rome. Here we see the time-honoured Roman strategy of giving the local native aristocracy a stake in Roman rule. In his policy of terror followed by appeasement of the wealthy, Didius was merely blazing the trail that Agricola would follow some 200 years later in Roman Britain. Despite their subjugation, it might be said that the Celtiberi wreaked a terrible revenge on Rome. It was while travelling to Numantia that Tiberius Sempronius Gracchus saw the social deprivation prevalent in the Italian countryside, and his attempts to remedy this in his tribunate of 133 BC sparked off the civil wars of the Late Republic in Italy which were to last for a century and end in the downfall of the Republican system.

The stand at Numantia proved to be the last major uprising against Rome. In 123 BC the Balearic Islands were annexed to Citerior, and by 120 BC at the latest a Roman road ran along the entire Mediterranean coast of the peninsula. Warfare continued, but on a smaller scale. Internal turmoil at Rome deflected ambitions, and pressing troubles, such as the incursion of Germanic tribes into Gaul, and more impressive fields for winning glory and wealth were found elsewhere, especially in the East.

The first century BC was marked less by wars against Rome than by an extension of Roman civil wars into the Iberian peninsula, which were to culminate in Caesar's final triumph over his enemies in 45 BC at Munda, possibly modern Bailén, in Andalusia. In 82 BC a Roman political refugee, Quintus Sertorius, was asked by the Lusitani to lead them. His skillful generalship caused considerable trouble, inflicting defeats on Roman forces in both Ulterior and Citerior. Although Sertorius cultivated the Iberians by a deft use of local religion and by setting up a school at his headquarters in Osca, modern Huesca, to educate the sons of Iberian aristocrats in Roman ways (something which also conveniently provided him with hostages for their continuing support), he was fighting a Roman, not an Iberian, war and his intention was always eventually to return in triumph to Rome. The command against Sertorius was given to Pompey who, after initial setbacks, forced Sertorius on to the defensive. In 72 BC Sertorius was assassinated by a subordinate who proved easy prey for Pompey. On his return to Italy, Pompey paused to found Pompaelo, modern Pamplona, named after himself, and erect a massive triumphal monument on the Pyrenees at Col de Perthus to celebrate his victory in what had been essentially a Roman civil war fought abroad.

Pompey's great rival, Caesar, first set foot in Spain in 68 BC as an adjutant to the governor of Ulterior, and returned as governor of the province in 60 BC when he led a campaign against the Lusitani. It would have been at this time that he met the Phoenician banker Balbus of Cadiz who became a lifelong backer and financial supporter. Balbus' reward for his support was a grant of Roman citizenship to his home town. Such ad hoc reasons probably lie behind the other grants of Roman legal status to various towns, such as Evora in Portugal, prior to the Emperor Vespasian's grant of 'Latin rights' to all the Hispanic communities. Balbus and his nephew, also named Balbus, who were both to reach consular rank at Rome, had great ambitions for their town, on which they spent vast sums of money creating a new classicizing quarter. However, the old was not entirely extirpated. Cadiz's coinage still bore legends in neo-Punic, and the huge temple of Hercules, in fact a syncretized version of the Punic god Melqart, continued to hold its rites in ancestral fashion throughout the Imperial period.

During the Roman Republican period Spain remained largely outside the cultural influence of the classical world. Few settlements of Romans were to be found, and the majority of these were devoid of legal status. In 171 BC a group of *hybridae*, sons of Roman soldiers and native mothers, obtained 'Latin' status for their town at Carteia, near modern Algeciras, but no other similar group is attested. Most settlers were merchants who gathered together in ad hoc 'Roman quarters' of Iberian towns. These groups were sufficiently large to erect buildings in Seville and Córdoba, and their attempts to preserve some form of Roman life were serious enough to afford amusement to the culturally snobbish. Cicero sneers at the 'thick-sounding' poets of Córdoba who entertained the governor of Ulterior in the 70s BC. Rome's impact on native culture was mixed. Roman tribute brought about the minting of coins and a degree of monetization of the Iberian economy. These coins slowly moved from using Iberian to Latin script, suggesting a gradual diffusion of the Latin language. The forms of Roman law were used by governors in their dealings with the native population, but this was for their own benefit, not the natives', and is no more proof that the Iberians understood what was being done to them than the Conquistadores' use of Spanish legal forms shows that Mesoamericans understood the law of the Spanish Golden Age. Oddly, as Rome found the more urbanized Iberians had a familiar social structure,

The siege of Numantia, later immortalized by Cervantes, marked the high-point of native resistance to Rome in the peninsular. Scipio Aemilianus eventually forced the surrender of the town after surrounding it with seven camps linked by a wall ten feet high containing over 250 towers. The later Roman town seen here preserved the orderly plan of the earlier Celtiberian city. The Greek historian Polybius, an eyewitness of the campaign, singles it out as one of Rome's most bitter wars.

she was inclined to disturb them less than the more unfamiliar groups she found further north and west. Hence, ironically, there are more physical signs of 'Romanization' in the less advanced parts of the peninsula than elsewhere.

Caesar, after his opponents' downfall, began for the first time a phase of large-scale settlement in the region, a policy followed by his successor the Emperor Augustus. Twenty-two *coloniae* were planted in Spain. These towns, composed of Roman citizens, were run in accordance with Roman law, and in some cases, such as Mérida in Estremadura, a deliberate attempt to overawe the native population by the sheer scale of building is evident. (This is easily appreciated by a visit to the town's museum, itself a building of considerable architectural interest.) But it is unlikely that the *coloniae* were intended to 'Romanize' the peninsula, and they are best seen as the fulfilment of pledges made to a Roman audience and, in some cases, punishment for pre-existing towns who had backed the wrong side in the civil wars. Nevertheless, if Rome's commitment to Iberia in the past had seemed questionable, now there could be no doubt that she intended to stay.

Augustus redivided the peninsula into three provinces: Baetica, roughly modern Andalusia and southern Estremadura, with a capital at Córdoba; Lusitania, approximately modern Portugal, with a capital at Mérida; and Hispania Citerior, the remainder of the peninsula, with its capital at Tarragona and hence often referred to as Hispania Tarraconensis. At the time of the division the Cantabrians still remained outside the Empire. Augustus campaigned against them in person from 26 to 25 BC, and almost died there through illness. The peninsula was finally subdued in its entirety by Augustus' deputy Agrippa, in 19 BC, almost 200 years after Gnaeus Scipio had arrived in Ampurias. Although occasional acts of violence did occur—the governor of Tarraconensis, Lucius Piso, was murdered by the Celtiberian Termestines of the Duero valley in AD 26—the region was now mainly at peace and only one legion, the VII Gemina, was retained in the peninsula, based at León. As a point of comparison, Roman Britain, with one quarter of the land mass of the Spanish provinces, required no fewer than three legions to police it.

The early imperial period saw an upsurge in the building of Roman

The *casus belli* of the Second Punic War, Saguntum was later rewarded with a grant of full Roman citizenship, a rare honour in the peninsula. The Levantine towns eagerly embraced Roman culture and the Roman theatre, built in the reign of Tiberius, which was constructed by the local ruling class, is a sign of its wish to integrate into the Roman World. The town was a major port for the export of Spanish wine to Rome.

structures not only at the formal *coloniae*, but also elsewhere. This change was a voluntary one: its impetus came not from Rome, but from the local aristocracy who were now determined to integrate as firmly as possible into the wider Roman world. Examples of these initiatives are legion, and include not only civic buildings but also the 119-arch aqueduct at Segovia and the Alcántara bridge which crosses the Tagus near Cáceres at a height of 150 feet and is the tallest bridge in the Roman Empire. There was no general plan to this development, and buildings often arose as the result of a local opportunity. The town of Belo, close to Gibraltar, for example, used the wealth generated by Emperor Claudius' expedition to Mauretania, for which it was a supply base, to create an urban centre for itself. A striking exception to this trend is found in the north-west of the peninsula, where Celtic settlements of round houses known as *castros* remained and were to persist until the fourth century AD.

This variation makes it impossible to regard the Emperor Vespasian's grant of 'Latin rights' to all the region's communities in around AD 71 as a reward for progress towards some Roman ideal. The grant did provide a stimulus for building in some towns such as Munigua, modern Mulva, where a massive temple complex, closely based on the temple of Fortuna at Praeneste in Italy, was erected, and Toletum, modern Toledo, where a large circus for chariot racing was constructed. But Vespasian's reluctance to allow the town of Sabora, near Ronda in Andalusia, to raise extra revenue which would have been spent on building projects for fear that the Saborans would default on their tribute should serve to warn us that the grant did not have a 'Romanizing' intent per se. Rather, it appears that the Emperor felt the need to appease the local aristocracies of the area at a time when his own position was in some doubt. His grant ensured that many local notables became Roman citizens, showing their desire to gain status, but not necessarily that all of them were 'Romanized' or indeed wished to become so.

The region's towns exhibit a civic life substantially similar to that found in the rest of the Empire and, after Vespasian's grant, one regulated, at least in theory, by Roman rather than native law. Latin is the only language found on inscriptions, though it is clear that other languages persisted alongside it in some areas—the Termestines who murdered Piso spoke Celtiberian, and a native language was spoken by some in Valencia as late as the sixth century AD. Penetration of Roman customs into the peninsula therefore varied widely, and it is impossible to speak of 'Roman Spain' as a single cultural entity. In those areas most in contact with Rome, such as the Levant and the Ebro and Guadalquivir valleys, a strongly

'Romanized' culture grew up. Here we find mosaics and paintings which would be at home in any wealthy Roman's home, but in more remote areas, like the Asturias, many of the old pre-Roman ways remained in place. Tombstones here, for example, though written in Latin remain crudely carved and often have spiral and rosette patterns alien to Roman art. Depictions of animals and humans here have a crude, stylized as opposed to a naturalistic Roman form. The tribe, rather than a town, also firmly remained the main focus of loyalty.

During the early imperial period Spain produced some notable figures, the most famous being the Seneca family who formed part of the Roman settler community at Córdoba. However, of these only the orator, 'the

The north and west of the peninsula were considerably less influenced by Rome than other areas. This funerary inscription is carved, albeit crudely, in Latin, but the *Dii Manes*, or shades of the departed, to whom it is dedicated, should probably be seen as local, rather than Roman, gods of the underworld. The anthropoidal shape of the stone and style of its carving are completely alien to Roman traditions.

Elder Seneca', spent any significant portion of his life in Spain. Though born in Córdoba, his sons, 'the Younger Seneca', teacher, confidant, and victim of the Emperor Nero and Junius Gallio (who judged St Paul when governor of Achaea), and his grandson, the epic poet Lucan, who was also to perish at the hands of Nero, all moved to Rome in their early youth never to return. The settler population of Baetica also gave Rome two emperors, Trajan and Hadrian, both of whose families came from Italica, and a possible third in Marcus Aurelius. Hadrian we know was mocked for his provincial accent, but apart from their speech, these provincial Romans would have been indistinguishable from other sections of the Roman aristocracy. The agricultural writer Columella, a contemporary of the Younger Seneca, was also a son of Baetica. From further north Quintilian, a native of Calahorra in Tarraconensis, was appointed as professor of rhetoric at Rome by Vespasian, while the poet Martial, who enjoyed the favour of his son Domitian, was aggressively proud of being a native Spaniard rather than descended from settler stock and, unlike many famous Hispano-Romans, returned to live in his native land.

In the first and second centuries AD Baetica was by far the wealthiest of the Iberian provinces. Her main source of wealth was olive oil, exported via the Guadalquivir to Rome, where an entire hill, the Monte Testaccio, is composed of broken Andalusian oil amphorae. Garum, a condiment made from rotted fish, was also an important export, and was made along the coast in all three Iberian provinces. The Greek writer Aelian, in his *On the Ways of Animals*, preserves a story of Spanish garum merchants suffering at Dicaearchia in Italy from raids on their stock by a garum-loving octopus. Although Italy was a major market for these products, they were sold elsewhere too, including in Britain.

Mining also continued to be important. The Mons Mariana, from which the modern Sierra Morena takes its name, was a major source of silver and copper, and mining for gold rather than silver in the north-west contributed substantially to the revenues of Tarraconensis. Pliny tells us that gold production here in his day was over 60 tons per annum. Other sources of income included wine grown in the Ebro valley, Spanish wool and woollen manufactures, and, apparently, dancing girls from Cadiz.

The later Empire saw a decline in the region's fortunes. In AD 171–3 Baetica suffered serious raids from Mauretania. Further attacks were to follow at the beginning of the third century. At the same time Tarraconensis suffered from the depredations of army deserters from Gaul. Nor were these the only external difficulties. In 193 the peninsula supported Clodius Albinus, the losing claimant to the purple. The victorious emperor, Septimius Severus, was swift to take his revenge by confiscating many of the oil estates in the south. While this did not harm production, it did damage the region's internal economy. Conspicuous expenditure by the local aristocracy was the life-blood of civic culture in the Roman Empire. Such attacks made the wealthy both less willing and less able to contribute to communal life. This particular blow was compounded by a general instability in the Empire, disrupting communication and trade. By the middle of the century discontent had grown to such a degree that the Spanish provinces joined the secessionist Gallic Empire from 258 to 270, renouncing allegiance to Rome altogether. The secession seems to have been a period of complete chaos. Hoards of coins, both great and small, and hence reflecting trouble spanning all social classes, reached record levels. Their owners of course never returned to reclaim their wealth—many probably perished before they could do so.

Stability was finally restored to the Roman world by Diocletian in 284, but at the high price of increased centralization and bureaucratic control which only exacerbated the underlying problems facing the Empire. Following a general trend, Tarraconesis was now subdivided into three smaller provinces which, along with the other two Iberian provinces and that of Mauretania Tingitana in North Africa, formed the 'diocese' of the Spains. Each province had its own bureaucracy, in addition to a diocesan bureaucracy, probably based at Córdoba, where the Vicar of the Spains held sway. The result of these changes was a far higher burden of taxation on the local aristocracy, with little by way of return. This produced an inward-looking local elite which, unlike its predecessors who had willingly spent their money to create an urban landscape of which they were the undisputed masters, was eager to avoid civic obligations, preferring to invest in private ostentation. The third and fourth centuries, therefore, see a sharp decline in public building in the peninsula and the rise of highly luxurious private town-houses and villas. Moreover, despite its exactions, the state no longer provided security, and many looked to individual landowners' villas and the enormous estates that surrounded them for protection. The villas therefore became states within a state, often sporting their own private armies. This rural and private luxury stands in stark contrast to the total decline of Cadiz, once one of the wealthiest cities of the Western Empire boasting over 500 members of the Equestrian order, the Roman squirearchy, but described in the fourth century AD by Avienus as an 'abandoned heap of ruins'.

Further impetus to this trend was provided by the rise of Christianity. Again wealth was diverted from civic building projects and endowments

The House of Cantaber at Condeixa a Velha. This luxurious peristyle house, complete with its own baths, was probably built in the third century AD. It would have been at home in any part of the empire and shows the degree to which the local aristocracy of the peninsula had adopted a Roman life-style. It marks the beginning of a trend in the Later Roman Empire for aristocrats to display their wealth and underline their dominance of society through the erection of private rather than public buildings as had previously been the case.

to the needs of the church; another alternative power structure and one which was eventually to outlive the secular state. It is unclear when Christianity first arrived in the peninsula. Claims that Saint Paul visited Iberia are unlikely to be true. Nevertheless, the early church grew in strength and Bishop Hosius of Córdoba was one of Constantine's close confidants even prior to the Emperor's legalization of the faith. A large mausoleum at Centcelles near Tarragona, whose dome is decorated with mosaics depicting hunting and incidents from the Old Testament, is probably the resting place of Constantine's son, the Emperor Constans, who was murdered in 350.

As well as a formal church structure, other more zealous forms of Christianity also rapidly appeared in the peninsula. Priscillian of Avila, a wealthy landowner, renounced the world and founded an extreme ascetic movement which grew in strength in the north of Spain. Despite protests in his support from other Christian luminaries such as St Martin of Tours, Priscillian became the first Christian to die at the hands of a Christian emperor, Magnus Maximus, in 385. Nominally the charge was heresy, but it is likely that Priscillian merely fell foul of the power politics of his day. Another wealthy Spaniard, Maternus Cynegius, zealously destroyed pagan shrines when Praetorian Prefect in the East. The final prohibition of paganism in the Empire in 392 was brought about by a Spaniard who had come to the purple, Theodosius, now known as Theodosius the Great and the last ruler of the unified Roman Empire.

Enthusiasm for Christianity was also reflected in the literature produced in the area in the late Empire. Aurelius Clemens Prudentius (348–c.405) from Calagurris, modern Calahorra, wrote a substantial amount of devotional poetry of high quality which shows his familiarity with the pagan classics. Some of his hymns remain in use to this day. Iuvencus, another high-born Spaniard, (*fl.* 330) wrote a paraphrase of the gospels composed of verses from Virgil to make the Bible acceptable to fastidious readers, and Paulus Orosius, a priest from Braga and a pupil of St Augustine, wrote the first history of the secular world from a Christian perspective in his *Anti-Pagan History*. Christianity also provided new inspiration for the plastic arts, as can be seen from the Centcelles mosaics and the fine marble sarcophagi found in the peninsula, many displaying explicitly Christian themes.

In the end the burgeoning Imperial bureaucracy, despite its size, was no longer able to command the loyalty of local groups. In 407 armies of the pretender Constantine III invaded Spain to detach it from the Western Empire, now ruled over by Theodosius' son, Honorius. Little resistance was encountered. Constantine pressed on into Gaul to fight Honorius himself. The commander he left behind in Spain, Gerontius, promptly rebelled against him and established a local Spanish aristocrat, Maximus, as 'Emperor of the Spains' with a court in Tarragona. Maximus' rule was short lived. Taking advantage of the chaos in the Empire, the barbarian Suevi, Vandals, and Alans poured into the peninsula. Meanwhile Honorius defeated the usurper Constantine, but was able to re-establish Roman control only of Tarraconensis. Maximus fled to live among the barbarians who now controlled the bulk of the peninsula. While Rome claimed the entire area, Roman Spain had in fact shrunk back to its proportions of the third century BC and continued to diminish in size. The last town to fall to the barbarians was, ironically, Tarragona, the city established by Scipio as Rome's bridgehead in the peninsula. It succumbed to Euric's Visigoths in the mid-470s, bringing to a close almost 700 years of Roman involvement in the area.

It would be impossible to overestimate Rome's impact on the Iberian peninsula. Marineus, professor at the University of Salamanca in the fifteenth century, was exaggerating, but not absurdly so, when he claimed, 'we should have no doubt that whatever memorable thing we come across in Spain is due to the Romans'. Rome had impressed herself physically on the landscape, providing a framework which allowed transport, manufacture, and agriculture to flourish. However, her most lasting legacies were mental rather than physical. The Latin language provided the base from which the region's romance languages would evolve and a vital intellectual link to the rest of Europe. Roman rule, by unifying the region into an identifiable unit, was responsible for creating the notion of a Hispanic as opposed to a purely local identity, and in this sense Spain itself can be seen as a Roman invention and Spanish history as having its beginning in the Roman period. Although some areas were less affected by Rome than others, the aristocracy and—importantly—the late-Roman clergy all firmly identified themselves with Roman culture and styled themselves Romans, continuing to do so long after the demise of Roman rule in the peninsula. This triumph over hearts and minds was to ensure that Rome's legacy remained central in the region long after the legions had departed.

2 Visigothic Spain 409–711

ROGER COLLINS

HE chronological boundaries of this period in Spanish history are defined by two invasions. The first of these was that of the Alans, Sueves, and Vandals, who crossed the Pyrenees in September or October 409, and put an end to Roman imperial rule over much of the Iberian peninsula. Although this process was not completed until the Visigothic conquest of the last imperial enclaves in the 470s, the collapse of the defences of the Pyrenees in 409 began the transition to the rule in Spain of a series of monarchies whose ruling families were of Germanic origin. At the other end of this period in 711, invaders from the south, comprising mixed forces of Berbers and Arabs, brought about the collapse of the Visigothic kingdom, and with it the end of the existence of a unitary state exercising authority over virtually the whole peninsula. This would only be recovered during the brief period (1580–1640) in which Portugal was subject to the rule of the Habsburg kings of Spain.

The invaders of 409, like the Visigoths after them, should not be envisaged as uncontrolled marauding hordes bent only upon loot or destruction. They were relatively few in numbers, and effective largely because they were unopposed. In terms of their material culture they were very similar to the Roman provincials amongst whom they came to live, and several of these confederacies had long experience of living on the edge of or even within the frontiers of the Roman Empire. Indeed, much scholarly argument is being devoted at the moment to the questions of how such groupings were formed, of what elements they were composed, and what roles they actually played in bringing about the decline and fall of the Roman Empire in the West. Older views that saw the Goths, Vandals, and others as tribal peoples with a tight ethnic cohesion and continuous histories reaching back to the periods described by Tacitus or even Caesar are now largely discounted. It seems more likely that such

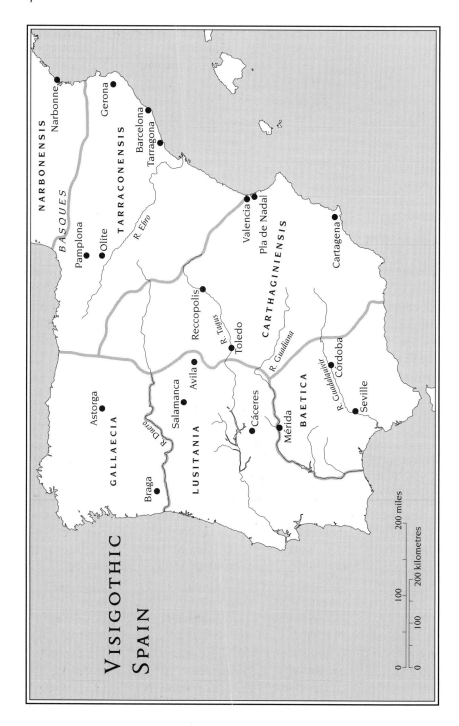

VISIGOTHIC SPAIN

confederacies were continually forming and reforming themselves, drawing in new elements of population, while losing others, and re-creating their sense of ethnic identity around a series of origin myths, with a special role possibly being played by a continuing ruling dynasty whose authority may have rested on rather nebulous claims to hoary antiquity and divine descent. At every stage intermarriage with local populations contributed further to the heterogeneous nature of the ethnic mix.

In the case of the Visigoths, the real processes of the formation of a sense of common identity and a shared history probably developed in the Balkans in the later fourth century. Large numbers of refugees from across the Danube were admitted into the Empire in 376, only to rebel two years later because of the ill-treatment to which they were subjected by the Romans. Although victorious in a historic battle at Adrianople in 378, in which the Emperor Valens was killed, they were subsequently brought to make a treaty with the Empire because they were unable to sustain themselves without Roman assistance. The Emperor Theodosius I (379–95), who was of Spanish origin, then used them as a major element in his armies in a series of civil wars, but following his death they became increasingly independent under the leadership of a series of kings, supposedly members of an ancient Gothic royal line called the Balts, who led them across much of western Europe, frequently in the service of the Roman emperors. The notorious sack of Rome in 410 was the result of the failure of a new Roman government to honour the agreements with the Goths that had been made by its predecessor.

In general, the 'barbarian' confederacies in the fifth century took on the role and filled many of the functions of the former imperial army, increasingly little trace of which can otherwise be found at this time. The 'barbarian' armies, under their own leaders, became linked to the Empire by treaties, and protected regions that were entrusted to them, receiving payment in kind through the imperial taxation system. On the other hand, while on the move or in periods of political turmoil, they took what they needed from the regions through which they passed, and this, in the case of Spain in the years 409 to 418 and in the 450s and 460s, could lead to the destruction recorded in the brief chronicles of the time.

Moving as are these accounts of the sufferings of particular parts of the peninsula, such periods were relatively short-lived. Thus, a treaty was probably made between the invaders of 409 and a rebel emperor called Maximus, who was set up in Barcelona in 410/11. In consequence the Alans and Vandals were established in the provinces of Baetica (the south of modern Spain) and Lusitania (essentially central and southern Portugal), and the Sueves occupied Gallaecia (modern Galicia and northern Portugal). What this meant in practice is not clear, in that the nature of the Roman system of *hospitalitas*, used to accommodate virtually all of the peoples from across the frontiers who became established in imperial territories in this period, remains controversial. It could have involved a distribution of lands expropriated from Roman owners, upon which they could settle and thus maintain themselves, or it could have been a fiscal device, whereby the tax owed on a fixed percentage of a Roman landowner's property became payable directly to the Germanic 'guests'. This interpretation would envisage the latter as remaining primarily as garrisoning forces, not settled on the land. This would certainly seem to have been the case in Spain in the early fifth century, as the various groups of invaders remained mobile, probably still concentrated into armies.

The legitimate western Roman imperial government, now based in Ravenna in Italy, regained control of most of Gaul during the years 411–13, not least through a treaty with the Visigoths, who had made themselves masters of much of the south-west of what is now France, with Narbonne as their capital. As allies of Rome the Visigoths entered Spain in 416 to reimpose the authority of the legitimate emperor, virtually eliminating the Alans and one of the two sections of the Vandal confederacy. In 418 they were withdrawn, leaving the task unfinished, and were re-established in Aquitaine. In the aftermath the Hasding Vandals, who had absorbed the remnants of the Alans and the Siling Vandals, were able to take over much of the south of the peninsula and resisted attempts by Roman and Visigothic armies to dislodge them. However, in 429 they crossed to North Africa and established themselves more securely in the Roman provinces there. This left the Sueves as the only remaining element of the invaders of 409 still in Spain. Under their kings Rechila (438–48) and Rechiarius (448–56) they took over the former Vandal territories in the south, and made the Roman city of *Emerita Augusta* (Mérida) their capital. Rechiarius converted to Christianity, the first of the German rulers in Roman territories to do so. He also began to expand his kingdom into the Mediterranean coastal areas still under direct imperial rule.

This proved fatal to the Suevic monarchy in Spain. As part of a wider agreement between Rome and the Visigoths in Gaul, their king, Theoderic II (453–66), led his army into Spain to put an end to Suevic

A highly decorated pilaster from a late sixth century church in Mérida, reused in the ninth century in a doorway leading to the *aljibe* or cistern in the Arab fortress. Such carved pilasters were typical of the architectural style developed in Mérida and its hinterland in the Visigothic period.

expansion. In 456 Rechiarius was defeated near Astorga, captured, and executed. The Sueves, now under a series of rival war leaders, were pushed back into Gallaecia, and the other territories they had controlled were occupied by Visigothic garrisons. This process was taken further in the reign of Theoderic's brother Euric (466–84), whose armies in the mid-470s overran the last regions of the peninsula, principally the province of Tarraconensis (Catalonia and the Ebro valley), still under Roman imperial rule. Thereafter all of Spain, other than the vestigial Suevic territory in the north-west, formed part of the Visigothic kingdom, which was still centred on south-western Gaul.

It is possible that more of the Visigoths crossed the Pyrenees and began settling in the Iberian peninsula in the 490s; though at no point were they ever more than a small minority of the population of the Iberian peninsula. It has not proved possible to establish the exact nature of the Gothic settlement. Older views that associated the large but materially poor cemeteries found in various parts of central Spain with the presence of Gothic populations in these areas are now discounted. Certainly the Gothic aristocracy, which is to say those members of this society that had sufficient wealth and status to have their own followings, seem to have been distributed across the whole of the peninsula, filling a variety of administrative and military posts of Roman origin. Their households and following will have accompanied them, and it may be assumed that they also began to build up local power bases and to recruit supporters and allies amongst the indigenous Hispano-Roman populations. Whether a difference in language was a bar to their integration into local society is not clear, as there is no evidence at all of the use of Gothic in Spain. The only certain linguistic contributions to the Spanish language, which only begins to emerge as distinct from Latin in the tenth and eleventh centuries, that can be attributed to the Visigothic presence are a small number of titles and a rather larger body of personal names, including a number that have remained popular to the present, such as Alfonso.

The royal government was transferred south of the Pyrenees following the defeat and death of Euric's son Alaric II (484–507) at the Battle of Vouillé. The victorious Franks and their Burgundian allies then overran most of the Visigothic kingdom in Gaul, other than a small area around Narbonne and Carcassonne, known as Septimania. Only the intervention of the Ostrogothic king Theoderic (493–526), who had been Alaric II's father-in-law, prevented further losses. For several decades the Visigothic kingdom in Spain and Septimania was under Ostrogothic rule, exercised first from Italy by Theoderic himself and then, after the brief and inglori-

A view of the foundations of what has been suggested was a royal palace in the city of Reccopolis (Zorita de los Canes, province of Guadalajara), founded by King Leovigild in 578. Continuing in more limited occupation after the Arab conquest, this site was finally abandoned in the late eighth or early ninth century.

ous reign of his grandson Amalaric (526–31), by one of his generals, called Theudis (531–48). With Amalaric's murder in Barcelona, following another humiliating defeat by the Franks, ended the dynasty of the Balts, that had ruled the Visigoths almost continuously since 395. Thereafter no royal house managed to establish an unchallenged right to rule, and none lasted longer than three generations.

Because of the very limited quantity and the restricted nature of much of the subject matter of the literary sources relating to this period, it is primarily archaeology that can, albeit within limitations, offer the best evidence for the way life was led by the different orders of society in Spain in the sixth and seventh centuries. While the neglect or reuse of the great public buildings of the early Roman Empire can be documented from as early as the second century, this was matched by the rise of new forms of public building, churches, baptisteries, pilgrim hostels, and hospitals (*xenodochia*) in the late imperial period. Such developments continued under Visigothic rule, as can be deduced in the case of Mérida both from the narrative history of its bishops written around 630 and from extant remains of some of the churches and other buildings that they erected in the second half of the sixth century.

Such activities and the general rise in the social and economic importance of the episcopate at this time probably need to be seen against a background of the increasing disengagement of the old Hispano-Roman urban aristocracies from town life. The large town houses, that in many cases had been refurbished or extended in the fourth century, are found abandoned or divided into numerous smaller dwellings in the Visigothic period. In Mérida, for example, the existence of burials of the Visigothic period within the rooms of what had been one of the grander town houses of the early imperial period, located close to the Roman theatre and amphitheatre, is clear evidence of the physical contraction of the city by this time. However, it has also been shown that another urban villa, close to the city centre, that had been the property of a single family in the fourth century, was being occupied by eight separate households in the Visigothic period. It is thus not possible to say that urban contraction was a symptom of or was caused by a shrinking in the population of a city such as Mérida. Other sites, such as Valencia, have also produced evidence of urban continuity in this period, with new constructions, even if of inferior quality, being erected over earlier Roman ones. The chronicle written around 602 by John of Biclar also records that the Visigothic King Leovigild (569–86) built two new towns. One of these, on the fringes of Basque territory, has been identified with Olite in Navarre, but this has never been confirmed archaeologically. The other, named Reccopolis after his second son and successor Reccared (586–601), has been located near to the village of Zorita de los Canes in the province of Guadalajara, and excavations have revealed the existence of fortifications, a church, houses that seem to have continued in use until at least the late eighth century, and the foundations of what has been interpreted as being a Visigothic palace.

Similarly, while many of the great rural villas of the later Roman Empire can be shown to have been deserted or destroyed in the upheavals of the fifth century, others continued in occupation, and some quite palatial new ones were first constructed under Visigothic rule. One such late villa, recently excavated at Pla de Nadal near Valencia, had its entry flanked by towers, perhaps indicative of the more troubled state of the countryside at this period, with banditry endemic and the authority of the royal administration liable to periodic violent fluctuations. This administration might even depend upon the resources that could be drawn from the great estates of the Hispano-Roman aristocracy. According to the contemporary Byzantine historian Procopius, King Theudis relied for his own protection upon the private army that he raised from the slaves owned by his Hispano-Roman wife.

The organization of rural life in the Visigothic period is very difficult to reconstruct. It is clear that, as in the later Roman Empire, there existed numerous great estates, worked by a servile population. Some of these were owned by the Visigothic monarchs, either as their personal heritable property or by virtue of their office. It is a notable feature of the seventh-century law code, known as the *Forum Iudicum* or 'Judge's Book', promulgated in 654, that a distinction is made between the two categories of royal estate. It is also clear from literary sources and from inscriptions that great landowners, including the kings, founded private churches on their estates, for their personal use and that of their dependants, and in some cases to secure the presence of men of noted sanctity, who lived as hermits in chambers built around the main body of the church. Their holiness might be expected to reflect upon the patron who supported them. Several examples of such churches have been found in Spain. One in particular, San Juan de Baños, can be shown from an extant inscription to be dated to the year 661 and to have been built on the orders of King Reccesuinth (649–72).

Archaeology has shed some light on another section of rural society in the Visigothic period through recent excavations of one or more of what appear to be village sites. One such, in the province of Salamanca, has revealed the existence of half-a-dozen or more simple stone-built houses, each attached to its own walled stockholding enclosure, with the whole complex being surrounded by a stone perimeter wall. This site is also important for the discovery in it of several of the slate documents that give some tantalizing glimpses of the legal, economic, and even educational life of a number of rural communities in the Visigothic period. Unfortunately, in this case the documents found on the site throw no light on the problem of the exact nature of this settlement. It may have been an independent village of small landowners and stock-rearers, or the village, its inhabitants, and their animals may have been entirely owned by a secular or ecclesiastical magnate.

The slate documents, of which over a hundred are now known, have

been dated to various points in the sixth and seventh centuries. They have been found in excavations, but also just lying in the open countryside in a variety of locations in the provinces of Salamanca, Avila, and Cáceres. The texts they contain have survived by virtue of their being scratched on stone, but unfortunately the friable properties of slate have meant that none have been preserved complete. They do, however, indicate the importance, even in rural society, of the making of records and the use of writing in all forms of legal and commercial transaction. The records of legal disputes and of sales and exchanges can be compared with the much greater quantity of such documents written on parchment that have been preserved from the late eighth century onwards. The similarity both in the procedures used and in the formulae employed in the texts make it quite clear how the legal and administrative practices of the Christian states after the Arab conquest continued those of the Visigothic kingdom.

Amongst the other, generally more significant and permanent forms of record to be found amongst the slate documents, are also a number of what have been interpreted as school exercises. These can be as simple as practice alphabets, but can also include copies of didactic texts and various numerical exercises. Although giving no clue to the precise contexts in which they were made, these documents add substance to the impression to be drawn from the literary sources that a relatively high level of literacy was maintained in Spain in the Visigothic period. References in letters, notably in the collection formed by Bishop Braulio of Saragossa (631–51), prove that not only the Visigothic kings but also other members of the secular aristocracy owned private libraries. Some of the monarchs were noted for their own writings. Best-known is Sisebut, who probably wrote a *Life* of the Frankish bishop, Desiderius of Vienne, and who certainly was the author of a sophisticated poetic epistle on the subject of eclipses. A handful of his letters to various correspondents also survive. Another royal poet was Chintila (636–9), who composed a verse dedication for a gift sent to Pope Honorius I.

The Goths in both Spain and Italy were followers of Arianism, a heresy that had developed in the Roman Empire in the fourth century, which denied the equality and co-eternity of the Son in the doctrine of the Trinity. These beliefs had been accepted by the Goths as a result of their having been converted to Christianity in the Balkans at a time when this

One of over one hundred documents scratched on slate and dating from the fifth to seventh centuries found at a number of rural sites across the western regions of Spain. This one has been dated to the late seventh century, and contains lists of names and quantities, probably of grain, but its exact purpose remains unclear.

heresy had enjoyed imperial support. Although this set them at variance with their Catholic (i.e. orthodox) subject populations, there was little or no religious conflict between the two groups before the 570s. This was in marked contrast to the Vandal kingdom in Africa (which existed from 442 to 533), where there were long periods of persecution directed by the Arian kings against the Catholic episcopate and clergy. In the early sixth century several regional councils were held, particularly in the north-east, in the period of Ostrogothic rule, and a small representative assembly of the whole church in Spain, in the form of eight bishops, met at the Second Council of Toledo in 527 or 531. By the end of the century a far more significant, regular, and large-scale programme of conciliar activity was initiated by the holding of the Third Council of Toledo in May 589, at which sixty-two bishops were present and others sent senior clergy to represent them. This, however, resulted from the solving of a series of political and military problems that had gravely weakened the kingdom, and from the final resolution of the problem of the Arian–Catholic divide in the church.

The middle of the sixth century was a period of considerable instability for the Visigothic monarchy. A new king, Theudisclus (548–9), was murdered like his predecessor, and his successor Agila (549–54) suffered a humiliating defeat at the hands of local rebels in Córdoba, and faced the revolt of a Visigothic noble by the name of Athanagild in Seville. Agila was assassinated by his own men at Mérida, and the kingdom fell into the hands of Athanagild (554–67). During this war, one or other of the two contestants had appealed to the Eastern Roman or Byzantine emperor Justinian I (527–65) for assistance. The expedition sent from Constantinople in 551 established an enclave of imperial territory along the Mediterranean coast from the Guadalquivir valley to the north of Cartagena, which became the seat of a Byzantine governor. Despite a series of campaigns by Athanagild's successors, it was not until the 620s that the Byzantine forces were finally expelled from their last strongholds in the south-east.

Athanagild was the first of the Visigothic monarchs to make Toledo his capital, his predecessors having favoured Seville and Mérida. He was followed in this by Leovigild (569–86), who also introduced new regalia and ceremonial, including the first use of a royal throne, to enhance the image of kingship. He also issued a new style of coinage in his own name instead of that of the emperor in Constantinople, as had been the practice since the fifth century. More practically, throughout the 570s he conducted a series of very successful campaigns that restored royal authority over much of the north and of the south of Spain, including Córdoba, which had been independent since its revolt against Agila around 550. Some Byzantine fortresses were also taken, though it would not be until the 620s that the dwindling imperial enclave centred on Cartagena would finally be eliminated. In 584 Leovigild also conquered and put an end to the small Suevic kingdom in Galicia, which had formally converted to Catholicism, under the influence of Bishop Martin of Braga, in the early 570s.

It seems that Leovigild intended a division of his kingdom between his two sons. In 580 he established the elder of them, Hermenegild, who had recently married a Frankish princess who was also a granddaughter of Athanagild, as subordinate ruler in the south, probably with Seville as his capital. However, the following year Hermenegild rebelled and soon after appealed for Byzantine aid against his father. It is not clear whether Hermenegild's revolt was inspired by his conversion from the Arian form of Christian belief that was the norm amongst the Goths to the Catholic theology of the majority Hispano-Roman population, or whether this followed the outbreak of the rebellion and was a consequence of it. Dynastic politics may also have played a part, as there are suggestions in the sources that Hermenegild had been persuaded into revolt by his stepmother, who was also the widow of Athanagild. Leovigild did not move against his son until after the latter's conversion and appeal to the

A coin of the Visigothic King Leovigild (569–86) of the new style, minted in Toledo in the 580s. There is a stylized bust of the king, with long hair but no other symbols of royalty, on both obverse and reverse. The royal title which runs from one side onto the other reads LEOVIGILDVS REX IVSTVS, and is followed by the mint name TOLETO.

SOROR MEA FLOREN
TINA ACCIPE CODICEM
QUEM TIBI COMPO
SUI FELICITER
AMEN

Byzantine court. In campaigns in 583 and 584 he captured the cities loyal to Hermenegild in the south, and forced him to surrender. Sent into confinement in Valencia, Hermenegild was killed in 585, probably on his father's orders.

This episode brought to a head the problem of the existence of two rival churches within a revitalized and reunified Visigothic kingdom. The Arian–Catholic divide was also ceasing to correspond to an ethnic separation between Goths and Hispano-Romans. A synod held in Toledo in 580 had modified Arian theology, and under Leovigild's persuasion the Catholic bishop of Saragossa had converted. At the same time an increasing number of Goths, particularly in the south, had become Catholics, and in some cases had risen to high office in the church. They resisted all of Leovigild's attempts to persuade or coerce them back into the Arian fold. The final resolution came with the personal conversion of the new king, Reccared (586–601), in 587, which was formalized along with that of the kingdom in the holding of the Third Council of Toledo in May 589. By this time most of the practical problems of absorbing the Arian episcopate and clergy into the Catholic church had been resolved, and the last attempt at revolt by Gothic Arian bishops and their lay supporters was crushed in 590. After this the religious divide ceased to exist.

The importance of the final resolution of this problem should not be underestimated, in that it then allowed the Hispano-Roman population, and in particular its lay and clerical elites, to rally round the Visigothic monarchy. The latter, for its part, had by now reunited virtually all of the peninsula, and was able to provide the church with the political conditions that made possible its subsequent flourishing under the leadership of a succession of outstanding bishops, firstly of Seville and then of Toledo.

Bishop Leander of Seville (d. 599/600) had been closely involved in the personal conversions to Catholicism of the rebel Hermenegild and then of his more successful brother, Reccared. Few of Leander's works, which were mainly directed against Arianism, have survived. He was succeeded as bishop by his brother, Isidore (d. 636), who was to be both the most prolific and most influential of the ecclesiastical authors of the Visigothic period. His twenty-book *Etymologies* was a vast encyclopaedia of late-antique learning, which became widely disseminated across western Europe soon after his death, and remained a standard work of reference

A depiction of Bishop Isidore of Seville (died 636) and his sister, the nun Florentina, to whom he dedicated his work 'Against the Jews'. This comes from a manuscript written in north-eastern France around the year 800.

throughout the Middle Ages. His briefer historical writings, a chronicle and the *History of the Goths, Sueves, and Vandals*, served to place the Goths and their past into the wider framework of both Roman and biblical history. Isidore dedicated these and others of his writings to some of the Visigothic kings whom he served. He remained the dominant figure in the church of his day, and was responsible both for the directing of the Fourth Council of Toledo in 633 and for the compilation of the first version of the *Hispana*, a collection of the acts of ecumenical, African, Gallic, and Spanish church councils.

After Isidore's death the leadership of the church in Spain passed to a series of bishops of Toledo, who not only encouraged the centralizing of secular authority in the hands of the monarchs who normally resided in their city, but also matched it by attempting to unify the ecclesiastical organization and discipline of the kingdom under the direction of their own see. While not all of their works have survived, a number of these bishops, in particular Ildefonsus (657–67) and Julian (680–90), were the authors of works that circulated widely both within Spain and across the Pyrenees for centuries to come. Another of these bishops, Eugenius II (647–57) was a noted poet, and like his successors a major contributor to the great body of liturgical compositions that is one of the glories of the Visigothic church. This line of bishops, and Julian in particular, also established the unchallenged authority of the see of Toledo over the other metropolitan and suffragan bishops of the kingdom. They also succeeded in ensuring that royal legitimacy, initially dependent upon the support of the aristocracy and army, also had to be guaranteed by the new king receiving unction and undergoing other inauguration rituals exclusively in Toledo and only at their hands. This became the norm from 672, if not earlier.

The secular narrative history of the Visigothic kingdom in the seventh and early eighth centuries is not as easy to write as that for the preceding period, as there is an almost complete lack of the necessary sources. In comparison with the detailed accounts of such substantial texts as the *Ten Books of Histories* of Gregory of Tours (d. 594) or Bede's *Ecclesiastical History of the English People*, which illuminate so much of early Frankish

Christianity took a firm hold in Spain in the Later Roman period. Optimus' epitaph written in awkward Latin reads 'Optimus, behold the Lord Who takes the greatest care over matters of gravity, has given you the divine mansions of heaven which He had promised. You rest at peace in the House of Christ.' The House of Christ may refer to the shrine of Bishop Fructuosus and his deacons, Eulogius and Augurius, who were martyred in the town's amphitheatre in AD259 and probably buried in the same necropolis as Optimus.

and Anglo-Saxon history, Isidore's historical writings, are disappointingly short. After this there follows a complete dearth of contemporary historiography in the Visigothic kingdom, broken only by the *History of Wamba* of Bishop Julian of Toledo, a short and highly rhetorical account of King Wamba's accession in 672 and his campaign against the rebel Count Paul in 673. Not until after the Arab conquest would historical texts be written in Spain. Some of these cast light back on to the period before 711, but this is strongly coloured by the events of that year. In rival historiographical traditions in the north and the south of the peninsula different Visigothic monarchs and dynasties were held responsible for the disaster that then befell the kingdom and its inhabitants.

Some additional information can be gleaned from references in non-Spanish sources, such as the later-seventh-century Frankish *Chronicle of Fredegar*, and from other forms of evidence, such as coinage. From the latter, for example, it is possible to know of the existence of two Visigothic kings, Iudila and Suniefred, who are not recorded at all in the literary evidence. Some contemporary events are to be found reported in the law codes and in the acts of the numerous plenary and regional councils of the Spanish church in this period. From such sources emerges the evidence of the participation of one of the bishops of Toledo, Sisbert (690–3), in a failed conspiracy against King Egica (687–702), about which almost nothing else is known. The chronology of the period can be worked out, more or less, from a series of king-lists, recording the lengths of their reigns, but these can be contradictory.

By such diverse routes it is possible to produce at least an outline of the events of the period between the holding of the Third Council of Toledo in 589 and the Arab conquest of 711. Of Reccared, following his achievement of the formal conversion of the kingdom and its Gothic population, surprisingly little is known. His early death in 601 left the throne in the hands of an infant son, Liuva II (601–3), who was soon deposed and murdered following a conspiracy amongst the court nobility led by his successor Witteric (603–10), who in turn would be murdered by his courtiers. The next king, Gundemar (610–11/12), is best known through the survival of some of the letters sent to him by one of his military commanders in Septimania, a Count Bulgar. Sisebut (611/12–20), an unusually learned

The votive crown given by King Reccesuinth (649–72) to an unknown church, probably in Toledo. Such crowns were used liturgically, being suspended over the high altar during the major ceremonies of the year. This, along with several other crowns and liturgical ornaments, was discovered at Guarrazár near Toledo in 1849. The pendant letters record the donor's name.

The depiction of a royal anointing from the tenth century León Antiphonal (León Cathedral MS number 8, folio 271ᵛ), a copy of a lost manuscript dating to the reign of the Visigothic King Wamba (672–80). The receiving of unction, a liturgical ceremony that could only be performed in Toledo, became the central feature of the formal processes of Visigothic king-making in the later seventh century.

monarch, died in mysterious circumstances, leaving a young heir in the person of Reccared II, whose own death the following year is never explained by Isidore.

As with Liuva II and subsequently in the case of Tulga (639–42), a minor had little hope of retaining the throne. On the one hand Visigothic kings had traditionally been the leaders of their people in war, a role that could not credibly be filled by a child, and on the other the factionalism and competition for power amongst the aristocracy required the deploying of considerable political skill on the part of the monarch, who was the ultimate source of patronage both at court and throughout the kingdom. This role, too, could not be taken by a ruler too young to exercise authority in person. His removal, then, became one of the options open to the factions vying for power. Even adult kings who were successful militarily found it difficult to retain power in this society. Thus the monarch who replaced Reccared II, Suinthila (621–31), who had both been a successful general in the time of Sisebut and also completed the eviction of the

Byzantines from their last strongholds (*c.*625), was himself overthrown in a military rising.

This was led by Sisenand (631–6), who obtained the assistance of the Frankish King Dagobert I (623–38/9) for his revolt. The reward for this was to have been part of the loot carried off from Rome by Alaric after the famous sack of 410, which had then come to be part of the Visigothic royal treasure. Such treasures represented not only a financial reserve for the monarchy, but more importantly embodied the history and traditions of the people. In this particular case the Goths would not let Sisenand part with the promised payment, and he had to send a sum in gold coins instead. It has been suggested that the, relatively few, later-sixth- and seventh-century hoards of Visigothic coins that have been found in France derive from this transaction.

Sisenand was clearly aware of the danger that he might suffer a similar fate to his predecessor, and, probably on the advice of Isidore of Seville, sought to hedge the royal office around with spiritual protection. He wanted the bishops to threaten supernatural sanctions, in the form of the excommunication of offenders, against conspiracies. He was thus the first king since Reccared in 589 to call together a full council of the church in Spain and in Septimania. The problem in practice was that, although the bishops assembled in council complied with Sisenand's requests, and threatened anathema against any who should plot against the king and his family, the distinction between a legitimate monarch and a usurper could only be made clear by the outcome of a revolt. In other words, should a rebel succeed in overthrowing the established ruler, this in itself made it clear that he had divine support and was thus a legitimate king.

It was thus perfectly logical for the same bishops who had promulgated these acts and threatened spiritual sanctions against plotters and usurpers not to have raised any opposition to the successful rebel Chindasuinth (642–53) when he overthrew and imprisoned the child King Tulga (639–42). The successful outcome legitimated the new king's actions. Chindasuinth himself, who was said to be in his eighties, took more direct and secular action to try to ensure the protection of himself and his dynasty. The *Chronicle of Fredegar* reports that he had several hundred Gothic nobles executed in the aftermath of his succession, eliminating actual and potential opponents. He also enthroned his son Reccesuinth (649–72) as co-ruler during his lifetime, to ensure a smooth succession. This he certainly achieved, but his son's lack of heirs meant that the dynasty died with him in 672, leaving the succession to be decided by the court aristocracy.

The reigns of Chindasuinth and Reccesuinth are notable not least for their legislative activity. The first code of law issued by a Visigothic king to have survived, at least in part, is that fragment ascribed to Euric, but which may be the work of his son Alaric II. The latter certainly issued an abridged version of the Roman *Code of Theodosius* in 506, which came to be called *The Breviary*. Although an individual law of Theudis has been found, no further codifications are known to have been made until the time of Leovigild. His revision and amplification of his predecessors's work has not survived, although it is thought that much of it was absorbed into the very substantial code promulgated by Reccesuinth in 654. This has come to be known as *Lex Visigothorum* or 'The Law of the Visigoths'. Although its application would be limited and modified from the tenth century onwards by the various sets of local *fueros* issued by kings and other founders of towns, this Visigothic code, which came to be known by the vernacular form of *Fuero Juzgo*, would apply over much of Spain until at least the thirteenth century. It was also the body of law that was administered by and for the Christian communities under Islamic rule in the centuries following the Arab conquest.

Divided into twelve books, it was a systematic statement of law that abrogated all previous codes. It has been seen as the first 'territorial' code of the Visigothic monarchy, which is to say it applied to all persons within the frontiers of the kingdom. Earlier codes are, in such an interpretation, to be taken as applying to either the Roman or the Gothic sections of the population, but not both. However, there are strong grounds for doubting this, and for suspecting that all of these codes could be taken as applying to all subjects of the Visigothic kings. This is certainly the case with Reccesuinth's code, which also sought to be comprehensive. Cases that were found not to be covered by the individual laws that it contained had to be sent to the king for decision, and rulings on them might be expected to be added to future versions of the code.

Reccesuinth is commemorated not only in his law-book and in his church of San Juan de Baños, but also in the impressive gold liturgical crown, decorated with semi-precious stones and the record of his gift in the pendant letters hanging from the bottom of it, that may now be seen in the Museo Arqueológico Nacional in Madrid. This, like another (now lost) full-size crown that was given by Sisenand, and a series of still extant smaller crowns and crosses given by lesser patrons, must have been presented to one of the major churches of the kingdom, perhaps in Toledo. It was in the countryside not far from the city that this treasure was found in 1849. Such liturgical crowns were never worn, but were hung over the

The church of San Juan de Baños, near Palencia. An extant inscription over the chancel arch records the foundation of this church by King Reccesuinth in 661, but it has recently been suggested that the present building derives from a later reconstruction in which the original elements were reused.

main altar of the church to which they were given on special festivals, such as Easter Sunday. Although documentary records show that such gold and silver crowns, which publicly displayed the munificence of the benefactor who presented them, were numerous in the early Middle Ages, very few have survived. That of Reccesuinth is by far the finest.

He seems to have had no heirs, and on his death in 672 the court nobility gave the kingdom to one of their own number, by the name of Wamba (672–80), but he was immediately challenged by rivals in Septimania, of whom the most effective was a Count Paul. Although a triumphal account of Paul's defeat in 673 was soon written by the Toledan deacon Julian, Wamba's relationship with the church was thereafter uneasy. His attempts to establish two new bishoprics were considered uncanonical, and when he fell ill and appeared near to death in 680, it was the same Julian, recently made metropolitan bishop of Toledo, who manoeuvred his removal from the throne. Although in later versions of the story it is claimed that Julian poisoned him to bring this about, it seems more probable that Wamba did genuinely fall ill, and as was then customary adopted the penitential state in expectation of his death. However, he recovered, but the church, led by Julian, decreed that as a penitent he could not resume his secular activities. He was obliged to retire into monastic life, while a Visigothic noble called Ervig (680–7) was made king in his place.

In 681 the new monarch issued a revised and expanded version of Reccesuinth's law code that is particularly notable for the substantial increase in the number of laws it contains relating to the Jewish population of Spain. Reccared had taken over some of the legislation of the later Roman Empire concerned with the Jews, such as, for example, the prohibition on their owning Christian slaves. But it was in the reign of Sisebut that the Visigothic kings began to frame laws of their own, intended to restrict the liberties of their Jewish subjects or to coerce them into conversion. Sisebut himself, who may have been responding to encouragements sent from the Emperor Heraclius (610–41) in Constantinople, attempted to impose conversion by decree on the entire Jewish population of Spain. This was condemned after his death by the bishops assembled at the Fourth Council of Toledo (633), but they refused to allow Jews who had been forced into conversion to return to their own faith.

The history of the treatment of the Jews in the seventh-century Visigothic kingdom makes sombre reading, not least because it has almost exclusively to be written in terms of the increasingly severe and arbitrary rules and restrictions handed down by secular and clerical legislators. There is no evidence from this period, unlike later centuries, as to how far, if at all, those regulations and prohibitions were translated into practice, or as to what relations between Christians and Jews were like at a local level. It is clear that increasing numbers of Jews will have been driven into conversion by the legal restrictions imposed upon them, even if the crudely direct methods of Sisebut were never again attempted. In the 690s those Jews who were still practising their religion were accused by Egica of conspiring with their fellow believers beyond the frontiers, and they were to be punished by enslavement and the forfeiture of their property. This may have been a fiscal measure intended to benefit the royal finances, but the accusation may also be a reflection of the worries that were then being felt concerning the rapid expansion of the Arabs through the former Byzantine provinces of North Africa.

Little more is known of the reign of Egica, who had secured the succession through his marriage to his predecessor's daughter and a promise to protect the interests of the former's family and supporters. Both wife and promise were repudiated soon after his accession, and subsequently Egica survived a conspiracy (*c.*692) in which the then bishop of Toledo, Sisbert, was implicated. It may be that this led the king into trying to resolve any problems over his own succession by making his son Wittiza joint ruler very soon after. No difficulties ensued when Egica died in 702, but Wittiza's early death in 710, when probably only in his early twenties, led to a crisis. A civil war between noble factions ensued. A King Roderic (710–11) gained control of Toledo and probably most of the south, while a rival monarch, Achila II (710–13) can be seen from his coins to have ruled over Barcelona, Narbonne, and the Ebro valley. There may have been other contestants. It was during this period of turmoil that the Arabs, who had completed their conquest of Roman North Africa in 698, launched their largely Berber armies across the straits of Gibraltar. Although the evidence is unclear and contradictory, the defeat and death of Roderic and the capture of Toledo seem to have followed in 711 or possibly 712. By 714 the Muslim armies had reached Saragossa, and the last Visigothic strongholds fell with the conquest in 720 of the vestigial kingdom of Achila II's successor Ardo (713–20) around Narbonne. In the same period new administrative and fiscal structures were being put in place in Spain by a succession of Arab governors. Seville and then Córdoba replaced Toledo as the administrative centre of the peninsula, breaking with the traditions of government of the Visigothic monarchy.

By the end of the seventh century, if not earlier, the sense of separate Roman and Gothic identities in the Visigothic kingdom had ceased to exist. There are no more Romans to be found, and after 711 it is as Goths that the inhabitants of the areas of the peninsula not under Arab rule feature in documents and literary texts amongst themselves and their neighbours across the Pyrenees. It used to be thought that this was caused principally by the abolition of a separate legal system for the Roman population in the mid-seventh century. However, it seems more reasonable to believe that royal laws applied to all sectors of society, from the time of Euric if not before. In reality, the Roman identity was more of a legal than an ethnic one, in that it derived from the notion of citizenship. With the processes described above of intermarriage and local assimilation taking place across the kingdom, and with the enthusiastic support given to the monarchy by the church from 589 onwards, the creation of a new common sense of a Gothic identity seems to have been increasingly embraced as the seventh century progressed, at least in the upper levels of society. Simply put, the Goths could have come to be seen as the ancestors of the modern Spaniards in the way that the Franks are so regarded

systems, intermarriage with the indigenous Christian and Jewish populations, shifts of religious allegiance between Judaism, Christianity, and
Islam, all combined to produce a thorough cultural mix. In northern
Spain the Basque and Cantabrian peoples, who had been less affected by
Romano-Visigothic Christian culture than their neighbours to the south,
were spilling out from their mountains onto the plains. The north-east
continued in the early medieval period to offer ease of movement to and
from southern Gaul as it had done from prehistoric times. Migration of
peoples, ethnic mixture, a dappled and speckled cultural map: these were
the fundamental characteristics of early medieval Spain.

Until the eleventh century the Muslims were politically dominant
in al-Andalus (as their new conquest was always known in the Arabic-
speaking world). The Umayyad dynasty, immigrants to Spain after the
takeover of their Syrian power-base by the rival Abbasids, presided as
amirs (756–929) and subsequently as caliphs (929–1031) from Córdoba
over most of the peninsula, saving only the refugee Christian principalities in the north. In this choice of capital they shifted Spain's political
centre of gravity southwards from the valley of the Tagus to that of the
Guadalquivir. The move did not simply reflect environmental preferences.
Córdoba's proximity to the Straits of Gibraltar draws attention to the
critical importance of the Maghrib to medieval Andalusi history. Africa
might be a source of wealth, as in slaves or recruits for the amiral army or
the gold laboriously brought across the Sahara from distant Timbuktu.
She might be a source of hostility from land-hungry Berbers or puritan-
ical Islamic zealots. Whether valued or guarded against, the African connection was one that Andalusi ruling circles neglected at their peril—or
which modern historians neglect at a cost to their understanding.

The great mosque which the Umayyad rulers built in Córdoba in the
eighth century on the site of the former Christian cathedral and subsequently enlarged in the ninth and tenth centuries was an architectural
manifesto of Islamic triumphalism. Many among the indigenous population adopted the faith of their conquerors. Conversion to Islam was a
gradual process, difficult for the historian to measure, but probably at its
most intense between about 850 and 1000. It was uneven in its incidence,
probably more widespread and thoroughgoing in urban and suburban
than in rural areas. It seems likely that in the remoter regions there were
numerous village or valley communities which preserved a rudimentary
Christianity untouched by Islam. Surviving written sources tell us almost
nothing at all about these Christian enclaves; little by little archaeologists
are revealing their material culture to us. Convert and non-convert alike

borrowed much of the non-religious culture of their rulers, most notably the use of Arabic as the language of everyday life. That is why there are so many loanwords from Arabic in modern Spanish, from *aceite* to *zoco*, so many place-names of Arabo-Berber formation such as Alcántara or Benidorm or Guadalquivir. Arabic versions of Christian scriptural texts survive in manuscript, as do Christian gravestones incised to the memory of the deceased with Arabic lettering, witnesses to the penetration of the native culture by the language of the conquerors.

The civilization and learning of Middle-Eastern Islam as well as its religion and language also put down roots in Spain during the ninth and tenth centuries. Trading networks linked al-Andalus to distant parts of the Islamic world—Egypt, Iraq, Iran, even India. Ambergris from the Atlantic was traded in Baghdad, textiles from Bokhara made their way to Spain. Improved techniques of irrigation were introduced and new crops to benefit from them such as rice, spinach, and sugar-cane. An imported aesthetic as well as the desire to impress visiting dignitaries informed the palaces and gardens of the Guadalquivir valley, the most famous among them the immensely grand and elegant palace-complex at Madinat al-Zahra, not far from Córdoba, built by the caliph `Abd al-Rahman III (912–61). Under the enlightened patronage of this ruler and his biblio-phile son the Caliph al-Hakem (961–76)—during whose reigns the power of the Umayyad dynasty reached its apex—a court culture of great richness and diversity flourished in fields as various as poetry and histori-ography, calligraphy and music, botany and medicine, mathematics and astronomy, ivory-carving and metalwork.

Centralist and nostalgic historiography, both medieval and modern, has tended to exaggerate the degree to which the caliphs of Córdoba brought into being the institutional machinery of a bureaucratic state dur-ing this period. There can be little doubt that something like this did exist within a variable radius of the capital. But the further one trav-elled away from Córdoba, the less heavy lay the caliphal hand. The ties of locality, the pressures brought to bear of those who made or main-tained locality, remained as strong as they had been under Romans or Visigoths. Even in parts of southern Spain not remote from Córdoba a dis-affected soldier like 'Umar ibn Hafsun (d. 917) could maintain a bandit state-within-a-state in the mountains round Ronda for a generation. The sophisticated culture of the caliphal court never lapped the austerer world of the northern marches. Contemporaries called these the 'front teeth' of al-Andalus. They were military zones, defended by castles such as that of Gormaz, in its day the most advanced piece of military architecture in Europe. Power lay in the hands of local bosses who commanded the networks and the military retinues to guarantee deference and security: *caciques*, a later generation would call them. Such, for example, was the Tujibid family of the north-east marchlands of the Ebro valley round Saragossa, whose members ran their own show to all intents and purposes independently of their nominal sovereigns at Córdoba from the late ninth century until the extinction of their dynasty in 1039.

The Christian principalities of northern Spain were modest indeed when compared to their imposing Muslim neighbour. Their origins were diverse. To the north-west, in the Asturias, a refugee principality claiming a tenuous continuity with the Visigothic monarchy dimly took shape in the second quarter of the eighth century. In the western Pyrenees a Basque principality, later to become the kingdom of Navarre, emerged in circumstances even more obscure a little later. On the southern flanks of the eastern Pyrenees in Catalonia a group of counties, collectively known as the Spanish March, was organized on the fringes of the Frankish empire by Charlemagne and his son in the early years of the ninth century. Though maintaining a nominal allegiance to the Carolingian dynasty of West Francia (i.e. France), these counties had in actuality drifted into effective independence by about 900.

These nuclei of Christian identity grew up almost imperceptibly on the ragged edges of al-Andalus where the Islamic presence had barely registered. From these bases they began to expand towards the south. The expansion of the Asturian kingdom was the most striking. By about 950 its political centre of gravity had shifted to the city of León on the southern side of the Cantabrian mountains, it had absorbed the north-western territory of Galicia, and it had spawned subordinate frontier counties, sometimes politically restive, of Castile to the east and of Portugal to the west. The traditional judgement that the territorial expansion of these statelets was urged on by the imperative of *Reconquista*, though now much less convincing than it once seemed, should not be summarily set aside. The rulers of Asturias and León claimed to be the heirs of the Visigothic monarchy. This claim was a significant theme of the historical writing undertaken at court under the sponsorship, perhaps in part the authorship, of King Alfonso III (866–910). One chronicler praised his forebear Alfonso II (791–842) for restoring at Oviedo 'all the ceremonial of the Goths, just

The castle of Gormaz, towering above the valley of the River Duero near Soria, was one of the so-called 'front teeth' which defended the northern frontiers of al-Andalus in the tenth century.

San Pedro de Roda, in Catalonia, with a church of the early eleventh century, was a monastery fortified to resist human enemies as well as supernatural ones.

as it had been in Toledo'. The surviving pre-Romanesque churches of this period in the Asturias deliberately harked back to the monuments of a royal Visigothic past: for instance, Alfonso II's church of San Julián de los Prados (or Santullano) at Oviedo, or Alfonso III's church of San Salvador de Valdediós a little further east. The law which regulated everyday life in the Asturian-Leonese kingdom was the *Lex Visigothorum* codified by seventh-century Visigothic kings. The intermittent use of the title *imperator*, 'emperor', by the rulers of Asturias and León from the tenth century onward seems to have indicated their hegemonial pretentions. Their propagandists looked back to the victory over a Muslim army at Covadonga (719?)—probably in reality a skirmish of no great military significance—

as the opening act in a drama of liberation. One remarkable work, the so-called *Crónica Profética* or 'Prophetic Chronicle' composed in 883, even looked ahead optimistically to the imminent collapse of Islamic dominion in Spain and the restoration of Christian authority. Such heady notions as these must have held some appeal, varying in potency as to time and circumstance, for a small elite of kings, courtiers, and clergy; but they need to be set in the context of earthier and less articulate social forces.

Demographic pressure was one such. The abundant documentation surviving from early medieval Catalonia has enabled historians to demonstrate that the eastern Pyrenean valleys were so densely populated in the ninth and tenth centuries as to be pressing at the means of subsistence. Though the evidence is sparser, a similar state of affairs may be detected in the mountainous regions of Aragon, the Basque country, Castile, the Asturias, and Galicia. There was, thus, an enormous reservoir of the land-hungry to furnish colonists for the plains to the south, plains which had been to a great degree depopulated so as to form a buffer zone between Muslim and Christian. This demographic imperative was fortified by economic habit. The economy of the Christian communities of early medieval Spain, as of their Islamic neighbours in the northern marches of al-Andalus, was overwhelmingly agrarian. Not only were there no big cities like Córdoba or Seville, there were hardly any towns worth the name. Exchange of goods beyond basic staples like iron or salt was rare. Coin circulated sluggishly at best and in many areas not at all. Itinerant pedlars, craftsmen in wood or leather or metal, suppliers of grain and meat to hungry ecclesiastical or princely households there may have been; but no bourgeoisie, no merchant class. This agrarian economy was a mixed one in which pastoral farming was prominent. Livestock need, ideally, variety of pasture according to the changing seasons. Territorial expansion made possible a routine of pastoral transhumance between mountain and plain, underpinned by an agriculture geared to necessities in grain and grape and oil, in pork and eggs and apples.

Diverse sources shed a little light on migration, settlement, and economy. Place-names in León and Castile first recorded in the tenth century as *Gallecos* and *Villa Vascones* indicate migrants from Galicia and the Basque lands respectively. In 943 the Castilian monastery of Cardeña, near Burgos, acquired pastures in the Duero valley sixty miles to the south, clear evidence of transhumant pastoralism. In the diocese of Braga, in northern Portugal, the phenomenal rate of church-building in the tenth and eleventh centuries attests a thickening of village settlement. In Catalonia, Abbess Emma of the nunnery of San Juan de las Abadesas, daughter of Count Wifred the Hairy of Barcelona, in some twenty years between 892 and 913 settled the country round about with a score of villages and over a thousand people. In 978 Count García of Castile founded a religious house for his daughter Urraca at Covarrubias: the endowments included land *per populare*, 'to be settled', and big herds of livestock—500 cows, 1,600 sheep, and 150 brood-mares. In these two and in other instances the role of forceful aristocratic women in organizing settlement is notable.

Settlement was laborious and often dangerous. Colonists were exposed not only to the risks of crop failure and cattle disease but also to lightning raids from al-Andalus by camel-borne predators intent on supplying the slave markets of Córdoba. Unsurprisingly, therefore, initially independent peasant farmers enjoying economic and legal freedom tended to drift or to be nudged into dependence upon more powerful proprietors who could protect them from hardship or attack. In Catalonia ecclesiastical landowners—Abbess Emma herself is a good example—were buying up peasant plots and turning their proprietors into tenants from the early tenth century onwards. Doubtless secular landowners were doing likewise, invisibly to us because their archives have not survived. References to 'evil usages' or 'customs' (*mali usatici, malae consuetudines*) begin to crop up in the documentation from about the year 1000. These 'usages' comprised such burdens as heavier rents, the imposition of labour services, the establishment of costly lordly monopolies over essential operations such as milling, the binding of peasant families to their land so that they could not move away and might be sold or donated with it, and fines for such offences as adultery. Unsurprisingly, the rhythms of social change displayed widely varying nuances and a confusingly diverse vocabulary at different times and in different regions. What was beginning to happen in Catalonia in the tenth and eleventh centuries can be traced on the plains of León and the valley of the Duero in the eleventh and twelfth, in central Portugal in the twelfth and thirteenth. As a rough and ready generalization, however, the trend was all in the same direction, and in the longer term the beneficiaries of colonization were ecclesiastical corporations such as bishoprics and monasteries, and the secular aristocracy. Its victims were the peasantry, on whom the pressure of seigneurial demand weighed ever more heavily.

The few surviving contemporary narratives relating to the tenth century, whether of Islamic or Christian authorship, focus their attention upon the military doings of the secular elites of their respective communities. Thus we hear of the daring raid of `Abd al-Rahman III on

Pamplona in 924, of his defeat at the hands of King Ramiro II of León at Simancas in 939, of the hammer-blows of the all-powerful vizir Almanzor whose armies sacked Barcelona in 985 and León in 988. But the cultures which faced out across the frontier zone about the year 1000 were not uniformly nor invariably hostile. The zone itself was permeable. Christian knights took service as mercenaries in caliphal armies. In 1010 the counts of Barcelona and Urgel contracted to supply 9,000 troops to serve in al-Andalus: Muslim chroniclers would remember it as 'the year of the Catalans'. A tenth-century prelate, Rosendo, successively bishop of Mondoñedo and Compostela, installed a Cordoban chef at the monastic house he founded at Celanova in Galicia. Jewish merchants intermittently visited the north to sell the silk textiles and other luxury goods which were so prized as status trophies among the Christian aristocracies of León or the Spanish March. There were permanent migrants as well. Although a somewhat grudging toleration was extended to Christians under Islamic rule in accordance with Koranic precept, emigration from al-Andalus to the friendlier north was always a tempting option. In the middle years of the ninth century, for example, the Galician monastery of Samos, originally founded in the seventh century, was revived with royal encouragement by an abbot named Argericus, a recent arrival from al-Andalus. These migrants, usually known as Mozarabic or 'Arabized' Christians, have left a strong imprint upon the art and architecture of the Christian north, notably in the robust graphic art with its vivid colours— once seen never forgotten—of their illuminated manuscripts. It was probably through the agency of the Mozarabs that some inklings of the scientific culture of al-Andalus leaked through to the culturally retarded north. The earliest surviving set of 'Arabic' numerals in western Christendom was committed to writing in a Navarrese monastery in about 976. When the great French scholar Gerbert of Aurillac wanted to pursue the study of mathematics as a young man in the 960s, it was to the Catalan monastery of Ripoll that he went. In Catalonia he came into contact with Mozarabic Christian and Jewish intellectuals who taught him to use the abacus, a skill which he subsequently passed on to his fellow-countrymen in France. The abacus is a simple device, but in an environment of desperately elementary mathematical knowledge in early medieval Christendom it had as liberating an effect as the computer has had in our own day.

Far-reaching changes occurred in eleventh-century Spain, seismic upheavals which re-drafted the cultural landscape. In the first place, the unitary political authority in al-Andalus represented by the caliphate of Córdoba dissolved in a welter of disputed successions and military *pro-*

nunciamientos. After two decades of civil war the last caliph was deposed in 1031. The caliphate was replaced by a number of successor states, petty principalities typically based on a town and its surrounding hinterland. These principalities are known to historians as the *taifa* states, a term derived from an Arabic word for 'faction' or 'party'. Factious they certainly were, their rivalries and conflicts resembling those of ancient Greece or Renaissance Italy (whom they resembled also in their artistic creativity). Rendered vulnerable by these internecine conflicts, the *taifa* states laid themselves open to exploitation by predators. The Christian rulers of northern Spain quickly learnt how to manipulate their Muslim neighbours, and successfully operated what has been termed a protection racket by which they offered military assistance in return for the payment of tributes, known as *parias*, in the gold coin of al-Andalus. These arrangements were sometimes formalized in written treaties, as for example the two treaties agreed between Sancho IV of Navarre and al-Muqtadir the ruler of the *taifa* state of Saragossa drawn up in 1069 and 1073: Sancho was to be paid the very considerable sum of 1,000 gold *dinars* every month. The kings of León-Castile, especially Alfonso VI (1065–1109), and the counts of Barcelona, especially Ramón Berenguer I (1035–76), were notably skilled manipulators who enriched themselves mightily. The tone of these exchanges is vividly conveyed to us in the remarkable autobiography of ʿAbd Allah ibn Buluggin, ruler of the *taifa* state of Granada between 1073 and 1090, which contains graphic accounts of his hagglings with Alfonso VI. Kings and counts were not alone in thus profiting. Freelance mercenary soldiers could also operate in these turbid waters. The most famous but not the only such man was the Castilian nobleman Rodrigo Díaz, known as *El Cid*, 'the Boss' (d. 1099). He was not in his lifetime what legend would later make him, a Christian hero and Castilian patriot who fought to push the Muslims out of Spain: eleventh-century realities were less straightforward than this. Rather, Rodrigo was a skilful soldier of fortune who enriched himself in the employ of a variety of paymasters, both Christian and Muslim, and ended up as his own man, tribute-taker and prince of the *taifa* of Valencia on the Mediterranean coast.

The flow of gold from Muslim into Christian Spain in the eleventh cen-

The pyxis of Al-Mughira, made for a member of the caliphal family in AH 357 (= 968 AD), is among the finest examples of Andalusi ivory carving. Luxury artworks of this sort were highly prized and eagerly coveted by the Christian elites of northern Spain and trans-Pyrenean France.

tury had far-reaching effects. It assisted in the consolidation of secular authority. The counts of Barcelona, for example, deployed their new-found wealth in the systematic purchase of castles, rights, and territories, which gave them the edge over any rivals for hegemony in the Spanish March. Ten such purchases are recorded from the single decade of the 1060s. In León-Castile Ferdinand I (1037–65) and his son Alfonso VI used their wealth to endow a nobility of service, a cadre of loyalists who would strengthen the royal hold over distant parts of their kingdom such as Galicia. They spent it on the embellishment of their royal city of León, many of whose monuments and treasures may still be admired. They also dispatched a generous proportion of their gains to a monastic destination beyond the Pyrenees.

During the period between the eighth and the eleventh centuries, Christian Spain had been to some degree, though never entirely, isolated from the developing culture of Carolingian and Ottonian Europe. Of course, there were as ever regional nuances: the Catalan counties of the Spanish March remained culturally a part of the Carolingian world long after they had ceased to be so administratively. With some such qualifications, however, it is broadly true that the further west one travelled in Christian Spain at this epoch the more culturally conservative a scene one would encounter. A small but significant indicator: with very few exceptions the literary works generated by the Carolingian Renaissance were not to be found in the libraries of great monastic houses such as Silos, Sahagún, or Celanova. Piety sparked the mechanism which hauled Christian Spain out of isolation. One manifestation of it took the form of pilgrimage to one of Christendom's holiest shrines. At some point between 818 and 842 what was believed to be the tomb of the apostle St James the Greater was discovered in Galicia at the place which now bears his name, *Sanctus Jacobus*, Sant'Iago, Santiago de Compostela. His cult was enthusiastically promoted by clergy and kings, notably Alfonso III. From the tenth century pilgrims to his shrine were beginning to trickle over the Pyrenees from France: a bishop of Le Puy made the journey in 951, an archbishop of Rheims ten years later. During the eleventh and twelfth centuries they were flooding in from all other parts of western Christendom as well. The earliest traceable English pilgrim to Compostela visited the shrine in about 1100. The church and town of St James did very nicely

Muslim gold in Christian hands. This illustration in a Catalan manuscript of the late twelfth century portrays Count Ramón Berenguer I of Barcelona (1035–76) and his wife Almodis paying in gold coin for the purchase of the counties of Carcassonne and Razès from the viscount of Béziers.

out of the pilgrim traffic. Already in the tenth century predators from distant places had found the place worth their while to sack, a band of Vikings in 968, Almanzor's army in 997. By the twelfth century much of the paraphernalia of international tourism can be discerned in guidebooks and accoutrements, ritual and souvenirs, songs and stories, Basque phrase-lists, exorbitant lodging-houses and fraudulent money-changers. The great Archbishop Diego Gelmírez (d. 1140) was able to rebuild St James's cathedral church on the grandest scale and to a design which was intended to facilitate the movement of large processions of pilgrims.

A second manifestation of piety was the act of largesse referred to above. In the mid-eleventh century the great Burgundian monastery of Cluny became the favoured recipient, in return for the expert prayers of the monks, of annual payments of Muslim gold from the royal family of León-Castile. A network of Cluniac monastic 'colonies' grew up in Spain, and the incoming Cluniac monks set about reforming what they saw as a tradition-bound and lamentably outmoded Spanish church along the most up-to-date lines sketched out by the idealists of the age of the Hildebrandine reform of the Papacy. The leading spirit among these innovators was Bernard of Sédirac, Frenchman, monk of Cluny, colleague and friend of that other Cluniac monk Pope Urban II, who became successively abbot of Sahagún (1080–6) and archbishop of Toledo (1086–1124). During Bernard's lifetime, and in great measure owing to his agency, the church in León-Castile underwent modernization on Franco-Papal lines. French clergy from Bernard's *équipe* were jobbed into bishoprics, such as Jerónimo, native of Périgord, successively bishop of Valencia under the Cid and, after the evacuation of the city in 1102, of Salamanca until his death in 1120. Church councils were held to condemn abuses and proclaim standards of excellence. An ancient and cherished liturgy was swept away. New texts of canon law began to circulate. A new script, *francesa* or 'French writing', that is, the Carolingian minuscule of France, gradually ousted the older 'Visigothic' script. An unprecedentedly close relationship with the Papacy was established. No papal legate had ever visited the churches of León-Castile, to our knowledge, before about 1067; over the ensuing ninety years nine cardinals paid legatine visits, five of them more than once. Routines and institutions of church government were imported from France, cathedral chapters, diocesan synods, and episcopal visitation.

This intensification of contact with western Christendom beyond the Pyrenees was not confined to the kingdom of León-Castile. French bishops were to be encountered in Navarre and Portugal. Norman knights fought in Catalonia, even establishing there for a couple of generations in the twelfth century a semi-independent principality at Tarragona. When the kings of Aragon expanded from their mountain nucleus round Jaca down into the valley of the Ebro they did so with the aid of French aristocratic adventurers from Poitou and Béarn to whom they were related by marriage. When they sought to repopulate the countryside and the semi-deserted towns such as Saragossa, it was to France that they looked for settlers. French members of new religious orders, Cistercians, Augustinians, Premonstratensians, founded houses in Spain. French entrepreneurs—shopkeepers, craftsmen, hoteliers—were to be found in towns along the pilgrimage road such as Pamplona, Logroño, Burgos, León, Astorga, and Lugo. Rulers imported techniques of authority from France, such as the use of written orders or mandates, and sometimes the bureaucrats who wielded these techniques on the king's behalf, such as Gerald of Beauvais who managed Alfonso VII's writing-office between 1135 and 1149. French architects designed the new cathedral of Santiago de Compostela built between 1078 and 1124, and markedly French influence can be detected in Spanish Romanesque sculpture. The famous French troubadour Marcabrun visited the court of Alfonso VII, and in his celebrated poem *Lavador* hailed Spain as a place of 'cleansing' where French knights might win spiritual merit in warfare against the enemies of Christ. Old French epic poetry influenced Spain's greatest epic, the *Poema de Mio Cid*, composed perhaps in the last quarter of the twelfth century.

Immigrants from France doubtless brought ideas with them as well as skills and fashions. During the eleventh century notions about the holiness of warfare against the enemies of the church were gaining strength. Ideas would be translated into action in the crusading movement initiated by Pope Urban II in 1095. Hitherto, Christians had tended to look upon Islam with a bewildered lack of curiosity. Little by little this was replaced by militant hostility in which Spain, like Syria and Palestine, became an arena of religious war.

The tribute-taking of the eleventh century had rested upon the coexistence of Christian and Muslim societies within Spain, for the simple but compelling reason that needy rulers had no wish to kill the goose that laid the golden eggs. Coexistence was not invariably harmonious, nor were considerations of territorial gain in addition or as an alternative to pecuniary advantage altogether absent. Ferdinand I had conquered Coimbra in 1064. Alfonso VI took Toledo in 1085, a prize of special resonance as the ancient capital of the Visigothic kings. These goings-on were watched with dismay from across the Straits of Gibraltar. A fundamentalist Islamic sect, the Almoravids, had grown up south of the Atlas in the middle years of the eleventh century and gradually extended its grip over northern Morocco. Fatally, the *taifa* rulers paid little attention to these developments. The Almoravid leaders, simple and direct of vision, saw only that Islamic law was being scandalously flouted in al-Andalus by the payment of tribute to infidels. In 1086 Almoravid troops crossed the Straits, inflicted a heavy defeat upon Alfonso VI at Sagrajas near Badajoz, and subsequently took steps to close down the *taifa* regime. Within a few years all the *taifa* states of southern Spain had disappeared. It was as a captive of the Almoravids in Morocco that 'Abd Allah of Granada, dethroned, composed his memoirs. Al-Andalus was once more reunited, but now under an intolerant, militant Islamic leadership.

In such a manner as this was religious hostility stoked up on both the Christian and the Islamic side of the religious divide in Spain in the late eleventh and early twelfth centuries. One symptom of it was the appearance of military orders in Spain. A religious order composed of men who took vows, like monks, to devote their lives to spiritually meritorious warfare against Islam was a characteristic product of the crusading era. The most famous such order was that of the Temple, or Knights Templar, so called because its headquarters in Jerusalem stood on what was believed to have been the site of King Solomon's temple. The Templars began to acquire recruits, properties, and military responsibilities in the Iberian peninsula in the second quarter of the twelfth century. Native orders in imitation of them began to be founded a little later. In León-Castile the order of Calatrava was founded in 1158, that of Santiago in 1170—St James thus assuming a new role as patron saint of Christian warfare against Islam—and that of Alcántara in about 1175. In Aragon the order of Mountjoy and in Portugal the order of Avis were also established in the early 1170s. Their troops were to make significant contributions to the campaigns of the Reconquest, and their castles to the consolidation of a Christian hold upon new territories. Their rewards, as we shall see, made them rich and powerful.

In terms of political power the Almoravids did not last long. Removed from their Moroccan homelands they rapidly succumbed to the temptations of a softer environment, thus fulfilling a cyclical pattern in Berber cultural evolution which would first be described by the great fourteenth-century Tunisian scholar Ibn Khaldun. From the 1120s they were being challenged simultaneously by the rise in Morocco of yet another fundamentalist sect with a confusingly similar name, the Almohads, and by successive native Andalusi risings against their occupation of Spain. In some

St James as a warrior who championed Christian warfare against Islam. This Romanesque tympanum from the cathedral of Santiago de Compostela, sculpted *c.*1200, is among the earliest surviving representations of *Santiago Matamoros*, 'St James the Moor-Slayer'.

respects history seemed to be repeating itself. As Almoravid dominion crumbled in al-Andalus authority again fragmented into petty statelets known to historians as the 'Second Taifas'. Christian rulers again exploited this weakness either by tribute-taking or by territorial aggrandisement, or by both. Alfonso VII of León-Castile (1126–57) raided deep into Andalusia, conquered Córdoba in 1146 and Almería, medieval Castile's first window on to the Mediterranean, in 1147. His anonymous contemporary panegyrist presented him to the world in the guise of an Old Testament king, fighting holy wars at the head of a chosen people. But this phase of heady Christian expansion in the middle years of the twelfth century was checked by intermittent Almohad intervention in Spanish affairs, followed by their full-scale takeover of al-Andalus, complete by 1173. Almohad power continued strong for a generation, but then became enfeebled as the Almoravid had beforehand. A decisive Christian victory was won by Alfonso VIII of Castile at Las Navas de Tolosa in 1212. In its aftermath a great push forward by the three main Christian kingdoms had by 1250 reduced Islamic dominion in Spain to the amirate of Granada.

The three Christian monarchies were those of Aragon, Castile, and Portugal. (Navarre hung on as an independent monarchy until the early sixteenth century, but its geographical position excluded it from the territorial spoils of reconquest.) This political fragmentation was the major institutional legacy of the early medieval period. Never again, save briefly between 1580 and 1640, would the entire land-mass of the Iberian peninsula be united under a single authority as had been the case for the first seven centuries of the Christian era. The last ruler to style himself 'Emperor' was Alfonso VII; the hegemonial claims implicit in the title were quietly dropped thereafter. Partition treaties which shared out prospective conquests of Muslim territory among Christian rulers—the first such agreed in 1150—took this political divergence for granted. The consolidation of divergent institutional practice—legal, fiscal, municipal—was a consequence of political fragmentation. In later centuries this would pose formidable obstacles to the ambitions of a centralizing Castilian bureaucracy.

Of these three monarchies that of Portugal was the least considerable. The county of Portugal, roughly the northern third of the modern state, hived off from its Leonese-Castilian parent in the second quarter of the twelfth century. Its first independent ruler, Afonso Henriques, assumed the title of king in 1140, secured recognition from the pope and, grudgingly, from his cousin Alfonso VII, conquered Lisbon in 1147 with the aid of an Anglo-Flemish naval force—the first post-conquest bishop of Lisbon was English—and was active in the resettlement of his newly won territories in central Portugal, notably with the help of the Cistercian monks of Alcobaça and the Templars based at Tomar. By the middle years of the thirteenth century the Algarve had been reconquered and Portugal had taken on the territorial contours which, with only minor modifications, have been hers ever since. Portuguese ships were already beginning to probe the Atlantic coasts of the Maghrib in search of plunder or trade, harbingers of the activity which would later yield a worldwide empire.

The kingdom of Castile, definitively united with León from 1230, was the biggest of the Spanish kingdoms. Ferdinand III (1217–52) exploited the victory of Las Navas to bring under his sway colossal areas of Andalusian countryside, dozens of towns great and small, and two southern coastlines with their ports, in the Mediterranean (Cartagena) and in the Atlantic (Cadiz). Ferdinand's conquests could be presented as glorious Christian crusades by his propagandists such as the historian and myth-maker Archbishop Rodrigo of Toledo (died 1247). Pursuit of *gloire*, how-ever, rarely makes kings wealthy. In choosing the option of territorial conquest Castilian kings deprived themselves of income from tribute and laid upon their own backs the expensive burden of responsibility for re-settlement. Castilian rulers had not developed the more sophisticated bureaucratic, fiscal, and legal machinery which enabled English or French kings to cream off an income from their subjects. They had not needed to, having been so long sustained by a 'slash and burn' public finance of trib-ute and plunder. Desperate for cash, they could and did plunder their own subjects, notably the most vulnerable among them, their churchmen. Ferdinand III forced the Castilian clergy to contribute heavily to his cam-paigns and he gave them very little in return. There is a hoary old myth that the Castilian church feathered its nest with the spoils of the Recon-quest: the truth was precisely the reverse; the church was bled white to finance it. An impoverished church, debauched and bullied by its secular protector—and it is surely one of Spanish history's most singular ironies that Ferdinand III was later canonized—was an ineffective church in its primary pastoral role. Judged by the standards proclaimed by Pope Inno-cent III and the bishops of Christendom assembled at the Fourth Lateran Council in 1215, the Castilian church of the thirteenth century was in a deplorable condition.

Another consequence of royal poverty was the practice of seeking con-sent for extraordinary levies of taxation. It had long been regarded as desirable for kings to rule with the counsel, if necessary the restraining counsel, of their greater subjects. Gradually, from the late twelfth century onwards, under the influence of both fiscal pressure and the revived study of Roman law, the seeking of consent became more frequent and the cir-cle of consenters was widened to include, notably, representatives from the towns. It is believed that the earliest recorded attendance of urban delegates at such a meeting of a royal court occurred at León in 1188. But what was beginning to happen in Christian Spain was matched by simi-lar developments, the summoning of assemblies variously called estates, diets, parliaments, and so forth, in other western European monarchies. The *cortes* (Catalan *corts*), as such assemblies came to be known in the Spanish kingdoms, had not become a fully formalized institution by the end of our period, but already they had shown themselves capable of playing a significant constitutional role.

The Andalusian countryside was sparsely settled, its towns and cities depleted by the flight of refugees, sometimes—as in the case of Seville in 1248—deliberately depopulated by the wholesale expulsion of their Muslim inhabitants. Spanish kings had long been in the habit of granting codes of municipal privilege, known as *fueros* (Portuguese *forais*, Catalan *furs*), to individual towns in order to encourage and regulate the process of resettlement. The Andalusian *fueros* of the thirteenth century not infrequently sound a note of desperation in the inducements they hold out to attract settlers (and in the sort of settlers they were prepared to take), and the magnitude of the concessions offered served to dilute and undermine the exercise of firm royal authority. The evidence of the *fueros* suggests that it was harder to attract settlers in the thirteenth century than it had been at earlier dates. This is a little curious, if historical demographers are correct in presenting the twelfth and thirteenth centuries as a time of steady population growth in western Europe. Possibly the evidence merits critical re-examination. Be this as it may, it would appear that earlier sources of people to resettle the vacant spaces of southern Spain and Portugal had dried up by about 1200. The northern mountainous zone had ceased to yield a surplus, and immigration from France seems to have slackened after about 1150.

In these circumstances it made the soundest economic sense to specialize in activities which were not labour-intensive. From the thirteenth century onward the large-scale ranching of cattle, horses, and above all sheep was developed by those who did best out of the conquest of Andalusia and the Algarve, namely the military orders and the aristocracy. In 1169 King Afonso of Portugal promised to the Templars one-third of all his conquests to the south of the Tagus. In 1174 Alfonso VIII of Castile conceded a fifth of his prospective landed conquests to the order of Calatrava. Enormous concentrations of property grew out of concessions such as these. In southern Estremadura the orders of Alcántara, Santiago, and the Temple each acquired nearly a quarter of a million acres (300,000 hectares). The great noble houses of Castile—Lara, Castro, Guzmán, and others—also assembled very extensive landed estates in the south. The ranchers set up their own cartel, the *Mesta*, to safeguard their interests, particularly in the protection of their flocks and shepherds on the *cañadas* or sheepwalks which led from winter pastures in Estremadura or La Mancha to summer grazing in the upland territories of Old Castile. The merino sheep, introduced from the Maghrib probably about 1250, is tough, does well in a hot, dry climate, and grows fine wool. The clip fed a domestic textile industry, and soon a foreign one in Flanders and England. Export of merino wool quickly became Castile's primary commercial activity.

Aragon is shorthand for *Corona de Aragón*, the 'Crown of Aragon', the title employed for what was not a single monarchy but a federation which came into being piecemeal in the course of the twelfth and thirteenth centuries. The Catalan county of Barcelona was yoked to the kingdom of Aragon by a dynastic marriage in 1137. Naval and military enterprise in the thirteenth century, lovingly and vividly chronicled by King James I (1213–76) in his *Llibre dels Feyts*, his 'Book of Deeds' or autobiography, enlarged it. The Balearic Islands were added in 1229–35, the principality of Valencia in 1238.

No attempt was made to unify or standardize the institutions of the separate components of the federation. The ruler's rights and powers, and the mode of their exercise, varied as between Aragon, Catalonia, and Valencia. Yet the federation pulled together, on the whole successfully, perhaps because of its very diversity. Aragon proper was a predominantly rural region. By contrast with Andalusia or the Algarve, its territory to the south of the Ebro retained its Muslim peasantry after conquest in the twelfth century, though gradually assimilated to Christian culture: kings were thus here relieved of the problems of resettlement. The principality of Valencia presented a contrast again. The city of Valencia itself was cleared of its Islamic inhabitants in 1238, like Seville ten years later, but in its rural hinterland the Muslim peasantry remained intact, far outnumbering the Christian settlers who were brought in from further north. Here among these Muslims under Christian rule, known to historians as Mudejars, the Islamic faith and the Arabic language would continue to thrive for several centuries; and there could be no question of the amassing of huge landed estates by the nobility or the orders as in Castile or Portugal.

The expansion of the city of Barcelona was the most striking feature of the economic and social history of Catalonia in the twelfth and thirteenth centuries. During this period it emerged as one of the great urban success stories of the medieval world, comparable with Genoa and Venice though unfortunately receiving less attention from historians than those over-indulged Italian cities. Initial growth was primed by the tributary gold of the *taifas* in the eleventh century and sustained by buoyant agrarian output in the town's hinterland. Barcelona was the first city for several centuries in western Europe to mint gold coin (from c.1020). A check to growth was administered first by the Almoravids and then by the Genoese, the latter bought with the promise of lavish trading privileges on the Mediterranean coast by the Emperor Alfonso VII in return for naval help with his conquest of Almería in 1147. But Almería could not be held, and several of the big mercantile families of Genoa got their fingers badly burnt by overextending themselves in investments which did not pay off. The bourgeoisie of Barcelona could step into the trading gap thus created. Their abundantly surviving documents show them diversely active—women as well as men, in an open and fluid social structure—as industrial and craft entrepreneurs, property developers, and bankers to kings, churchmen, and magnates. The extension of the Aragonese-Catalan maritime empire—by 1300 it included Sardinia, Sicily, and Malta, and would soon encompass an outpost in Greece—provided bases for the skippers who plied throughout the Mediterranean and beyond into the Black Sea. The men and women in the counting-houses of Barcelona had to keep a weather eye on markets as distant as Tunis or Trebizond.

Early medieval Spain was multicultural in the sense of being culturally diverse, a land within which different cultures coexisted; but not in the sense of experiencing cultural integration. Toleration for Christians and Jews as 'Peoples of the Book' is enjoined by the Koran. But in practice it was limited—Christians under Islamic rule were forbidden to build new churches, to ring church bells, to hold public processions—and sometimes it broke down altogether. In 1066 there was a pogrom in Granada in which its Jewish community was slaughtered. Thousands of Christians were deported to slavery in Morocco in 1126. Thoroughly dismissive attitudes to Christians and Jews may be found in the Arabic literature of al-Andalus. It is a myth of the modern liberal imagination that medieval Islamic Spain was, in any sense that we should recognize today, a tolerant society.

Much the same could be said of the fortunes of the Mudejars and Jews under Christian rule. They were reluctantly tolerated, not out of principle but out of pragmatism: because they could be useful. Seville offers an instructive example. Ferdinand III's 'ethnic cleansing' in 1248 was designed to render it an exclusively Christian city. However, when a few years later it became apparent that it would be impossible to repopulate it with Christian settlers, Muslims and Jews were permitted to settle there. We can chart the process in Seville's *Libro de Repartimiento*, literally a 'book of partition', a register of urban property showing how it was shared out in the years after the reimposition of Christian rule. The urban *fueros* suggest that the religious minorities were subject to all sorts of discrimination designed to maintain their subjection. For example, it was made difficult for

A Christian knight in all the arrogance of victory rides down a Muslim in the submissive posture of defeat. This sculpture of *c.*1200 from Tudela in Navarre is an eloquent statement about cross-cultural relationships in medieval Spain.

Mudejars to bring lawsuits against Christians, and they tended to be fined more heavily than Christians for the same offence. A dismissive arrogance towards Muslims and Jews is displayed in literature such as King James's autobiography and in art.

Inter-communal relations in medieval Spain are difficult to investigate because so much of the evidence is that of legal prescription, which is not necessarily a reliable witness to everyday social reality. When *fueros* required that Christians, Muslims, and Jews should use the municipal bathhouses on different days of the week, it is a nice point whether we may assume that this hygienic apartheid invariably occurred. Only rarely can we test prescription against reality. We have evidence that Christian churches were being built near Córdoba in the ninth century, despite the ban alluded to above. We have evidence that, despite the prohibitions of the *fueros*, sexual relations between Muslims and Christians did occur. We hear of Christians accompanying Islamic or Jewish friends to mosque or synagogue. We can name many Jewish doctors who treated Christian patients. When Queen Berengaria, the mother of Ferdinand III, was laid to rest in 1246 her head reposed upon a pillow whose crimson silk cover was decorated with Arabic lettering proclaiming the standard pieties of Islam. We know that from time to time Muslim dress was fashionable in smart Christian circles. Such instances as these should make us cautious of generalizing. However, we are on reasonably secure ground in assuming that throughout our period the dominant authority, whether Islamic or Christian, would take steps to be, and to be seen to be, dominant. Religious and cultural minorities were there to be exploited for their skills, but in other respects to be kept firmly down.

Muslim and Christian were simply not interested in one another. The great Cordoban poet and scholar Ibn Hazm (994–1064) composed a work known as the *Kitab al-Fisal* or 'Book of Sects', a treatise demonstrating and celebrating the rightness of Islam. He had learned a considerable amount about Christianity from the Christian texts available in Arabic translation—but only in order to refute it. Ibn Hazm's attitudes can be exactly matched on the other side of the religious divide a century later. Peter the Venerable, Abbot of Cluny, commissioned a translation of the Koran and other Islamic texts into Latin in the course of a visit to Spain in 1142. He did this not out of any sympathetic interest in Islam, but simply in order to refute it, which he duly did to his own satisfaction in a work whose tone is indicated by its title, *The Abominable Heresy or Sect of the Saracens*.

The translators whom Peter engaged were two foreign scholars working in Spain, the Englishman Robert of Ketton and the German Hermann of Carinthia. Their primary motive in going to Spain had been to locate Arabic works on astronomy, geometry, and mathematics and to translate them into Latin. They were, in this, following after an interval in the footsteps of Gerbert of Aurillac. Robert and Hermann were only two of a large number of scholars who were attracted to Spain in the twelfth and thirteenth centuries by the lure of Graeco-Arabic philosophical and scientific works and the technology which accompanied them. The transmission of this corpus of learning to western Christendom—especially of the works of Aristotle with the commentaries upon them by the Andalusi polymath Ibn Rushd (1125–98, better known as Averroes)—was to have far-

The great mosque of Córdoba was built as an assertion of Islamic piety and triumph by successive rulers of al-Andalus between the eighth and the tenth centuries. Its *mihrab*, illustrated here, indicates the *qiblah*, or direction of Mecca, towards which Muslims must turn in prayer.

Ferdinand and Isabella, the *Reyes Catolicos* or 'Catholic Monarchs', whose marriage brought about the dynastic union of Aragon and Castile: famed for their conquest of Granada, their expulsion of the Jews from Spain and their patronage of Columbus.

reaching consequences for the development of European intellectual culture in the thirteenth and fourteenth centuries.

Early medieval writers commonly employed the term *Hispania* to indicate what Arabic speakers called al-Andalus, that part of the Iberian peninsula under Muslim rule. But the *Hispania* which, with the exception of Granada, had been repossessed for Christendom by 1250, had lost even that degree of cultural identity which it had had under Romans or Visigoths. There were the political and institutional divergences already discussed, and the uneasy religio-cultural bandings and overlappings of Christian, Muslim, and Jew. Linguistic diversity was more complex in 1250 than in 700, with the admixture of Arabic, the diffusion of Basque, the fragmentation of proto-Romance into Galaico-Portuguese, Castilian, and Catalan. French cultural fashions in architecture and art, in literature, and in aristocratic values and behaviour had mingled with native traditions. There were lines of tension. The perennial strain in the peninsula between centre and periphery had been made more intense by the rise of Barcelona and the beginnings of maritime enterprise in Atlantic and Biscayan harbours. Translated into social terms, there was an incipient conflict of values between a military landed nobility which drew most of its wealth from ranching, and the urban and commercial culture of the bourgeoisie of Barcelona or Bilbao, Valencia or Seville. In a slightly different form, comparable strains can be detected in the southward thrust of the Reconquest itself. As the itinerant Castilian royal court increasingly favoured residences at Toledo, Córdoba, or Seville, there were places like Oviedo and León which simply got left behind, lapsing into the subdued provincial backwaters they have remained ever since. The same could be said of the Crown of Aragon. Racial, communal, and cultural mixture was a source of anxiety to authority in church and state. Could Muslim subjects be relied upon to be loyal to Christian kings? Were converts from Judaism or Islam genuine, or were they bogus, crypto-converts who might revert to a former religious allegiance? In crude material terms, kings were impoverished by the Reconquest. Ferdinand III was a less wealthy ruler than his forebear Alfonso VI. Those who profited—the military orders, some aristocratic families, some towns—would be the less amenable to control, harder for kings to manage. Church and peasantry alike experienced, in different fashions, burdensome pressures which stifled freedom and initiative.

The sheer diversity of medieval Iberian society, emphasized at the outset of this chapter, renders useful generalization difficult. Medieval Spain has been called 'a society organized for war', and a 'colonial' or 'frontier'

society. Such perceptions or characterizations may have validity when applied to the ever-shifting frontier zone but are less convincing when used to describe the ever-more-extensive regions behind its lines. One may doubt whether, say, the tradespeople of Pamplona who served the needs of pilgrims to Santiago thought of themselves as part of a society organized for war; or the nuns of remote Cines near the Atlantic coast of Galicia; or the market gardeners of the irrigated *huerta* of Valencia, whether living under the rule of the caliphs, the *taifas*, the Cid, the Almoravids, or King James I; or the dons who taught theology and law at the young university of Salamanca.

Iberian society was already too complex to be susceptible of such simple classifications. There was plenty of variety and vitality in the Iberian peninsula by the mid-thirteenth century. Perhaps there was more vitality than harmony. A duty, from a certain point of view, had been done; but at a heavy cost. Later ages would have to pick up the bill.

This celestial globe, made in one of the *taifa* states probably not long before Alfonso VI's conquest of Toledo in 1085, embodies the sophisticated knowledge of astronomical science in the Islamic world which attracted western European scholars to study in Spain in the twelfth and thirteenth centuries.

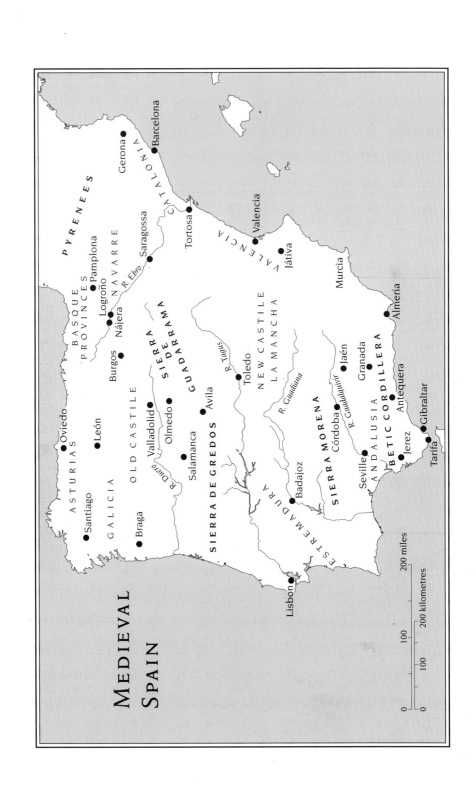

MEDIEVAL SPAIN

Barcelona
Gerona
PYRENEES
Pamplona
CATALONIA
Saragossa
R. Ebro
NAVARRE
Logroño
Tortosa
VALENCIA
BASQUE PROVINCES
Nájera
Valencia
Burgos
SIERRA DE GUADARRAMA
Játiva
OLD CASTILE
NEW CASTILE
Oviedo
ASTURIAS
León
Valladolid
Olmedo
Ávila
LA MANCHA
Murcia
Almería
Santiago
GALICIA
Salamanca
SIERRA DE GREDOS
R. Tagus
Toledo
R. Guadiana
Jaén
Granada
BETIC CORDILLERA
Braga
R. Duero
Córdoba
R. Guadalquivir
Antequera
Gibraltar
SIERRA MORENA
Seville
ANDALUSIA
Jerez
Tarifa
ESTREMADURA
Badajoz
Lisbon

0   100   200 miles

0   100   200 kilometres

4 The Late Middle Ages
1250–1500

ANGUS MACKAY

N addition to the documentation held in royal, seigneurial, ecclesiastical, and urban archives, the historian of Spain from the mid-thirteenth century down to the accession of the Catholic Kings, Ferdinand and Isabella, has at his disposal splendid series of chronicles. The authors of almost all of these concentrated on the events of the royal courts and the deeds of the kings or their enemies, either because their salaries were paid by the monarchy or because they attached themselves to particular political factions. As a result, the evidence of such works has to be used with a necessary degree of caution. An outstanding example of such a chronicler would be the chancellor of Castile, Pedro López de Ayala (1332–1407). He deserted one king and supported his rival. When the latter usurped the throne, Ayala skilfully defended his desertion in his chronicles. Is his evidence about the defeated king's character and tyrannical behaviour to be taken at face value? Of course there were exceptions to these chroniclers obsessed with the royal court. One constable of Castile, for example, retired from the royal court and settled in the town of Jaén. As a result, the chronicle of Miguel Lucas de Iranzo contains fascinating accounts of the tournaments, entertainments, plays, and frontier military activities that characterized the life of this town and its extended region.

In surveying the history of Spain during this period certain obvious themes require consideration. The first of these is that of the Reconquest, that is, the process whereby the Christians attempted to win back the lands which had been lost to the Muslims when the latter invaded and overran most of the Iberian peninsula in 711. Starting long before the period dealt with here, the Reconquest appeared to stagnate during the Later Middle Ages. Yet the sense of Spain's 'manifest destiny' (that is, the task of the Reconquest) had not been lost. Indeed, even foreigners helped with this sacred task. In June 1329, for example, Robert the Bruce, the hero of the Scottish Wars of Independence, lay dying. He had always wanted to participate in a crusade against the infidels, and he now planned to do so posthumously. His heart would be embalmed, put into a casket, and entrusted to a contingent of Scottish knights who would take it into war against the infidels in the Holy Land. But in the event the Scottish knights, led by Sir James Douglas, went to Spain. There, in Andalusia, at the Battle of Teba de Ardales, Douglas threw the casket into the middle of the Muslim enemy and the Scottish knights charged to rescue it. They were almost all killed, but the casket was recovered and taken back to be buried in Scotland at Melrose Abbey. Bruce had achieved his wish, but he had done so in Andalusia. Was Andalusia another Holy Land, another Jerusalem? Chaucer's fictitious knight participated in the reconquest of Algeciras in 1344 and he crossed the straits to fight the Marinids in North Africa.

Did Spain perhaps provide an alternative route to Jerusalem? There certainly existed a belief in a Last World Emperor who, at the end of days, would resign his *imperium* directly to God in Jerusalem at Golgotha. In Spain this tradition, suitably influenced by Joachimite ideas and prophesies attributed to St Isidore of Seville, produced a Spanish messianic king and world emperor known variously as the *Encubierto* (the Hidden One), the *Murciélago* (the Bat), and the New David. The beginning of each new reign, therefore, aroused eschatological expectations. Was the new king the *Encubierto* or the Bat who would defeat the Antichrist in Andalusia, retake Granada from the Muslims, cross the sea, defeat all Islam, conquer the Holy City of Jerusalem, and become the last world emperor? When would the Hidden King reveal himself?

The problem was that reality had to match eschatological expectations, and this coincidence was not achieved until after 1480 at the end of the period under consideration in this chapter. Suddenly, between 1480 and 1513, there was an explosion of exuberance as contemporary events made eschatology credible. As the successes of the Catholic Kings, Ferdinand of Aragon and Isabella of Castile, multiplied, so too did the prophetic texts, commentaries, and even ballads which identified Ferdinand as the *Encubierto* or the Bat who would conquer Jerusalem and then the whole world. Nor was all this the work of obscure and humble fanatics. It was proclaimed and elaborated at the highest levels, as can be seen by the letter of revelation which the grandee Don Rodrigo Ponce de León, marquis of Cadiz, circulated to the great nobles of Castile in 1486. The secret, the truth, had been revealed to him by a mystic. What was it?

...the illustrious, powerful, and great prince, King Ferdinand, king and lord of the kingdoms of Castile, Aragon, and Sicily, was born under the highest and most copious planet that any king or emperor ever was...There will be nothing in this world able to resist his might, because God has reserved total victory and all glory to the rod, that is to say the Bat, because Ferdinand is the *Encubierto*... And he will subdue all kingdoms from sea to sea, and he will destroy all the Moors of Spain, and all renegades to the Faith will be completely and cruelly destroyed because they are mockers and despisers of the Holy Catholic Faith. And not only will his Highness conquer the kingdom of Granada, but he will subdue all Africa, and the kingdoms of Fez, Tunis, Morocco, and Benamarin... And he will conquer the Holy House of Jerusalem...and with his own hands he will raise the banner of Aragon on Mount Calvary...and he will become Emperor of Rome...and he will keep the Roman see empty for three years; and then, by God's will, he will install an Angelic Pope...and not only will he be Emperor but he will be Monarch of all the world...

Spain, therefore, provided an alternative crusading route to Jerusalem. Certainly, the holy city was not far from people's minds. Robert the Bruce had died in 1329. For his part King Ferdinand the Catholic received a message from God shortly before his death in 1516. This message was passed on to the king by the celebrated female visionary known as the Beata of Piedrahita, and it assured him that he would not die until he had taken Jerusalem.

Given the successes of Ferdinand and Isabella, it is hardly surprising that they have traditionally been regarded as 'early modern' monarchs who established a 'Renaissance state' and supposedly 'unified' Spain, even though the Kingdom of Castile and the Crown of Aragon retained their distinctive institutions and customs. By contrast, the Later Middle Ages seem to have been bedevilled by disunity, civil wars, and chaos. For example, although the Reconquest started long before the period being dealt with here, it appeared to stagnate during the fourteenth and most of the fifteenth centuries until it was brought to a triumphant conclusion when the Muslim Kingdom of Granada fell in 1492. This has often been regarded as Spain's *annus mirabilis*, for not only did the Christians fulfil their 'manifest destiny' by taking Granada and completing the Reconquest, but in the same year Christopher Columbus discovered America. Unfortunately, 1492 was also the year when the Catholic Kings expelled the Jews from Spain. As far as the period under consideration here is concerned, it witnessed Spain's involvement in the Hundred Years War in Europe, the breakdown of what is known as *convivencia* (a form of relative religious tolerance), the emergence of contrasting constitutional trends in

the Crown of Aragon and the Kingdom of Castile, the beginnings of a maritime and territorial expansion in the Mediterranean and Atlantic, and cultural developments of extraordinary vitality and interest. While adopting a narrative structure of political events, this chapter will attempt to do justice to these important themes.

At the start of this period the reigns of James I of Aragon (1213–76) and Alfonso X of Castile (1252–84) provided intriguing contrasts in terms of successes and failures. As his own *Book of Deeds* (*Llibre dels feyts*) illustrates, James I of Aragon, 'the Conqueror', had a high opinion of himself, perhaps deservedly so, given his resounding victories over the infidel in Spain. Certainly, Pope Innocent IV was impressed enough to regard him as a champion of Christendom who might recover Palestine and the Holy Land.

In 1229 James I conquered Muslim Mallorca, then acquired the other Balearic islands of Menorca and Ibiza, and took the Muslim Kingdom of Valencia in 1238. To a large extent, however, these successes were due to James's willingness to come to terms with the Muslims and allow them to retain some of their own civil and religious institutions. This was particularly true with respect to the Kingdom of Valencia, even after Mudejar rebellions subsequently led to further expulsions of the Muslim population. In general terms, the northern part of the kingdom was almost entirely cleared of Muslims, but the central and southern regions, with the exception of the city of Valencia and its countryside, remained predominantly Mudejar. Játiva provides a good example. Its Muslim military governor (*qa'id*) and the hundred leading men of the town did homage to James I and became his vassals. Here and elsewhere the Muslims retained many of their mosques, and indeed on one occasion the king complained about his sleep being disrupted by a nearby muezzin noisily summoning the Muslim faithful to prayer. Above all, the Muslims who remained continued to use their agrarian institutions and manpower, the countryside being mainly tenanted by Mudejars. In many areas sophisticated irrigation techniques were to benefit the agrarian economy, notably those in and around the city of Valencia, and at Játiva James himself described the patchwork landscape of irrigated farms (*huertas*), villages, and the watercourses or *acequias* on which the inhabitants depended. In the 1270s James

A fourteenth-century Valencian altarpiece shows James I of Aragon (1213–76) assisted by St George, the patron saint of crusaders, in battle against the Muslims. His success led Pope Innocent IV to view him as the Christian champion who might recover the Holy Land.

was to complain about the shortage of Christian settlers available for the task of repopulation; there were several predominantly Christian cities, but there were also many towns in which Muslims and Christians lived together, and a countryside mainly tenanted by Mudejars living in Moorish villages.

Matters turned out otherwise in the Kingdom of Castile. Ferdinand III (1217–52) invested the great city of Córdoba, the former capital of the Muslim caliphate, in 1236, and in 1248 he gained the prize of Seville. After describing the conquest of Seville, a chronicle goes on to explain why this event was so momentous:

There are many other noble and great features about Seville apart from all those which we have already described. There is no town as pleasant or as well situated in the world. It is a town to which the ships come daily up the river from the sea. Ships and galleys and other sea vessels dock there inside the walls with all kinds of merchandise from all parts of the world. They arrive there frequently and come from all kinds of places: from Tangier, Ceuta, Tunis, Bougie, Alexandria, Genoa, Portugal, England, Pisa, Lombardy, Bordeaux, Bayonne, Sicily, Gascony, Catalonia, Aragon, and even France and many other places from across the sea, and from the lands of both Christians and Moors. So how can such a city, which is so perfect and plentiful and where there is such an abundance of goods, not be so excellent and so prized? Her olive oil is sent throughout the world by sea and land—and this is to omit all the other plentiful riches which are to be found there and which it would be tedious to recount here . . .

There were other successes, too numerous to narrate in detail. The essen-

tial point is that the Christians were now virtually masters of all Spain, apart from the Muslim kingdom of Granada, and even in this case its rulers had entered into a vassalage relationship with Castile which obliged them to hand over substantial sums of money as tribute payments (*parias*) at regular intervals. Muslim Granada was to last until 1492, but in many ways its independence had already been seriously eroded. Even today, the enlightened tourist can understand this point by looking at the paintings which cover three domes in the Hall of Justice of the Alhambra palace of Granada. They date from the fourteenth century, but what they reveal is that this last stronghold of Islam in Spain had already been in some way invaded. Islam was hostile to artistic representations of living beings, yet these scenes, which depict elements of chivalric legends to be found in Christian Europe, are particularly intriguing. In fact, this 'invasion' of Granada has even raised doubts about the artists who were involved. Were they Muslims who 'borrowed' from the northern Gothic style? Were Italian or French artists involved? In any case, the scenes seem to derive from tales and legends contained in the northern Arthurian cycle of legends involving characters like Tristan and Isolde, Enyas, and Lancelot.

A cultural invasion of Muslim Granada? In these scenes painted on the ceiling of the Hall of the Kings in the Alhambra, Christian and Moorish nobles and ladies are engaged in chivalrous pursuits such as fighting, hunting, and playing chess. Islam forbids figural art, yet these were commissioned by an Islamic ruler; a sign that the tolerant coexistence of the two religions was still possible when this last great Moorish palace was completed in c.1350.

Of course there were to be episodes of Muslim resurgence after Ferdinand III's conquest of Seville. In 1264, for example, the Mudejars of Andalusia, the Muslims of Granada, and Marinid troops from North Africa mounted a serious uprising. This rebellion failed and the consequences were far-reaching. Previously, resistance in Córdoba and Seville had led to the expulsion of Muslims, but there were many other areas where a speedy capitulation to the Christians enabled the inhabitants to keep their lands and customs. However, the rebellion of 1264 led to a radical change in Castilian policy and the Muslims were expelled in place after place until only a very few of their *morerías* or settlements were left. As a result, the need for Christian settlers to colonize these lands became particularly acute, and a policy of the orderly distribution of land among these settlers, known as *repartimiento*, was put into effect. The *repartimiento* of Ecija, for example, was a deliberate attempt to repopulate the deserted town and to create villages or *alquerías* in its rural areas. But the shortage of manpower was evident. The *repartimiento* of Jerez revealed that there were more houses than settlers, and in a few cases places which had been colonized were once more abandoned and depopulated for a time. But the Reconquest drive southwards had already meant that since the thirteenth century the land available in the Kingdom of Castile had grown at a faster rate than its population, and this had led to a marked increase in pastoralism and the numbers of sheep. These had to be moved between summer and winter pastures, and this transhumance was catered for by three main north–south routes (*cañadas reales*) and many tributary tracks. All were marked by stone pillars 1.5 metres high at 100-metre intervals. In the thirteenth century the Crown set up a royally recognized association of stockmen known as the *Mesta*, and derived valuable revenue from royal taxes levied on the movement of sheep.

As we have seen, to all this the city of Seville provided a striking exception. Its repopulation total of about 24,000 inhabitants made it the largest city in the peninsula after Barcelona. Its population was cosmopolitan: the vast majority of settlers came from places in northern Castile, such as Burgos and Valladolid, but Catalans also came in fairly large numbers, there were men from Aragon, Galicia, and Portugal, the Genoese and other Italians were prominent, there were some French, Bretons, and Germans, and a small *morería* continued to exist. Many Jews also came after the city's reconquest, and their community was to become one of the most prosperous of its kind in the peninsula.

Alfonso X of Castile was not politically successful. He spent money prodigiously, endlessly demanded taxes from his subjects, and manipulated the coinage. He pursued grandiose ambitions which proved failures, and he alienated members of his own family, the nobles, and many in the towns to a dangerous extent. For example, he invested a great deal of time and money in a futile attempt to secure the Crown of the Holy Roman Empire; he vainly pressed his dynastic claims to Gascony, eventually yielding his rights to his sister, Leonor, who was to marry the heir to the English throne; he tried to impose his sovereignty over Navarre; and he quarrelled ignominiously with his younger son and eventual heir, the future Sancho IV (1284–95).

Yet these political disasters must be counterbalanced by Alfonso X's (1252–84) outstanding cultural achievements, which were to earn him the sobriquet of *el Sabio*, that is, 'the Wise' or 'the Learned'. To a large extent these achievements depended on the transmission of learning from classical, Arabic, and Hebrew sources of knowledge. Of course, such a process had begun much earlier, notably in the various twelfth-century centres of translation, of which the most famous was that based in Toledo. But Alfonso X provided the essential royal patronage for a revival in this work. Everything from history to chess interested the king, and he also seems to have deliberately promoted the vernacular rather than Latin. Castilian was to be the language of law, history, and official chancery documents, and it by no means restricted the cultural vistas surveyed, as the *History of Spain* (*Estoria de España*) and the unfinished history of the world or *General Estoria* demonstrate. The famous law code of the *Siete Partidas* was an even greater project, which systematically dealt with every possible aspect of political and social life, and was strongly influenced by Roman Law. It was resisted by the nobility and towns, committed as they were to regional, local, and social *fueros* (customary laws), and it was not until the closing years of the reign of Alfonso XI (1312–50) that the *Partidas* were to be promulgated as the law of the land.

But in some ways it would be a mistake to exaggerate the 'modernity', the scientific endeavours, and the erudition of Alfonso the Wise. Although he used the Castilian vernacular in his chronicles and chancery records, and much later Castilian would become 'the language of Empire', he also used Galician-Portuguese in poetry, and his scientific interests were paralleled by his Marian devotion. If some were to end up thinking that he was too learned, even perhaps a heretic, then it should be remembered that his devotion to the Virgin Mary was to become an essential part of that Catholicism which would, much later, be questioned by the Protestant Reformation but reaffirmed by the Catholic church.

All these contradictions can be beautifully and literally illustrated by the magnificent miniatures and Galician-Portuguese poetry of the *Cantigas de Santa María* (*Songs in Praise of the Virgin Mary*). Here men and women are rescued from the most awful predicaments: Parisian thieves, pregnant abbesses, murderers, and even those guilty of infanticide. How do the *Cantigas* explain these miraculous escapes from certain damnation? In each case, the sinful person (be it a robber, a drunken dice-player, or even a pregnant abbess) is saved by his or her devotion to the Virgin Mary. Elbo, the Parisian thief, is a good example: he always prayed to the Virgin before going out at night to steal, and his faith was enough to save him (*sola fide*). The phrase *sola fide*, of course, recalls Martin Luther and the Reformation. But well before the Reformation the message of the *Cantigas* was clear: faced with a rather grim Father (God), men should try to influence his Son (Jesus) by recourse to the latter's mother (the Virgin). The classic case was that of Teófilo. To become a bishop, Teófilo made a pact (a feudal pact) with the Devil. He even went down to Hell to swear his allegiance. But the all-powerful Virgin went down there as well in order to save him.

The death of Alfonso X's eldest son caused a juridical and dynastic crisis. Who was to succeed to the throne, the deceased elder son's oldest son, Alfonso, or the elder son's brother, Sancho? The latter, relying on past customs, used the Cortes to back his claims. He became king as Sancho IV (1284–95), but was soon confronted with complicated problems. Concluding an alliance with Aragon, he quickly had to prepare for war against the Marinids of Morocco who, led by the emir Abu Yaqub, landed in Spain in September 1291. Realizing that control of the straits was vital, Sancho IV laid siege to Tarifa, captured it, and then successfully defended it against further Muslim attacks. To the north, his problem of opting for an alliance with either Aragon or France was compounded by the fact that leading nobles at his court were opposed on this matter.

In the Crown of Aragon the Aragonese nobility had already defended their interests and forced concessions from James I in the Cortes of Ejea of 1265, and they had laid the basis of a powerful 'Union' which almost became a governmental institution during the reign of Peter III (1276–85). The latter's attempts to strengthen royal power and curb the nobility might have succeeded but for the aftermath of his conquest of Sicily in 1282. Excommunicated by the pope—who proclaimed a crusade against

The *Cantigas de Santa María* (Songs in Praise of St Mary) were composed by the learned King Alfonso X of Castile (1252–84). The miraculous powers of the Virgin Mary are the dominant theme of over 100 illustrations, but the daily life of the mixed world of Christians, Jews, Mudejars, and Muslims, along with details of dress, weapons, architecture, and customs, are faithfully depicted—a unique source of social history.

Como os mouros sacaron ó Conde du Soum da galea.

Elli poseron dentro ouro e prata r el no qs tillar se non un liuro.

Como os mouros tornar o Conde a sa compa

Como o conde foi na crimda euuez os mouros bon uero r bronsse.

Como o conde contou aagente toro quell auuera con os mouros.

Como uero dali auante muitas gêtes aaql logar loar santa Gl.

The Spanish landscape still reflects the violence and conflict which Spain suffered for centuries. Avila, set 3,400 feet above sea level, with its thick granite walls reinforced by eighty-eight towers, was one of many fortified cities protecting the local population from the ebb and flow of battle. In the Middle Ages more effort and energy was expended on rebellion and private war than was ever devoted to the confrontation with Islam.

him, freed the nobles from their allegiance, and offered the crown to Charles of Valois, son of the king of France. Peter III tried to avoid the dangers of invasion and civil war by capitulating to his opponents. At the Aragonese Cortes of Saragossa in 1283 he had to agree to a *privilegio general*, binding himself to respect the privileges and customs of the nobility and townsmen of Aragon and Valencia, and accepting demands that the Cortes should meet annually and have greater powers. With respect to Catalonia, Peter III capitulated to similar demands three months later at the Cortes of Barcelona. Such decisions were far from being temporary in nature. Alfonso III (1285–91) fell foul of the Aragonese Union and, apart from facing military threats and the disruption of royal revenues, he was forced to grant even greater concessions in the *privilegio de la Unión* of 1287.

In Castile, the minority of Ferdinand IV (1295–1312) led to anarchy. His uncle, Juan, justified his hopes of becoming king himself by claiming that Ferdinand IV was illegitimate. James II of Aragon (1291–1327) allied himself with the young king's enemies and even urged that Castile should be partitioned. In 1296 Castile was invaded from all directions, but Ferdinand IV's energetic mother, María de Molina, thwarted the invaders, a success for which she received little thanks from her son when he came of age in 1301. He concluded an alliance with James II of Aragon in 1308 which projected further territorial shares at the expense of the Muslims: Granada was reserved for conquest by Castile, but whereas previous treaties had allotted the entirety of this Muslim kingdom to Castile, the important port of Almería was reserved for Aragon. Christian sieges of Algeciras and Almería failed, but Ferdinand IV did capture Gibraltar in 1309 (it was to be lost again in 1333). Ferdinand IV died at the early age of 28 in 1312.

In the Crown of Aragon the ideal of regular yearly meetings of the Cortes proved to be impossible in practice. In 1301 triennial meetings were stipulated for the Catalan Cortes, the same principle was established for the Cortes of Valencia, and six years later James II and the Aragonese Cortes agreed to biennial meetings. But although the ideal of yearly meetings failed, the powers of the Cortes in the Aragonese federation were substantially enhanced by the emergence of a standing committee which continued to exist between meetings. This institution, which was known as the *Diputació* or *Generalitat*, did not emerge in Aragon and Valencia until 1412 and 1419 respectively, and in both these cases they never acquired the same political importance as the Catalan *Generalitat*.

The Catalan *Generalitat* originated in the late thirteenth century, when the Cortes chose delegates to continue dealing with outstanding problems after the representatives dispersed. Their main duty was to cater for the collection of taxes voted by the Cortes and ensure that the resulting income was used for the specific purposes which had been agreed. In 1359 this temporary committee became a permanent institution, and from 1365 onwards it established its headquarters in Barcelona. At this point it consisted of seven *diputados*: two clergy, two nobles, and three townsmen. However, it would be a mistake to regard the Cortes of the Crown of Aragon and institutions such as the Catalan *Generalitat* as being genuinely representative. They only represented privileged social groups, namely the oligarchs of the towns and countryside, and this in effect meant that some two-thirds of the population were excluded.

The long reign of Alfonso XI of Castile (1312–50) was characterized by impressive victories over the Muslims, the imposition of greater royal control over the towns, reforms in the administration of justice, and intrigues by the nobility which would eventually become part of a serious dynastic and international crisis after the king's death. The most resounding success was the famous Christian victory at the Battle of Salado in 1340. The Marinids of Morocco, who already controlled Algeciras and Gibraltar, laid siege to Tarifa. Alfonso XI, helped by contingents of knights from the other Spanish kingdoms and even from abroad, forced the Muslims to give up the siege of Tarifa, and then decisively defeated them in a bloody battle on the banks of the River Salado. The booty was immense, but of greater significance was the fact that the battle ended the threat of Moroccan invasion and marked a significant turning-point in the Reconquest of Spain. Indeed, Alfonso XI and his allies soon went on to lay siege to Algeciras, which eventually surrendered to the Christians in 1344.

Alfonso XI was engaged to the daughter of his cousin, Juan Manuel. The latter, a political arch-conspirator, was to acquire fame as a literary personality; indeed, he consciously used a cultivated prose style and carefully deposited his works in a monastery in order to ensure their survival. His most famous book is the *Libro de los enxemplos del Conde Lucanor et de Patronio*, a collection of stories and fables derived from Arabic, Christian, and Jewish sources, but he also wrote a treatise on hunting and falconry, as well as briefly chronicling contemporary events.

Alfonso XI broke his engagement to Juan Manuel's daughter, and married the daughter of the king of Portugal. However, he clearly disliked his wife and openly flaunted his long affair with Leonor de Guzmán. His wife bore him his only legitimate son, subsequently to be known as Peter 'the Cruel', but his mistress bore him ten illegitimate children. In itself the latter fact would hardly have raised any problems. Kings and princes were usually subjected to arranged marriages for dynastic reasons, and were almost expected to have mistresses because true love, so to speak, existed outside marriage. Besides, it was also the century of the *Book of Good Love* (*Libro de Buen Amor*), whose author, Juan Ruiz, archpriest of Hita, used his poetic masterpiece to relate hilarious and obscene adventures, pen religious lyrics to the Virgin Mary, a satire on clerical concubinage, and deliberately play on the concept of 'Good Love' as being both the love of God and the search for sexual love. But in terms of marriages arranged for dynastic purposes, the consequences of Alfonso XI's involvement with Leonor de Guzmán were to be momentous.

Peter I (1350–69) was an authoritarian king, and it was his more savage acts that earned him the sobriquet of 'the Cruel'. The kingdom was soon plunged into a civil war in which Peter was challenged by a coalition of nobles led by his bastard half-brother, Henry of Trastámara. But as both sides sought support outside the kingdom, Castile gradually became another theatre of operations in the prolonged European conflict known as the Hundred Years War, with the English supporting Peter and his heirs and the French backing Henry of Trastámara and his successors. At the head of professional mercenary soldiers, Henry invaded Castile and proclaimed himself king in 1366. Peter fled to Bayonne, and with the help of the English he too mounted an invasion of Castile, defeated the Trastámarans at Nájera in 1367, and regained the throne. But his triumph was short-lived, and he was finally overcome and murdered by Henry at Montiel in 1369, the latter becoming king as Henry II (1369–79).

During the civil war Henry of Trastámara had deliberately used propaganda against the Jews, and their communities (*aljamas*) suffered severely. It is true that Henry II and his successors in the Trastámaran dynasty of kings would continue to rely on the abilities of Jews and *conversos* (that is,

This portayal of a Spanish Jew, wearing the compulsory red and yellow badge of identification, appears in the chapel of Santa Lucia in Tarragona. In the early Middle Ages Jews were tolerated and accepted as part of the community, but following the great pogroms of 1391 they began to suffer severe persecution, and were eventually expelled from the peninsula in 1492.

those Jews converting to Christianity either voluntarily or under duress). But, despite some royal protection of those minorities, ugly incidents of anti-Semitism continued. The most serious of these was the great pogrom of 1391. Beginning in Seville on 6 June, it quickly spread to other Andalusian towns, and thereafter to Toledo, Valencia, Mallorca, Barcelona, Gerona, Logroño, Lérida, Jaca, and even Perpignan. The killings and the fear of further persecutions led to mass conversions. In Seville, for example, synagogues were forcibly changed into churches and the city's Jewish quarter virtually disappeared. Later, from 1449 onwards, a series of anti-Semitic pogroms would again disrupt many towns, culminating in the pogrom of 1473 which, starting in Córdoba, led to massacres in many Andalusian towns.

In 1371 the duke of Lancaster, John of Gaunt, married Peter the Cruel's eldest daughter and claimed the throne of Castile. The most serious threat to the Trastámaran dynasty came in the reign of John I (1379–90). In 1381 Lancaster's brother led an abortive campaign in Portugal. The heiress to the throne of Portugal, Beatriz, was married to John I of Castile, and when Ferdinand I of Portugal died the Castilian king asserted his claims to this neighbouring kingdom. It turned out to be a disastrous move: the Master of Avis was proclaimed king of Portugal in 1384, and the Portuguese, assisted by English archers, won a famous victory over the Castilians at the Battle of Aljubarrota (1385).

The disaster at Aljubarrota prompted John I to undertake institutional and military reforms in collaboration with the Castilian Cortes. But the crisis was not yet over. In 1386 the duke of Lancaster landed in La Coruña. In the event his invasion proved a fiasco, and the truces of Leulingham and Monçao (1389) brought the Spanish phase of the Hundred Years War to an end. Gaunt surrendered his claim to the Castilian throne in exchange for a large indemnity payment, a substantial annual pension, and the marriage of his daughter Catherine to John I's heir, the future Henry III of Castile (1390–1406).

The French continued to benefit from Castilian naval power. In 1372 a Castilian fleet linked up with French forces to defeat the English at La Rochelle, and three years later the Castilians attacked and burned English ships in the Bay of Bourgneuf. Castilian galleys also attacked Rye, Lewes, the Isle of Wight, Plymouth, Hastings, Portsmouth, Dartmouth, Winchelsea, and even sailed up the Thames to burn Gravesend. The magnificent chronicle of *El Victorial* by Díez de Games provides eyewitness accounts of Castilian naval operations, including raids along the English coast from St Ives to Southampton and expeditions into the Mediterranean.

Before his early death in 1406 Henry III of Castile had envisaged problems which might arise during the long minority of John II (1406–54). He arranged for the kingdom to be governed by his wife, Catherine of Lancaster, his brother Ferdinand, and the royal council. Ferdinand, who was to be the dominant personality during the regency, captured the Moorish stronghold of Antequera in 1410, and when King Martin I died in the same year he put forward his claims to the Crown of Aragon. But Martin had died childless and there were several conflicting claims to the succession. The political, religious, and even 'artistic' ways by which Ferdinand succeeded in winning his claim are worthy of more consideration because of the light they throw on this period.

The issue of conflicting claims to the Crown of Aragon was resolved by a special commission of electors who, at the so-called Compromise of Caspe in 1412, chose to *elect* Ferdinand as king. In the face of rival claims, therefore, Ferdinand first of all had to secure his own election and then, subsequently, try to convert his elective kingship into something more substantial (after all, what can be bestowed by election might later be withdrawn or at least circumscribed). As far back as 1403 Ferdinand, then a Castilian prince, had founded his own chivalric order of the Jar and the Griffin in honour of the Virgin Mary at the Annunciation. What better ploy, then, than to present himself as the Virgin's favourite and predestined claimant to the throne of Aragon? Prior to the election at Caspe, paid court hacks in Castile busily engaged themselves in presenting Ferdinand as the Mariological candidate whose special devotion to the Virgin was also coupled both to his chivalric order and to his undoubted successes in war against the Muslims. Clearly a kingship which was both elective and predestined was either impossible or, for want of a better way of putting it, somehow Calvinistic in nature. In any case, Ferdinand played his particular concept of kingship for all it was worth.

At his coronation at Saragossa in 1414, therefore, the clergy were kept well out of the way and the king virtually did everything himself. It was Ferdinand alone who approached the altar, Ferdinand who, with his own hands, took up the crown and put it on his own head, and Ferdinand alone who took up the sceptre with his right hand and the orb with his left. One problem remained. It was customary for the ceremony of knighthood to form part of the coronation. How would Ferdinand cope with this? No one was allowed near him: he took the sword of knighthood off the altar himself, put it on himself, and then, slapping of the face being *de rigueur* in knighthood, he slapped his left cheek with his own right hand.

To those present at the coronation, and indeed to those reading the account of it, the point must have been obvious enough. But what about the amazing coronation banquet which followed? So much happened that only part of the proceedings, which involved platforms and wheels up in heaven filled with the Seven Deadly Sins, God, angels, archangels, princes, prophets, and apostles, as well as an enactment of the Coronation of the Virgin, can be described. Here, then, in part is what happened in the banqueting hall:

Before the first dish there came a beautiful golden griffin as big as a horse, and he had a crown of gold round his neck, and he moved forward belching out fire and thus making room between the people for the dishes to pass through...

The king being at table and having received water for his hands, the first dish was brought in very solemnly through the door of the hall. And on the trenchers there were peacocks with their tails raised up and their bodies covered with leaves of gold and the arms of Aragon, and on their high necks they had the device or stole of the order. And in front of them there were *juglares* [*jongleurs*, minstrels] making such a noise that nobody could hear anybody else, and the griffin went in front belching out fire from side to side, scattering people...

And then the *mayordomo* entered with the second dish, with the trenchers and dishes full of capons and golden pies with various living birds and many other dishes. And the *jongleurs* went before the said griffin, who belched out fire throughout the hall, making a path for those who were carrying the dishes. And behind the griffin and in front of the second dish there was a huge float in the form of a painted wooden castle on top of carts. And in the middle of this castle there was a very large silver pitcher [or jar: *jarra*] of the Virgin Mary with white lilies. In the castle there were six damsels singing very sweet songs to hear. And on the edge of the castle there was a very large crowned eagle of gold who had a collar of the order or *devisa* of the pitcher [*jarra*] of the King of Aragon round his neck. And the pitcher or jar which was in the middle of the castle gyrated when they moved it. And in this fashion the second dish entered the hall.

And then God the Father moved the heavens and all the angels and archangels played their instruments, and patriarchs and prophets sang their marvellous songs, and the first cloud which had appeared before the king's table moved in the air, and on it there came an Angel who held a beautiful pitcher [*jarra*] of gold with its lilies in his hand. And he sang a verse, saying that he was the ambassador of the resplendent Virgin who sent him [the king] the pitcher which he should always carry with him in his conquests...

The *retablo* (altarpiece) of Archbishop Sancho de Rojas (left) showing the Virgin and Jesus crowning Ferdinand of Antequera. Seeking to consolidate his position following his election to the throne of Aragon in 1412, Ferdinand presented himself as the ruler chosen by the Virgin Mary.

And when the Angel had finished with his embassy, he returned to paradise. And in this way the dishes arrived at table, and the pies were opened and the birds flew out around the hall.

And when the griffin saw the castle before the king's table, he made for it in order to fight the eagle, and with the griffin there came men dressed as Moors with shields in their hands. And when the eagle saw this he climbed down from the castle onto the ground, and in spite of them he reached the king's table and made reverence to him, and then he returned to the castle which the griffin and Moors were besieging. And the damsels who were guarding the castle fought them, and when the eagle saw this he went to fight the griffin, pecking at the Moors; but he did not actually clash with the griffin but only made a show of going to fight him. And at this point the pitcher or jar opened up and a beautiful boy emerged from it dressed with clothes in the form of the arms of Aragon, with a sword in his hand, and with great valour he made to go against the griffin and the Moors. And then they all fell down on the ground as if dead and very terrified of the boy's bravery, and the griffin fled, and the eagle climbed back onto the edge of the castle. And in this manner the king and the other people finished the banquet.

What on earth does it all mean, or how do we read or decode it? Obviously there is a connection between Ferdinand's chivalric order of the Jar and the Griffin and the events of the banquet, but the readings must be more explicit, otherwise extraneous interpretations might creep in. An obvious example might be the opening up of the pies which allowed the birds to fly round the banquet hall, which strongly insinuates a reading along the lines of the nursery rhyme: 'And when the pie was opened, the birds began to sing. Wasn't that a dainty dish to set before a king?' But, in fact, one of the Spanish words for a bird is 'ave', and this must be linked in turn to the angel's words at the Annunciation: *Ave Maria gratia plena.*

While keeping his regency in Castile, Ferdinand had enhanced his family's powers in both kingdoms. His eldest son succeeded him as Alfonso V of Aragon (1416–58). In Old Catalonia peasant unrest (*remensa* movements) was already endemic. But, in addition, the importance which the kings of the Crown of Aragon attached to their Mediterranean possessions had already entailed important institutional repercussions for their realms in Spain because of their absence. From the late fourteenth century lieutenants-general or viceroys appeared in Sardinia, Sicily, and Mallorca, and this pattern was to be repeated in Aragon, Catalonia, and Valencia as a result of Alfonso V's prolonged absence in Italy. But although he was chiefly interested in Italian politics, taking control of southern Italy after the death of Joanna II of Naples in 1435, Alfonso V supported the intrigues of his brothers in Castile. One brother, the *infante* John, inherited vast landed power in Castile, and by marriage he also became King of Navarre in 1425. Subsequently, he succeeded his brother in the Crown of Aragon as John II (1458–79).

When John II of Castile finally came of age, the members of what is frequently referred to as 'the Aragonese party' were entrenched in power and controlled the resources of royal patronage. But the Castilian king, ably helped by the royal favourite Alvaro de Luna, waged a protracted struggle to break the power of the Aragonese party. During these years the balance of power continually changed, but the Aragonese party was finally defeated at the crucial Battle of Olmedo in 1445. Eight years later the great Alvaro de Luna fell victim to a court intrigue and was executed by royal command (1453), the king himself dying the following year. Despite the troubles and political unrest, the long reign of John II of Castile was remarkable for the way in which a form of royal absolutism was developed. The king (or perhaps it was Alvaro de Luna, behind the scenes) was inordinately fond of using his *poder real absoluto* (absolute royal power) to make law unilaterally, to assert that he was above the law, and that he was God's vicar. It is true that he occasionally consulted the Cortes, and he sometimes declared that the laws which he promulgated were to be as valid as if they had been made in the Cortes. But such concessions could hardly disguise the fact that royal power was theoretically increasing greatly while the powers of the Cortes were rapidly declining.

Culturally, the same reign was also of considerable significance. The king and some of his courtiers took an interest in humanism, which can be defined as a revival of classical studies, and in some cases specific political programmes were propounded. For example, the secretary of Latin letters, Juan de Mena, presented John II with a long poem, *Laberinto de Fortuna*, which was a sophisticated attempt to win support for Alvaro de Luna's policies. But the significance of humanist scholarship was limited. Of greater impact were the subtle love poems by *cancionero* poets and the chivalric or courtly festivals, such as the visually intricate 'happenings' or tableaux held in Valladolid in 1428. Rather than the Italy of the Renaissance, such cultural manifestations recall the civilization of the Burgundian ducal court.

Ironically, the next reign, that of Henry IV of Castile (1454–74), was to reveal the extent to which theory and practice could diverge. Anarchy, fomented by unscrupulous nobles, dominated much of the reign, and in an infamous tableau known as 'the Farce of Avila' an effigy or statue of the

ffenar G. de goejas alcalte de bur
gos guarda de nuo señor el Rey

ffenar G. de ayelca.

Johan G. de ayelca.

alffon G de camargo el moco.

king was deposed. This reign of civil wars and anarchy was followed by that of the 'Catholic Kings', Ferdinand and Isabella. Did they usurp the Castilian throne, wresting it from Henry IV's putative daughter, Juana? If the Catholic Kings and their propagandists are to be believed, Juana was not the king's daughter. The king's enemies alleged that he was both impotent and homosexual. After his death Ferdinand and Isabella won the civil war of succession, and Juana was exiled to Portugal. Entering a nunnery, she was never to return.

The Hidden One (or the Bat), alias Ferdinand the Catholic, reconquered Granada in 1492, and Jerusalem would be the next objective. But, needless to say, the signs could be read in a different way. For the Jews the successes of the Catholic Kings could be seen as the birth-pangs of the Messiah and the beginning of the ingathering of the exiles:

And it is well known that in 1475, in Spain, began the reign of the wicked Queen Isabella, she who has brought upon us all these evils, and that in 1483 began the period of forty-five years and the principal sufferings and affliction, for in that year the she-bear expelled Israel from all of Andalusia, and from thence to this very day the afflictions have not ceased...until 1492 when came the general expulsion of all the Exiles of Jerusalem who were then in Spain.

Indeed, even as far as some of the Christians were concerned, time, geography, and history could be changed. Ferdinand the Catholic hardly needed to conquer Jerusalem, because Jerusalem was in Spain. During 1490–1 a grotesque show trial was put on by the Spanish Inquisition. This case, which is known as that of the *Santo Niño de la Guardia*, came to its climax just three months before the Edict of the Expulsion of the Jews. The trial purported to prove that a motley collection of Jews and *conversos* from the village of La Guardia (near Toledo) had crucified a young Christian child. Although the gruesome details were, of course, fabricated, the objectives behind staging such a trial were effectively secured. Most obviously, the devilish conspiracies of Jews, as revealed by the trial, justified their expulsion from Spain. Less obviously perhaps, the trial validated certain Christian doctrines which, though central to the faith of Catholicism, had always proved problematical. Why would Jews bother to desecrate hosts unless these hosts were in fact in some way the body of Christ?

Knights depicted in the *Libro de la Cofradía* (confraternity) *de San Pedro de Sántiago*. Faced with the insecurities of fourteenth-century urban life, many men joined a confraternity, an artificial 'family' encompassing all aspects of religious and social life. The emphasis was on the enactment of ceremonies in honour of God, the Virgin, and the saints, and on providing dignified funerals and masses for departed members.

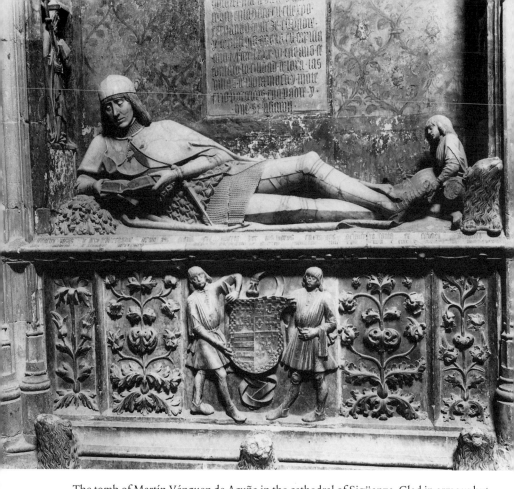

The tomb of Martín Vázquez de Acuña in the cathedral of Sigüenza. Clad in armour but also reading a book, he represents the ideal of the cultivated warrior cherished by the Castilian aristocracy of the later Middle Ages. Too often precedence had to be given to arms over letters because of the crusade against Islam, and as a consequence humanism developed more slowly and fitfully in Spain than in neighbouring countries.

Why would they bother to re-enact the Crucifixion unless they too believed in the authenticity of the original Crucifixion? But if Spain now had its own Christ-child from La Guardia and its own Crucifixion, might it not also contain Jerusalem? In some sixteenth-century devotional works woodcut illustrations make the point abundantly clear. For not only do we see the child of La Guardia on the Cross, but the landscape around Toledo and La Guardia is presented as the exact equivalent of Jerusalem and its environs.

Spain would become the champion of the Catholic or Counter-Reformation, and it has often been portrayed as intolerant and dedicated to the task of rooting out and suppressing heresy. Yet there was another important legacy. Most of this chapter has devoted attention to two kinds of protagonists during the centuries in question—those who were politically active in ruling and participating in the Reconquest, and those who were important as writers or artists. It is obvious that in some cases these roles were difficult to combine: after all, despite his cultural achievements, the reign of King Alfonso X was in many ways a political disaster. Yet towards the end of this period the ideal of combining 'arms' with 'letters' began to emerge. To some extent we can begin to see this in the famous elegiac verses which Jorge Manrique wrote in 1476 in memory of his father, Rodrigo Manrique, master of the military order of Santiago. In his poem, the *Coplas por la muerte de su padre* (Verses on the Death of his father), the son celebrated his father's loyalty to the Crown and his military prowess in campaigns against the Moors. Today, however, we would hardly remember Rodrigo Manrique were it not for the poetry of his son. Similarly, Iñigo López de Mendoza, marquis of Santillana (1398–1458), was described by his nephew, Gómez Manrique, as removing all prejudice against letters and as 'the first man of our times to conjoin science and chivalry, the breastplate and the toga'. Visually, this combination of 'arms' and 'letters' can still be seen today in a tomb in the cathedral of Siguenza. It shows a nobleman, Martín Vásquez de Acuña, dressed in armour but at the same time propped up on one elbow reading a book. This legacy of combining military prowess with cultural sophistication would be inherited by Spain during the Golden Age or *Siglo de Oro*.

5 The Improbable Empire

FELIPE FERNÁNDEZ-ARMESTO

HE paradox of Spain recalls Dr Johnson's dog, who surprises you so much by walking on hind legs that you do not expect him to do it well. Similarly, no one should expect a poor and naturally ill-endowed corner of the world to make a good job of conquering so much of the rest of it; nor of inaugurating, in the same period of dramatic expansion in the sixteenth and early seventeenth centuries, an era at home of extraordinary artistic creativity and social peace, so lustrous that it has always been known, by almost universal acclaim, as 'Spain's Golden Age'.

The historical tradition has tended to take for granted Spanish cultural achievement and political preponderance and to have puzzled instead over the problem of Spain's subsequent decline. Yet the former phase was very much the more wonderful. While western Europe endured more than a century of Spanish preponderance, a sort of *Wunderkind* monarchy grew improbably into the world's farthest-flung imperial experiment. After this, to revert to a subordinate place in the wars and counsels of Europe and, ultimately, to shrink to modest dimensions among the empires of the world was a regression to normalcy—like the dog returning to all fours.

To explain the uncharacteristically rampant posture Spain adopted in this period, historical tradition has identified some tempting but tendentious areas of enquiry. The precocious 'modernity' of a unified nation-state has been alleged, by scholars with an appropriate political agenda, to have given Spain an advantage. Religious uniformity has been seen as the starting-point of worldly power, supplying unity of purpose and encouraging militant zeal. A crusading mentality has been detected, inherited from the Middle Ages, or its secular equivalent, an ideology of *Weltpolitik* adapted from ancient European traditions of universal empire. Contradictory claims about the virtues and vices of national character have been invoked: sobriety and austerity are supposed to have deserved success, while thriftlessness and improvidence are said to have gilded the 'golden age' with reckless overspending, so that its grandeur becomes a mere appearance of greatness—a flashy purchase with unsound credit. Seekers of explanation have foraged among luck and emerged with two explanatory accidents: a 'power vacuum' created by French impotence and a temporary bonanza brought by the fortuitous acquisition of American silver. Those who incline more to determinism are hard to surprise but have their own passionless doctrines. Spanish achievement, for instance, is predicted by the pattern of 'challenge and response': an empire of escapees from poverty, a civilization of genius disciplined by insufficiency.

Rejecting most of these traditional approaches, a great deal of recent scholarship has tried to describe a true-to-life society in 'early modern' Spain. As the resulting picture grows, it looks more and more convincing as a conspectus of people equipped to do what they did: no unified nation-state but a political framework which worked for a while; no 'modern' centralization of power, but a widely diffused ethos and habit which made obedience come easily; no bonanza but a modest measure— by the standards of the time—of fiscal productiveness; no heroic prowess, but a dogged ability to keep armies in the field and fleets at sea; no uniformity of culture, but a disposition to peaceful change; no peculiar virtues and vices, but some special merits—in particular, a relatively large educated elite with values which favoured technical innovation and creative arts. At the same time, the paradox at the heart of the subject abides: the fragility of the achievement is always apparent, its durability always impressive.

The Ringmaster's Whip: The Nature of the State

If you stand in the square of the Escuelas Menores in Salamanca and look up at the old university façade, you can see a medallion. It depicts— clearly enough, when the sun shines slantwise on the golden stone and picks out the carvings with fine shadow—a king and queen of Aragon and Castile or, as they liked to say, of Spain. In some ways it is a typical example of the iconography of Ferdinand and Isabella, designed to project an image of power and unity. The figures are ponderously crowned and symmetrically arrayed, according to the Renaissance aesthetic dominant at the time, around a central axis formed by a royal sceptre, which they reach to clasp with matching gestures. Yet this work, executed in the generation after the monarchs' deaths, contrasts in one striking particular

with the portraiture authorized in their lifetimes. The king, this time, is bigger than the queen. While they were alive, an inflexible rule of equipollency allowed no artist to represent one of them as greater than the other.

In the 1520s, when the face of the university was carved, Castile was again under the rule of joint sovereigns: but the queen mother, Joanna I, was a nominal monarch, presumed to be mad and carefully isolated from affairs of state. Her son, Charles—the Holy Roman Emperor Charles V— was in effective sole command and it suited the needs of the times to represent his male supremacy as a continuation of previous practice. It was not, however, how Ferdinand and Isabella themselves wanted their relationship to be perceived. Almost all the documents of their reign in Castile were issued in their joint names, even when only one of them was present. They were said to be 'each other's favourite', 'two bodies, ruled by one spirit', 'sharing a single mind'. As well as of unity, their propaganda made a display of mutual love. Love-knots and yoke-and-arrows were their most favoured decorative motifs. The conjugal yoke bound weapons of Love. Presentation copies of royal decrees were illuminated with pictures of the monarchs exchanging kisses—ritual *oscula* rather than erotic *basia*, but kisses nonetheless.

Propaganda is usually devised as a mask for truth. In their early years together, the reasons for Ferdinand's and Isabella's single-minded cultivation of a united image lay in the rivalry and discord they felt obliged to disavow. For when Isabella first emerged as a candidate for the Castilian throne during the civil wars of the 1460s, she suffered from an almost crippling physical disability, of which only a husband could relieve her: she was a woman—and according to the physiology of the time, before Falloppio had sliced his way into women's bodies and found how they really work, a woman was regarded as nature's bodged attempt to create a man. The presence of Ferdinand at her side in all her self-representations was a calculated display of essential equipment. It was not meant to proclaim a project for the political unification of their respective inheritances, but to cope with an immediate emergency.

In exchange for parity of power with Isabella in her lifetime, Ferdinand

The imperial and humanist trappings which surround Ferdinand and Isabella on the façade of the University of Salamanca reflect values of their grandson's reign, when the work was executed. Symmetry and equipollency were typical of portraits in their lifetime, but Ferdinand is here slightly more prominent than his wife, not for reasons of realism, but to legitimate Charles V's superior authority over his mother, who was nominally joint-sovereign.

was obliged to forgo not only his own immediate claim to the throne, but also his right to its reversion in favour of his offspring by his wife. The rivalry between them is apparent between the lines of the address she is said to have delivered at a conference in Segovia in 1475, when her differences with her husband over the government of the realm were settled: 'My lord...where there exists that conformity which by God's grace ought to exist between you and me, there can be no dispute': by implication, the conformity was lacking and the dispute obvious. The image of unity, in short, papered over the cracks in the monarchs' alliance. Theirs was the equality of Tweedle-dum and Tweedle-dee. The monarchs' mutual love may have become a fact, but it began as an affectation.

Their propaganda has impressed and often convinced historians. Whenever the political context has demanded myths of power and unity, the memory of Ferdinand and Isabella has been summoned to supply them. In 1640, when the cohesion of the monarchy was threatened by the revolt of the Catalans, a Jesuit wit published a work which elevated the king, 'our immortal hero', as a prophet and exemplar of peninsular unification, 'born in Aragon for Castile'. In 1938, as an act of resistance against the 'reds' whose armies closed about him as he wrote, a nationalist historian praised Isabella as the 'foundress of Spain'. The Franco regime used the names and emblems of its presumed predecessors to justify its work of centralization and discouragement of minority cultures. The yoke-and-arrows became the symbol of the Falange. In historical atlases, the impression of a peninsula almost unified is strengthened by the apparent disappearing trick which blends the formerly distinct kingdoms—Castile, Aragon, Granada, Navarre—into a single colour by the time of Ferdinand's death in 1516, though at best this signifies only the fortunes of a single dynasty, not the elimination of political diversity. In 1467 one of Isabella's two brothers spited the other by putting the cherished creatures of the royal zoo to the sword: deer, bear cubs, and a leopard were slaughtered and only one elderly mountain goat was spared. Spain is sometimes thought of as an uncontrollable menagerie, full of intractable 'historic communities' and unassimilable separatist tendencies, which might be tackled by centralization enforced by tough discipline or by a destructive policy—a hecatomb like young Prince Alfonso's in which centralizing governments have tried to bury separatism. Ferdinand and Isabella are commonly seen as the first and—by some accounts—the peculiarly effective wielders of the ringmasters' whip.

The vagaries of dynastic history had often brought Iberian kingdoms into personal union. Occasionally these arrangements had proved permanent. In some cases they had induced particular rulers to arrogate imperial titles over the whole peninsula or had led gradually to the spread of uniform institutions and the creation of a common elite. The union of Aragon and Castile, considered from one point of view, was another such episode. Contemporaries, however, instantly recognized it as something special. They began to speak loosely of the monarchs 'of Spain': Ferdinand was the last ruler to contemplate dividing his peninsular kingdoms among their heirs. Spanish unity—such as it was—was in part a function of Castilian strength, which had been gradually growing, relative to that of other peninsular kingdoms. Ferdinand and Isabella confirmed the trend by adding new conquests to the crown of Castile. There was now a hegemonic power in the peninsula, where once there had been a ring of states in equipoise, and in 1580 even Portugal, the last peninsular state outside the Castilian system, became by inheritance a realm of the ruler of the other kingdoms. Nothing in the subsequent history of Spain can be understood except against the background of this dynastic revolution.

It produced a single system of states in an unprecedented combination, but poorly articulated, with every kingdom, and some parts of every kingdom, distinguished by peculiarities of law and custom. It was a world riven by particularism—an 'unamalgamating bundle', as it still seemed to Richard Ford, even in the nineteenth century when conscious policies of centralization, undreamed-of in our period, had wrought their effects. For these were vast and intractable kingdoms, almost unembraced by institutional unity. Government was collaborative, mediated through local and regional networks of devolved authority. In remote places, the monarchs' authority was more ritual than real. When royal letters arrived, officials would kiss them and place them on their heads in token of submission and read them aloud in a public place to anyone who would listen, as if they bore some fragment of the persona of their senders, with the reverence due to relics of the saints; but, like saints' relics, royal letters were usually powerless to change people's lives. After the rite of reception, they might be laid aside for 'obedience without compliance'.

The monarchs were 'absolute' only of some laws; and, in any case, in an era when the concept of statute was in its infancy, absolutism was intelligible more readily in terms of the untrumped right to dispense justice rather than the untrammelled right to legislate. Moreover, despite the growing importance of secular political theory throughout our period, sovereignty was not understood in terms of supreme power in the state or absolute control of the laws, but as a constraining relationship to

God. As the humanist canon of Toledo, Alonso Ortiz, warned, 'Monarchs have only God to fear, and if ever that fear is overcome, they fall headlong into the abyss of vice.' A strict standard distinguished kings from tyrants: the service of their people, the public good. Chroniclers could still quote the medieval adage: 'The voice of the people is the voice of God.' Therefore royal government, though not necessarily by consent, was always with advice, from the people narrowly defined—a small political nation. Kings were not obliged to take counsel with peasants except through their lords, or with townsfolk save through the urban corporations.

Still, Castile, by comparison with most European states, proved 'faithful'—manipulable, that is, to royal will, with a population willing to contribute to the costs of the crown. The monarchs' Aragonese dominions, on the other hand, were notoriously intractable. There—according to many comentators—the allegiance of subjects was conditional on the king's part of the bargain: the defence of their customs and liberties. Far more than among the Castilian dominions, the states of which the Crown of Aragon was composed retained representative assemblies and peculiar, indefeasible laws of their own. Spanish rulers could not have taken a uniform approach to their realms, even had they wished to do so. Nor, except in connection with religion, do they appear to have so wished until the eighteenth century. Like the Burgundian dominions under the Valois dukes or those of the British monarchies of the seventeenth century, the Spain bequeathed by Ferdinand and Isabella was a dynastic agglomeration, capable of concerted action and—given time—of political symbiosis, but still divided in itself by conflicting interests and divergent traditions.

The networks of power were spread mainly by traditional means: by patronage and propaganda, by personal monarchy and persuasion, backed by canny judgement in securing the collaboration of potentially rival sources of authority in the realm. Ultimately, obedience depended not on the power of the monarchs but on the willingness of their subjects. When it could not be purchased or coerced, it had to be cajoled or inspired, ransomed out of the riches of myth. Machiavelli's portrait of Ferdinand as an embodiment of *Staatspolitik*, who wore gay colours to celebrate his son-in-law's politically convenient death, has created a deceptive image of a 'modern' monarch, actuated by secular values. The real Ferdinand is better classified as a 'medieval' figure, trying to live out the millenarian expectations with which prophetic utterance endowed him—the 'promised prince' who would raise his banner in Jerusalem and rule the world until its appointed end. Columbus claimed to have brought a smile to the monarchs' lips by promising that the profits of his projected enterprise would contribute to the cost of conquering Jerusalem. The smile is usually supposed to have been ironical: the smirk of hard-headed realists amused by the dreamer from Genoa. But it is more likely to have been a smile of pleasure—a grin of recognition as their propaganda was reassuringly reflected back.

The prophetic tradition surrounded the monarchy throughout the sixteenth century and even, in some respects, clung hazily in the vicinity of the susceptible Philip IV. Charles V was depicted as the Last World Emperor—indeed, while things went well for him he convincingly looked the part. Philip II was the subject of a similar prophecy at birth, though he did not encourage the tradition, perhaps doubting its orthodoxy. He preferred another family myth which sacralized his dynasty: the role of the Habsburgs as guardians of the Blessed Sacrament. He also cultivated a royal vision with popular roots, which you can still see embodied on the main façade of his foundation of El Escorial. The kings carved there are not kings of Spain but of ancient Israel, leading a chosen people through trials of faith, just as Philip tried to do in a life of unremitting and ultimately unrewarding duty. His successors lived in the shadow of the same self-perception, practising stoicism in adversity or wielding 'the sword of the faith'. 'Reputation' mattered more than realities. The gap between resources and achievements was filled with subjects who shared the propaganda-vision of the monarchs as warriors in a sort of externalized psychomachia, a cosmic battle of good and evil, in which Moors, Jews, heretics, and fautors of heresy were on the other side.

Loose mesh is often the most elastic but it is doubtful whether traditional techniques of government would alone have been sufficient to stretch the monarchy across the world. To evoke obedience, commands had to be communicated, and in our period the art of political communication was transformed. Ferdinand and Isabella were heirs of a personal style of monarchy. Unlike the monarchs of France they had no thaumaturgic touch with which to reach across the ranks of society; but they received humble petitioners at weekly audiences with 'generous faith in hearing the petitions and plaints of all who come…to ask for justice'. They made their presence felt in person, as they crossed the country from town to town, taking the court with them, in sixty-two ox-carts. They spent most of their time crawling along the historic highway of the kingdom between Toledo and the Duero valley; but they also penetrated the parts other monarchs did not reach. They made a royal progress to Galicia and were as familiar to their subjects in Andalusia as in any province of their kingdom. The web-like spread of their itinerary marks the only sort of 'unification' they can confidently be said to have essayed.

They maintained, so far as we can judge, the most active chancery in Castile's history. The reach of royal communications had been extended by one technical revolution—the use of paper—in the fourteenth century; Ferdinand and Isabella presided over another—the use of printing. This was a novelty but it was also, in a sense, the counterpart of tireless travel—transmitting fragments of the royal presence. Ferdinand's successor was peripatetic by inclination: an old-fashioned monarch, who liked to do business in person; but he took the paperwork revolution further. He began the habit—perfectly exemplified in the reign of his son, Philip II—of spattering official dispatches with annotations. Bureaucratic immobility tended to fix government in particular locations: the higher judiciary in Valladolid and Granada; the court and councils of state, including those of the kingdoms of Aragon and Portugal, in Madrid or Valladolid. A decision-making environment was created by Philip II in the purpose-built palace-monastery of El Escorial. The characteristic royal monuments of the Middle Ages had been mausolea: henceforth, they were palaces. The tapestries, formerly favoured for ease of transportation, as the same scenes of Solomon and Hercules were unrolled at every royal stopover, were gradually displaced in royal art collections by paintings and sculptures. Government became 'curialized' concentrated in a few highly literate hands. Philip III and Philip IV—respectively out of laziness and incapacity—ended up reliant on *válidos*, men of business of quasi-regal power, who controlled the flow of documents and the corridors of the court.

Still, Spain never became a bureaucratic, centralized or 'modern' state in our period, though the professional bureaucracy grew and new institutions of education—consciously elitist residential colleges in university towns—developed to renew it: on the contrary, there was a 'seigneurial revival' in the sixteenth century, as Charles V and Philip II alienated taxes, rents, and jurisdictions into the private hands of local potentates for administrative convenience, economy, or ready cash. There was a sense, however, in which the overseas empire acquired by Castile became a type of 'modern' statehood. For here, where time and distance armoured the

The kings who dominate the entrance-court of the Escorial are monarchs of ancient Israel—including, in pointed justification of Philip's reformist ecclesiastical policy, Josiah, Jehosaphat and Hezekiah: the scourges of the priests and purifiers of the temple. More generally, the façade expresses a concept of Spain as the new Israel, embarked on a sacred history, enduring trials of faith.

colonies against peninsular control, the Crown was jealous of its power. Hereditary offices were few; elected ones were of little account; justice was the preserve of royally appointed bureaucrats; ecclesiastical patronage was in the king's hands. The administration aspired to regulate the most minute details of the lives of its subjects in Manila and Michoacán, down to the weight of the burdens that native labourers were allowed to carry and the identity of individuals allowed to wear swords in the street. With the exception of a few estates of broadly 'feudal' character and some ecclesiastical 'peculiars' where the rights of the Crown were effectively farmed out to religious orders, the overseas empire was run, with all the distortions and inefficiencies that derived from the intractability of time and space, from Madrid.

The Political Nation: i. The Nobility

Spanish monarchs were successful as long as they ruled a compliant society. Aristocratic co-operation was indispensable. The palaces of the *ricos hombres* of the time show wealth and prowess united to exclude interference and crush resistance: solid and angular, impregnably built, richly embellished and sometimes crowned with fantastic galleries or sumptuous balustrades, though the most startling examples—the Mendoza palaces of Guadalajara—represent an attempt at local domination which, in this city, the family could never be quite sure of. A dozen of the most powerful lineages commanded incomes greater than those of any bishopric except that of Toledo, which was, by repute, the second most valuable in Christendom.

The monarchs sensed no conflict of interest with a class who were their natural allies in the government of the monarchy and whose very status was a function of traditions of service to the Crown. They were deft in their handling of their privileged position as matchmakers in the aristocratic marriage market. In partial consequence, intermarriage made a well-knotted tapestry of the Castilian high nobility: in 1502 two Mendoza cousins were granted a dispensation to marry on the grounds that they were even more closely related to all the other suitable candidates.

The king and queen were participants in the prevailing aristocratic ethos—the cult of chivalry and of 'the love that conquers all'. A Venetian ambassador remembered the conquest of Granada as 'a war won by love ...What man is so vile, so lacking in spirit, that he would not have defeated every powerful foe and redoubtable adversary, risking a thousand lives rather than return to his lady in shame?' Even kings who did not care for jousting, like Philip II, were responsive to chivalric values, celebrated aristocratic companionage in the hunt, and imposed freely on traditional *noblesse oblige* when they wanted cost-effective service in war and government. If chivalry had not still been shaping society in the early seventeenth century, Cervantes's satire would have lacked bite.

The alliance of nobles and monarchs meant that the inequitable savageries of an unrestrained master-class sometimes went unpunished or were even encouraged. The most barbarous case under Ferdinand and Isabella was that of Don Fernando de Velasco, brother of the lord constable of Castile, who burned to death some drunken yokels who had mistaken him for a Jewish rent collector. In reply to the bereaved families' complaints, the king maintained that Velasco had acted nobly by avenging the insult. At the same time, the most conspicuous instances are not always the most typical, and although it would be wrong to speak of a transformation of the nobility, there are signs in some cases of a pacification of their habits, part of which was owed to the influence of court life. Unwittingly—no doubt—the monarchs began the process of domestication which would eventually create a court-aristocracy in Spain.

Writers questioned the true nature of nobility, pointing out, under the influence of Aristotle and his commentators, whose works were widely diffused in fifteenth-century Spain, that gentility lay in the cultivation of virtue: 'God made men, not lineages.' Diego de Valera put forward a concept in which elements of nobility were linked to intellectual distinction: 'I know', he declared, 'how to serve my Prince not only with the strengths of my body but also with those of my mind and understanding.' Hostility persisted between 'arms and letters', but in the court, where aristocracy met and married with bureaucracy, a world of mixed values took shape. Noblemen began to send their sons to universities.

Nobility was also associated with wealth: 'ducats make dukedoms', quipped Góngora, Spain's greatest Baroque poet, 'and crowns coronets.' This was not the result of the 'rise of capitalism' but an ancient fact. It coexisted with plenty of *hobereau* poverty, like that of the knight in *Lazarillo de Tormes*, whose toothpick was the prop of his pretence that he could afford to eat, or the two noble bootblacks of mid-seventeenth-century Ciudad Real. Noble status or self-belief could derive from royal fiat, or one's place of birth, or one's inherited exemption from certain fiscal obligations, or one's 'pure' blood, untainted by Moorish or Jewish ancestry. Above all it was conferred and sustained across the generations by service to the Crown.

Noblemen of every kind of pedigree could agree on the ennobling virtue of such service. Most of the great lineages of the period were not of truly ancient blood: most of the *vieille garde* were descended from warriors from the northern mountains who had fought in the civil wars of the fourteenth century; the newest recruits were royal servants of another sort—bureaucrats who married into and aped the warrior dynasties. More than by any other single development, the greatness of Spain was guaranteed by the fusion of interests between aristocracy and Crown. In a continuing carve-up of the exploitable potential of the realm—which has been mislabelled as a 'feudal reaction'—potential rivalry between Crown and aristocracy was choked by a glut of shared power. Uniquely among European monarchies of the period, Spain experienced no serious aristocratic rebellion. The real power-struggle was not between Crown and nobles but between nobles and towns.

The Political Nation: ii. The Towns

When Hernán Cortés arrived on the fringes of the Aztec world, almost his first act was to create a municipality and have his men elect him mayor. This has been interpreted as an attempt to legitimate his dubious authority and as a gesture of solidarity with urban rebels in Castile. But, at

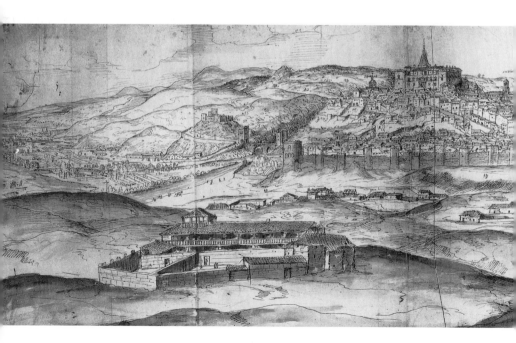

another level, it was the normal reflex action of a Spaniard in such circumstances. On a savage frontier, when two Englishmen meet they form a club; Spaniards found a city. Castile, according to the early-seventeenth-century moralist Juan Pablo-Mártir Rizo, was 'a kingdom made of cities'. The impression Spain made on Machiavelli was of great desert lands interspersed with cities. Anton van Wyngaerde painted these staging-posts of civilization for Philip II—the album of an urbane kingdom. Historians routinely call early modern societies 'rural', but Spain imagined herself, thought herself urban.

Municipalities of appropriate status could—if they kept rivals at bay—exercise lordship in their own right and mulct profits of jurisdiction not only within their own walls but in dependent lands around them. In the disputes which arose, Ferdinand and Isabella almost always favoured the noble lineages against the urban patriciates. In a famous case, the monarchs stripped Segovia of two villages and 1,200 vassals and gave them to

Anton van Wyngaerde was one of many Flemings Philip brought to Spain in the 1570s to enrich the arts and enhance scientific and encyclopaedic projects: van Wyngaerde was a surveyor as well as a portrayer of the cities of the realm. Toledo was beginning an era of relative decline, as the new courtly centre of Madrid began to draw aristocrats and the growth of Seville and Valladolid had a magnetic effect on religious communities.

the courtier-bureaucrat whom they elevated to be marqués de Moya. The citizens beat their children to fix the affront in their memories, but despite unremitting petitioning from the city the Crown never relented. The partisanship shown to the great family of Velasco in the struggles to control the town council of Burgos is recalled today by the towering dome of the family's funerary chapel; the crushing weight of their palace, with the monarchs' monograms exhibited like favours, dominates the town.

Power in Burgos was uneasily shared between a mercantile patriciate and the Velasco family, hereditary Constables of Castile. The buildings and art-works the Velasco endowed were proclamations of ambition—especially the crushingly huge funerary chapel, begun in 1482 and finished in 1494 in the characteristic Burgos style, developed through cross-fertilization with the German and Flemish artists who found work and established dynasties in the city.

A few years after Ferdinand's death, Crown and aristocracy together crushed the last efforts of some Castilian towns to recover their lost regime of liberties. The insurrection of 1520 was provoked in part by unease at the accession of a foreign ruler: Charles V, a Netherlandish prince, provoked sentiments in Spain not unlike those his Spanish son, Philip II, was to inspire in the Netherlands. In part it was the overflowing of a mood of *grande peur* caused by rumours of a hearth tax. But it was also the outcome of long-accumulating resentments—the unfulfilled rebelliousness of two generations of declining civic autonomy.

Rebellion erupted out of the violent frustrations, the cycles of vengeance spinning out of control which typified factional squabbles on city councils. Burgos in the years before the revolt was rent by the dissensions of the court-connected faction of the Orense and de la Mota families and another allied with the greatest aristocratic dynasty of the region: the Constables of Castile, for whom control of Burgos was the great prize of regional politics. By 1520 there were nine members of the de la Mota family on the Council: 'Fortune', said one of their enemies acidly, 'rewards those whose merits are beyond our comprehension.' Urban rebellion—and the unrest which occasionally broke out in isolated instances—was not usually a sign of democratic outrage but a baring of teeth in elite power-games.

City status was a habit of mind, rather than a function of size. Only a handful of Spanish towns could rival the scale of the conurbations of Flanders or Italy. In the course of the sixteenth century Seville and Madrid swelled to the metropolitan dimensions of a Naples or Rome. Seville had about 55,000 people in 1534, over 100,000 by 1570. Madrid's population grew in the same period from about 12,000 to nearly 40,000 and would more than double in size in the following generation. These came to rank among the great cities of Christendom for size, and over the century as a whole, most settlements of urban status or pretensions tended to get bigger: 234 out of 370 places which made reports on their own changing dimensions in the reign of Philip II admitted to growth. Most towns grew disproportionately, drawing population from the countryside in an era of general demographic buoyancy: the number of taxpayers disclosed on Castilian censuses increased by about three-eighths from 1530 to 1591, but the normal ceiling was represented by the populations of 30,000 or 40,000 of Valladolid, Barcelona, and Valencia. Cities of undeniable prestige were tiny: Burgos had only about 6,000 people in 1530, León only 3,600 in 1591.

Nor could towns easily be defined by function. Valladolid was a city of *fonctionnaires.* Its prosperity derived from the Court of Chancellery—the highest court of appeal, save the king himself, in the realm, which was unique to Valladolid until the growth of the kingdom obliged Charles V to establish another at Granada. Its floating population was of litigants-in-waiting: here courtiers died, waiting for their cases to come up. Here religious orders congregated to be able to throng and lobby the court. Of the 6,750 heads of household who appear in the census of 1530, 2,000 or 3,000 lived directly off the chancellery. Burgos, by contrast, was a city of merchants—an inland emporium whose character was defined by its 7,000 to 8,000 mules, the makings of the caravans which plied between the pastures of the plateaux and the ports of the Cantabrian coasts. Its civic chronicler likened it to Venice. A Venetian ambassador acknowledged a certain similarity: 'the majority of its inhabitants', it seemed to him, 'are rich merchants.' In Ciudad Real, by contrast, there was no local thalassocracy: the town had no merchant councillors before Juan de Rojas in the late seventeenth century—and even he diversified, as he grew in wealth, from trade into investment in land. Only Barcelona quite kept the character of an ancient city-republic, sending its own ambassador to court with a retinue allegedly as magnificent as that of the papal nuncio. But there were many sizeable communities by the standards of the time: most of the population, over most of the country, was concentrated in settlements of 1,500 to 2,000 people. Though small villages by today's standards, they cultivated a consciously urban self-image.

Early modern Spaniards, for all their urban prejudices, can be said to have discovered the rural face of Spain. The frequency of famine encouraged scientific agronomy; ennui with court life encouraged the poetry of meditations of rural *soledades*; nature mysticism alerted its practicioners to previously under-appreciated scenic beauties; above all, the godly drive to reform popular culture spread evangelizers through a previously under-evangelized countryside. Civil peace was imposed on the towns by *force majeure*; it was spread through the countryside by a sort of Spanish Reformation.

The Peaceful Reformation: i. 'Popular' Religion

Ferdinand and Isabella achieved startling triumphs in their drive to 'constitute Spain to the glory of God': the founding of the Inquisition, an unprecedented depth of ecclesiastical reform, the conversion—at least in name—of a large number of the conquered Moors, and the painful eradication of Spanish Judaism. Subsequent monarchs imitated them with excessive zeal. Charles V expelled the remaining Moors from most of the kingdom. Philip II forcibly dispersed the descendants of the Moors of Granada in response to a rebellion. Philip III expelled virtually all descendants of Moors—some 275,000 of them—in full awareness that the economic consequences would be disastrous. All the monarchs of our period tried to burn heresy out of the kingdom. The Inquisition acted as a social safety-valve for the complaints of the poor and unsophisticated, who could never indict their neighbours or challenge their social superiors in ordinary courts. After the reign of Ferdinand and Isabella it was by no means the bloody tribunal vulgarly supposed, but it did more harm than good by encouraging vexatious and spurious accusations of heresy. It ought to have been socially 'functional'. In practice, however, it had a divisive and depressant effect, spreading insecurity with its secretive procedures and vast web of informers, setting neighbours at loggerheads, and inducing an atmosphere of fear.

If religious uniformity was the aim of such policies, they were bound to fail: it was not heretics or infidels who fatally compromised unity, but the infinite variety of Catholic tradition itself. The Tridentine clerical elite brought the universal cults of the Virgin Mary and the suffering Christ as part of an effort to make the church 'truly one'. Villagers responded by adapting the proffered symbols to their local need for tutelary deities. Christ and His mother were stripped of their universal significance and became the Christ of this place, the Virgin of that. Strict horizons were imposed on local religion by saints greedy for devotion, who enforced the discipline of rotating feast-days and fast-days with demonic urgency: indeed, demons too were everywhere—whipping Sor María de la Cruz by night, inciting Sor Isabel de Jesús to prostitution, impersonating Christ and the saints in countless unverified visions.

Where the strength of local cults occluded people's sense of belonging to a universal church, the saints of a spiritual *patria chica* did demons' work for them. Local religion was the patch on Christ's seamless robe, the boil on his perfect body. In Catalonia, priests struggled against parti-coloured local piety in a country where—as a modern expert says—there were 'more advocations of the Virgin than kinds of sausage'. In Castile, when 'our Lady of Riansares or the Christ of Urda... are valued above other Marys and Christs', the Church seemed to dissolve, according to clerical critics, into competing churches.

Many of the ceremonies still enacted today in expiation of parish and municipal vows, from Barcelona to San Vicente del Realejo in Tenerife, originated in the seventeenth century. Everywhere devotion ticked away to the traditional rhythms of the countryside, with feasts and fasts adjusted to the oscillations of dearth and glut. The god of rural Christians still looked like a demiurge, personifying a Nature who was not always benign. Some of the excesses commonly ascribed to 'popular' or 'local' religion were rites peasants practised to appease her: the mock trials and excommunications of locusts, rats, and swallows, the aspersion of vine pests with water from St Gregory's shrine. Water shortages inspired acts of collective penance, like the procession of flagellants bearing a statue of the Virgin which Don Quixote mistook for the abduction of a noble lady. This was a religion of survival in this world, rather than salvation in the next. Of 745 vows analysed by William Christian, Jr., from reports drawn up for Philip II, 82 per cent were made in response to disease or natural disaster—in most cases, plague or infestation by pests.

St Teresa of Avila had her first vision of Christ after hearing a Franciscan preach about his order's mission to the Indies. 'There is another Indies waiting to be evangelized here in Spain', said her celestial voice. It was a common saying of the late sixteenth century that 'within Spain there are Indies and mountains of ignorance', and as the clergy made increasing spiritual demands on their flocks, so the oceans seemed to narrow. 'I don't know why the fathers of the company go to Japan and the Philippines to look for lost souls,' wrote a Jesuit correspondent in 1615, 'when we have so many here in the same condition who do not know whether they believe in God.' In 1603 the prior of a Dominican house in Santillana on the Cantabrian coast complained that the inhabitants of his region 'know little of faith and are... victims of a thousand superstitions'.

The clerical elite answered this challenge by mobilizing to invade the countryside—the parts of Spain earlier evangelizations had not reached. The sixteenth-century encounter of the godly with the under-evangelized could be represented as a struggle of learned against popular religion or of universal against local Christianity. In Spain it was, at least in part, a confrontation between rural and urban spirituality. 'The life of the church', wrote Pedro de Oña in 1603, 'is the life of a city, not of a village', and clerics were indeed inclined to despair before the problems of irrigating rural wastelands with the waters of salvation. In an obvious sense, Oña was right: in a land where at least 1 per cent of the population enjoyed benefit of clergy, it seems incredible that there was a shortage of priests: yet such was the concentration of religious communities and parishes in urban settings that for much of the country outside town-walls the sight of a priest and the opportunity to receive the sacraments could be a rare event. In towns, by contrast, bishops complained that communion was taken with excessive frequency by some worshippers: 'many people receive the Holy Sacrament every day, for which they cannot have made due preparation.' To the problems of clerical immobility, inertia, and undermanning was added the impenetrability of the wilder parts of one of Europe's most mountainous countries. In the broken uplands, in remote Galicia, and along inaccessible seaboards, complained Spanish bishops at the Council of Trent in 1565, 'to go to Mass on feast-days and carry the Blessed Sacrament and hear confessions' priests had to face arduous mountains and swollen rivers. There were complaints that even in the diocese of Toledo not all districts could be provided with a priest's services.

Customs too entrenched to change could be sacralized. One common endeavour was the appropriation of social rituals. Marriage is the most obvious example: in the sixteenth and seventeenth centuries, in most of Europe it was revolutionized by successful campaigns to suppress clandestine marriages and to bring all unions under clerical bans. Ostensibly the Spanish Inquisition was a tribunal of faith. In practice, most of its efforts in the second half of the sixteenth century were devoted to getting laymen's sex lives under priestly control. Bigamy became one of the most frequent causes in the Inquisition's courts in the 1560s and 1570s; fornication was the tribunal's major preoccupation for the rest of the century. Sex had never been something of which church leaders had unequivocally approved; but they were united in thinking it did least harm when licensed by themselves. Their campaigns were motivated by charity as well as power-lust. It seemed vital, as a saintly lobbyist claimed in 1551, 'to invalidate all marriages where there is no witness', because 'an infinite number of maidens have been deceived and undone, sinning with men and trusting in the promise of marriage made to them; and some have left their parents' house and gone to their perdition'.

As well as in the countryside, the evangelizing efforts of the early modern period were concentrated wherever crowds uprooted from the traditional environment and disciplines of parish life needed urgent ministrations from the godly. The movement worked best, perhaps, in the army, not only because of the large and active corps of chaplains that developed in the late sixteenth and seventeenth centuries, when Spain's armies were the biggest in Europe, but also because it was a home-from-home for deracinated men, removed not only from the structures of the parish but also from the comforts of family life. The Spanish army, with its avowedly crusading vocation, needed religious inspiration. Specifically, religious men—those of frustrated religious vocation or strong inclinations towards religiosity—seem to have been attracted to the soldiering life. Jerónimo de Pasamonte, for instance, claimed explicitly to have been led into soldiering by his want of means to train for the priesthood. His fellow-autobiographer, Alonso de Contreras, tells of seven months he spent as a hermit in an interlude of his soldier's life, claiming never to have been so happy as in his poor and lonely cave—and this from a notoriously libidinous and hard-living picaroon who seems to have been addicted to his own adrenalin. The new, evangelically aware orders of the Counter-Reformation, of whom the Jesuits were the most conspicuous and dynamic, were attracted to army chaplaincies for the same reason as they felt drawn to the slum-ringed boom-towns like Seville and Madrid and to the dense, servile native populations of the New World.

The Peaceful Reformation: ii. Popular Mysticism

The characteristic Spanish religion of our period was mysticism. When St John of the Cross escaped from prison, his first thought was to read his *Dark Night of the Soul* to the nuns among whom he took refuge. The pious virgins and their supervisors apparently had no difficulty understanding or, at least, excusing the incandescently erotic language. Spiritual fulfilment is not, presumably, much like sexual satisfaction; but 'one makes these comparisons,' St Teresa said, 'because there are no suitable ones'. After the sublimities of the poets, analysis makes the whole subject seem ridiculous, but it has to be attempted because mysticism plays such an important part in our story.

In the sixteenth century, mysticism was, so to speak, the Protestantism of Catholics—the means whereby, without unorthodoxy, the faithful soul could cleave the trivial round of good works and routine obligations, slicing through the active life of a Martha to Mary's 'better way'. Mystics dodged to God around the sacraments, ducking the hierarchy and bucking the authority of a mediatory church. If it was in the nature of mainstream Protestantism to cultivate a personal relationship between the Christian and God, how much more did mysticism do so, by igniting

El Greco (1541–1614) has been re-evaluated as a more-or-less typical mannerist by recent scholarship. Yet really nothing about him was typical and mysticism is far more prominent than mannerism in his mental world: especially in works of the last few years of his life, like this *Visitation*, in which visionary shapes seem to half-materialize from what one of El Greco's favourite texts—the Byzantine mystical treatise ascribed to Dionysius the Areopagite—called the 'cloud of unknowing'.

Titian's allegory usually called *Spain Coming to the Aid of Religion* was traditionally supposed to be a celebration of the Holy League which won the battle of Lepanto in 1571. Really, however, it was a more generalized propaganda-piece, which could be reproduced in different versions with suitable variations—substituting, for instance, a serpent of heresy for a malevolent Turk—and bestowed as a diplomatic gift.

the soul with tongues of fire and fanning them with the rush of wind. Licensed mysticism kept great saints inside the Catholic Church at a time when many ardent seekers after God could only feel freed for their quest by espousing Protestantism.

It should not be supposed that this was an exclusively elite devotion, limited to privileged ranks. Mysticism was part of the active Christianity which evangelically minded propagandists tried to promote among ordinary people. St Teresa and St John of the Cross were genuine evangelists of mysticism. St Thomas of Villanueva devoted entire sermons to counselling his congregations in mystical techniques. Popular handbooks of Catholic devotion by Diego de Estella and Luis de Granada included—albeit not at a sophisticated or adventurous pitch—some of the same advice. Though a soulless art-criticism has tried to demote El Greco from mystic to mannerist, he was saturated in mystical reading and his works—especially the late paintings in which figures seem translated into flame or atomized in cloud-like blurs—are among the most vivid memorials of the Catholicism of the Reformation era. Well represented in his work is a favourite exercise in meditative mysticism in the sixteenth century, easily taught to ordinary people: contemplation of a starry night. On such a night, in an amusing poem, Fray Luis de León strove earnestly for the mystical effect without achieving it. As a form of Christian discipline suitable for cultivation throughout society, mysticism had one outstanding advantage: it was cheap; for those who could procure one, a mystical ecstasy was as vivid an introduction to God as any work of art, without having to be paid for.

The Peaceful Reformation: iii. 'Official' Religion

In the right foreground, Religion wilts, downcast, with arms, cross, and chalice fallen from her grasp. Only the Spanish monarchy, entering, stage right, like a buxom Amazon, can save her, while the chaste fortitude of the figures in the foreground contrasts with the phallic malevolence of the enemy—serpent or Turk in different versions—in the rear. Titian's great allegory, *Spain Coming to the Aid of Religion*, was probably designed in the early 1570s, when the building of the Escorial was nearing completion and the Holy League against the Turks was taking shape. It has come to symbolize, in a certain tradition of Spanish self-flattery, the relationship between Spain and the church idealized by propagandists of the time: Spain as the sword of the Lord and of Gideon, the sling of David, the champion of the faith.

The court's propaganda was reflected back in submissions from around the country. In 1575 the citizens of Las Mesas near Cuenca likened to the Samaritan woman's plea to Christ their own appeal to Philip II as 'the heir of the Catholic Kings ... whose Catholic renown you have inherited'. In 1590 Fray Antonio Baltasar Alvarez, self-appointed topographer of Spain's spiritual landscape, pictured Spain as a redoubt of beleaguered Catholicism in an image curiously reminiscent, in inverted fashion, of the English propaganda that extolled the beleaguered 'Protestant isle': 'Of the whole of today's world there is no part where our true God is not persecuted and ill-used, save only for this little corner called Spain, where, in refuge from the world He has deigned to seek a welcome for His great mercy's sake.'

Philip II's title of 'Catholic King' was hereditary, but he was anxious to display its particular application to himself. His faith was deeply felt, not conveniently affected, after something like a conversion experience at the end of the 1560s—connected, perhaps, with the tragic end of his son and heir Don Carlos, who, having shown signs of violent madness, died imprisoned by his father's command. Yet, at the same time, Philip's Catholic image concealed certain ironies. In his youth he had been quite differently portrayed, as a prince of the pagan Renaissance, in gilded armour. After his conversion he continued to quarrel with popes, protect heretics when it suited, ally with them at need, and cheerfully secularize church property. His personal spirituality, with its liturgical austerity, its Old Testament allusions, and its strenuous exercises in mental prayer, had in some ways more in common with the Reformation than with main-stream Catholic practice. His own choice of regular pious reading contained almost nothing that would have offended Luther, but was altogether in the tradition of late-medieval personal piety, scriptural reflection, mystical devotion, and critical self-examination which helped to inspire the Protestant reformers in their search for a direct and personal experience of God.

At one level, the defiance of Protestantism seems embodied in granite and blazoned in art in the Escorial; yet those kings over the gate include Protestant heroes like Josiah, Jehosophat, and Hezekiah, who humbled

Apart from Titian, no painter received more commissions from Philip II than Antonis Mor (1512–75), a Fleming who became court painter in the Netherlands from 1552. Philip's esteem began with this portrait of 1549. Our conventional image of the monarch as austerely black-clad dates from later life, when he was often obliged to wear mourning. His self-perception in his prime is reflected in this gilded vision of princely splendour and *sprezzatura*.

the high priests and cleansed the temple of filth. Even the custodian of the Blessed Sacrament was not far, in cultural terms, from his confessional enemies. His ecclesiastical policies, too, resembled those of other sixteenth-century kings—'Erastian' policies of arrogating patronage to the Crown, enforcing secular jurisdiction on clerics, dissolving houses of religion, or imposing reforms at royal initiative.

It has long been recognized that the religious culture of literate people in early modern Spain was not *sui generis* but intelligible in a European perspective. It has been found, for instance, by one school to have been saturated in 'Erasmianism'—the critical, Christian-humanist piety particularly associated with Erasmus of Rotterdam. Other scholars have drawn attention to the shaping flow of Franciscan currents from one of the great international mendicant orders. It is now possible to see the same writings in an even broader context which embraces the Reformation. The trend in contemporary scholarship is to re-evaluate the Reformation in a new light as part of a great evangelizing movement, common to western and eastern Christendom in the sixteenth century: an 'age of transition' to a more intense and committed form of Christianity, embraced more widely at different levels of society and education than ever before.

The kernel of the devotional reading inherited by sixteenth-century Spaniards from the past was the corpus published by Cardinal Cisneros—grand inquisitor, regent of Spain, patron of education. In the cardinal's eyes, the primitive and patristic church was seen through the eye of traditional faith, not refracted through the brilliant but prismatic lens of the classically inspired humanist curriculum. He favoured works which emphasized Scripture, mysticism and the appeal from a profoundly penitent conscience to the direct exercise of God's grace. Cisneros's mental world, considered from this point of view, looks rather like that of Luther, concerned to investigate the most direct routes of access between Man and God. If Cisneros helped to forestall Protestantism in Spain, it was rather by over-trumping in advance the appeal of the reformers than, as used often to be alleged, by the supposed efficacy of his attempted ecclesiastical reforms. The Cisnerian devotional corpus anticipated some of the devotional and scholarly features of Erasmus's Christian vision without sharing all the same sources or having a specifically humanist pedigree. We ought not to say—to adapt a famous phrase—that Cisneros laid the egg which Erasmus hatched, but that the same egg was incubating spontaneously, as terrapins' eggs are said to do, in the warm and propitious soil of Spain.

The Costs of Reputation

Spain's peaceful Reformation was not enough to keep her out of the wars of religion which crippled other early modern European states. For nearly a century from the 1560s the Netherlands bled the strength and treasure committed in defence of Spanish kings' fortuitous rights as hereditary rulers of those rebellious and divided provinces. The monarchy was racked and almost snapped by the strain of the greatest religious war of the period—the Thirty Years War, which, like the First World War, unleashed all the horsemen of the apocalypse and added a fifth: the nemesis of great states. These were the most demanding conflicts, but they piled their oppressive weight on a monarchy already buckled by constant warfare on far-flung fronts: the 'defence of Christendom' against the Turks in the eastern Mediterranean, the 'pacification' of wild frontiers in America and the Philippines. From 1580 the burden of defence of the scattered Portuguese empire was added: mud forts in Laristan, sugar-lands in Brazil, shipping lanes along the Benguela current—all attractive to predatory enemies, either because they were rich or because they were easy pickings. A decorative scheme for Philip IV's palace in Madrid, designed by Velázquez and executed in part by Zurbarán, likens Spanish victories, with some justice, to the labours of Hercules: astounding tasks, achieved against the odds, in widely separated and contrasting environments.

The monarchy endured with amazing fortitude. Military clout is a morally objectionable measure of the success of a state: it at least has the merit of being objectively quantifiable. Between widely separated defeats in major pitched battles—Cerignola in 1497 and Rocroi in 1643—the forces of the kings of Spain acquired a reputation for invincibility. They had no secret formula in tactics or technology; such long-term success cannot be convincingly ascribed to commanders of genius. It was made by sinew and spirit—logistics and morale.

'Everything', as Philip II said, 'comes down to one thing: money and more money.' Though all European states in our period were fiscally intractable, Castilians—until late in the seventeenth century—were singularly amenable to royal demands. The evasion and delay with which tax-demands were always greeted was experienced by Cervantes himself when he visited the notoriously miserly peasants of Ecija as a royal purveyor in 1587: they resisted by every legal means, with commendable invention, even getting the novelist locked up for a while in the prison of the Inquisition. But they paid up in the end. In emergencies, taxpayers showed an extraordinary spirit of sacrifice: when the armada sent against England came to grief in 1588, scores of cities voted voluntary contributions. It was understood, according to a writer of 1621, that kings, though physicians of their kingdoms, were no leeches and had to 'avoid occasions for bleedings' in order to build up 'the blood and substance of the body of which they are the head'. When Philip IV came to the throne in 1625, his lament for 'my poor taxpayers of Castile'—who, he said, had given 'more than their life's blood' to sustain the reputation of his predecessors—showed, perhaps, that he was a victim of a conventional rhetoric, for his sincerity is beyond doubt.

Evidence, however, was accumulating to suggest that the limits of fiscal resilience were being approached. Critics of taxation grew bolder and more insistent as the reign of Philip IV lengthened and the costs of monarchy grew more burdensome. 'The treasure of kings', wrote a theorist at the end of the reign, 'is in having prosperous subjects.' By this period, moralists who wrote on taxation stressed the sinfulness of deputies who voted for excessive taxes, as well as of subjects who denied Caesar his due. This shift of priorities was expressed in the vernacular in works intended for ever wider readerships: a vital part of the political culture which had paid for Spain's victories was being eroded. Philip IV's anxieties over the moral proprieties of taxation were as intense towards the end of his reign as at its start; the difference was that he had the encouragement of homespun counsels from his favourite correspondent, the cloistered nun Sor María de Agreda. 'For the love of God,' she told him in 1661, 'I would that taxes could be moderated for the poor.'

Next to taxes, the silver mines of the New World were most important in royal finances. From the mid-1550s until the 1620s a huge increase in output was contrived and sustained, but its importance was essentially psychological: deceptively 'unending' new wealth encouraged the kings' foreign creditors and helped to make possible the dazzling ambition of royal projects in the reign of Philip II. But the value to the treasury of American bullion was always small in relation to the tax-yield. One measure of financial wizardry is having so much that you can safely borrow more. 'I have never been able to get this business of loans and interest into my head', said Philip II, whose income in 1584 was officially— and probably rather conservatively—estimated at less than 6 million ducats, when his debts amounted to nearly 74 million. Figures like these were sustainable as long as the tax-yield increased and the bullion flowed in. By the 1620s it was becoming apparent that the fiscal potential of

Castile was nearing exhaustion and that silver production was tumbling into decline.

The moral, as Napoleon said, is to the material as ten to one. The monarchy's resources of morale began to give out even before the cash. The self-image of Spaniards in conquistador-literature of the mid-sixteenth century—a godlike, God-led race, chosen for victory—was displaced by self-deprecation: the 'low life' version of Spain depicted in picaresque literature, the pamphleteer's vision of a 'nation under enchantment, outside the natural order of things'. Peoples can talk themselves into decline: the prominent themes of moral and political discourse about the state of Spain from the end of the sixteenth century onwards were convictions or fears that God had deserted his Spaniards, that they had failed the trials of faith, and that they were following earlier empires—albeit somewhat prematurely—into ruin. We can now date the erosion of morale, with some confidence, to the 1590s. It was a decade of egregious imperial pretensions: Philip II launched attempted conquests of France and England and contemplated campaigns against Cambodia and China; but it was also the threshold of retrenchment. The peace with France of 1598 was followed by a treaty with England in 1604 and a truce with the Dutch rebels in 1609. The monarchy was retreating into peace.

Spain might have enjoyed a prolonged golden age or, at least, a protracted mood of *enrichissez-vous*, symbolized by the breathtakingly corrupt regime of the duke of Lerma, Philip III's favourite, who moved the court from Madrid to Valladolid and back in order to profit from real-estate speculations in both cities. A sudden and terrible crisis of mortality made such a future impossible. The plagues that were chiefly responsible were, perhaps, a fatal trick of Spaniards' weakness for city life: in the repeated and unprecedented pestilence of the last decade of the sixteenth century and the first of the seventeenth, nearly a tenth of the population of Castile is believed to have been wiped out.

The demands of imperial defence continued in peacetime. Corroded morale became dangerously obvious in a series of army mutinies. American bullion revenues began to cause anxiety from 1610. The outbreak of the Thirty Years War had already begun to tug Spain back into an unaffordable grand strategy of even wider intervention when, in 1621, Philip III died and a new regime began in an atmosphere of moral rearmament and a grim burst of optimism: commitment to recover the 'reputation' of the monarchy and the favour of God. Against a background of shrinking resources and growing commitments there was only one way to make reality of these ambitions: exempt classes and privileged kingdoms would have to be exploited as thoroughly as 'the king's poor vassals of Castile'.

During twenty years of stupendous effort, from the early 1620s to the early 1640s, this policy became identified with a *válido* of transcendent power and unmatched energy: the count of Olivares. In some respects he was the supreme courtier. His career took off when he kissed the king's chamber-pot; the summit of his achievement was marked when he sat down to dine at the king's table. He was also an indefatigable man of business with a real vocation for power—a jerky gait, restless habits, and 'a passion to command'. He had himself painted in frankly kingly poses. He presided over Spain in the worst of times. He needed *encore un effort* from the nobility but, like the senatorial patriciate of the late Roman Empire, the nobles had got used to trading for local power their traditions of service at the centre. Olivares needed an army as good as Philip II's; but lacked the manpower, the professionalism, and the pay. He needed, above all, money from the fiscally privileged—but that alerted all the suspicions of the peripheral kingdoms of the peninsula, with their comfortable tax regimes. There seems in retrospect an air of the bunker about Olivares's last years. Impotently, he swivelled armies and fleets on the map while rebellions multiplied and invasion struck. The union of peninsular kingdoms, with which our period opened, seemed threatened with imminent dissolution at his fall.

The gravest threat arose from the attempt in 1640 of Catalan rebels to withdraw their principality from the monarchy. The policy of secession was a response to the strain of war and an expression of outrage at unaccustomed demands from the Crown. But like the contemporaneous 'Great Rebellion' in England, Catalonia's was hastily extemporized and reluctantly espoused. Most of its leaders belonged to families of the commercial patriciate of Barcelona. They found themselves caught between two fires: on the one hand, a traditional, millenarian rebellion of peasants exasperated by soldiery, banditry, and warfare; on the other, the unruly army of occupation with which Olivares intended to keep them in order. In the circumstances, they opted to appeal to the only possible third force: France. They proclaimed Catalonia a republic under the government of the King of France…as in the time of Charlemagne, with a contract to observe our constitutions'.

Gradually, the French and the rebels became disenchanted with each other. In 1648 peace on other fronts gave Spain a respite just when France, afflicted with war-weariness and a royal minority, was distracted by civil wars of her own. A great plague from 1650 to 1654, which reputedly

The summons to repentance painted in 1672 for the Chapel of the Hospital de la Caridad, Seville, by Juan Valdés Leal (1622–90) is part of a scheme which continues with good works, the sacraments, death and glorification—appropriate for an aristocratic confraternity who cared for the terminally sick with their own hands. The symbols of vanity include an engraving of the triumphal arch erected in celebration of the Spanish victory at Nordlingen.

claimed 30,000 lives in Catalonia, sapped the will to continue the rebellion and gave moralists a scourge for troubled consciences. By 1652 the rebellion was confined to Barcelona, which submitted after a siege of thirteen months. The principality was treated so leniently by the victors that a similar crisis was bound to recur: the structural problems of Catalonia's relationship to the rest of the monarchy were unmodified.

It seems remarkable that so much was salvaged from the crisis of the mid-seventeenth century. Of all the parts of the monarchy whose loyalty

The spectacular cult of penance associated with Sevillan Holy Week processions—
re-enactments of calvary—took on its present appearance in the seventeenth century.
The artistic style was established by carvers in the hyper-realistic tradition of the school
of Juan Martínez Montañés, while the boomtown era of the city's history gave way to
plagues, crises, and introspection. The hoods are of medieval pattern, designed to preserve the anonymity of the penitent during public acts of contrition.

was strained or whose conquest loomed, only Portugal, the northern
Netherlands, Jamaica, and two Catalan provinces were permanently lost.
Nor was material recuperation, of a sort, beyond Spain's extraordinary
powers. The plagues abated in the second half of the seventeenth century.
The levels of silver production recovered from the 1660s. But by the

standards of the fatal ambitions of the time the monarchy had failed: by the time of Philip IV's death in 1665 not even his debt of 22 million ducats had been enough to repurchase 'reputation'. The Spanish art and literature of the late seventeenth century remained distinguished for technical dexterity, baroque display, lively realism, religious exaltation. Yet it does seem, in retrospect, to evoke a society in retreat from worldly ambition: excelling in the depiction of the insubstantiality of life's dreams, suffering, death, decay, and *vanidades*—the glories of blood and state trivialized or left to rot. The canvas in which Juan de Valdés Leal summoned worshippers to repentance in the chapel of the Hospital de la Caridad in Seville shows a skeletal reaper, with limbs outstretched, surrounded by the débris of greatness: the books of the wise, the arms of the valiant, the memorials of art, the arch of triumph. His work belonged to a new mood in Seville—once the capital of picaresque *espièglerie*. In the second half of the seventeenth century devotional style was dictated by the chillingly penitent confraternities whose sacrificial calvaries still dominate everyone's image of Holy Week in the city. The gilded youths of the boom years became sombre confrères of the Hospital de la Caridad, burying the plague-dead and tending the buboes of the poor with their own hands. Prosperity had turned, like Don Juan's revelries, into a feast of the dead.

The essential ingredients of Spanish power in the world—willing taxpayers and a service-oriented aristocracy—were getting ever harder to wrest from the nation. While the aristocracy's traditional ethos eroded, the practical limits of such service were narrowed by economic constraints. The reasons for the mounting insolvency and inertia of the great families of Spain in the later seventeenth century are unclear; yet the facts seem incontestable. Statistical evidence accumulated by recent scholarship bears out the general accuracy of a Venetian ambassador's judgement in 1681: 'There is hardly a noble who does not live off the king's treasury or who, in the absence of royal pensions, could keep himself on his own income. Because of this, the principal lords, attracted by offices in Madrid, have abandoned their estates from which they draw empty titles rather than material benefit.' The description was exaggerated but the predicament was genuine. It had been mounting conspicuously, as family after family reported imminent or actual bankruptcy, since the mid-century crisis.

The monarchy was therefore seriously ill equipped when a similar crisis occurred on Philip IV's death in 1665. The situation was one of classic weakness: a royal minority, a female regency, and unpopular favourites chosen, in defiance of the Crown's 'natural' counsellors, by caprice of the queen. Unreconciled as yet to the loss of Portugal, Spain was committed to war on one front; meanwhile, an opportunist French invasion opened another. The self-proclaimed strong man of the age, Don Juan José of Austria, the royal bastard who had been the hero of warfare against the Portuguese and Catalan rebels, tried various strategies for working government into his hands. Eventually, in 1676, he seized power by threat of brute force.

He was a blusterer and a hustler somewhat in the style of Olivares and, like Olivares, he aimed to galvanize the country into a renewal of united effort. He had, however, to contend with the onslaught of all the horsemen of the apocalypse: plague, war, famine, and inflation. He died in 1679, defeated by intractable problems, with no prospect, as a satirist sneered, 'that the people will be relieved, the kingdom saved, and our fortunes improved'. His best legacy was a spell of peace, which he conjured out of negotiations with France without further sacrifices of territory. His worst was an empty treasury and a crisis of falling tax returns which his successors made worse by introducing a bold new system of taxation, designed to cut out tax-farmers: the revised assessments which accompanied the exercise reduced the yield, probably by around 20 per cent.

Meanwhile, a new shadow loomed over the monarchy: the prospect of a future without an heir to the throne. Charles II has usually been depicted as a *fainéant* halfwit, with no virtue save a sort of myopic piety. In reality, he was a conscientious and reflective king, unable to contend with wretched health. His efforts to rule without a favourite were well meant, though their result was to make the direction of government diffuse and incoherent. He failed, however, in the most basic duty of a monarch: to engender a successor. He tried expedients of every kind—rapid remarriage on the death of his first wife and even, in 1699, treatment by an exorcist on the grounds that his impotence might be the result of drinking a witch's brew. The politics of the western world came to be dominated by the 'Spanish question': what would happen to the empire when Charles died? In consequence, the country was to be denied the spell of peace she needed.

French invasions, launched in the 1690s as a way of pressurizing Charles into decreeing a French succession—which he finally did, just before his death in 1700—turned Spain into a battleground of European armies, which contended for the Crown like buzzards for a bone. Yet this sorry consequence should not be taken as evidence that Spain had been prostrated by an inevitable decline, or should be classed as a 'sick man of Europe' fit only for dismemberment by the surgeons: on the contrary, the covetousness of other states was excited by the value of the spoils. The story of the late seventeenth century should be seen, perhaps, less as one of unrelieved decline than of recovery repeatedly retarded or prevented by war. The 'Spanish preponderance', achieved in Spain's era of improbable empire, was unrecoverable, but the monarchy would demonstrate its habits of resilience and survival again in the new century.

6   Vicissitudes of a World Power
1500–1700

HENRY KAMEN

Rise of a World Power

'LL other empires began through violence and force of arms,' a Spanish commentator noted in 1597, 'only that of Spain began through just means, since the greater part came together through succession.' The claim was by no means exaggerated. The combination of territories that came to form the vast Spanish 'empire' could not have been put together by systematic conquest, for the territories of the peninsula did not have the manpower or arms adequate to the purpose. The union of the crowns of Castile and Aragon in the persons of Ferdinand and Isabella began the chain of hereditary links that brought Spain's empire into existence.

The element of conquest in the empire was small. Castilian expeditions began occupation of the Canary Islands in 1483. The arms of Ferdinand and Isabella that put an end to the civil wars in the peninsula and achieved the occupation of the Muslim province of Granada (1492) was a temporary force, recruited annually and disbanded altogether when the Reconquest was over. Special forces had to be recruited to take part in the Italian campaigns against the French in Naples, where the Spaniards remained after 1504 as a token force rather than an occupying power. In subsequent years further small expeditions devoted themselves to occupying key fortresses on the North African coast, such as Oran and Algiers. Throughout the period the main enemy was neighbouring France, and it was to achieve security of the frontier in the Pyrenees that efforts were made to retain Perpignan. The annexation (1512) of Navarre followed. Apart from Granada, the African forts, and the Canaries, none of these territories was formally 'conquered': no troops stayed behind to occupy them, and each retained complete independence in government. What united Naples, Navarre, and other states was common allegiance to the Crown of 'Spain', a word that foreign commentators soon came to identify with the rulers of Castile and Aragon.

The emergence of Spain into the international arena was dramatically highlighted by two major events: the discovery of America in 1492 and the succession of the Habsburgs to the throne of Spain in 1516. It was a long time before Spaniards recognized the importance of the discoveries of Columbus and his successors in the New World. The first generation of Spaniards in America limited their activities to the Caribbean. Nearly thirty years passed before the first famous expeditions of conquest were launched. In 1521 Hernando Cortés overthrew the empire of the Aztecs and in 1532 Francisco Pizarro seized the last supreme Inca, Atahualpa. Their feats have often been mythified as a victory of few over many, of European arms and expertise over primitive cultures. The success of the

The successful conquest of the great Aztec nation by a small number of Spaniards under Cortés, inspired others, such as Pizarro in Peru, to emulate the achievement. In reality, Spanish successes would have been impossible without the help of Indian allies. In this illustration the Indians of Tlaxcala, who contributed to Cortés's capture of the Aztec capital Tenochtitlán, greet the Spaniards with friendship.

conquistadors was in reality no mystery. Both Pizarro and Cortés were fortunate in being able to exploit the state of civil dissension in the American empires, and Cortés's attack on Tenochtitlán would have failed but for the inestimable help of thousands of Indian allies who were revolting against Aztec rule and gave the Spaniards clear superiority. All over the continent, during the subsequent decades, conquistadors were able by ruthlessness and guile to make headway against the natives of America. By the mid-sixteenth century Spanish settlers were firmly entrenched in the New World. The government in Madrid, which had taken no direct part in the conquest of America, and had expended neither soldiers nor ships in the enterprise, woke up to find itself master of the richest continent in the world.

Apart from treasure, the New World had little to offer Spain. Between about 1500 and 1600 over 150,000 kilograms of gold and 7.4 million kilograms of silver reached Spain from America. Settlers in the new territories who did not have access to this wealth were obliged to create their own resources, through exploitation of the soil and of native labour. In this way sugar plantations began to spread through the Caribbean and then on the mainland; other crops followed. In the process, the indigenous population was slowly wiped out. On the island of Hispaniola, the Dominican friar Bartolomé de Las Casas attributed 'the total destruction of those lands' to the combination of sugar-milling and Indian slavery. Adventurers in search of new opportunities, like Hernando Cortés, left the Caribbean in search of wealth elsewhere. As the white man came to settle, bringing with him his own tools and animals, the biological environment of the continent began to change. By 1600 wheat, hitherto unknown, was the most widely cultivated crop in the New World. Indians were deprived of their lands and living; in Peru, a pre-conquest population of some 9 million had fallen to some 600,000 by 1620.

In contrast to the slow and almost imperceptible extension of empire in the New World, the succession of the young Charles V to the throne in 1516 had an immediate impact. A good section of the Castilian elite showed, by its participation in the short-lived revolt of the Comuneros (1520–1), its rejection of the foreign Habsburg dynasty. The election of Charles as Holy Roman Emperor in 1520, however, promised to identify Spaniards with a new, more exciting destiny. The new emperor spent most of his active life out of the peninsula, but he was quick to show his deep appreciation for his Spanish inheritance, which soon began to contribute to his military expenses and which convinced him of its capacity to resist the heresies that were spreading through Germany. In their turn,

Spaniards for the first time began to learn from Europe. The writings of Erasmus introduced Spanish intellectuals to the humanist culture of the north. Spanish soldiers like the young duke of Alba served on northern European fields. Scholars, like the emperor's confessor Hernando de Soto, settled in northern universities and published their works in Germany. With opportunities for expansion in both Europe and the New World, Spain's elite began to identify itself enthusiastically with the destiny of the Habsburgs.

Maintaining World Hegemony

Spain's leadership of a world monarchy brought considerable benefits. The provinces associated with it paid only limited taxes, which had in any case to be spent within the borders of each province. But they contributed substantially through their trade, which tended to be orientated towards Castile; and they were able to furnish soldiers and cash grants to help finance wars. Thanks to this, the relatively poor Spaniards were able to accomplish the extraordinary feat of building up a world empire backed by very limited military power. The earliest of the so-called 'Spanish' military victories, won by the forces of Philip II over the French at St Quentin (1557), was in reality achieved by an international army commanded by Netherlanders, in which Spaniards formed only 12 per cent of the men. The Netherlanders and Italians were always at the forefront of the 'Spanish' imperial achievement, notably through their military skills but even more surely through the immense economic aid they offered. It was the Genoese fleet, commanded by admiral Andrea Doria, that in 1528 allied itself to Charles V and so brought into existence Spain's naval power in the Mediterranean. From then on, Italians were at the forefront of Spain's imperial role. The most glorious of 'Spanish' naval victories, scored over the Turks at Lepanto in 1571, was won by a force to which the Italians contributed two-thirds of the ships and troops, though the bulk of the financing came from Spain.

Possession of an empire also brought responsibilities. Probably the most vital problem was that of control. The insuperable distances of the empire—America was an average of three months away—required efficient postal services and methods of consultation. The Crown had always functioned adequately through its officials in each province of the monarchy. Charles V saw no need for an overall system of imperial administration. In Castile, however, where the Crown came eventually to be based, the Habsburg rulers followed the practice of Ferdinand and Isabella in establishing 'councils' that were in effect government departments to strengthen links between the centre and the provinces. Two types of council were created: those that ran the administration of Castile (the all-important Council of Finance, for example), and those that were largely consultative and included nobility from the respective regions (the Council of Aragon, formed in 1494; the Council of Italy, formed 1555). Despite the growing tendency for Castile to interfere more and more in the affairs of other territories, at no time did the monarchy become a centralized organism. There was normally scope for considerable autonomy in all the regions. Properly speaking, Spanish 'imperialism' was really a vast exercise in international co-operation between Spaniards, Italians, Germans, Flemings, and the innumerable people of varying profession and nationality who stood to gain from service under Europe's one 'superpower'.

'With as many kingdoms as have been linked to this crown,' Philip IV stated in 1626, 'it is impossible to be without war in some area, either to defend what we have acquired, or to repulse my enemies.' The very extent of Spain's dominion invited aggressive intentions. In the early sixteenth century the king of France proclaimed, with every good reason, that the New World discovered by Columbus was the heritage of all mankind and not a private possession of the king of Spain. 'I would like to see', he is said to have stated, 'the clause in Adam's will that excluded me from my share when the world was created.' Necessities of defence and war were a priority from the earliest days, but Spain in fact played a surprisingly muted role in the policies of Charles V. There was, for example, no 'Spanish' army serving him in the field. Spanish soldiers constituted less than a fifth of Charles's army in Italy in the 1520s, less than a sixth of that serving him in Germany in the 1540s. The real rise of Spain as a military force occurred only in the reign of Philip II. After the 1560s the king dedicated himself to building up naval defence in the western Mediterranean: by the 1570s he possessed a navy there four times greater than his father had ever possessed. From 1580, when Spanish forces occupied Portugal and united it to the Crown, it was the turn of the Atlantic. A powerful new fleet was constructed, with the primary purpose of defending the seas against England and keeping the American trade routes under surveillance. In those years the size of the armed forces under Spanish control also increased dramatically. In the one year 1587 it was estimated that throughout his

A Flemish tapestry of the Emperor Charles V as conqueror of Africa, conveys the confidence of the early years of his career. Spanish financial resources, drawn in part from America, became the principal mainstay of his wars, and Spanish fidelity to the Catholic Church inspired him to spend his last years in the peninsula.

AFRICAE
SVBIVGATORI

dominions Philip II had over 100,000 soldiers (not all, evidently, from the peninsula) in his pay.

The next major problem was financial stability, seriously compromised by continuous wars. Charles V, as head of a multinational empire based on his German territories, took wars in his stride, and spent the greater part of his active life on the battlefield. He built up the territory of the Netherlands through conquest, personally defended Vienna against the Turks, won over the Genoese to lead his naval forces in the Mediterranean, and led in person the successful campaign that captured Tunis from the North African princes in 1535. But it was all done at a high price, usually borne by the Castilian exchequer. He himself recognized that his most reliable funding was in the peninsula: 'I cannot be sustained except by my realms of Spain', he stated in 1540. By the end of his reign the war debt of the Castilian treasury absorbed 68 per cent of ordinary income. Ramón Carande's extensive study of Charles' financial system shows that the emperor during his reign borrowed nearly 29 million ducats from European bankers—mostly Italians and Germans—on which he paid an average rate of interest of 32 per cent. Philip II managed to extricate himself from war by the Treaty of Cateau-Cambrésis in 1559, but the debt remained. In 1565, on the eve of intervention in the Netherlands, it absorbed 84 per cent of Castilian revenue. By the end of Philip's reign, the total state debt was eight times higher than annual income. A generation later, during the ministry of Olivares, over 93 per cent of state expenditure was being directed to foreign policy.

A part of the debt was funded through bullion from America, particularly during the reign of Philip II, when the mines of Zacatecas and Potosí began to pour out their treasures. Apart from what the Crown claimed as its due (the royal *quinto* or fifth), income came from numerous taxes in the New World. The total officially received by the state from America during the reign of Philip came to over 64.5 million ducats. Incalculably higher amounts were imported by private traders, entered the peninsular economy and set in train an inflationary spiral that in its early stages was beneficial to production but in the long run seriously affected the cost of living of ordinary Spaniards. But American silver was never adequate for the government's needs, and in any case was usually pledged in advance to the Crown's bankers. The real burden of financing empire came more and more to fall on the Castilian taxpayer. Philip's annual income from regular sources tripled during his reign; over the same period the burden on the Castilian taxpayer increased by some 430 per cent, at a time when nominal wages had increased only 80 per cent. War,

The great mine at Potosí in Bolivia, first tapped in 1545, was quarried for over a century for its rich veins of silver, and a whole community of producers, machinery, and slaves came into existence at the foot of the mountain. Symbol of the riches that Spain received from the New World, Potosí's riches were soon overtaken by the silver mines of Mexico.

as many Castilian commentators came to recognize, brought no perceptible benefits, and probably impeded the process of economic growth. Profits that might have been invested in the domestic economy were in practice expended on military enterprise. Moreover, war triggered a long chain of state bankruptcies that continued their run, unabated, into the seventeenth century. Unable to recover from the debt burden created by Charles V, the Castilian treasury under Philip II declared itself bankrupt every twenty years; under his successors the bankruptcies were aggravated by soaring monetary inflation, the highest of any European state.

Since Spain relied continuously on the collaboration of its partners in the monarchy, it ironically dedicated little attention to its own military status. At the peak of its role as an imperial power, it remained an unmilitarized and largely defenceless country. Charles V's wars had been fought outside the peninsula and did not affect the nation directly. 'The peace

that has reigned here for so many years', commented a Spanish government official in 1562, was to blame for the country's military backwardness. In consequence, throughout the reign of Philip II the peninsula was extraordinarily vulnerable to attack, a situation that explains the constant fears of a possible Turkish invasion. In order to put down the rising of the Granada Moriscos in 1570, the state had to import virtually all the necessary arms from Italy. In 1596 the English occupied for three weeks, with no resistance whatever, one of the most important ports in the country, Cadiz.

The consolidation of imperial machinery and finance, however, was inevitably seen by other European powers as aggressive. As early as 1559 the Venetian ambassador had observed, in a phrase that may be applied to his entire reign, that Philip II aimed 'not to wage war so he can add to his kingdoms, but to wage peace so he can conserve the lands he has'. It was a vain hope, encouraged no doubt by the satisfactory peace treaty of Cateau-Cambrésis, but soon shattered by the reality of international power politics. Even then, it is a fact too frequently forgotten that Spain was the only imperial power in Europe's history never to have annexed any territory from its neighbours. The continuous wars into which the nation was dragged were logical results of imperial obligations, foremost among them the elementary duty of defence.

From Charles V's capture of Tunis in 1535 to the successful raising of the siege of Malta by Turkish forces in 1565, Spain's concern for its own defence was focused entirely on the Mediterranean. In his magnificent survey of these years, Fernand Braudel has traced the long-term drama of a divided Christendom confronted by an expanding, aggressive Turkish empire. The Spanish peninsula was exceptionally vulnerable, with a large resident population of Muslims (the so-called Moriscos, never adequately Christianized) who gave their surreptitious help to Muslim corsairs raiding the coasts of Valencia. This long phase of conflict drew effectively to an end after the notable naval victory at Lepanto (1571), celebrated by one of its participants, Cervantes, as the greatest battle of all time, and greeted everywhere in the west as a major repulse to the Ottoman empire. The success came in time to allow Spain to devote more resources to the suppression of discontent in the Netherlands, where the duke of Alba had

Ottoman expansion in the sixteenth century was the principal threat to western Christendom, especially in the Mediterranean, where Muslim sea-power went long unchallenged. Eventually an alliance between Venice, the papacy and the Spanish crown enabled the Christian powers to inflict a crushing naval defeat on the Turks at Lepanto in 1571. This reconstruction comes from the Church of La Magdalena, Seville.

gone in 1567 with an army of 10,000 men. The Flemish nobles were anxious to preserve their privileges and rejected the increased role played by Spain in their affairs. Both Flemings and Spaniards disagreed about the measures necessary to control the rise of heresy, an issue that offered Philip II a timely excuse for armed intervention. In the months after his arrival in Brussels, Alba put into effect a tough policy of repression through a Council of Troubles that the Netherlanders more appropriately termed a 'Council of Blood', responsible for the arraignment and execution of over a thousand persons, both Catholic and Protestant. Philip II evidently felt that severity to presumed rebels would crush dissension, but Spanish methods served only to strengthen opposition and eventually provoked the outbreak of a national uprising of the people of the Netherlands, led by William of Nassau, prince of Orange.

Spain's foreign policy was never consciously expansionist. It therefore required considerable effort on the part of Philip II to explain why in 1580 he sent his armies in to annex the neighbouring kingdom of Portugal. He had the strongest hereditary claim to the throne (left vacant by his nephew Sebastian, who had taken the Portuguese army to fight the Muslims in Africa and had perished there in 1578). He was also influenced by fears of intervention by the English and the French, who backed the rival candidate, Antonio, the prior of Crato. In the event, after its occupation by the king's army Portugal was guaranteed its autonomy within the empire, and Philip made Lisbon his capital for over two years. But the annexation helped to confirm the image of a power-hungry Spain. The empire was now at its peak. Spain's flag had been planted in the Philippines and in Buenos Aires. Within this vast network of power the weakest point was the tenacious resistance of the Dutch rebels.

The Dutch revolt became the great nightmare of Spain's imperial destiny. It consumed increasing amounts of money from a heavily indebted exchequer, pushing the Crown into further bankruptcies. Before 1566 the total annual military expenditure of Castile in Spain, the Mediterranean, and Flanders never reached 2 million ducats; in the 1570s it was over 4 million, by 1598 it was estimated at 10 million. The greatest single drain on finance was the Netherlands, to which in the 1570s the government

By the late sixteenth century, English naval intervention in the Netherlands and in America represented the principal threat to Spanish interests. When Philip II sent the Great Armada in 1588, it failed to make contact with the troops needed for an invasion, and was scattered first by English action and then by the North Sea winds. The illustration is an imaginative reconstruction of Spain's greatest military disaster.

was sending an average of 1.5 million ducats a year. After the assassination (paid for by Spain) of William of Orange in 1584, England stepped forward as protector of the Dutch rebels. A number of other considerations, notably English aggression (by sea captains such as Francis Drake and John Hawkins) against Spain's territories in the New World, alerted Philip to the new threat. His response was the preparation of a naval expedition, with the purpose of invading England and ensuring a compliant western Europe in which it would be easier to resolve the Dutch question. But the great Armada, which cost 10 million ducats to prepare, was dogged by continuous problems. Mary Queen of Scots, who would have been Philip's candidate for the English throne in the event of a successful invasion, was executed in 1587 after taking part in a conspiracy against Queen Elizabeth. The intended commander of the fleet, the veteran marquis of Santa Cruz, died inopportunely. When the Armada set sail in 1588, commanded this time by the duke of Medina Sidonia, it failed to make the intended rendezvous with troops from the army in Flanders, was harassed by superior English naval forces, and driven by winds into the North Sea. After a terrifying voyage round the Atlantic coast of Ireland, nearly half the fleet managed to return to port in Spain, but a total of possibly 15,000 men had perished. The English were jubilant; for Spain, by contrast, it was probably the darkest moment of the century. No other single event served more to convince both government and people that peace was necessary. After the failure of yet another expedition against England nine years later, Philip's own chief admiral advised him: 'if Your Majesty decides to continue the attempt on England, take care to make preparations in good time and in good quantity, and if not then it is better to make peace.'

Losing Control

In 1600 an official in Madrid commented that 'the war in Flanders has been and is the ruin of Spain: the ministers are against it, and the people demand that an end be put to it'. Spain's own general in Flanders conceded in 1607 that 'there is only one course to take: to end this long and costly war'. The pressures that had been growing against the conservative and imperialist policies of Philip II now came to the surface, initiating among Spaniards a century of debate and disagreement that found their expression in the writings of the publicists known as *arbitristas*. The move towards peace was affirmed in the peace treaties signed by Spain with its chief opponents in the early years of the reign of Philip III. One of the

BRIELE.

The capture of the small port of Brill by the rebels in 1572 began the most important phase of the Dutch revolt. In attempting to recover control of the Netherlands, Spain faced extraordinary obstacles that it never managed to overcome. In the print, Spanish forces besiege the town by land and sea.

treaties was a truce (1609) with the rebel Dutch, guaranteed to last for twelve years.

But peace was not an option that Spain could choose at will. In the half-century after the death of Philip II it became clear that the empire was under steady pressure on all fronts from other European powers, notably the Dutch, who consolidated their trade with Asia and began a military and commercial penetration of Brazil. If Holland were not stopped, a minister argued in Madrid, 'we shall lose the Indies, then Flanders, then Italy, and finally Spain itself'. The outbreak of a local war in Bohemia in 1618 constituted the first step towards what was to become the Thirty Years War, which threatened to spread rapidly into other areas of the continent, and impelled Spain to recruit soldiers once again. The expiry in 1621 of the twelve-year-long truce with the Dutch confirmed the need for military preparedness.

The Spanish position was, more than ever, one of defensiveness. 'To promise ourselves that we can conquer the Dutch,' a minister admitted, 'is to seek the impossible.' Yet could an imperial power ever limit itself only to a defensive role? Others saw Spain's intervention in the German Thirty Years War as frankly aggressive. By 1625 both England and France were also at war against Spain. The crisis passed for the moment. The new king, Philip IV, could report proudly in 1626 that 'we have had all Europe against us, but we have not been defeated'. Certainly the military successes of these years were striking. In 1625 three significant victories showed that the empire could strike back: the port of Bahia in Brazil was recaptured from the Dutch; General Spinola in the Netherlands recaptured Breda, a feat immortalized in Velázquez's great canvas *The Lances*; and an English fleet was repulsed from Cadiz.

The run of successes was short-lived. Over the next few years Spanish power was rapidly whittled away. In 1628 a Dutch admiral captured the entire treasure fleet from America as it was setting out across the Atlantic from Cuba. The military scenario changed decisively when France entered the Thirty Years War directly, declaring war on Spain in 1635. Spanish observers had little doubt that it was a grave moment. Though France had little military achievement to its credit, it had enormous resources. Spain, by contrast, had spent the last three-quarters of a century at war. Over the next generation its enemies successfully attacked all the most vulnerable points of the monarchy. The Dutch admiral Tromp decisively destroyed Spain's naval power at the Battle of the Downs (1639), and in Germany Spain's allies suffered serious reverses. 'God wants us to make peace,' complained Spain's chief minister Olivares, 'for he is depriving us of all the means for waging war.' The worst was yet to come: that year, 1640, Catalonia and then Portugal rebelled against the Crown and threatened to destroy forever the unity of the peninsula. Three years later, in 1643, when Spain's army in Flanders attempted to invade France it was annihilated by a French army commanded by the young duke of Enghien, later famous to history as the great Condé. The defeat by no means disabled Spain; but it was significant as the first occasion since the rise of Spain's empire that one of its armies was totally routed in battle.

'Peace is necessary,' a government minister wrote in 1645, 'whatever the cost.' Negotiations for settling the Thirty Years War had already been opened in the cities of Münster and Osnabrück. There seemed to be no way to avoid a total collapse. In 1648 the Catalan and Portuguese revolts were still unsubdued, in Aragon there was a plot to secede, in Sicily and Naples revolution was triumphant, and epidemic and rebellion were tearing the peninsula apart. In the peace treaty signed at Münster in October, Spain finally recognized the Dutch United Provinces as an independent state. France largely dictated the peace agreements, known collectively as the Treaty of Westphalia. And France decided that though peace had come to Germany the war with Spain must go on.

Spain's weakness was all too clearly shown up by its inability to exploit the civil war (known as the Fronde) that preoccupied France between 1648 and 1652. A brief spurt of military successes in 1652 (most notably, the recovery of Barcelona from the French) did not serve to reverse the tide. The declaration of war by Cromwell's England in 1655 had a decisive impact. English naval forces seized the island of Hispaniola, and Robert Blake's navy destroyed the Indies treasure fleets in 1656 and 1657. It was a cowed Spain that acceded finally in 1659 to the Peace of the Pyrenees with France: the monarchy lost the Catalan counties on the Pyrenees frontier, and several fortresses in the Netherlands. Spain also agreed to the marriage of the Infanta Maria Teresa to the young Louis XIV of France. The peace marked the end of Spain's century-long hegemony in Europe. From around 1560, when Philip II began to build up Spanish imperial resources, to around 1660, when those resources visibly crumbled, the nation had dictated the course of international politics.

Economic realities, rather than imperial dreams, began thereafter to haunt government policy-makers. From the early seventeenth century much of western Europe began to experience the classic aspects of depression: falling production and prices, accompanied by trade contraction. Scholars have determined that in Spain a principal cause of difficulties was demographic crisis. Birth-rates fell in much of the interior of the peninsula from around 1580, and population levels were further hit by major epidemic around 1600. The worst epidemic experienced by Spain in early modern times was that of 1647–52: in the realms of Valencia and Mallorca one-fifth of the population died, in the cities of Barcelona and Seville approximately one-half.

It was a time of crisis in which Spaniards questioned all their traditional values. A long-standing tradition among scholars has placed emphasis on the negative aspects of this reaction: the emphasis among some *arbitristas* on the 'decline' of their society, the attention among writers to the theme of disillusion (*desengaño*), the preference among some artists for religiosity and pessimism. The burden of empire had fallen most heavily on Castile, and logically it was Castilians who were most vociferous in their reaction. Why, many asked, should it be Castile that had to bear the burden of empire? Other writers actively rejected the whole imperial history of Spain. Nothing had gone right, argued Lope de Deza in 1618, since other states 'such as the Indies, Flanders, and Italy, have been incorporated' into the

After nearly eighty years of campaigning in the Netherlands, the Spanish war machine was visibly unable to cope. The evocative painting of the siege of Aire-sur-la-Lys by Snayers, set in the winter of 1641, shows the town's extensive walled fortifications

confidently dominating the entire area of the canvas, while the cold and ragged Spanish conscripts huddle into the foreground. A few years later, in the Peace of Westphalia (1648), Spain formally accepted the independence of the Dutch.

monarchy. America, still viewed as the shining jewel in the crown, did not seem so for some: 'the poverty of Spain has resulted from the discovery of the Indies', proclaimed Sancho de Moncada in 1619. Perhaps the most sardonic voice was that of the poet Francisco de Quevedo. Writing in 1604 to a correspondent in the Netherlands, he commented: 'In your country we consume our soldiers and our gold; here we consume ourselves.'

In perspective one can see that the reaction was not limited to these negative attitudes. The profundity of Spain's crisis forced thinkers to question not only economic policy (the special concern of the *arbitristas*) but also all the postulates on which official policy was based. Attacks were launched against maldistribution of wealth, against racial prejudice, against social injustice. In the provinces of the empire regional pretensions came to the fore. The revolts of Portugal and Catalonia were only one part of a malaise that could be found throughout the monarchy. There were plots aimed at separatism by nobles in Andalucia in 1641 and in Aragon in 1648. The very serious separatist revolt of Naples in 1647–8 threatened to fragment the Mediterranean empire irreparably. In Galicia in 1657 printed pamphlets appealed to the secession of Portugal as a precedent. One of the little-known voices of the century was that of Juan de Palafox, a saintly Aragonese prelate who spent many years as a bishop in Mexico, battling against the Jesuits there, and then as bishop in his native Aragon, battling against ignorance and superstition among his own people. In a commentary written around 1650, he contemplated the impending ruin of Spain's empire and criticized the excessive predominance of Castile. Spain, he felt, would only succeed in its mission if it recognized that variety of thought and culture was preferable to a stolid imperial conformity.

The succession to the throne in 1665 of a chronically invalid child, Charles II, immediately made Spain the centre of international rivalry. There was no direct heir after him, and Charles was unable to sire children on either of his two wives, Marie Louise of Orléans (1679) and Mariana of Neuburg (1689). The European powers, led by Louis XIV of France, meanwhile came to several secret agreements to partition the monarchy in the event of there being no heir. At the same time several nakedly aggressive campaigns by the French gnawed away at Spanish territories throughout the world. At the Peace of Aix-la-Chapelle (1668) Spain ceded major cities in the Netherlands, at that of Nijmegen (1678) it ceded to France the provinces of Franche-Comté and Artois, and at that of Rijswijk (1697) it gave France the island of Hispaniola in the West Indies.

Charles surprised the world by living on to rule for thirty-five years, and sprung a final surprise by leaving the throne to the grandson of Louis XIV, the duke of Anjou, with the stipulation that no part of the monarchy should be alienated. He did not leave a barren inheritance. After decades of questioning and crisis, Spain was ready to adapt itself to the standards of the rest of Europe. The elite was reading European philosophers, and the Inquisition was largely inactive. A new scientific movement was spreading among younger intellectuals. Isolation from Europe was recognized and regretted: in 1687 the Valencian doctor Juan de Cabriada lamented that, 'like savages we have to be the last to receive the innovations and knowledge that the rest of Europe already has'. Don Juan José of Austria, chief minister from 1677 to 1679, was a notable patron of pro-

The impressive *auto de fe* staged in the Plaza Mayor of Madrid in 1680, captured here in the painting by Francesco Rizzi, was the last great display put on by the Spanish Inquisition. Its pomp contrasted with Spain's real problems of economic crisis and military disaster at that period.

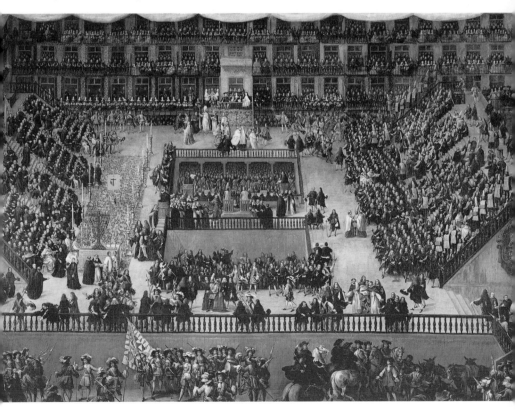

7 Flow and Ebb
1700–1833

RICHARD HERR

HE history of Spain under the first five Bourbon monarchs— Philip V (1700–46),* Ferdinand VI (1746–59), Charles III (1759–88), Charles IV (1788–1808), and Ferdinand VII (1808–33)—can be divided into two distinct periods. During the eighteenth century the country and its overseas empire enjoyed a recovery from the afflictions of the last Habsburgs that culminated in the relative splendour of the reign of Charles III. Thereafter the wars, passions, and suffering introduced by the French Revolution and the imperial ambitions of Napoleon Bonaparte consumed the country, brought on Spain's first experiments with democratic monarchy, and led to the loss of most of its empire.

Flow

When Philip, duke of Anjou, accepted the realms of the Spanish monarchy bestowed on him by the will of Charles II, he had to defend his claim against the Habsburgs of Vienna, who could not brook the transfer of the main part of the family estate to the grandson of their arch-enemy Louis XIV. The leading elements of Castile rallied around Philip V, as the best hope to preserve intact the Spanish empire in Europe and America. Their counterparts in the Crown of Aragon originally accepted him, but when war began they transferred their allegiance to the pretender, the Archduke Charles, for they feared Philip would copy the absolutism of Louis XIV. Austria was joined in 1702 by Britain and the Netherlands and a year later Portugal, who feared a possible dynastic union of Spain and France. Castile had only the support of France. Philip was twice driven

---

* In 1724 Philip V abdicated in favour of his son Louis, perhaps hoping to inherit the crown of France from the sickly Louis XV, but he returned to the throne when Louis I died seven months later.

temporarily from Madrid; however his army won the two major engagements of the war, at Almansa in 1707 and Brihuega in 1710. Exhaustion, and Charles's withdrawal from Spain to become the next Holy Roman Emperor, eventually brought the international contenders to accept peace. Philip's army had taken control of Aragon and Valencia in 1707, but Catalonia escaped his grasp. The Allies now evacuated Catalonia and left its inhabitants to the mercy of the Castilian and French forces. Barcelona withstood desperately a two-months siege but finally surrendered in September 1714.

The Treaties of Utrecht (1713) and Rastatt (1714) ended the War of the Spanish Succession. Spain had failed to preserve all its territories, for Austria received the Spanish Netherlands and the Spanish possessions in Italy except for Sardinia, which went to Savoy. Britain had captured Gibraltar and the island of Menorca, and it kept them. Spain did preserve its American empire intact, but it was forced to concede to Britain the monopoly of the slave trade with its colonies known as the *asiento*. Along with the slaves went permission to send one 500-ton ship each year with merchandise, which became a cover for a massive British contraband trade.

The fortunes of Spain under the Bourbons continued to be tied to the nature of their involvement in the European international arena, as they had been in Habsburg days. The loss of its territories in Europe offered Spain the possibility of turning its energy to America, but it could not exorcize the spell of Europe, or more precisely, Italy. Philip's second wife, Isabel Farnese of Parma, a young and dominating consort, hungered for Italian territories for their son Charles, because his older half-brothers had prior claim to Spain. Upon the extinction of the Farnese line in 1731, Charles received its lands. Three years later a Spanish army recovered Naples and Sicily from Austria, and Charles became king of the Two Sicilies. When he left in 1759 to succeed his half-brother on the Spanish throne, his enlightened rule had made Naples the intellectual centre of Italy.

The War of the Austrian Succession (1740–8) saw Spain again challenging Austrian predominance in Italy. In 1739, however, it engaged in a naval conflict in America to halt Britain's smuggling under pretence of the *asiento*. Although the 'War of Jenkin's Ear' was brief, it marked a turning point. After 1748 Britain replaced Austria as Spain's major enemy, and Spain's wars were fought to defend its overseas empire and to recover Gibraltar and Menorca. The Bourbon rulers had at last sloughed off the European millstone worn since the marriage policy of Ferdinand and Isabella in order to make the most of the world of Columbus.

In Spain as elsewhere in Europe, the eighteenth century witnessed a passion for the building of palaces. Philip V's summer palace of San Ildefonso, known familiarly as La Granja (the farm), in the sierra above Madrid reflects the courtly elegance of Versailles, where he had grown up. Its elegant façade, formal gardens, and flowing fountains encourage the pursuit of pleasure, a stark contrast to the cold walls and overpowering church dome of Philip II's Escorial. Here the dome is modest, but it remains at the centre of the building, unlike Versailles where the king's quarters were at the centre and the chapel an afterthought at one side. Like the Spanish Enlightenment, the Spanish Bourbon monarchs were imbued with Spain's Catholic identity.

Ferdinand VI initiated a naval policy aimed at creating a force that, together with the French navy, would match that of Britain. Unfortunately for Spain, the efforts never succeeded in producing ships or crews as good as those of its rival. Allied with France by what was known as the Family Pact, Spain took part in both the Seven Years War (1762–3) and the War of American Independence (1779–83). In the first, France lost Canada to Britain, but Spain protected its position, for France compensated it with Louisiana for the loss of Florida. (Spain would return Louisiana to France in 1800, when the two countries were again at war with Britain, and Bonaparte would promptly sell it to the United States.) In the second war Charles III put his heart into the recovery of Gibraltar, keeping it under siege for over a year. A stubborn British defence foiled the Spanish forces, but they recaptured Menorca and Florida in briefer operations.

Philip's victories over the realms of Aragon allowed him to resolve the problem that had haunted the Habsburgs: how to rule effectively the different realms of the peninsula. The Thirty Years War and the War of the Spanish Succession had revealed the peril presented by the *fueros* (charters) of the eastern kingdoms, for they protected them from wartime levies and justified their rebellions. Philip made sure this would not recur. In 1707 he abolished the *fueros* of Aragon and Valencia, reducing these kingdoms 'to the laws of Castile and to the use, practice, and form of government that exists and has existed in it and in its tribunals without any difference whatsoever'. The Council of Aragon, which dated from 1494, ceased to exist; its affairs passed to the Council of Castile. The highest officials of Valencia and Aragon would henceforth not be viceroys but captains-general. Similar reforms were effected in Catalonia by the decree of 1716 called the Nueva Planta, with the added proviso that the Castilian language must be used in all levels of justice. The Cortes of these territories also disappeared. Philip had convoked those of Aragon and Catalonia at the beginning of his reign, but in 1709 he incorporated the *procuradores* of Valencia and Aragon into the Cortes of Castile and in 1724 those of Catalonia. Although the Cortes of Castile met only twice more, at the beginning of new reigns in 1760 and 1789, to recognize the prince of Asturias as future king, they had become in effect if not in name the Cortes of Spain.

These measures, coming at the same time as the Act of Union that joined England and Scotland into Great Britain with a single parliament, were part of the common European development toward strong, independent sovereign states, ready always to take advantage of a neighbour's weakness and mindful of the danger that one's own disunity entailed. Centralization of the Spanish monarchy was not complete, however, for the Basque provinces and Navarre, which had stood by Philip, maintained their *fueros*. These caused little problem in the eighteenth century, but would be a thorn in the side of the Crown after 1833. Barring the Basque and Navarrese, no institutions could challenge the king's word as the *parlements* and provincial estates did the kings of France, even after Louis XIV.

The government of Castile, now that of Spain, was also being modified to make it more effective. Philip had inherited a conciliar form of government from the Habsburgs. Pre-eminent was the Council of State, which dealt with war and diplomacy, but the most powerful was the Council of Castile, which acted as high court and consultative body. Its *fiscales* (advisory attorneys) received petitions and projects and formulated proposals that the council reviewed and, if approved, submitted to the king for his acceptance as royal cedulas, decrees, or in rare instances pragmatic sanctions, reserved for the most important matters of state. A parallel Council of the Indies handled questions of the empire, while other councils dealt with finance, war, military orders, and the Inquisition. The structure was cumbersome, and Philip introduced a pattern drawn from Louis XIV of secretaries (we would call them ministers) to act in an executive fashion for the various branches of government: state (foreign affairs), finance, justice and ecclesiastical affairs, war, and navy and Indies.

Thus arose a dual government structure, part conciliar, part departmental. Gradually the secretaries took over more attributes, particularly in administration, leaving the various councils, except for the Council of Castile, as little more than high courts. The Council of State continued to exist under the Bourbons, but it lost its authority and appointments to it became purely honorific. In this way the eighteenth-century rulers paved the way for a contemporary structure of government.

Always on the mind of the royal counsellors was how to strengthen the state economically in order to face its international competitors, for coin has ever been the sinews of war. Freed from the *fueros* of the kingdoms of Aragon, Philip introduced new taxes on property and income. Intended to produce revenue comparable to that from Castile, by their simplicity they nevertheless showed how oppressive and inefficient the Castilian sales and excise taxes were. Ferdinand VI made a serious attempt to modernize the Castilian fiscal system. In 1749 he established in each province an intendant, an official copied from France and tried briefly by Philip V, who represented the king in matters of policy and finance. Under the direction of the Secretary of Finance, the marquis of La Ensenada, the intendants carried out a detailed survey of the individual properties and incomes in all the towns of Castile, a remarkable effort that revealed the capacity of Spain's royal servants when provided with leadership. The 'cadaster of La Ensenada' showed how low the tax-rate could be if noble landowners and ecclesiastical bodies paid their full share. The result frightened the privileged groups, and they managed to hold off the introduction of the reform until Charles III abandoned it. The royal taxes of Castile remained complicated and inefficient, contracted out to tax farmers who kept what they collected above the agreed price.

The Catholic church played a major role in the politics and economy of the country, as it had done for centuries. It was the Crown's most powerful ally. In war it would rouse the people against the enemy, against

Protestant powers now as they had against Muslims in the Middle Ages. The Castilian clergy made the War of the Spanish Succession a crusade against the British, accused of sacking churches and raping nuns. In return kings had placed large territories under the jurisdiction of bishops and monasteries. The church also provided the most reliable royal income, for two-ninths of the tithes went to the Crown (the *tercias reales*) and also the full tithes of the richest farmer in each parish (the *excusado*). Received in grain rather than money, this income was protected from inflation and rose automatically as population growth extended the area under cultivation.

The church's social role was commensurate. A large landowner could push a second son into a rich benefice, the priest in his cassock dominated his village, and a peasant boy could shine as a monk or friar. For centuries persons close to death had bequeathed a share of their wealth to a religious foundation or charitable fund. According to the cadaster of la Ensenada, the property of the church and its endowments produced a fifth of the income from agriculture in the provinces of Castile, mostly from lands rented to the cultivators.

Since Ferdinand and Isabella, Spanish monarchs had the right to present candidates for Spanish bishoprics and enjoyed complete temporal authority over the church in Granada and the Indies, known as the *patronato universal*. With this background, and angered by Clement XI's support of the archduke Charles, Philip V moved to extend royal control of the Spanish church. After lengthy vicissitudes, his campaign culminated under Ferdinand VI in the concordat of 1753. It confirmed the Crown's right of presentation of bishops and extended it to other high church offices, declared ecclesiastical property to be taxable, and reduced the fees collected by Rome from Spanish supplicants. Charles III moved further, reaffirming the *exequatur*, the need for royal approval for the publication of papal bulls and breves in his realms.

In the eighteenth century the Catholic church was plagued by internal divisions on matters of doctrine, forms of worship, and the role of the papacy, and it faced challenges from lay rulers over questions of temporal authority. Many Catholic rulers desired to limit the authority of the pope and the Roman curia, and they found support among clergymen who believed the church had become morally corrupted. The latter focused the blame on the Jesuits, whom they accused of teaching lax morality. They became known as Jansenists after the French group whose doctrines the papacy had condemned. The issues were fought out in Spain as they were elsewhere. The Spanish Jansenists objected to ornate church embellishment, extravagant processions, and other conspicuous demonstrations of faith, which they said detracted from the true spirit of devotion. The Spanish Inquisition, traditional in its outlook, banned the reading of theologians who put forth the Jansenist position. Priests who admired their works loathed and feared the Holy Office. They would not burn, but it could ruin their lives.

Charles III was ill-disposed toward the Jesuits. The loyalty of their missionaries in America was suspect, and in Spain his counsellors resented the alliance of Jesuits in university faculties with prominent families that resulted in their former students obtaining high posts in the royal councils and the church. Among the less affluent students who had suffered from this network was Pedro Rodríguez de Campomanes, who as *fiscal* of the Council of Castile became the king's leading adviser in economic matters.

The kings of Portugal and France had expelled the Jesuits from their kingdoms. An excuse to follow their example came from an unexpected quarter. Three years of bad harvests had by the spring of 1766 produced food shortages that brought hunger to the cities of central Spain. The common people of Madrid also resented the high-handed efforts of the Secretary of Finance, the Italian marquis of Esquilache, to clean up and police their city. On Palm Sunday crowds rose in reaction to an attempt to enforce an old order banning traditional capes and hats on the grounds that they concealed the identity of evildoers. Three days of fierce tumults drove the king to flee to Aranjuez, and sent Esquilache packing to Italy. Rioting over the cost of bread spread to some seventy other places. Sensing the need for someone whom the public could respect, Charles named the count of Aranda, a general and a grandee, president of the Council of Castile, where he and Campomanes would provide leadership for a programme of reform. In Madrid and elsewhere timely concessions followed by a firm hand restored order.

The *motín* (riot) of Esquilache was the most serious threat to royal authority in Castile since the Comuneros of 1520, and it marked a turning point in the Bourbon period. A secret commission concluded that the Jesuits were part of a conspiracy that had incited the Madrid riots, whereupon Campomanes drew up an indictment of the Jesuits as 'instigators and centre of dissention' in Spain and America. Charles III ordered their expulsion from his dominions in 1767. Some 5,000 Jesuits were deported, to settle eventually in the Papal States. A large majority of Spain's bishops, many of whom owed their place to the king's nomination, informed the pope that they approved of the expulsion. Six years later, in response to pressure from France, Spain, and Portugal, the pope abolished the Company of Jesus.

Charles III confiscated the Jesuit properties and banned the teaching of their doctrines. His advisors exploited the situation to impose royal authority on the universities. Pablo de Olavide, a collaborator of Campomanes familiar with the intellectual world of Europe, was named intendant of Seville in 1767. In taking over the Jesuit properties in the University of Seville, he modified its curriculum to reject scholasticism in favour of Cartesian logic. Inspired by his example, Campomanes convinced the Council of Castile to instruct the other Spanish universities to revise their philosophy curricula by including modern physics, astronomy, and epistemology and the law of nature and of nations. Although most faculties managed to avoid serious reform, within the leading universities professors and students were becoming familiar with modern science and political theory.

The educational reforms responded to a spirit of Enlightenment that was spreading among educated Spaniards. It flowed from many streams. The most conspicuous source of new ideas was the writings of a Benedictine professor at Oviedo, Benito Jerónimo Feijóo. His *Teatro crítico universal* (9 vols., 1727–39) and *Cartas eruditas* (5 vols., 1742–60), unmasked common superstitious devotions and practices and described foreign scientific and medical advances in an entertaining style that delighted generations of readers. The city of Valencia became another centre of contemporary thought, with the humanist Gregorio Mayáns and the professor of medicine Andrés Piquer. At the court of Philip V, Gerónimo de Uztáriz and José del Campillo y Cossío produced works urging the need to increase Spain's manufactures, commerce, and population. They wrote in the tradition of the *arbitristas* of Habsburg times, but their ideas reflected the mercantilist thought of Louis XIV's minister Colbert. After mid-century the royal servants Bernardo Ward and Campomanes argued for the need to loosen economic regulations. Although Spaniards did not contribute significantly to the contemporary advances in physical sciences, they excelled in botanical research in both Spain and America. The botanical garden of Madrid, founded by Ferdinand VI, soon achieved first rank.

After mid-century foreign works began to appear in Spanish translations, notably those of economists and botanists. The Inquisition of course banned the works of the leading *philosophes*, Montesquieu, Voltaire, Rousseau, and others, yet interested Spaniards learned about them from smuggled books or other sources. However, the deism and atheism that scandalized good Christians abroad found virtually no audience south of the Pyrenees. Spain had a true Enlightenment, but it took a different form from that of northern Europe.

What excited people was the practical side of new ideas, those that could improve the country. This spirit inspired the institution most typical of the Spanish Enlightenment, the societies of *Amigos del País*. In 1764 the king gave approval to sixteen Basque noblemen for a society of 'friends of the country' to encourage agriculture, industry, commerce, and the arts and sciences. Their activities impressed Campomanes, and his influence led to the founding of similar bodies in Madrid and over fifty other places in Spain and America. The most active, with the Economic Society of Madrid in the lead, did much for their regions, publicizing new methods of farming and manufacturing, founding vocational schools, offering prizes, holding public meetings, publishing their memoirs. Commoners, enlightened priests, and aristocrats rubbed elbows at the meetings, and Charles III ordered the society of Madrid to admit ladies, who took charge of a school for girls. Spanish women headed commercial houses and ran peasant farms, but the inclusion of women in a chartered society was an innovation.

The patriotic and egalitarian spirit of the *Amigos del País* reflected a vision of the ideal society that inspired Spain's governing elite. Its central figure was a small farmer who tilled the fields he owned, producing rich harvests and filling his home with warmth, joy, and love of his country. This was an ancient ideal, voiced anew by writers in the eighteenth century. Joining the farmer would be the good artisan, producing common goods for ordinary people, and the simple, dedicated priest, teaching moral virtue. Prosperity of the multitude would bring well-being to the nation.

In this ideal landscape idle aristocrats and sumptuous churches were out of place, and poverty-stricken labourers would disappear. Charles III and his counsellors would agree with Montesquieu that monarchy required a nobility, but privilege entailed service to society and compassion for inferiors. Francisco Goya captured the spirit of well-ordered social relations in the pictures of Spanish life he designed for the royal tapestry factory.

This spirit called for a new kind of king. Philip V shared the European mania for palaces inspired by Versailles. He began construction of the massive palace of Madrid, and in the sierra near Segovia built the delicious summer residence known familiarly as La Granja. Charles III maintained the palaces and court etiquette, but he changed the image of monarchy. A widower, he led a chaste and relatively simple life, finding diversion in the hunt, on foot with a few servants. He could be seen on horse or in an open shay, which he drove himself, removing his hat to any well-dressed person or cleric and nodding warmly to those of lower rank. The royal portrait made traditional by Louis XIV called for majestic robes and setting, but Goya painted Charles III in rough hunting costume with his gun and his dog, the only hint of majesty a ribbon across his chest. Royal portraits by Titian and Velázquez furnished him with precedents, but Goya conveyed a warmth and simplicity befitting more the father of a new republic than a divine-right monarch.

After the *motín* of Esquilache of 1766 government policy began to reflect this new spirit. Freed from wars in Europe and strengthened by an expanding economy at home and in America, the king of Spain could enjoy the luxury of social reform, convinced it would produce prosperity. Privileges and distinctions came under attack. He abolished the ban on hidalgos (lesser nobles) engaging in manual labour so that they need not 'live idly or badly occupied and become a charge on society'. Municipal offices were opened to occupations hitherto considered dishonourable— tailor, shoemaker, tanner, smith, and carpenter.

Local government was a concern, particularly in the large towns of Andalusia. Many municipal councillors, *regidores*, owned their office, purchased from the king by an ancestor, and they ran their towns like oligarchic republics, untroubled by the miserable existence of their day-labourers. Many rioters of 1766 blamed the town councils for their hunger. Charles III adopted a proposal of Campomanes to create new members of municipal councils called deputies of the commons, to protect the interests of the community. They were to be chosen by all lay heads of household. By mobilizing the ordinary townsmen through popular elections, Campomanes hoped to break the hold of the *poderosos*, the powerful ones.

The reform did not produce the desired effect, for the evidence suggests that the new officials, rather than defend the commoners, were often corrupted or marginalized by the *regidores*. A case in point involved a royal project aimed at forestalling future food shortages. The king ordered

Hunting was an inescapable kingly diversion, which re-enacted rites of knightly companionage. Lucas Cranach was the court painter of Frederick of Saxony and therefore became one of the chief propagandists for Charles V's enemies. His master, however, was captured in battle in 1547 and Charles seized the chance to extort Cranach's services from his prisoner. At the age of 78, in 1550, Cranach joined Charles's court and, assisted by his son, produced a prodigious series of works.

municipal governments to distribute common lands as small farms to landless and poor residents, first in Estremadura, then in La Mancha and Andalusia, and in 1768 in all Spain. Complaints soon came in that the best lots were going to the wealthy, while poor farmers, short of capital, were losing their allotments for failure to pay their stipulated annual fee. The reformers in Madrid were imbued with the Enlightenment faith that good laws could reform society. They now seem naive. Royal decrees had little effect on ingrained social customs and attitudes, and the king, like other early modern rulers, lacked an adequate network of loyal agents to enforce his laws.

Where the countryside was empty, however, the king and his advisers could create their ideal communities. As part of the strategy for highways, they founded new colonies along the wild stretches of the road to Seville where travellers were prey to bandits, in the Sierra Morena and west of Córdoba. Olavide was given charge of the project. The settlers received hereditary leases to family-size farms with newly built houses, tools, and livestock. Farms could not be merged, churches would be small, religious orders were banned, and town governments would always be elected. The first settlers were German Catholics, chosen for their reputed sobriety and industry, but soon Spaniards were more numerous. Olavide boasted of the large grain harvests, but the main cause was most likely the virgin soil. The townsmen also raised hemp, flax, and silk, and local weavers turned out woollens and linens, the reformers' ideal rural economy. The strict rules were abandoned in the nineteenth century, but the towns, many now centres of rich agriculture, still exhibit their democratic origins, rectangular streets, simple churches and houses, a living tribute to Charles III.

Another spirit also infused the royal policies of the century, a belief gaining currency in contemporary Europe in the benefits of economic freedom within state borders. In large measure it was a response to a pop-

Francisco Goya (1746–1828), the son of an Aragonese artisan who rose to be the First Court Painter of Spain, developed a unique style that has had a profound influence on modern art. His later work would be dominated by an obsession with social injustice, the supernatural, and the evils of war; but his first major commission, a series of paintings to serve as models for tapestries for the royal palaces, depicted the gamut of the king's subjects living in a society at peace with itself. In *The Crockery Vendor* Goya, perhaps symbolically, gives front stage to the figures at the popular market and places the aristocratic carriage in the background. The exchange between the vendor and the attractive customer appears to be sliding into a sly flirtation (abetted of course by the traditional crone), while the elegant lady seems equally disposed to appeal to the two well-dressed soldiers. Beneath the trappings of social hierarchy common human emotions unite everyone.

ulation increase that was common to most of Europe. Some 7.5 million Spaniards in 1712 became 10.5 million in 1786. After mid-century urban food shortages, such as that which preceded the *motín* of Esquilache, encouraged the royal counsellors to abandon traditional forms of regulation and trust market forces to produce supplies. A market economy was no stranger to rural Spain; recipients of rents and clerical tithes that were paid in kind furnished urban markets, and small owners and tenants also sold excess harvests and livestock. The grain trade was by tradition closely regulated, however, to keep down the price of bread. In 1765 the king freed the grain trade. The new faith in economic freedom also affected the Mesta, the privileged group of owners of migrant sheep, that had for centuries been guaranteed the use of the pastures it rented. Campomanes, appointed its president, arranged for the abolition of this right; owners could henceforth enclose their fields for planting. He also warned of the stifling effect of family and ecclesiastical entails (*mayorazgos* and *manos muertas*) that prohibited the alienation of real property, but the time was not yet ripe to act, and in fact many rural properties were being bought and sold, and buildings in Madrid frequently changed owners.

Imperial policy also moved toward economic freedom. The expanding economy of the American empire was multiplying the market for European goods. Challenged by foreign interlopers, the Crown struggled to secure this market for domestic products. Cadiz replaced Seville in 1717 as seat of the Casa de Contratación, the royal office in control of shipments to America, and remained through the century the major port for colonial trade, with a flourishing international community of merchants of French, Irish, Basque, Catalan, and Sevillan origin. They began to lose their American monopoly, however, when Philip V decided to copy the trading companies of northern Europe. In 1728 he founded the Royal Guipuzcoan [Basque] Company of Caracas with a monopoly of trade with Venezuela, which fed the growing vogue for chocolate. In 1755 came the Catalan Company in Barcelona for trade with the West Indies except Cuba. Charles III introduced a different policy in 1765 when he opened all the West Indies to shippers of Barcelona and seven other ports of Spain. Happy with the results, in a *reglamento* of 1778 the king authorized

The new agricultural colonies of Sierra Morena and Andalusia were seen as the major achievement of Charles III's reign, which would stamp his image upon contemporaries as an enlightened ruler. La Luisiana, founded in 1768 between Córdoba and Seville, was one of four chief towns. The small town square and modest church fulfil the plan to make the colonies productive communities of peasant farmers and artisans, free from large landowners and religious orders.

these ports to trade with all colonies in America except Mexico, which remained the preserve of Cadiz until 1789. Spain and its empire were progressively becoming a vast free trade area, attempting to protect itself from the outside world.

Many of the goods flowing to America through Spanish ports were of foreign origin, but easier trade with the colonies spurred a growth of domestic industries. The Basque provinces were turning out iron and copper wares, Valencia was known for its silks, and the traditional Catalan woollen industry prospered. Merchants of Barcelona also responded to the contemporary European fashion for elegant cotton cloths by establishing primitive factories to print 'indianas' for Spain and the colonies.

In the central meseta the major force driving the economy was the market of Madrid, home of the royal court and government, of absentee aristocrats, and wealthy religious institutions. Unlike other European capital cities it could not be provisioned by water, and by the 1780s an average of some 700 carts and 5,000 pack animals every day in good weather were needed to supply food and fuel to its nearly 200,000 residents. Attracted by rising prices for their crops, Castilian peasants were turning pastures into wheat fields, and Andalusian landowners were switching to marketable products like wine and olive oil.

The government sought ways to improve the economy of Castile. Reflecting French practice, it created a number of royal factories to provide domestic substitutes for foreign luxury goods, notably porcelains, glass, and fine cloths. Most were located in Madrid and other cities of central Castile. The largest, at Guadalajara with some 800 looms, produced fine woollens in the hope that stylish Spaniards need no longer wear Spanish wool woven in Britain. The royal factories ran at a loss, however, in large part because of the cost of transportation in central Spain. La Ensenada made improving the roads a major royal objective. Reflecting political centralization, a comprehensive plan of 1761 aimed to join Madrid with the ports of Andalusia, Valencia, Catalonia, and Galicia. The network was partially completed when the crisis of the 1790s interrupted it.

Overall Spain's economy was healthy; so far as one can determine, per-capita income was growing, promising a prosperous future. Paradoxically, although Castile had established political control of the country, economically it was losing out to the periphery, due in large part to its lack of easy access to the sea. Here grain prices fluctuated sharply depending on the impact of the weather on harvests. In contrast, the peripheral regions were part of the western maritime economy. Their cities could be fed by grain from France, Sicily, and North Africa at world prices, and the

Mediterranean coast exported wines, nuts, and dried fruits to northern Europe. The large estates of Andalusia shipped grain, olive oil, and wine to domestic and foreign markets. Its populous towns and stratified class structure were a different world from the peasant villages of Castile. Spain was becoming divided into three distinct regions that foreshadowed nineteenth-century politics: the underdeveloped interior; oligarchic, agrarian Andalusia; and the prosperous periphery of the north and east.

The period of most active reform ended after a brief six years. The haughty spirit of the count of Aranda aroused the ire of the king, and in 1773 Charles III removed him from the presidency of the Council of Castile and appointed him ambassador to Versailles. The reformers thereby lost their main protector, and Olavide became the sacrificial victim. Clerics who resented his university reforms and strict control of religious institutions in the agricultural colonies denounced him to the Inquisition. The Holy Office arrested him, and after keeping him two years in prison in 1778 pronounced him guilty of heresy, in penitent's garb, on his knees with a taper in his hands, before an audience of royal officials, aristocrats, and clerics. Although sentenced to eight years confinement, Olavide soon escaped to France, apparently with the connivance of the sympathetic Inquisitor-General. France gave him a hero's welcome.

In 1776 the king named as his secretary of state José Moñino, a former *fiscal* of the Council of Castile recently given the title count of Floridablanca. The king also made Campomanes a count and raised him to governor of the Council of Castile. Charles III took Floridablanca into close confidence, and in 1787 at his suggestion ordered the various royal secretaries to meet weekly under his presidency. This Supreme Junta [committee] of State anticipated a modern cabinet and gave Floridablanca unchallenged authority. Floridablanca and Campomanes dominated the last years of Charles III's reign. They continued to support reform and the spread of enlightened thought, but without the aggressiveness of the sixties. In this spirit the 1780s collected a rich harvest from seeds planted since the Bourbon accession.

Peace with Britain in 1783 brought on a decade of economic prosperity. Market-oriented agriculture supplied growing demands in Spain's cities and abroad. The *reglamento* of 1778 freeing trade with the Indies could now take effect, and exports to the colonies rose to perhaps twice their pre-war level. The king profited along with his subjects. In Catalonia trade with America rocketed, in wines, in metal goods, and above all in textiles, driving forward its industries. Every year saw more establish-

Improving internal communications was a major concern of eighteenth-century European governments. Ferdinand VI and Charles III devoted much attention to building roads. The plan of 1761 to tie Madrid to the major ports, although not completed, improved travel notably, especially in mountainous regions. The best roads were in areas of prospering communities—the Basque provinces, Catalonia, and Valencia. One of the finest ran from Valencia to Barcelona, completed under Charles IV. This section, with its bends and bollards, conquered the Coll de Balaguer, which previously had to be scaled on foot, 'the despair of travellers', as the French observer Alexandre de Laborde called it. This road permitted scheduled mule-drawn diligences to connect the two places, as they did other cities in Spain.

ments that turned cotton cloth into elegant *indianas* for the luxury markets in Spain and America. Although much of the cloth they used was imported, cotton printing made Catalonia a major centre of the early industrial revolution. The English reformer Arthur Young, in a brief visit to Barcelona, noted the euphoria: 'There is every appearance as you walk the streets of great and active industry. You move nowhere without hearing the creak of stocking engines.'

In Madrid a similar excitement pervaded the arts and letters. Goya had become the most fashionable portrait artist. In 1789 Charles IV would make him court painter and complete his triumph. Spain's best writers incited each other to test new thoughts and new styles: José de Cadalso, who circulated manuscripts of his *Cartas marruecas* satirizing Spanish society; Tomás de Iriarte, poet and playwright critical of the values of the upper classes; and the much sought-after young poet and court judge, Gaspar Melchor de Jovellanos, a protégé of Campomanes and former member of Olavide's circle in Seville. He was a patron of Juan Meléndez Valdés, Spain's greatest poet of the century, whose social philosophy stirred his students in humanities at the University of Salamanca, and who in turn inspired the poets of the next generation, Nicasio de Cienfuegos and Manuel Quintana. Their verses shifted easily from pastoral themes of love to social criticism and contemporary science. Playwrights, Jovellanos among them, sang of the national heroes, Pelayo and the defenders of Numantia, teaching patriotic duty and enlightened virtue.

A flourishing press produced elegant editions of *Don Quixote*, *El Cid*, and other classics, and translations of contemporary foreign works, especially in political economy. Periodical journals published in Madrid reached beyond the main cities to priests, notaries, and other subscribers tucked away in provincial towns. Luis Cañuelo voiced the thought of the Jansenists and economists through biting satire in *El Censor* (1781–7), until the authorities decided he had gone too far and silenced him. Valladares de Sotomayor's *Semanario erudito* (1787–91) revealed past ills of the country by printing 'the instruction that many wise Spaniards have left us', and other journals publicized the latest intellectual news from abroad.

Within a generation, cultured Spaniards would experience nostalgia for the prosperity, the feeling of progress, and the intellectual ferment that characterized the last years of Charles III. Crabbed clerics and refractory *poderosos* resented royal reforms, but no one openly resisted a respected monarch. Beneath them the vast majority continued as ever earning their livelihood, trading in local markets, gathering for religious festivals and personal rites of passage, and experiencing the joys, the rivalries, and the physical ills that mark all lives: Basque smiths, Catalan weavers, Valencian ceramists, Galician fishermen, Castilian shepherds, Andalusian rural labourers, and peasants, muleteers, potters, spinners, widows everywhere. The froth of new ideas did not concern them. Very soon, however, matters of state would embroil their society, the monarchy would quake, and the Old Regime would come to an end.

Ebb

Charles IV has gone down in history as the inept successor to his father. While less decisive in character, he does not deserve this harsh judgement. He took his responsibilities seriously and had a strong concern for the

welfare of his people, but he was unable to preserve Spain's well-being amidst the whirlwind that the French Revolution unleashed on Europe.

As prince of Asturias, the new king had consorted with a group of aristocrats who admired the count of Aranda and resented the power of the count of Floridablanca, an upstart in their eyes. Nevertheless, Charles IV kept Floridablanca at the head government. Authority had tempered Floridablanca's spirit, and the news from France of a self-proclaimed National Assembly that rejected royal authority affronted his code of legitimate polity. He determined to keep Spaniards ignorant of French events, mobilizing customs officers and Inquisitors to confiscate French publications and censoring Spanish journals. Papers and reports slipped through, however, and some of the Revolutionary reforms found admirers in Spain. In his anxiety, Floridablanca, like many other enlightened Europeans, came to suspect activities he had recently promoted. In 1791 he stopped the publication of periodical journals, and he discouraged the activities of the *Amigos del País*. He had Campomanes and Jovellanos, the most prominent partisans of reform, removed from their key positions.

For all his authority, however, the French tide overwhelmed Floridablanca. Louis XVI, anxious about the security of his throne, pressed his Spanish cousin to state publicly his approval of the new French constitutional monarchy. In February 1792 Charles IV responded by dismissing the ageing curmudgeon, abolishing the Junta of State that he had controlled, and naming Aranda in his place. Aranda sought to support the French king; nevertheless, the overthrow of Louis XVI in August 1792 followed by the declaration of the French Republic revealed his impotence. The king dismissed him in November.

Charles IV surprised his court by naming as first secretary Manuel Godoy, a guardsman in his twenties with an attractive figure, whom the king had recently made a grandee. Aranda's friends attributed his rise to the influence of Queen María Luisa, whom they accused of making him

Since the days of Louis XIV it was accepted that monarchs should appear in their portraits with the robes and other accoutrements of rule. Following this tradition, Raffael Mengs, whom Charles III brought to Spain at the beginning of his reign, depicted his patron in full armour. At the end of Charles's reign, Goya replaced the attire of state with the dress of the king's favourite diversion, the hunt, the only hint of majesty a ribbon across his chest. Goya had for inspiration a portrait by Velázquez of Philip IV in hunting attire with gun and dog, but in his day Goya's portrait reflected the new concept of monarchy that Charles and his ministers had evolved, a king close to his people, 'Padre de la Patria,' as medals struck in Mexico called him. Goya conveyed a warmth and simplicity more in keeping with that other 'Father of his Country', Charles's republican ally across the Atlantic, George Washington, than with a divine right monarch.

her lover. The more likely explanation is that Charles IV, eager to be free of his father's advisors and impressed by the capacities of Godoy, found in him a loyal servant, a trust that Godoy would honour until the king's death in exile in 1820. Except for two years after 1798, he would remain the dominant figure in Charles IV's reign.

Godoy's first major challenge came from France. The French Convention, after executing Louis XVI in January 1793, anticipated the response of Spain and Britain by declaring war on them. The Spanish war was fought at both ends of the Pyrenees. A Spanish advance in 1793 was followed in 1794–5 by French invasions of Catalonia and the Basque provinces. Both regions organized their own defense, but Godoy, suspicious of their loyalty to Madrid, negotiated peace in 1795, ceding to France Spain's half of the island of Santo Domingo in return for French evacuation of northern Spain. Charles IV rewarded Godoy with the title 'Prince of the Peace'. Two years later he permitted Godoy to marry the king's own cousin, a mark of great favour.

Peace provided Spain only a brief respite. Britain, still at war with France, suspected a Spanish–French agreement, and its navy attacked Spanish shipping. Spain responded by signing an alliance with the French Republic in August 1796 and soon declared war on Britain. The Family Pact had been revived, although the French branch of the family was gone. The Treaty of Amiens of March 1802 ended the war of Britain against Spain and France, but a year later France and Britain renewed hostilities. Charles IV attempted to remain neutral; however, Bonaparte demanded payment of a 'neutrality subsidy' and Britain renewed attacks on Spanish shipping. Spain once more declared war on Britain in December 1804.

Seldom have wars that saw little open conflict been so disastrous for a country. The British navy cut off most trade between Spain and America. By 1798 the merchants of Cadiz were in dire straits. The cotton industry of Catalonia, unable to get raw materials or reach its best customers, came to a virtual halt, and the workers turned to soup lines provided by the captain-general. Peace in 1802 brought a brief recovery, but after 1804 the British blockade again wrecked the colonial trade. Spain was losing its American market to Britain, and the euphoria of the eighties was gone.

The wars were a fiscal disaster for the Crown, which lost both American remittances and customs duties. New taxes conceived in an enlightened spirit to hit the wealthy and spare the labouring classes produced little more than ill will. An easier resort was to increase the money supply, reviving a measure introduced by Charles III in the War of American Independence, of issuing interest-bearing notes called *vales reales* that circulated as legal tender. After 1793 Charles IV issued new *vales reales* in larger and larger quantities. The public rapidly lost faith in them and exchanged them well below face value. The king and his advisers were racked by the knowledge that royal bankruptcy had brought on the French Revolution. Charles IV allowed Godoy to resign in March 1798, leaving others to find a solution to the fiscal crisis. The task fell to the new secretary of finance, Miguel Cayetano Soler. His solution initiated a policy of profound consequences.

In 1795 Jovellanos finished a report on agrarian reform commissioned by the Economic Society of Madrid. His *Informe en el expediente de ley agraria* is the masterpiece of the Spanish Enlightenment. It responded to a major preoccupation of Charles III's reformers: the negative impact on agricultural production of the vast properties in entail of the church and aristocracy. Jovellanos admired Adam Smith, and he argued that entail should be relaxed, if not abolished. The free play of the market would give efficient small farmers control of the land and it would flourish. Jovellanos pushed to its logical end the notion of economic freedom that had marked Charles III's reforms and tied it to the small-farmer ideal. Here in one theoretical framework were united the germs of liberal economics and liberal democracy. The nineteenth century would show that they were unnatural bedfellows, for freeing the land market would benefit capitalist landholders more than smallholders. Spain's eighteenth-century reformers, however, ignorant of the future, saw no inconsistency in the two aims.

These arguments provided Soler with the inspiration he needed. In September 1798 the king decreed the sale at auction of the properties in the hands of the church that supported hospitals and other charitable institutions, benefices, and religious activities like memorial masses. In 1806, when the supply was drying up, the king got the pope's permission to sell one-seventh of the properties directly owned by churches and religious orders. The king also gave owners of *mayorazgos* permission to sell properties, but the response was very modest. The proceeds of all sales would be applied to redeeming the *vales reales*, while the Crown would pay the prior owners 3 per cent interest.

By 1808 a vast number of lands and buildings, perhaps a sixth of the property controlled by the church, had passed into private hands. Persons who resisted social reforms could gain from ecclesiastical disentail, and it flourished. Spaniards—even those with *mayorazgos*—were discovering the benefits of a free market in real property. The process did not alter the social structure much, but it gave a chance for enterprising individuals of all levels, from hidalgos, priests, and royal counsellors, to merchants, bakers, and peasants, to acquire land and buildings, thus encouraging economic development. However, it angered conservative clergy, shredded the safety net of the poor, and established a precedent for later bankrupt governments.

Acts of God added to the monarchy's problems. Yellow fever, which was sweeping though the West Indies, reached Cadiz in 1800 and spread into Andalusia. Heavy rains spoiled the harvests of 1803 and 1804, and famine stalked Madrid and Castile. When the crises seemed to subside, Spaniards read in the *Gazeta* in October 1805 that the British navy had destroyed the combined French and Spanish fleets off Cape Trafalgar. Despite the best intentions, the proceeds of the sale of ecclesiastical properties had to be spent on the war and current emergencies rather than to redeem the *vales reales*. By 1805 these were being exchanged at scarcely half their face value.

The sad irony of the situation was that it obscured the enlightened spirit of Godoy's government. The *Amigos del País* resumed their activities, Spanish letters continued to flourish, headed now by Quintana and Leandro Fernández de Moratín. New critical journals came forth. In 1797 Godoy initiated a weekly journal, the *Semanario de agricultura y artes dirigido a los párrocos*, carrying useful information on farming and crafts that parish priests could disseminate. Not even Campomanes had conceived so obvious a way to spread the light.

The public seemed only aware of Spain's difficulties, and as a public is wont to do, they blamed their rulers, in this case Godoy. Ferdinand, the prince of Asturias, young, impressionable, and not too bright, became the centre of a campaign that involved the remnants of Aranda's party (Aranda had died in 1798). They spread the story that the queen and her lover were plotting to eliminate Ferdinand and become rulers after the death of Charles IV. Conservative clergy helped Godoy's sinister reputation to reach the common people. More and more Charles IV appeared a duped and complacent cuckold, incompetent to run his country.

Across the Pyrenees Napoleon, now Emperor of the French, anxious as always to squeeze as much as he could out of his Spanish ally, decided to exploit the dissensions in the Spanish court. He lent a sympathetic ear to approaches from both parties. In November 1806 Godoy negotiated a treaty with France to undertake the conquest of Portugal, with a share for himself. On his side Ferdinand responded favourably to Napoleon's confidential suggestion that he ask for the hand of a Bonaparte princess.

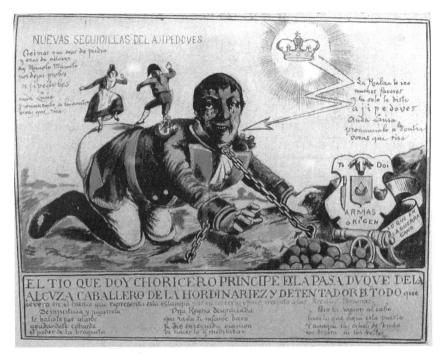

Manuel Godoy, Prince of the Peace, was ever the object of stories that he rose to power as the lover of Queen María Luisa. Rumours held that the two planned to make Godoy the next king. As part of an active campaign to destroy him, this libel is one of 35 cartoons known to have beem commissioned by the authority of the Prince of the Asturias, future Ferdinand VII, to be copied and distributed in taverns and similar places. Here popular vengeance ruins Godoy's ('Que Doy's') dream of a crown. A couple in popular Majo dress dances seguidillas on his back to the tune of scurrilous poetry that credits his success to his sexual prowess with the queen. To one side is a coat of arms with a butcher's knife and a pig's head, symbolic of his mock title 'Choricero' (sausage maker). María Luisa's reputed adultery, like the sexual corruption that Marie Antoinette of France was accused of by her enemies, brought discredit to the absolute monarchy and helped prepare its downfall. But in Spain the royal heir worked to blacken his own mother.

Napoleon could now intervene directly. A joint French–Spanish army conquered Portugal in November 1807, forcing the Portuguese royal family to flee to Brazil. The war was rapidly over, yet French troops continued to enter Spain. Spaniards were suspicious, but rumours had it that they were coming to save Ferdinand from Godoy. Godoy, with the royal family at Aranjuez, suspected treachery when the French approached Madrid, but before he could act, Ferdinand's associates incited a riot against him on the night of 17 March 1808. Godoy was discovered after two nights in hiding, and King Charles, demoralized and fearing for the life of his favourite, abdicated in favour of Ferdinand.

The *motín* of Aranjuez marked the end of the Old Regime in Spain. At the news, crowds in Madrid celebrated by sacking the houses of Godoy and his relatives. All across the country people rejoiced on learning of the accession of Ferdinand *el Deseado* ('the Desired One'). The popular celebration was the fruit of years of turmoil and disaster that had discredited the court and awakened an interest in national events among wide sectors of the population.

Charles IV soon regretted his hasty abdication and declared it null, as signed under duress. By now French troops had occupied Madrid and Barcelona and were spreading out through northern Spain. Both claimants realized that Napoleon's support would determine who kept the Crown. With a plot hatching in his mind, Napoleon invited Ferdinand to Bayonne in France, and had French troops bring Charles, María Luisa, and Godoy to the same place.

When Napoleon had both claimants in his presence, he pressured Ferdinand into returning the Crown to his father. Charles then assigned it to Napoleon, convinced that this was best for Spain. Napoleon gave the Crown to his brother Joseph, currently king of Naples and Sicily, and assembled a group of distinguished Spaniards in Bayonne to approve a written constitution for Spain. Joseph went off to Madrid, and Napoleon interned Ferdinand and Charles, María Luisa, and Godoy in different French chateaux.

Napoleon assumed that Spaniards would not object to a second change of ruler, but he was vastly mistaken. Ferdinand's departure to France raised anxiety, and the common people of Madrid, on 2 May 1808, rioted to prevent the remaining members of the royal family being taken to France. The French garrison crushed the rising brutally. Several other cities saw demonstrations, but the official Spanish bodies, from the Council of Castile down, condemned the rising and stopped the troubles.

A few days later the Council of Castile published the texts of the change of dynasty. This time the people, suddenly aware they had been robbed of their young idol, would not be quieted. Despite warnings that Napoleon was invincible, crowds in Valencia, Saragossa, Oviedo, and Seville forced the hesitant officials to proclaim war on the French in the name of Ferdinand VII. By June all unoccupied Spain was mobilizing for war.

Joseph Bonaparte, donning the mantle of an enlightened reformer, urged his new subjects to reject the senseless acts of a common rabble, and indeed the demonstrations frightened people of the better sort. Where French troops were in control many Spaniards co-operated with Joseph, former creatures of Godoy who sought to save their skins, believers in enlightened royal authority, but mostly simple persons trained to accept royal orders who saw no purpose in resistance. They became known as *afrancesados*.

Where the rising had succeeded, royal officials, high churchmen, and other persons of distinction formed provincial juntas that took command of their provinces in the name of Ferdinand VII. Needing to justify their rejection of the renunciations of their legitimate monarchs, they cited the sovereignty of the nation and the will of the people. Their words were revolutionary, but they were local notables and their spirit was basically conservative, seeking to take control of the situation. Presses, suddenly free from official censorship, flooded the country with sermons and proclamations of clergymen and others inciting the Spaniards to defend Religion, King, and Country against the godless French. Responding to appeals for help, on 4 July Britain ended its war with Spain. As a century earlier, Britain, operating out of Portugal, would support a Spanish rising against a new French dynasty in Madrid. And, as before, Britain would look for its reward in trade with the Spanish empire.

To everyone's surprise, the first major military encounter, on the road into Andalusia at Bailén, produced a Spanish victory on 19 July. The French prisoners were sent to rot in hulks in the bay of Cadiz, and Joseph fled from Madrid to Vitoria. The various juntas made contact, and in September their delegates met at Aranjuez and formed a Supreme Central Junta to rule in the name of Ferdinand. As its president it elected the venerable count of Floridablanca and among its members was Jovellanos, both of whom Charles IV had banished. Its main task was to organize the war effort, raising funds and armies, but its conservative spirit was evident in its decision to end the sale of church properties, despite its urgent need for money, and its attempt to activate the Inquisition to control the patriotic press because some writers were questioning Spain's political structure.

Napoleon, infuriated by the Spaniards' insolence, drove across the Pyrenees with a new army in November, and in December recaptured Madrid. Assuming the Crown himself temporarily, he abolished the Inquisition and then left his armies to finish off the rising. The Central Junta fled to Seville to escape Napoleon's clutches. Floridablanca died on the way. During 1809 it struggled to keep armies in the field. As a sign of its desperation, it authorized what it termed privateers on land, small bands of guerrillas who were to gnaw away at Napoleon's troops over the following years.

Jovellanos and others inside and outside the Junta urged it to convoke the Cortes, as the only legitimate authority in the absence of the king. A growing number of persons spoke of establishing a written constitution. Napoleon, following revolutionary doctrine, had given them one, but he was the enemy. Nor did Spaniards need this example. Since the 1790s Quintana and others had been saying privately that Spain's medieval Cortes represented a constitution and that Habsburg absolutism had destroyed it. Spain needed only to revive its ancient institutions, something a meeting of the Cortes could do.

The Junta's hand was forced by a rapid French advance into Andalusia in January 1810. It ordered elections for Cortes, both in the peninsula and in America. Its members fled to Cadiz, named a regency of five men, and resigned in unjustified disgrace. Jovellanos, broken-hearted, died on a ship carrying him home to Asturias. The last figures of Charles III's glory had disappeared, as had Spain's organized armies.

The new regency seemed powerless. Cadiz was under siege, and in Buenos Aires and Caracas colonists replaced royal authorities with supreme juntas nominally loyal to Ferdinand but not to the regency. King Joseph, with the country now at his feet, made a triumphal procession through Andalusia. At this critical juncture, Napoleon spoiled Joseph's victory by ordering his commanders to take over Catalonia, Navarre, and the Basque provinces, evidently planning to join them to France. This move destroyed any hope Joseph had of winning Spanish hearts.

Where Spaniards were out of French control, they were electing deputies to Cortes, and so were colonists in America. For deputies who were temporarily missing, persons from their regions present in Cadiz chose substitutes. The Central Junta had provided for the Cortes to have a second house of bishops and grandees, but the instructions for them to assemble were never issued. Enough deputies were in Cadiz for a first meeting to be held on 24 September 1810.

A majority of the members were committed to radical change in the monarchy, including a number of Jansenist priests. Led by Agustín Argüelles and Father Diego Muñoz Torrero, they gave the Cortes a strongly reformist bent, a sharp change in spirit from the Central Junta and the regency. They became known as Liberals, the origin of this as a political name. The first acts of the Cortes, symbolic of their mood, was to declare that sovereignty resided in them, as representative of the nation, and to proclaim freedom of the press in matters political. In the next years this freedom provided Spain with the novel experience of an active, partisan, and often vitriolic political press, pouring forth pamphlets and journals, not only in Cadiz but in other free cities.

In March 1812 the Cortes used the sovereignty they had assumed to proclaim a constitution. It declared that sovereignty resides in the Nation and defined the Nation as 'the union of all Spaniards in both hemispheres'. Spaniards would be Catholic, no other faith was permitted. The constitution established a limited parliamentary monarchy, with unicameral Cortes elected by a very broad male suffrage (servants, criminals, men without known income, and monks could not vote). The king was hereditary and inviolable and had a limited veto, but his ministers would be responsible to the Cortes for their acts. Regional differences, *señorío* jurisdictions, and noble privileges were abolished. Municipal councils were to be elective, thus eliminating hereditary *regidores*. The Liberals' constitution embodied the logical goal of enlightened Bourbon policies leavened with revolutionary liberty: a Catholic society of legal equals stretching across the Atlantic, without colonies or provincial privileges, but with the citizens themselves discussing their problems and choosing those who made the laws. Charles IV had brought enlightened despotism into discredit; ministerial responsibility would prevent a repetition of Godoy.

Within decades, imposing a uniform political system on all Spain would arouse hostility outside Castile, as it had a century earlier. For the moment, however, the prosperity of the late eighteenth century and the common struggle against the French had suppressed the momory of past regional conflicts. The immediate threat to the Liberal system came from a different quarter.

The Liberals, with their Jansenist sympathies, proceeded to abolish the Inquisition, as incompatible with the civil rights guaranteed by the constitution. Bishops' courts would henceforth judge religious transgressions. The conservative clergy, who had been biting their tongues, found here a cause they could exploit. They called the act an attack on religion, and the Liberals agents of Napoleon. They took their message to the nation using the freedom of the press the Liberals had provided and, with more effect, the pulpit, since most Spaniards were illiterate.

While the Cortes were refashioning the nation, the Spanish guerrillas had been harassing the French units, a war without mercy on either side, and slowly Spanish, British, and Portuguese forces led by the duke of Wellington went on the offensive. In August 1812 Joseph had to abandon Madrid temporarily and in March 1813 permanently. Allied forces destroyed his army at Vitoria in June 1813, and Joseph, accompanied by the leading *afrancesados*, sought safety in France.

The first regular Cortes elected under the constitution met in Madrid in October 1813, with a smaller Liberal majority. In December Napoleon recognized Ferdinand as king of Spain and sent him back, hoping for his friendship. The Cortes decreed that his first act must be an oath to the constitution, but Ferdinand gave his ear to a group of deputies opposed to the Liberal system. Assured of military support, in Valencia on 4 May 1814 he signed a decree declaring the meeting of the Cortes of Cadiz illegal and the constitution null and void. Most Spaniards, exhausted after a six-years war to bring back their 'desired' Ferdinand, celebrated the king's proclamation. Only in Madrid did a few small disturbances defend the Cortes. The king's military supporters arrested the leading Liberals, sent civilians to military forts in Africa, and interned priests in monasteries.

The institutions of the Old Regime were restored: the Council of Castile, *señoríos*, municipal councils, and the rest. Ferdinand's decree promised 'legitimate' Cortes, but they never were called. The pope re-established the Company of Jesus as a bulwark against revolution, and Jesuits were welcomed back to Spain. The Inquisition, given new life, undertook to root out and ban all Liberal publications. It searched out men who had joined the masonic lodges that King Joseph had introduced to attract leading Spaniards or which had been founded by Liberals in Cadiz. In Spain, as elsewhere under the Holy Alliance, the Restoration aimed to recover the legitimacy that rulers had enjoyed before the French Revolution. The actions of Ferdinand belied this legitimacy, however, because they made manifest that, rather than being an arbiter above its people, the monarchy favoured one section of it.

Despite Ferdinand's wide popularity, the supporters of the constitution did not give up. They included a number of officers who had fought under the Cortes, and the masonic lodges offered conspirators a form of association, complete with secret rituals and the mistaken reputation of having organized the French Revolution. In the following years military groups attempted several unsuccessful risings in favour of the constitution, and their leaders were executed.

Unlike Ferdinand's Spanish subjects, those in America did not welcome him back. Ferdinand sent off armies to restore Spain's sovereignty. Successful at first, they were losing out by 1818, when Argentina and Chile were free and Simón Bolívar was liberating northern South America. Another army was being prepared at Cadiz when one of its commanders, Rafael de Riego, on 1 January 1820 relieved his troops of the dread of service in the tropics by 'proclaiming' the Constitution of 1812. The general sent to crush Riego went over to his side and several cities of northern Spain installed constitutional city councils. Seeing no choice, Ferdinand announced on 7 March that he would 'lead his people along the constitutional path'. Spain had experienced its first successful *pronunciamiento*, a change of government imposed by the military; others would follow.

The Cortes was elected and met on 9 June. Its majority of Liberals took up where they had left off in 1814. The Inquisition was, of course, abolished, and they expelled the Jesuits. They promised a pension to monks who renounced their vows, and closed monasteries with fewer than twenty-four members. They sold ecclesiastical properties to redeem the national debt, now far greater than when Charles IV had taken this step. With the small-farmer society still their ideal, they voted to give vacant lands to veterans and landless peasants, and they abolished *mayorazgos*. They enacted free public education, needed for a literate electorate.

In the new era, the Liberal unity broke down. Outside the Cortes the masonic lodges multiplied, the more radical Liberals established patriotic clubs that excited the public, and the free press became ever more violent. Politicians seasoned at Cadiz and informed by exile controlled the legislature, headed by the poet Francisco Martínez de la Rosa. The radical agitation in the press and streets made them nervous. They looked to modify the constitution, with an upper house in the Cortes and a limited suffrage, as in Britain. They became known as *Moderados* or moderates. Opposing them, the *Exaltados*, the extremists, were committed to the constitution as it stood, with its unicameral democracy. Riego was their charismatic leader. They were strong in parts of the army and in the municipal councils of provincial capitals, through which they could influence elections to the Cortes. The elections of 1822 gave the *Exaltados* control of the Cortes, with Riego at their head.

Inside and outside Spain opposition built up against the regime. The new legislation hardened the hostility of the clergy. Guerrillas took up arms against the government, often led by monks. The army hunted down and killed some royalists. Blood had been shed in an incipient civil war. In 1822 the enemies of the constitution established a regency in northern Catalonia to rule for the king, who they said was no longer free.

Abroad, the Constitution of 1812, enacted by a people fighting Napoleon, was a beacon to partisans of constitutional government throughout Europe. Following Spain, in 1820 revolutions established constitutions in

The high point of Ferdinand VII's merciless vengeance on the Liberals was the execution of General Rafael de Riego in a small square in old Madrid on 9 November 1823. The man who began the Revolution of 1820 and later led the Exaltado party was for the conservatives the incarnation of irreligion and anarchy. Abandoned by his commanders and captured by the French forces that came to restore Ferdinand to absolute rule, he was brought ailing to Madrid and convicted of *lèse majesté*. To add insult to his suffering, his enemies had him conveyed to the scaffold in a coal basket pulled by a donkey before a jeering crowd. Generations of Spanish liberals, however, kept alive the *Hymn of Riego*, first sung in 1820.

Portugal and parts of Italy. The leaders of the Holy Alliance defeated the Italian revolutionaries and welcomed secret appeals from Ferdinand. British attempts at mediation failed because of the intransigence of the king, who wanted no constitution, and the *Exaltados*, who were confident the Spanish people would defend their sovereignty, as they had in 1808.

In April 1823, with the blessing of the Holy Alliance, Louis XVIII sent a French army into Spain to restore Ferdinand to his legitimate authority. No people rose, and the Spanish armies were no match for the French invaders. The Cortes fled to Seville and then Cadiz, taking the king with them. This time Cadiz did not hold out long against a siege, and the Cortes surrendered in September. Despite a promise of amnesty, Ferdinand decreed the death of leading Liberals, who were saved by the intervention of the French commander. Riego was, however, taken prisoner to Madrid, condemned, and dragged to his execution in a basket behind a donkey to add to his humiliation. Buyers of church properties lost them without indemnity and the Jesuits returned, but this time the Inquisition was not restored, because of French pressure.

The failure of the Constitution of 1812 meant the end of the enlightened ideal of an egalitarian society of small producers. The *Exaltados* claimed to represent the common people, but the sight of the Madrid crowd that had cheered Riego in 1820 jeering him on the way to the scaffold and celebrating Ferdinand's return a few days later shook their faith. The *Moderados* had already lost that faith. The ideal had been formulated in men's minds, not in the realities of Spanish society. An enlightened despot might work for the good of the common people, in whom he saw the strength of the monarchy, but the common people, still largely devout, would not defend a constitution that gave them a vote but, as their preachers told them, threatened their salvation. The other enlightened ideal, of a free market society, survived to be adopted by future *Moderados*, because it favoured the economically strong whom they would represent. Spain's constitutions would, until 1931, have two houses, and until 1891 male suffrage would be limited.

The vast empire in continental America also came to an end. The Liberals had deluded themselves that restoring the constitution would attract the rebels to lay down their arms, but its reforms threatened the Creoles of Mexico, and revolutionaries elsewhere had no intention of giving up independence and commercial freedom. Spain was left with Puerto Rico, Cuba, and the Philippines, crumbs from the imperial banquet that would eventually become loaves and fishes, softening the blow of the loss of the continents.

Loss of the empire marked the end of an era. The Bourbon rulers had ended the drain of continental Europe, and a splendid period followed. Spain could not escape the conflicts generated by the French Revolution, however, its rivals now attracted not by its continental territories but by the riches they believed lay in its American colonies. And as under the Habsburgs, involvement in European wars pulled Spain down. How destructive the period since 1793 had been is a matter of dispute. Castile suffered renewed famine in 1811–12 and tens of thousands died in Madrid. Yellow fever continued to scourge the country, Cadiz during the war, Barcelona in 1821. After 1815 rampant smuggling in Catalonia, the Basque provinces, and Andalusia defrauded royal coffers and broke down respect for the law. The public debt had mushroomed, while with America the Crown lost a major source of income. But the Spanish economy was mainly agricultural, easy to restore once armies and famines ended, and Europe would buy its specialties. On the other hand, the wars had largely closed off the Spanish American market and opened it instead to British manufactures. Cadiz fell to the level of a provincial port. The industrial periphery would recover with the markets of Spain and the West Indies, but the possibility of becoming a leader in the early industrial revolution had been dashed. Spain would no longer be a major international and economic power.

Thousands of liberal refugees now lived in Gibraltar, London, and Paris, and once again they plotted to overthrow the absolute monarchy. Their plans went awry and a number were executed. Help came instead, unexpectedly, from the king himself. Spaniards who had taken arms against the constitution had wanted to see more liberals executed, and fanatical Catholics were furious that the Inquisition was not restored, without which, they said, religion would not be safe. Malcontents drew together, calling themselves *Apostólicos*, and looked for leadership to the king's brother Don Carlos, the heir to the throne, since Ferdinand was childless. They argued again that Ferdinand was not free and their sympathizers rose in Catalonia in 1827. Ferdinand went to the front in person to disprove their claim, and the rising collapsed. He drew the lesson that he should court the mercantile classes and the more moderate liberals.

The July 1830 Revolution in Paris strengthened the liberal hand, for it placed a king opposed to absolutism on the throne of France, ending the threat of the Holy Alliance. In the same year Ferdinand's fourth wife, his young niece María Cristina, gave him a female heir, Isabella. In ending the War of the Spanish Succession, Philip V had introduced the Salic Law, which said women could not inherit the throne. The Cortes of 1789 had revoked the law, but Charles IV had not published their Pragmatic Sanction. Ferdinand did so during the queen's pregnancy; on its basis Isabella's birth deprived Don Carlos of the succession to the throne. Don Carlos promptly denied its validity. Ferdinand modified his government to attract *Moderado* support, and an amnesty freed political prisoners and allowed liberal refugees to return to Spain. As the king's health failed, Don Carlos's supporters prepared to place him on the throne by force of arms. Spain was headed toward civil war when Ferdinand died in September 1833.

8 Liberalism and Reaction 1833–1931

RAYMOND CARR

I

HE trickle of tourists who visited Spain in the 1830s professed to have discovered a country that had escaped the materialism of bourgeois Europe, preserving the human values of a traditional society that the advanced industrialized countries had lost. Ruled by what the British minister described as 'ragamuffins of the first order, bragging coxcombs, indifferent pupils of second rate actors of the Théâtre Française', such a society was deemed incapable of progress. Yet the professed aim of the native political elite, by the constitutions which it imposed on the country, was to convert Spain into a liberal parliamentary monarchy which would give power to the men of property and intelligence, seen as the advance guard of economic and social progress. Even the conservative constitution of 1834 professed to reconcile what it called the fundamental laws of the kingdom with the 'improvements demanded by the times and the progress of civilization'.

Yet all attempts at liberal constitutionalism which would make an elected Cortes the centrepiece of the political system failed to provide stable governments. Short-lived, bankrupt governments were confronted by the stubborn resistance of rural reactionaries. The Carlists, whose main strength lay in the Basque Provinces, with outposts in Catalonia and Aragon, pinned down the liberal armies in a savage and costly civil war that lasted from 1833 to 1839. Carlism was more than a dynastic conflict between Ferdinand VII's brother Don Carlos and the king's declared successor, his 3-year-old daughter Queen Isabella II for whom her mother, María Cristina, was to act as regent until she came of age in 1843. It was a crusade against impious liberals who persecuted and despoiled the church, combined with the defence of the local self-government granted by medieval privileges (*fueros*) of the Basque Provinces. Liberals were

The defence of Isabella II's claim to the throne during her minority against the reactionary Don Carlos had made her the symbol of liberal Spain. Coming to the throne as an inexperienced girl, she had little understanding of the conventions of a constitutional monarchy. Her support of neo-catholic reactionaries in her governments of the 1860s turned her into the personification of the 'traditional obstacles' to a genuinely liberal Spain. Discredited by a series of financial scandals, she was driven into exile by the Revolution of 1868. No beauty but sympathetic as a person, she was not a model of a respectable 'Victorian' monarchy; married to an allegedly impotent consort, her affairs were notorious.

'Jacobin' centralizers determined to impose a single constitution on all Spaniards. The old historic regions had been replaced by uniform provinces on the French model. Carlism was a war of a profoundly religious

countryside against liberal towns. To Carlists, Bilbao was Sodom and Go-
morrah. The failure of the Carlist armies to take Bilbao doomed Carlism,
plagued by factionalism, to defeat.

Liberals were therefore defined as those who defended the throne of
Isabella against Carlist reactionaries. The political battles of 1834 to 1868
were fought between the conservative wing of the anti-Carlist coalition,
the 'men of order' who came to form the Moderate party, and the 'defenders of liberty', the Progressives.

The weakness of liberalism lay in its lack of a solid social base in
a country where, even by 1900, almost two-thirds of the population
worked in agriculture and where 60 per cent of Spaniards were illiterate;
where the towns, the natural constituency of bourgeois liberalism, were
islands in a sea of rural ignorance. Both the Progressives and the Moderates were parties of notables struggling for power and patronage, ma-
nipulating an ignorant and apathetic electorate by extensive corruption.
Lacking any independent power base, the politicians appealed to the generals as their 'swords' to install them in power by the *pronunciamientos*, the
officer revolts which marked the alternation in power of Progressives and
Moderates in government. The major politicians were the generals who
had become national heroes, publicized in popular prints as defenders of
liberalism in the Carlist wars: Baldomero Espartero and later Juan Prim
were the 'swords' of the Progressives, Ramón María Narváez of the Moderates, and Leopoldo O'Donnell of the Liberal Unionists in the 1860s. But
the *pronunciamientos* were not a series of military coups and they rarely
resulted in bloody battles, becoming formalized affairs in which the
government *in situ* surrendered to the superior force of the rebel generals.
This military mechanism for political change is characteristic of underdeveloped countries with a weak civil society.

The generals saw themselves not as military malcontents but as party
politicians. All *pronunciamientos* had civilian support and a party programme. In this they were distinct from the military takeover bid planned
by the Nationalist generals in July 1936. Nor was it only ambitious generals who destabilized politics. María Cristina and her daughter, open
to criticism for their irregular private lives and questionable financial
dealings, consistently abused their constitutional prerogatives to appoint
ministers in order to favour the Moderates. The result was to turn the me-
chanics of liberal constitutionalism upside down. Instead of coming to
power as the result of an election, governments, installed by the court or
a successful *pronunciamiento*, could use the extensive powers of the minister of the interior over the local agents of a highly centralized government

to fabricate a comfortable majority from above. Electoral corruption was not unique to Spain; it was what was euphemistically called the 'moral influence' enjoyed by the Minister of the Interior that was to distinguish it from other countries.

The Moderates and Progressives came to be distinguished by their constitutional doctrines and the nature of their civilian support. The central doctrine of the Progressives was that the constitution should represent the sovereignty of the nation embodied in the minority of property-owners entitled to vote. If the constitution was subverted by Queen Isabella or, during her long minority, by her mother as regent in order to exclude the Progressives from office, then it was the duty of Progressives to save Spain from despotism by force. This could take the form of a creeping provincial revolution of town committees or, more usually, a classic *pronunciamiento*. All entailed an appeal to the Progressives' urban clientele: town mobs and the host of lower-middle-class *pretendientes* who 'pretended' to minor government posts as their only source of income; in the 1840s 3,000 *pretendientes* applied for a handful of such jobs in the Post Office. In a vast spoils system, just as generals after a successful *pronunciamiento* were rewarded by promotion and titles, Progressive politicians were expected to reward these modest clients. It was they who had organized committees of the towns and manned the barricades.

Once in power, the Progressives organized a National Militia to guard the conquests of the revolution. Open to all property-owning householders, the National Militia was the private army of radical town councils. Moderates regarded the Militia as ending the rule of the notables; they would now have to obey cobblers, tailors, butchers, and barbers in uniform.

It was the Progressives, as their name implies, who saw themselves as the champions of political, social, and economic modernization. Their 'Jupiter' was Juan Mendizábal (1790–1853), allegedly a Jew who had sought his fortune in the London money market. Swept to power by a rash of provincial town revolutions, in 1835 he became prime minister of a bankrupt state engaged in a life-and-death struggle with Carlism. His solution for establishing his government's credit was to confiscate the landed property of the church, first of the regular orders and then of the secular clergy, selling it off by auction with preferential rates to holders of government bonds. The Progressives were not enemies of Catholicism; their 'sword' Espartero was pious to the point of superstition. But to Catholics, as convents were turned into barracks or demolished, Progressives appeared as the sacrilegious allies of popular anticlerical street mobs.

The breach between advanced liberalism and a reactionary church was never to be healed.

The land sales were conceived as more than a fiscal device to ward off bankruptcy. The bible of Progressives was Florez Estrada's *Course of Economic Policy*, a regurgitation of the works of Adam Smith and his followers. To believers in the virtues of competition, the great defect of the Old Regime was the lack of a free market in land. Thus, not only the corporate, inalienable church land was 'freed' by sale to individuals; aristocratic entail was abolished, allowing nobles to convert a bundle of seigniorial dues into absolute property rights, with rents set by the market. To complete the market economy, the monopoly of guilds was abolished.

The attack on corporate property in the name of absolute individual property rights as a receipt for economic progress was the real liberal revolution of the nineteenth century. Later, it was seen by radicals as the great lost opportunity for an agrarian reform that would benefit a disinherited rural proletariat. Sold for cash or for discounted government bonds, land went to speculators with inside knowledge and government friends, to local notables and substantial farmers. The poor lost out in the liberal land revolution to the 'powerful ones' of rural society. Taxed and conscripted (the rich would buy out of military service), the propertyless were denied citizenship. The liberal constitutions confined the vote to property-owners, in the case of the Moderates' 1845 constitution to a mere 1 percent of the adult male population. The Progressives only differed in that they enfranchised their urban, artisan clientele.

In the 1840s the Democrat party emerged to channel the discontents of the excluded. Its strength lay in Barcelona, where an industrial proletariat was taking shape, and in the towns of Andalusia and the Levant. Rejecting the *juste milieu* of the Progressives, the Democrats demanded universal male suffrage, a distribution of rural land to the dispossessed, and the legalization of workers' associations to fight employers. The Democrat leadership was prepared to accept a democratic monarchy, but further to the left a vague Utopian socialism came to combine with republicanism, particularly in its federal form that would create 'from the bottom up' a Spain of self-governing units or cantons. The Republican party rejected the monarchy as illegitimate, unsuited to the modern age. The Progressives needed the support of the Democrats if they were to mount a successful *pronunciamiento*. The Democrats organized town committees (*juntas*) and could bring enthusiasts to the barricades. But the alliance was unstable. Progressive politicians and discontented generals wished to force the Crown to desert the Moderates and call them to office. The

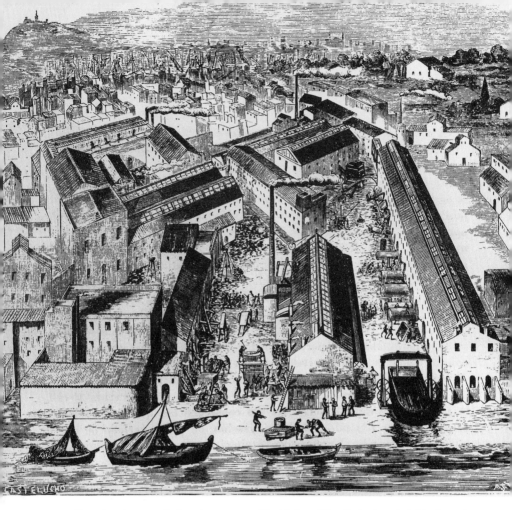

Barcelona's cotton industries, protected by high tariff walls, had made it 'the Manchester of Spain'. By the mid-century it had begun to diversify. The Maquinista Terrestre y Maritima became an important metallurgical and engineering enterprise. It made the first railway engine in Spain and suffered badly from the collapse of the railway boom in the late 1860s. With a large skilled workforce, it was troubled by strikes in the 1900s.

Democrats were not content with capturing the system in order to exploit it; by the 1850s they wished to jettison a corrupt court. In 1845 General San Miguel warned that barricades threatened property-owners with 'ruin, blood, and anarchy'. Once in power, respectable Progressives sought to escape the Democrats' embrace.

The Moderates were the oligarchs of liberalism as the defenders of order against the excesses of the Progressives. They included higher civil servants, successful lawyers and journalists, court aristocrats, rural notables, and the higher clergy. Burkean conservatives, they rejected the 'abstract' doctrine of the sovereignty of the nation in favour of a supposedly 'historic' constitution embodying the joint sovereignty of the king and the Cortes, a dogma embodied in their constitution of 1845. Secure in the support of the Queen Regent, they were determined to destroy the Progressives' power base: the elected town councils and their private army, the National Militia. When the Moderates sought, with the support of the Queen Regent, to destroy the Progressives' hold on municipal governments, the Progressives turned to their sword, Espartero. He forced María Cristina and the Moderate leaders into exile, ruling as regent from 1841 to 1843. The fatal weakness of both parties was an infinite capacity to form factions which made impossible the establishment of stable governments. In July 1843 the Progressives fragmented as the *políticos* resented Espartero's penchant for his military cronies. They were sent into the wilderness for ten years by a Moderate *pronunciamiento* captained by General Narváez.

The Progressives were Anglophiles, admirers of Bentham and Adam Smith. The Moderates were Francophiles, who saw in French administrative centralism an instrument to destroy the Progressives' hold over local government. Under their 1845 constitution, mayors were appointed by the central government; they became the Moderates' electoral agents, who could be relied upon to ensure the party a safe parliamentary majority. The Moderates' appeal to the 'material interests' of a rising class of capitalists by fostering economic progress and sound, efficient administration would provide stable government. It was as administrative reformers that they left their permanent mark, overhauling an antiquated system of taxation and creating an imitation of the French gendarmerie, the Civil Guard—a militarized police force that could be trusted with the defence of public order and property. The National Militia was abolished. University reform turned professors into civil servants, which they have remained. The Progressives' onslaught on church property had brought Espartero into open conflict with the Vatican. The Moderates, aware of the influence of the church as bulwark of the social order, came to terms with Rome in the Concordat of 1851. The Pope recognized the land sales in return for the state assuming the obligation of paying the clergy.

Narváez was a liberal in the sense that he intended to rule according to the constitution of 1845 provided it worked to exclude the Progressives from office. But the Moderates went in fear that a Progressive general would bring the European Revolution of 1848 to the streets of Madrid. For Juan Donoso Cortés (1809–53), the apostle of the absolutist reactionaries of the party, 'the question lies, not between dictatorship and liberty, but between the dictatorship of the revolution and the dictatorship of government'. Narváez abandoned his constitution, becoming a dicta-

Spain's larger towns and cities began to be modernized in the 1840s and 1850s. The first step was the destruction of the town walls; this allowed the building of housing developments outside the old limits. An essential element was the supply of clean water and its arrival was greeted with celebrations, as in this painting *La llegada de las aguas a Madrid* by E. Lucas Velásquez.

tor who, it was alleged, remarked on his deathbed: 'I have no enemies, I have shot them.' From military dictatorship, the court turned to civilian authoritarianism in the person of Bravo Murillo (1803–73), a former radical journalist and philosophy professor. His permanent achievement was characteristic of the Moderates as administrative reformers. He began

work on the Canal of Isabella II, which brought the fresh water supply which was essential if Madrid was to become a modern city. He had no taste for liberals who drafted constitutions and then disregarded them in practice, 'hypnotized by epaulettes'. He proposed a constitution which would reflect social reality and ensure efficient civilian government. His successor was a rich capitalist who, confronted by the opposition of the military oligarchs in the senate, exiled their leaders.

The result was the Revolution of 1854, a *pronunciamiento* of the exiled generals, led by O'Donnell, and of the Progressives loyal to their old hero Espartero, with the Democrats manning the barricades. In power for two

years the Progressives drafted a constitution based on universal male suffrage. But the coalition that had made the revolution fell apart in 1856.
O'Donnell forced Espartero's resignation, and the Progressives failed to
make another appeal to the barricades. Once more, the factionalism of the
liberal family made the officer corps the arbiter of politics.

The Revolution of 1854 was a political failure: the constitution of 1856
never came into operation. But to see only this political failure is to mis-
interpret the significance of the Progressive biennium. For the Progressives, the appeal to the 'material interests' became a regenerating creed:
capitalism, credit, and free trade would destroy the surviving remnants of
the Old Regime. The sale of the municipal commons was the last onslaught on corporative property in the name of absolute individual property rights. Once more, it was the poor who lost out. The Cortes of the
biennium concerned itself with every aspect of economic life: afforestation, railways, the electric telegraph, roads, banks. It was this legislation
(company and mining laws) that provided the legal structure for the prosperity and expansion which lasted until 1866.

The collapse of the two-year Progressive administration left the dour
O'Donnell as prime minister. His long ministry of four years and seven
months seemed to offer the prospect of political stability. O'Donnell was
an heir of the biennium in that he aimed to harness the 'material interests'
by a programme of economic expansion. In his novel *O'Donnell*, Benito
Pérez Galdós makes his heroine desert her Democrat lover after a mystical
experience before the residence of a rich capitalist. The prime minister
embarked on a series of overseas adventures in Mexico and nearer home
in Morocco to stimulate patriotic enthusiasm and keep the army occupied. It was in Morocco that Prim became a national figure, as O'Donnell
had become in the Carlist wars. But the Liberal Union, like every other attempt to create 'the harmony of the Liberal Party', fell apart. The Queen
now committed political suicide. Under the influence of the neo-Catholic
reactionaries of her court, she regarded the Progressives, who would have
served loyally if called to power, as revolutionaries to be excluded from
office. After trying a *retraimiento*—a boycott of politics as a protest against
corrupt electoral practices—the excluded had no alternative but to become revolutionaries. Prim, who had succeeded Espartero as 'sword' of

A poster celebrating the proclamation of the Second Republic. Alongside the traditional
female representation of the Republic, the ministers of the first government and below
them the leader of the Catalan movement and the two republican officers executed for
their attempt to overthrow the Dictatorship in 1930. The poster displays the optimism
of those heady days in the early part of the Republic when it was believed the government could reverse decades of social injustice and political corruption.

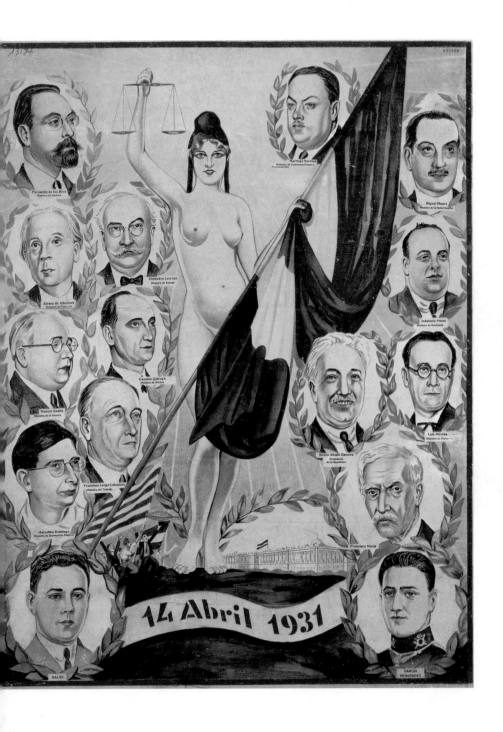

the Progressives, after a series of abortive Progressive *pronunciamientos* turned to the Democrats. The alliance was not to his taste.

The Revolution of September 1868 was a *pronunciamiento* of those politicians and generals denied office by Isabella's exclusivist reaction, the Liberal Unionists and Prim's Progressives. To widen their support the generals appealed to the restive Democrats of the towns. Isabella herself went into exile, and a provisional government of the September coalition was installed.

II

The distress which provided the Glorious Revolution of 1868 with its groundswell of popular support was the result of a general cyclical crisis, whereas earlier 'revolutions' had mobilized the discontents of the urban masses facing high food prices, the consequence of bad harvests. The years between 1852 and 1862 saw Spain's foreign trade double. The main railway network was laid down by the late 1860s. Factory chimneys had transformed the industrial landscape of Barcelona. The boom collapsed in 1866–7, as railway construction fell off and banks failed.

This crisis was typical of the speculative disasters of the more advanced European economies. But Spain was not on the edge of an industrial take-off. Confronted by a hostile geography which made railway construction a costly enterprise, and without cheap coal, it also lacked native capital and entrepreneurial skills. Where native capitalists had failed, it was for-eign capital and technical expertise that, in the 1860s and 1870s, created great enterprises to exploit the copper and pyrite resources of Huelva. It was foreign capital—mainly British—that established the open-cast iron mines around Bilbao that supplied south Wales with the low-phosphorous ore for its blast furnaces.

This issue has given rise to fierce controversy. Foreign capitalists have been accused of establishing colonial enclaves policed by foreign man-agers to exploit and profit from Spain's mineral resources. By allowing free import of railway goods, it was argued, the possibility of a flourish-ing Basque metallurgical industry was nipped in the bud. These national-ist arguments, resurrected by General Franco, are false. Without foreign

Gaudí (1852-1926) is now recognised as the most original architect of Catalan 'modern-ism'. Influenced by European developments, as a Catalan patriot he drew on local craft traditions, especially ironwork. Himself an austere Catholic, he was patronized by the Catholic conservative new rich, for whom he built apartments—the Casa Batlló was built in 1904–6. His patrons included the industrialist Count Eusebi Güell who intro-duced him to William Morris and Ruskin.

capital, Spain's mineral wealth would have stayed in the ground; had railways been dependent on the steel output of Basque forges, they would either not have been built at all, or been delayed for decades. The bulk of the profits of the Basque mining enterprises went to the British ironmasters, but some remained in Spain to be invested in Basque-owned blast furnaces, steel mills, shipyards, and banks. Progressives, as free-traders, fully realized the importance of foreign investment, providing the legal framework that made it possible.

In 1868 the major industrial centre of Spain remained the textile concerns of Catalonia, which had ruined the artisan enterprises of the interior and created Spain's first urban proletariat, providing the Democrats with a clientele whom they supported in their demands for associations to fight the employers. Modernization and new inventions—self-acting mules and steam-powered mills—set off bursts of Luddite machine-breaking and arson. But workers and employers could unite in one demand: protection against British cotton imports. The word 'Manchester', Richard Ford noticed in the 1830s, had become a term of abuse for Catalans. Particularly after the loss of exports to Cuba and Puerto Rico in 1898, the textile manufacturers demanded a total monopoly of the home market, secured by prohibitive tariffs. This inevitably put up prices for consumers and took away any incentive for Catalan manufacturers to become competitive in the world market.

This modest industrial and commercial growth was not matched by the performance of a relatively stagnant agriculture. There were few improving landlords or educated, prosperous farmers, as in England. No agricultural revolution could come to the handkerchief plots of Galicia, or the scattered fields of the Castilian peasantry in the dry meseta. As for the large estates, increased production came from extension of the cultivated areas, enlarged by mid-century land sales. There were dynamic export sectors: Andalusian sherry went to England, and the sherry trade made the fortune of the critic and essayist John Ruskin's family. The fruits of the Levant went to northern Europe. Spain was still a dual economy of rich and poor regions, where the absence of a national economy was evident in the sharp differences between regional prices.

Comparisons with the advanced industrialized societies of the north revealed a gap that made Spain's performance appear mediocre. Nevertheless, growth occurred, unbalanced and confined to the periphery as it was, leaving the interior a rural backwater. The 'material interests' were beginning to transform Spanish society as the squalid provincialism of the 1830s, portrayed by George Borrow's *The Bible in Spain*, gave way, at least in the large towns, to a more comfortable, bourgeois lifestyle. With the arrival of fresh water the picturesque water-sellers disappeared from the streets of Madrid, an early example of unemployment created by technological advance.

In this changing society the old aristocracy remained economically intact but, in comparison with the British aristocracy, had little political clout, except at court where its influence was disastrous. The new aristocracy which emerged in the 1830s and 1840s was one of notables, forming the core of the political elite: generals, speculators in real property, prominent political journalists, and lawyers. British observers were struck by what they called the 'democracy' of Spanish society: men of humble origins could rise to the top, the snobbishness and rigid class-distinctions of British society did not prevail in Spain. Espartero was the son of a carter. This social mobility, which had long existed in the church, remained a characteristic of political life. The great conservative leaders of the late nineteenth century, Cánovas and Maura, were obscure provincials; the contrast with their British contemporaries, Gladstone, the marquis of Salisbury, and Balfour, is striking.

The new aristocracy often exhibited the vulgarity and fashionable mimetism of *nouveaux riches* everywhere. José de Salamanca, who specialized in railways and real-estate speculation, installed the first private bathroom in Spain, and employed Napoleon's chef. Narváez, an Andalusian squire, built a palace in Madrid where he appeared, the British minister noted, 'literally covered in diamonds'.

The model to be imitated, from banking to architecture and the arts, was France of the Third Empire. As in Paris, the 1860s in Madrid were an age of financial and sexual scandals in which the court was involved. The Romantic movement, imported ready-made from Europe, swept over Spain; it produced one gifted poet, Gustavo Adolfo Bécquer, and an outburst of *costumbrista* literature describing 'typical' customs. Goya had no heirs. The art market of a newly confident bourgeoisie was supplied by conventional portrait painters.

Spanish cultural life appeared second-rate to foreigners. Nevertheless, the foundation of literary societies, especially the Athenaeum of Madrid (founded in 1837), was to establish the respectability of the intellectual in political and social life, and with it the beginnings of public, informed debate. But this debate could not acquire the salience it achieved in Britain and France. The press was tied to political parties and its circulation modest. The vulgarity, political corruption, and formal religiosity, the crude utilitarianism of the society of the 1860s were rejected by the new intelligentsia who were giving a respectable ideological foundation to Republicanism. Emilio Castelar (1832–99), a professor of philosophy, was Republicanism's greatest orator and a polemical journalist whose devastating attacks on the scandals of the court eroded the prestige of the monarchy. Sacked from his post, the ensuing demand for 'freedom of the professional chair' and freedom of the press became the watchwords of Democrats and Republicans. It is a curious comment on the cultural isolation of Spain that intellectual regeneration was the work of the disciples of an obscure German philosopher, Karl Krause (1781–1832). Krausism, a mystique rather than a philosophical system, is best described as a version of the Protestant ethic of self-improvement, laying great emphasis on education and, in contrast to imported positivism, on moral purpose rather than utility as a recipe for Spain's regeneration. The legacy of

The Flaquer family were bankers, seen here enjoying the comforts of bourgeois life. They were typical of a new urban middle class of successful soldiers, journalists, lawyers, bankers, and politicians which began to emerge in the 1840s. Many of them had profited from the sale of church lands in the 1930s and were to speculate in the railway boom of the 1860s. Few, outside Catalonia and the Basque provinces, were engaged in industry. Madrid long remained a city of artisans and civil servants.

Krausism was the ideal of an open, tolerant society. For this reason it was regarded by Catholics as a pagan heresy, a direct attack by the legatees of freemasonry and Protestantism on the educational and social influence of the church. The Krausists in 1876 founded the Institute of Free Education which became the private school of a liberal elite, and its Residence was later to become the Madrid home of Luis Buñuel, García Lorca, and Salvador Dalí.

III

The Revolution of 1868, with its constitution of 1869, is as much a landmark in Spanish history as the constitution of 1812 had been. It seemed to offer the prospect of a genuinely representative system. Yet it was to fail, as the September Coalition fell apart. For five years the statesmen of the September Revolution fought to stave off a relapse into anarchy which would turn men's loyalties back to the Bourbon monarchy as the only guarantee of political stability and peace. Each government in turn sought to stabilize the revolution at a point which suited its own interests—a process described as keeping the revolution on course. The key to the failure of these repeated attempts must be sought in the composition of the September coalition and the rival claims of its constituent elements to power and patronage. Who had 'made' the revolution? Who deserved the rewards?

It was not merely party rivalry in Spain itself which destroyed the optimism of September. The cancer of the September Revolution, sapping its vitality, was the Cuban war, legacy of twenty years of liberal neglect. In 1868 the richest remnant of the colonial empire was still subject to the absolute power of the captain-general and his allies amongst the Spanish community on the island. The native Creoles resented the presence of an administration staffed by Spanish *peninsulares,* while economically the Spanish connection was an anachronism, since the prosperity of their sugar plantations depended on exports to the United States. The Creoles would have been satisfied with a generous grant of autonomy. They rebelled for an independent Cuba only when such autonomy was rejected by the *peninsulares* and their allies in Madrid. The result was a savage guerrilla war that entailed the dispatch of Spanish troops to Cuba and forced the government to abandon the two promises which had given the Revolution its popular support: the abolition of conscription and of food taxes.

The Provisional Government of the Revolution, first under Serrano, the strong man of the Unionists as regent, and then with Prim, the Progressives' chief, as prime minister, struggled to create a constitutional monarchy which would command the loyalty of the September coalition of Unionists, Progressives, and Democrats. Their constitution of 1869 gave the Democrats what were called 'the Liberal Conquests': universal suffrage, the jury system, and the recognition of freedom of religion, but retained the monarchy for some suitable king. To the Democrats, 'a few gentlemen' had demanded the 'fruit that others [i.e. the Democrats themselves] had shaken from the tree'. The more extreme Democrats sought to 'bring the rebellion back on course' by a provincial uprising which was suppressed by the army. The disappointed provincial zealots became Republicans who were committed to the idea of a federal as opposed to a unitary Republic.

Prim, the strong man of the Progressives and the ablest military politician of the century, imposed his king, Amadeo of Savoy, only to be assassinated on the day the king entered Madrid in December 1870. Cold-shouldered by the Unionists who saw him as the Progressives' king, Amadeo could form no stable government as the Progressives fell into contention with the Democrat *políticos*. He abdicated in despair in February 1873.

The subsequent First Republic of 1873 dissolved in chaos. Soldiers, with the cry 'Down the epaulettes', refused to obey their officers. The four respectable presidents of the Republic could not restrain what one of them, Pi y Margall, himself the theoretician of federalism, called the 'puerile enthusiasm' of provincial zealots for the immediate installation of a Federal Republic without waiting for a vote of the Constituent Cortes. They set up self-governing, independent cantons in the towns of Andalusia and the Levant. Political fanaticism contained an undercurrent of primitive social rebellion. 'I have killed the richest man in Montilla', declared one small-town energumen for whom violence, as for many other provincial zealots, had become a way of life. General Pavía, having restored military discipline, decided it was the duty of his officers 'as soldiers and citizens' to save society and the *patria* from the anarchy of the Federal Republic. A few shots sufficed to dissolve the Constituent Cortes. A unitary Republic of order, facing the renewal of the Carlist war in the north, failed to re-establish 'the harmony of the liberal family'. Antonio Cánovas de Castillo (1828–97), who was to be the architect of a monarchical Restoration in the person of Isabella's son, the future Alfonso XII, wanted a civilian restoration by an organized party. An impatient brigadier restored the monarchy by a classic *pronunciamiento* at Sagunto in De-

In January 1873 the Cortes (Parliament) was on the point of declaring Spain a federal republic which would mean a descent into anarchy and the destruction of discipline in the army. General Pavía decided that it was his and his officers' duty 'as soldiers and citizens to save society and the country' (the *patria*) from a federalist ministry and chaos. A few shots in the air ended the Constituent Cortes of the Republic and the destiny of Spain fell into the hands of an artillery general. In July 1936 it was Franco and his fellow conspirators who took upon themselves the duty to save the *patria*.

cember 1874. Once more, what Cánovas called 'the miserable interests of militarism' had decided the political destiny of Spain.

Like the Revolution of 1854, the Glorious Revolution of 1868 was a political failure. This obscures its fundamental importance. A Catholic monarchy, sustained by a narrow conservative oligarchy, had been challenged by the assumptions of democracy and free thought. The 'liberal conquests' of the constitution of 1869, claimed Romanones, later a liberal prime minister of the Restoration, 'could never, never be reversed'. The groundswell that defeated the revolution was based on the cry of 'the Church in danger'. Convents had been desecrated and burned, mobs attacked priests. The freedom of religion of the constitution of 1869 had admitted 'heresy'. As the debates on the constitution revealed, the battle-lines were drawn between the proponents of an open, tolerant society and the Catholic church, for which Catholicism was the test of citizenship.

—¡Gracias á Dios que se ha ...ercado alguien!

The grant of universal male suffrage in 1891 did not turn Spain from an oligarchy of notables into a parliamentary democracy. The electorate was manipulated by the Minister of the Interior in order to provide safe majorities for the conservative and liberal parties. This widespread electoral corruption was possible because the rural voters were illiterate and abstained. Genuine electoral contests took place only in the large cities and even there abstention was high. At the polling station of this caricature only the dog turns up.

IV

The Restoration Monarchy and its constitution of 1876 survived until its overthrow by a general in 1923. It was the creation of the political philosophy of Cánovas del Castillo. An intellectual and historian, he had lived through a succession of *pronunciamientos* and revolutions and was determined to end them. The Revolution of 1868 was the consequence of the exclusive policies of Queen Isabella and her reactionary court. The restored monarchy of her son, Alfonso XII, must include all those who accepted the constitution of 1876: Progressives, repentant Democrats and Republicans—including Emilio Castelar, a former president of the Republic—would be allowed a legal existence provided they were prepared to abandon revolution.

His recipe for stable government was a two-party system which would allow a Liberal party and a Conservative party to alternate in power in what was called the *turno pacífico*. Between 1881 and 1885 those groups who considered themselves heirs of the conquests of the September Revolution had coalesced to form a Liberal party, capable of forming a government as the alternating party under their leader, 'the old shepherd' Práxedes Mateo Sagasta (1827–1903). Sagasta restored some of the liberties of the September Revolution—press freedom and freedom of association among them, lost in the conservative atmosphere of 1876. In 1892, the great triumph of the revolution, universal male suffrage became law.

Spain was now, on paper, one of the most democratic polities of Europe. The problem was to convert theory into practice, transforming a regime run by notables and 'political friends' into a parliamentary system where free elections would determine political power. The *turno pacífico* came into play when a ministry was 'exhausted' and the king appointed an alternative ministry of the party in opposition. The minister of the interior of the new ministry could obtain an overwhelming majority for the incoming ministry by a judicious use of the 'moral influence' provided by his control, in a highly centralized system, over judges, civil governors, and mayors. This institutionalized electoral corruption was called *caciquismo*, since its agents were called *caciques*, the term for an Amerindian chief and local bosses in general. Only with the emergence of mass parties could the system cease to be a machine for fabricating majorities. These did not emerge, partly because the notables showed little enthusiasm in organizing them, but above all because an electorate on the British model, as Cánovas confessed, did not exist in an overwhelmingly agrarian society where only 25 per cent of the potential voters could read. He turned a blind eye to electoral corruption. 'He did not dignify the base of the parliamentary regime with clean elections', wrote a journalist who admired him, and it was for this reason that his lieutenant Francisco Silvela deserted Cánovas and split the Conservative party. Bastard constitutionalism not only encouraged political fragmentation. It put a dangerous weapon in the hands of the king. As long as the system worked to provide him with clear choices between two strong parties, he could act as the neutral 'moderating power' envisaged in the constitution. Once the two-party system fragmented, as it did after 1909, he became a power-broker.

V

In 1898 this artificial system and somnolent public was shaken by what was known simply as 'the Disaster': overwhelming defeat at the hands of the 'sausage makers of the United States' as the allies of Cuban separatists. The consequence of defeat was the loss of the remnants of Spain's colonial empire: Puerto Rico, Cuba, and the Philippines. This national humiliation released a flood of self-examination. Why, at the moment when other Europeans were building empires, had Spain lost hers? Was Spain a decadent nation, or did it have, as the historian Altamira argued, powers within itself to stage a national recovery? This complex of pessimism and optimism coalesced into what was called regenerationism. 'Regenerationism', wrote a satirist: 'a tonic for weak nations. Recommended by the best doctors, apostles and saviours.'

Regenerationism was neither novel in content nor coherent. Joaquín Costa (1846–1911), son of an Aragonese peasant and a self-educated polymath, who became the prophet of regenerationism, had long meditated on the historical roots of Spanish backwardness. Regeneration would sweep away *caciquismo*—a term of universal condemnation which he coined—and allow the 'live forces' of society to enter political life. He hoped to combine the discontents of agriculturists and the grievances of the Chambers of Commerce in a national movement which would force the politicians to undertake an ambitious project for educational, social, and economic reform. In this endeavour Costa failed. Regenerationism, as he conceived it, rested on a myth: that the 'live forces' would respond to his call. But they did not. Without a public or a party, Costa appealed to an 'iron surgeon' to make Spain a democracy.

The literary renaissance of the generation of 1898 was an equally diffuse protest against the mediocrity of the cultural establishment that had antedated the Disaster. Spain's greatest writers, Galdós, the Dickens of

Spain, and Clarín (the pen-name of Leopold Alas), whose *La Regenta* is a psychological masterpiece, had published major works before 1898. Nevertheless, with the writers of what came to be called the 'generation of 1898' and their successors, Spain ceased to be a literary backwater. More important than the limited influence of Spanish writers abroad— the eccentric novelist Pío Baroja was translated into Russian—was their own familiarity with European culture. To the philosopher José Ortega y Gasset, Europe was the solution to 'the problem of Spain'.

What the rhetoric of regenerationism did was to give an urgency to critics of the Restoration Monarchy. It was the obvious shortcomings of a regime that had plunged Spain into the Disaster in '98 that gave old protests new impetus, as the ragged and disease-ridden defeated army returned to Spain. In retrospect, it is remarkable that the regime survived the Disaster. It did so because the protest movements, sharply divided from each other, proved incapable of providing an alternative to what all, including elements within the regime, saw as an artificial and corrupt system but which, nevertheless, had established roots in a country which the conservative regenerationist Silvela described as 'anaemic' and 'without pulse', and the poet Antonio Machado as a nation which yawned.

The protest and reform movements given new life by the Disaster included Catalan and Basque nationalists; socialists and anarchists; and the officer corps, humiliated by a defeat which they came to blame on the politicians who had sacrificed a heroic army to the demands of selfish party politicians.

For the Carlists, loyal to the heirs of Don Carlos, Alfonso XII was a usurper. Their attempt to install the Carlist pretender, a renewed Catholic crusade of the rural countryside against the 'Babylon' of Bilbao, had ended in defeat in 1878. Carlism had been the bulwark of Catholic reaction; but in the 1880s the Catholic right, obedient to the counsels of Pope Leo XIII, formed a party to defend the interests of the church within the system. This left the integrist wing of Carlism, which split from the main party in 1888, as survivors of an extreme form of Tridentine Catholicism, proclaiming the 'social reign of Christ the King'. The presence of this vociferous minority diminished the influence of those Catholics who might accept the liberal state as a 'lesser evil'. To integrists it was an absolute evil. Carlism in the Basque Provinces remained the protest of a deeply religious rural society threatened by industrialization. It revived during the Second Republic, as in the first, with the cry 'the Church in danger'.

The Republican movement, discredited by the anarchy of 1873, immersed in doctrinal struggles, with neither organization nor a programme beyond a belief in Republicanism as a self-evident political truth, became an affair of local clubs, with a wing that still looked for a 'sword' to overthrow the regime. They made little impact in rural Spain. Their strength lay in the great cities—Madrid, Barcelona, and Valencia.

The Republican revival after 1900 took two directions. Alejandro Lerroux, son of a veterinary surgeon and typical representative of the middle class, was an heir of the old urban revolutionary tradition of exploiting the discontents of the marginated workers living in the slums of the larger cities. A demagogue, his appeal to the Barcelona proletariat was based, less on any specific programme, than on his perception of the cultural gap between the working class and the self-satisfied bourgeoisie, with its contempt for the 'uncultured workers' and those who sought their votes. The main ingredient of his attack on bourgeois values was a revival of the violent anticlericalism of the 1830s. 'Pillage this decadent civilization, destroy its temples, tear aside the veil of novices and elevate them to the category of mothers.' This his followers did in an orgy of convent burnings in the 'Tragic Week' of 1909. His other appeal was to the non-Catalan immigrants who had flooded to the factories around Barcelona. They voted for his Republican party in his bitter electoral battle with Catalan nationalism, attacked as anti-Spanish. A corrupt but able machine politician, his Radical Republican party dominated Barcelona politics until 1914, by which time his working-class clientele was vanishing and he was on the way to becoming a respectable bourgeois politician.

The bourgeois wing of Republicanism, the Reformist Republican party created in 1912, was distinguished by the intellectual quality of its leadership; hence its attraction for the philosopher José Ortega y Gasset and the young Manuel Azaña, later to become the president of the Second Republic. Its ideal was a modern, democratic Spain with up-to-date social and educational legislation. If the monarchy of Alfonso XIII could provide this, well and good. If not, the monarchy must be replaced. 'I believe', wrote the reformist Gumersindo de Azcárate 'that a kind of fatality prevents the dynasty from solving the social and political problems of today. The only kind of government likely to provide a solution is a Republic.' His prophecy came true with the defeat of the monarchists in the municipal elections of April 1931 in the large towns, the result in no small measure of the erosion by the Republicans of the moral and political foundations of the monarchy as it failed to embrace democratization. But once again, as the results of the 1931 election revealed, Republican propaganda had failed to penetrate rural Spain.

The Tragic Week of 1909 was sparked off by the distribution of crosses by devout Catholic ladies to conscripts embarking for the war in Morocco. An outburst of traditional working-class anti-clericalism against 'the church of the rich' had been stirred up by Republican demagogues and anarchists: 12 churches and 40 convents were burnt or destroyed and a strike brought Barcelona to a standstill. The photograph shows Civil Guards rounding up suspects; some 1,000 arrests were made.

Catalanism, like Irish or Czech nationalism, fed on a combination of the memory of past splendours and a sense of 'victimization' by an alien, oppressor state. The medieval institutions that protected the liberties of a flourishing mercantile empire had been destroyed by Bourbon kings and liberal centralizers; its industry was threatened by the Anglophile liberal free-traders. Catalan industrialists clamoured for protection. The politicians of Madrid were parasites exploiting the profits of industrious Catalans. Starting in the 1830s as a literary renaissance of Catalan language and culture, the 1890s saw the emergence of political Catalanism demanding home rule for a Catalan-speaking region. For its leader, Prat de la Riba, the Spanish state was 'one of the great mechanical units formed by violence', holding Catalonia in a 'slavery vile as that of the Turks'. But both he and his disciple, Francesc Cambó, a self-made millionaire and born statesman, rejected the radical nationalism of their rhetoric; as regionalists, they fought for Catalan demands for home rule 'within Spain', by entering the political system. The party they organized, the Lliga, can be seen as the first modern party.

The problem of Catalanism was the diversity of its component parts. It included bishops and plutocrats, Federal Republicans, respectable citizens, and café bohemians. In 1906 all these elements, except for Lerroux, joined in a movement called 'Solidaritat Catalan' to defend civil liberties, surrendered to the army in the Law of Jurisdictions, and to demand autonomy for Catalonia. Solidaritat mounted mass demonstrations of 100,000 people, and defeated the local *caciques*, sweeping the board in the general election of 1907. Cambó hoped to use this strength to obtain satisfaction for Catalan demands. In this he failed. By 1914 all that Catalonia had won was the creation of the Mancomunidad representing the administrative union of the four Catalan provinces, a body which Prat de la Riba, as its president, used to promote Catalan culture and language as the basis for a national revival. Catalanism was no longer the affair of the literary enthusiasts of the 1830 Renaissance. There were now Catalan working-class choirs, while popular libraries spread enthusiasm for Catalan literature.

Cambó and the Lliga had sought a solution for Catalan demands for home rule 'within Spain' by a combination of threats and offers of collaboration with Madrid governments. But his vision of a Great Spain, regenerated by an autonomous Catalonia, found no understanding outside its borders, where home rule was seen as the first step on the road to separatism. At home in Barcelona Cambó was confronted with the Spanish nationalism of Lerroux, exploiting the indifference, if not hostility, of the working class to Catalan demands. To the Catalan left the Lliga, by co-operating with the politicians of Madrid, had made it an 'appendix of monarchical conservatism' and Spain, 'an oppressor state inferior to the nation it oppresses'. Political Catalanism shifted to the Republican left with the foundation of Catalan Action in 1922. The rhetoric of radical nationalism, combined with the intransigence of Madrid, turned the fears of Spanish conservative nationalists into a self-fulfilling prophecy. Colonel Francesc Maciá became the charismatic leader of a separatist movement. Catalans must fight for Catalonia as a free republic in a federal state.

Like the Catalans, the Basques saw themselves as victims, their ancient liberties destroyed by liberal centralizers as 'punishment' for the Carlist rebellions. But Basque nationalism never seriously challenged the Restoration settlement. It lacked the political clout of its Catalan counterpart. With little support from the local industrial oligarchy, its cultural, linguistic, and political roots were less secure. The most eminent Basque intellectuals, the philosopher Miguel de Unamuno and the novelist Pío Baroja, scorned Basque as a literary language though Unamuno regarded the Catalan poet, Jacint Verdaguer, patronized by the industrialist magnate the marquis of Comillas, as the greatest living Spanish poet. There was no such eminent figure in Basque literature. Native Basques had a strong sense of community but, unlike Catalonia, the Basque Provinces could not count on the memory of a single political unit with a glorious past. Sabino de Arana, who came from a Carlist family, the founder of Basque nationalism and its party, the PNV, saw the Basque-speaking community as being threatened by a flood of migrant Castilian speakers, the *maketos*, who came to work in the mines and factories around Bilbao. To save this community from adulteration Sabino de Arana invented a national unit, which he called Euzkadi, which would separate from Spain. The official language of this independent state would be Basque, which he saw as a means of excluding the *maketos* from the political community. His nationalism was essentially racist. The PNV shed his racist exclusivism, but unlike Catalan nationalism, it never moved to the left, but remained a Catholic conservative party whose legal tactics were to become unacceptable to radical nationalists and in the 1960s they were to adopt the terrorism of ETA. Catalan nationalism, given its wide social support and secure linguistic and cultural roots, had no need to resort to violence.

Organized working-class protest had existed in the form of associations since the 1840s. Its new strength had little to do with regenerationism as such. It was a consequence of industrialization. Its fatal weakness was its division, both ideological and geographical, between utopian revolutionary anarchists and pragmatic Marxist socialists who were prepared to act as a political party. The socialist party, the PSOE, was founded in 1879 and its trade union, the UGT, in 1880, both inspired by Pablo Iglesias, the son of a poor washerwoman. An austere moralist, Iglesias inherited from French Marxists his hostility to bourgeois Republicanism. Fighting elections alone, up until 1910 the PSOE never captured more than 30,000 votes in the whole of Spain. This political puritanism was rejected by Indalecio Prieto, and it was his alliance with Republicans that gave the PSOE seven deputies in 1923. Apart from the labour aristocracy of Madrid—Iglesias was a printer—the strongholds of socialism were the coal-mining districts of Asturias and the open-cast iron mines and metallurgical industries of Bilbao and its surroundings. The resort to violence in the UGT strikes of the 1890s was a sign of weakness when faced with the intransigence of the employers, who refused to accept

From the 1890s the Barcelona café Els Quatre Gats was a centre of the artistic revival known in Catalonia as 'modernism'. It was there that Picasso exhibited his early works; along with Santiago Rusiñol (b. 1861) and Ramón Casas (b. 1866), both from well-to-do bourgeois families. Casas in his early years was drawn to the struggles of the Barcelona working class. This 1894 painting by him shows the garrotting of an anarchist.

unions as participants in the settling of labour conflicts. As elsewhere in western Europe, the Great War of 1914–18 saw a dramatic increase in union membership. In 1917 the UGT abandoned parliamentary tactics, joining the anarchist union in a general revolutionary strike. A disastrous failure, the subsequent return to legality drove the men of violence into the small communist party.

The importance of the PSOE lay less in its power as representing organized labour (compared to Italian and German socialism it was a puny growth), than in its standing as the heir of the Republicans as critics of a 'feudal' monarchy. From Iglesias onwards it sought to create a moral alternative to a corrupt system. Its meeting-places (the Houses of the People) would educate the working class and wean it from the drunkenness and vice of the tavern.

The anarchist strongholds were among the Barcelona proletariat and the *braceros*, the landless casual labourers of the great estates of Andalusia, described by Gerald Brenan as the most wretched, semi-starving working class in Europe. Socialists had made little attempt to penetrate rural Spain, leaving the field to Catholic unions in Navarre and Castile, and to the anarchists in Andalusia and the Levant. The hold of anarchism in a major European country has puzzled historians; it is perhaps most simply explained by the hostility of employers and landowners to any form of labour organization, leaving violence as the only alternative. Andalusian anarchism could take the form of a messianic, primitive rebellion. But the *braceros* had concrete demands: the abolition of piecework and casual labour. After 1917, inspired by the Bolshevik Revolution, a wave of strikes and land occupations swept over Andalusia, driving the *señoritos* to the safety of the towns.

The Anarcho-Syndicalist union, the CNT, was founded in 1910–11 to organize the proletariat for a final battle against a decrepit capitalist society with feet of clay. But anarchists differed as to how this great revolutionary transformation of society should be achieved. To syndicalists, 'the day' would be the achievement of organized, permanently militant unions, engaged in direct action against the employers. But syndicalism had little appeal to what Victor Serge called 'the vast world of outcasts' of Barcelona, marginalized men who could find no outlet for their frustration except in a craving for violence. This could be accommodated by the strong, individualist tradition in anarchism. It took the form of 'propaganda by deed', bombing and assassinations. In 1893 an anarchist threw a bomb into the Lyceum Theatre, the social centre of the rich bourgeoisie, killing twenty-two people. Arrests and torture not only revived in Europe the Black Legend of Spain as the country of the Inquisition. In Spain itself it set off a cycle of revenge killings. Cánovas himself was assassinated in 1897. During and after the 1914–18 war the CNT organized massive strikes in Catalonia, met by employers' lockouts. Barcelona was the scene of a savage social war between CNT *pistoleros* and employers' thugs.

Like the socialists, the anarchists created in their lay schools an alternative culture, strongly anticlerical by tradition (seeing priests as the ideological soldiers of bourgeois civilization), and even embracing free love, vegetarianism, and nudism. But unlike socialism, its revolutionary utopianism, its rejection of the state, as a body irredeemably hostile to the working class which would use the army and Civil Guard brutally to suppress any organized protest, made anarchism incompatible with democratic politics. 'The day', the destruction of an immoral capitalist system, would be the result of a spontaneous street revolution or a general strike, with anarchists divided as to which would bring the inevitable triumph of the revolution.

Apart from Carlism, the protest movements of regenerationism shared a vision of a modernized Spain. The Catholic church, however, saw in modernization a threat that must be met by a return to the past. The religious unity of a confessional state, as Catholics conceived it, was lost with the limited toleration of the constitution of 1876. Secularism was making great strides; the lost ground must be recaptured in a counter-offensive. The church expanded the missionary activities begun by Queen Isabella's confessor, Father Claret, in the 1860s; a genuine intensification of devotional practices centred round the cult of the Sacred Heart of Jesus and the Immaculate Conception. Catholic Action, founded in 1894, aimed to mobilize the laity; the National Association of Catholic Propagandists the intellectual elite. 'Social Catholicism', inspired by papal encyclicals, would win back the alienated working class for Christ.

The spearhead of the Catholic counter-offensive was the religious orders, as they advanced to take over the welfare and educational functions that an impoverished liberal state could not finance. During the Restoration, female religious orders trebled; male orders grew tenfold. This spectacular growth alarmed liberals, who saw in the educational enterprises of the regular orders and the Jesuits an attempt to capture the moral high ground of society for a reactionary church. Both liberal anticlericals and Catholics indulged in conspiracy theories. The Jesuits were the secret army of the Papacy; Catholics saw freemasons infiltrating the liberal establishment. For the Catholic polymath Marcelino Menéndez y Pelayo, Spain had been 'poisoned' by the heirs of the Enlightenment.

The Catholic counter-offensive failed in its purpose of converting the urban working class and the rural proletariat of Andalusia. This was partly a consequence of maldistribution of resources. While the old city centres and hamlets of Castile and the north were served by an abundance of parish priests, for the poor of new working-class suburbs and on the great estates of Andalusia a single priest might minister to 8,000 souls. More importantly, the religious revival was financed by landlords and businessmen. The Basque industrialists founded in Bilbao the University of Deusto; the Catalan industrial magnate, the marquis of Comillas, financed the confessional trade unions of Father Vicent, the 'redemption' of prostitutes, and pilgrimages to Rome. 'Social Catholicism' boiled down to paternalism and respect for a hierarchical society where workers should learn obedience and employers Christian charity. Vicent's rigidly confessional unions were rejected by Iglesias as instruments for the creation of a docile working class. The one success came in the Catholic Castile and Navarre, where the National Catholic Agrarian Confederation gave struggling subsistence farmers the credit to survive.

The result of renewed militancy was to strengthen the religious commitment of the right; defence of the church became its sign of identity. On the left its most immediate effect was to revive the anticlerical violence of the 1830s and 1860s, directed against the church of the rich in the church burnings of the Tragic Week of 1909. For liberals, few of whom were freethinkers, the social and educational influence of the church stood in the way of progress which could only be guaranteed in the 'neutral', tolerant state that the politicians of the Second Republic, above all Azaña, sought to create. But a 'neutral' state was, to all but an intelligent minority of Catholics, a work of impiety.

The politicians of the Restoration were aware both of the artificiality and the corruption of the system they manipulated and of the dangers of 'revolution from below'. The 'revolution from below' must be met by a 'revolution from above', an overhaul of the system that would plug the gap between 'official Spain' and the excluded neutral mass, made voiceless by the machine of *caciquismo*. To the conservative leader Antonio Maura (1853–1925), a devout Catholic and austere man of order, the greatest orator of the epoch, 'revolution from above' took the form of a reform of local government that would sweep away *caciquismo*. His reforms met the uncompromising hostility of the Liberal and Republican parties, who formed the 'Block of the Left' with the cry 'Maura, no'. It triumphed in 1909, following Maura's severe repression of those responsible for the Tragic Week. King Alfonso XIII, fearing that Maura's unpopularity threatened the throne, dismissed him, although he was supported by a solid majority in the Cortes, appointing in his place the Liberal Segismundo Moret. To Maura, Moret had allied with the 'sewer' of the anti-dynastic parties and he refused to co-operate with him. The *turno pacífico*, the peaceful alternation of Liberals and Conservatives, the essential mechanism of Restoration politics based on the consensus between the parties, was under threat.

The Liberals' recipe for regeneration was to assert the claims of the state to regulate the mushroom growth of the religious orders dedicated to the education of the elite. A modern educational system was the precondition for a modern society. The tragedy of the religious issue was not merely that it set off a series of violent demonstrations and counter-demonstrations, but that it diverted the attention of the Liberal leader José Canalejas (1854–1912) from a programme of social and political reforms that might have made him the Lloyd George of Spanish liberalism. He was assassinated in 1912. Without him the Liberal party split into competing personal factions, at the same time that Maura's intransigence was threatening the unity of the Conservative party.

It was this fragmenting political system that faced a series of crises which, as elsewhere in Europe, were a consequence of the dislocations of the Great War of 1914–18. Spain, as a neutral, had profited from exports which enriched the employers but brought inflation and high food prices for the less fortunate. In 1917 the UGT, for once in alliance with the CNT, attempted to turn a railway dispute into a general strike. The Catalan parties in Barcelona organized an illegal extra-parliamentary assembly to press demands for autonomy and constitutional reform on Madrid.

Spain had a long-standing interest in Morocco. Granted by France and Britain a protectorate in northern Morocco, it was confronted with the task of pacifying the local tribesmen. In 1921, under the leadership of Abd el Krim, who had declared an independent Republic of the Rif, they massacred an army corps at Annual. The photograph shows Spanish troops defending the capital Tetuan against a rebel attack. In 1926 Abd El Krim was finally defeated. Franco made his name in the 'dirty war' of Morocco.

Finally the army staged a comeback. Always as much a bureaucratic machine as a fighting force, the promotion of officers fighting in Spain's Moroccan protectorate led the bureaucrats at home to set up Committees of Defence (*Juntas de Defensa*) to press for strict promotion by seniority, and better pay. Disguised as an essay in national regeneration by patriotic officers, these military trade unions became, in the words of a Liberal politician, 'a state within the state', blackmailing and bringing down governments as they veered between concession and repression.

The regime survived the crisis of 1917 because the protesters were divided. This concealed the fact that it was no longer capable of providing efficient, strong government, evident in a 'crisis of governability' which was the consequence of the fragmentation of parties that had proved fatal throughout the history of liberalism. The machinery which provided safe majorities for the two alternating parties was wearing out in the big towns like Barcelona and Valencia. In 1910 both a Liberal and a Conservative government saw their majority vanish in internal quarrels, and in 1919 Maura's minister of the interior failed to fabricate a majority. The formation of stable governments, whether of single parties, coalitions, or of 'national' governments, became increasingly difficult. Between 1902 and 1923 there were a record thirty-four governments, making any consistent effort of reform an impossibility. After 1898, for example, there had been repeated efforts to reform the army; yet between 1898 and 1909 this was the responsibility of twenty different ministers. The military press began to dismiss parliament as a talking-shop devoted to 'trivial matters', incapable of solving the problems either of the army or the country.

The constitution placed the formation of ministries from a fragmenting party system in the hands of the king, Alfonso XIII, who came of age in 1906. Brought up isolated from public opinion in what Harold Nicolson called the most hieratic court in Europe, he was surrounded by the flattery of his courtiers and the company of his aides-de-camp. Alfonso's exasperation at the difficulties of finding a strong ministry mutated into a conviction that the constitutional system was worn out. In a speech in 1921, to the dismay of his ministers, he declared that, within or without the constitution, 'he must impose his will and sacrifice himself for the *patria*'. He cast himself in the role of a one-man regenerator. Years later, his son called this speech 'little less than the beginning of a dictatorship'.

It was a disaster in Morocco, where Spain had been granted the protectorate over a barren strip inhabited by restive tribes, that led to the establishment of a dictatorship. In 1921 thousands of Spanish soldiers were brutally massacred by tribesmen in a retreat from the advanced post

of Annual, a tragedy that gripped public opinion as rumours of ineffi-
ciency and corruption among the officer corps filtered through a censored press. The left in the Cortes raised a demand for a parliamentary
inquiry and judgement of those responsible for the disaster, both the generals and politicians and the king himself. To avoid this humiliation, General Primo de Rivera (1870–1930), staged a *pronunciamiento* in Barcelona
in September 1923 and the king accepted him as a military dictator. It was
to be a fatal blunder. The king had broken his coronation oath to the constitution which legitimized the monarchy.

The abrupt demise of the liberal constitutional regime can be seen as a
European phenomenon. Insecure, faction-ridden democracies collapsed
into authoritarianism and dictatorship all over central and eastern
Europe, between 1923 and 1926, as what in Spain were called 'the comfortable classes' formed private armies to save society from Bolshevism.
The army, once the defender of the liberal state against Carlist reactionaries, now saw itself as the defender of a conservative social order.

VI

If liberalism as a political option based on truly representative, democratic
parties failed to materialize, it can be argued that the Progressives' dream
of a modern capitalist society was taking shape. Modernization was
reflected in the pattern of population growth. Spain's population had
grown from 11 million in the 1830s to 23.5 million by the 1920s, marked
by high fertility rates and a death rate persistently above European levels.
By the twentieth century it began to approximate to European patterns, as
the death rate began to fall. If the modest growth of the economy still left
Spain far behind the economies of the north and outdistanced by Italy, it
was sufficient, particularly after 1910, to modernize the structure of Spanish industry. Steam engines, and later electricity, powered modern flour-
mills, olive-presses, and engineering concerns. Beside the old artisan
establishments came large modern enterprises. The iron conglomerate,
the Altos Hornos de Vizcaya in Bilbao, employed 6,000 workers. The last
of the periodic famines, the *crises de subsistence* of the Old Regime, with the
consequent outbreaks of cholera, came in the 1880s.

Between 1875 and 1887 Barcelona was gripped by 'the Fever of Gold'.
The great industrial magnates survived the subsequent crash: plutocrats
like the López and Güell dynasties were active in textiles, flour-mills,
railroads, Portland cement, banking, gas, and shipping. In the Basque
Provinces the metallurgical concerns and shipyards, financed by the

Neutrality in the war of 1914–1918 allowed Spain's industrialists and ship owners to make large fortunes by supplying the belligerent powers. Hispano-Suiza, with factories in Valladolid and Barcelona, supplied airplane engines. The wartime prosperity collapsed in 1920. Hispano-Suiza continued to manufacture the luxury touring cars that were popular with the European rich. Only in the 1970s did Spain become a major exporter of cars to a mass market, the first success story of Spain's modern industrialization.

profits of iron exports to Britain, expanded after the 1870s. With Basque banks this created the most powerful industrial oligarchy, of a dozen families, in Spain. With heavy industry concentrated around Bilbao, Catalonia, its industries increasingly to be freed from dependence on expensive coal by electricity, began a process of diversification into chemicals and metallurgy. By the 1920s Barcelona was producing railway goods, marine turbines, and the finest luxury car in Europe, the Hispano-Suiza. Spain's neutrality in the war of 1914–18 brought large profits from exports to the belligerents, and further diversified Catalan industry. The Hispano-Suiza factories supplied the French air force with its engines; the wool industry of Terrasa and Sabadell the army with its greatcoats. The citrus fruits of the Levant flourished as an export crop. But prosperity did not reach the subsistence farmers of Galicia and Castile or the landless labourers of Andalusia, whose only escape from grinding poverty, as in Eastern Europe and Ireland, was emigration to the New World or to the growing industries of the Basque country and Catalonia. The absorption of this 'foreign' immigrant population was long to remain a problem for Basque and Catalonian nationalists. Emigration of the agrarian poor to the industries of the cities was, like labour militancy, part of a process of modernization. Bilbao doubled its population between the 1860s and 1920. By absorbing its surrounding smaller municipalities, greater Barcelona contained a million inhabitants by the 1920s. Already in the 1850s towns were demolishing their ancient walls, which restricted growth. New broad streets cut through Barcelona and Madrid; tramlines connected the old city centres to the new, insalubrious and disease-ridden working-class suburbs, breaking down the social promiscuity of the old city centres. Urbanization spread to the provinces. The growing prosperity of the fishing port of Vigo in Galicia was reflected in splendid assembly rooms (1866), a gymnasium (1861), and a theatre (1881), where Pablo Iglesias lectured and the most famous actors and actresses performed.

The Universal Exhibition of 1888 established Barcelona as a European city. Catalanism was inward looking in that it idealized the family farm as the depository of traditional Catholic values, but Catalans also prided themselves on being open to Europe's cultural influences. Barcelona's opera-house was among the first in Europe to stage Wagner; the city became a showplace of modernist and art nouveau architecture. Its genius Antoni Gaudí, an austere Catholic, built the palaces of the new rich. Lluis Domènech i Montaner, a political leader of Catalanism, combined in his Palace of Music (1905–8) Catalan motifs and the most daring use of iron and glass. It was in this cosmopolitan atmosphere that Pablo Picasso and Joan Miró absorbed the influence of France; the Dalmau Gallery in 1912 staged the first exhibition of Cubist art outside of Paris. The revival of local crafts in Catalonia was inspired by William Morris.

Madrid could not match the cultural vitality of Barcelona and its avantgarde architecture. The painter Dario de Regoyes, friend of James Ensor and Camille Pissarro, was scorned by the academic establishment in Madrid but welcomed in Barcelona. The great banks and new public buildings of Madrid were impressive in their sheer size and decorative exuberance, but essentially conservative. But Madrid was becoming a financial capital, as the Basque banks moved there. Renowned for its poor lodging-houses and crowded streets, Madrid began to take on the appearance of a modern European city. Alfonso XIII opened the Ritz Hotel there in 1910, and the Metro in 1919. An expanding service sector threw up a new professional class, which doubled in the 1920s. For the first time women found an alternative to domestic service in department stores and telephone exchanges. Urban renewal and expansion was accompanied by a cultural revival, as modernist writers in avant-garde magazines experimented with symbolism, imagism, and surrealism. The modernists were resolute elitists. José Ortega y Gasset, an early admirer of Proust, argued that the socially divisive art of the modernist elite should be the basis of a hierarchical society. 'The time is coming when, from politics to art, society will again be organized as it must be, into two orders: that of the men of excellence and that of the ordinary man.' The needs of 'the ordinary man' were met by the new mass entertainments: the cinema and football. This elitism reflected the scant diffusion of a liberal and democratic culture, inevitable in a country where an illiterate public lacked the popular press which had politicized the electorate of Britain and France. Madrid had thirty daily newspapers, the most important of which could hope for a circulation of only 80,000, whereas in France and Italy the major newspapers could reach a circulation of over 500,000.

In spite of modest advances towards modernization, contemporaries brooded on the gap between Spain and the advanced economies of northern Europe. The traditional explanation for this lag has been that a static agricultural sector, dominated by cereals, was incapable of creating a demand for industrial goods. Recently the balance of some of the blame has shifted to the lacklustre performance of the non-competitive native industry, and to mistaken economic policies designed to protect, on the one hand, the livelihood of subsistence farmers, and on the other, the established textile and metallurgical industries. Both interests possessed political clout. It was not that Spain, after the 1890s, in an age of protectionism had the highest tariff barriers in Europe. It was that they protected the wrong objects. In particular, by granting high protection to cereal producers tariffs not only kept in being a stagnant sector of the economy that could not provide a market for industrial goods, but also forced up food prices for industrialists. In return, the industrial interests demanded protection in the domestic market, thus avoiding any necessity to modernize in order to produce competitively for export.

The essential problem of liberalism, from the 1830s till its political demise in 1923, was the poverty of the interventionist state. It was not merely that this poverty reflected an economy struggling with considerable geographic, climatic, and cultural difficulties. Tax revenue did not cover expenditure and, after the Carlist wars, the state resorted to loans, on unfavourable terms. The servicing of this debt was an intolerable burden on the budget. Moreover, the state inherited a taxation system from the Moderates of the 1840s which was not merely designed to protect the interests of the dominant oligarchy and thus penalized the less fortunate, but which proved to be inflexible and incapable of mobilizing what wealth there was. Once the debt repayments and fixed expenditure on the army and bureaucracy had been met, there was little left for the infra-structural reforms for which the regenerationists clamoured, or for the in-vestment in a modern educational system seen by all reformers as the essential foundation of a modern society. Liberals like Canalejas and con-servatives like Dato were genuine, well-informed social reformers. But they were deprived of the means to finance even an adequate factory in-spectorate, much less to provide the 'New Liberalism' of Lloyd George. Even more important, there was no money to satisfy the professional de-mands of the army. Repeated economies fostered the grievances which were expressed in the military press.

VII

It was not surprising that the Catalan bourgeoisie and the Andalusian landlords, faced with the imagined threat of a Bolshevik revolution, gave Primo de Rivera's coup in 1923 a warm welcome as a relief from strikes. The independent liberals of *El Sol* had long argued that the 'old politics' condemned Spain to marginalization in Europe. Since 1898 intellectuals had become a force in Spanish society, but so deep was their distaste for the old politics that they were ready to give a Spanish soldier-politician, nineteenth-century style, the benefit of the doubt as a potential regen-erator. It was only later that Alfonso XIII reaped the penalty of his sup-port for Primo de Rivera. Apart from the ousted 'old politicians', most Spaniards regarded his 'perjury' as giving Spanish political life a long needed shake-up. Primo de Rivera saw himself as Costa's 'iron Surgeon', called to clear out corrupt and ineffective parliamentary politicians who represented only themselves, and to hand the country over to true pat-riots. A *bon viveur* and amateur politician, his intuitions would tell him what needed to be done; soldiers in politics tend to believe that complex problems can be solved by decrees, of which Primo issued an abundance.

It was as a politician that Primo failed. He could not create an alter-native to the constitutional monarchy he had destroyed. 'We are going to prepare Spain for a government by those who have never governed before.' But his attempt to create, in the National Political Union, a move-ment of patriots to replace party politicians attracted only a few right-wing enthusiasts and a collection of opportunists. Unlike Franco, he never saw himself as a permanent fixture; after a short, sharp dose of military discipline, he would return to 'normality'. But normality eluded him. In 1925 he summoned a National Assembly to forge a new, corporate constitution. Its debates only revealed the erosion of his support.

Primo had his successes, and his frequent speech-making tours, reported in a censored press, led him to think that he ruled a grateful country. The Moroccan tribes of the Protectorate were at last subdued. Part of his one-man regenerationism was an ambitious programme of state-financed public works, particularly dams, irrigation, and roads—he was much praised by the Automobile Association for bringing Spain into the motor-car age. These public works would provide the infrastructure for an industrial take-off. His ideal, inherited by Franco, was autarky, an enclosed, self-sufficient national economy where protection would force import substitution, weaning surgeons from buying foreign scalpels and Spaniards from drinking champagne. His combination of state intervention, covering all aspects of the economy from rabbit skins to petrol refineries, was dismissed by the Valencian economist Perpiña Grau as

After his coup of September 1923, which abolished the constitution of 1875 and put the old political class out to grass, Primo de Rivera ruled Spain advised by a military directorate of his fellow generals, illustrated here. The provinces were administered by subordinate officers. Government by military amateurs was abandoned in 1925 for that of civilian 'technocrats' who embarked on an ambitious programme of public works, cut short by the onset of the depression in 1929.

'suicidal'. Nevertheless, productivity and per-capita income rose sharply, probably a reflection of the European post-war recovery rather than the result of imposed autarky. For the first time in Spain's history the proportion of the population engaged in agriculture fell to under half, from 57 per cent to 45 per cent. The beginnings of an industrial revolution were reflected in the beginnings of a consumer society. The 18,000 cars of 1923 became 37,000 by 1929, the 63,000 telephones, 212,400. In his labour legislation, which created mixed committees to settle labour conflicts, Primo secured the co-operation of the UGT, happy to see its rival the CNT repressed. Largo Caballero, leader of the UGT, became a councillor of state.

Primo would never hope for the support of the 'old politicians' whom he had insulted and injured, and for whom the constitution of 1876 was still the sacred codex which had kept them in power. In 1928, with the help of the discontented officers, the Conservative leader Sánchez Guerra staged a feeble *pronunciamiento*. The Catalan bourgeoisie deserted him when he persecuted Catalanism only to encourage the renewed defence of Catalan culture and identity. Moreover, the saviour of society showed signs of becoming a dangerous social reformer. When his public works programme ran into financial difficulties, plans to reform the tax system were overwhelmed in what his finance minister called an 'avalanche of gold'. Primo had failed to retain the support of the PSOE which, under the influence of Indalecio Prieto, had rejected the UGT's collaborationism. Above all, the opposition of the politicians, former targets of the criticism of intellectuals, now secured their support. In an age of cultural revival the intellectual establishment became the dictator's bitterest critic. The exiled Unamuno became the symbol of the revolt of the intellectuals. The Valencian popular novelist Blasco Ibáñez published a violent, personal attack on Alfonso XIII. Students rioted in the streets and smashed busts of the king. Finally, an attempt by Primo to reform the army by abolishing strict seniority alienated the generals. They advised the king to dismiss him. In a last-minute attempt to recover the political ground lost by his recognition of Primo in 1923, Alfonso accepted their advice. Yet again the army was a prime mover of political change. But by then, not only Primo was expendable. The perjured king was also doomed, and with him the constitutional monarchy he represented. A popular explosion greeted the establishment of the Second Republic in April 1931. It was to bring Spain into the age of mass politics.

9 Spain from 1931 to the Present

SEBASTIAN BALFOUR

The Second Republic

HE proclamation of the Second Republic on 14 April 1931 was greeted with jubilation in the streets and squares of Spain. The new regime ushered in the first genuine democracy in Spain. In a country hitherto ruled by an oligarchy of notables, a privileged and largely intolerant clergy and an oppressive military establishment, the Republic promised modernity and social justice. Its supporters had high expectations. For the landless labourers of the South, it augured much-needed agrarian reform that would redistribute land and raise their pitiful living standards. For industrial and service workers, it promised better wages, union rights, and more bargaining power. For many others, the Republic meant sweeping social and cultural reform: it would extend rights to minorities, recognize the claims for autonomy of historic regions, educate and empower ordinary people. For its sympathizers in general, the coming of the Republic heralded a historic shift in power and wealth from a small minority to the vast majority of society. For radical sections of the left, it meant the first stage of a social revolution. The new government was thus entrusted with a huge burden of expectations.

On the other hand, the Second Republic was greeted with trepidation and angst in more private places, such as the officers' mess, the boardrooms, and the churches. Traditional sections of society viewed the Republic not just as a threat to their own interests but as a menace to the very identity of Spain. The Catholic church feared that the laicizing reforms they expected from the Republic would destroy the influence they exerted over society and open the gates to the old enemy: freethinkers, Protestants, and atheists. Landowners and industrialists shuddered at the prospect both of a rise in the cost of labour and of legislation imposing union and bargaining rights. Conservative military officers saw regional autonomy as the beginning of the break-up of Spain's territorial integrity

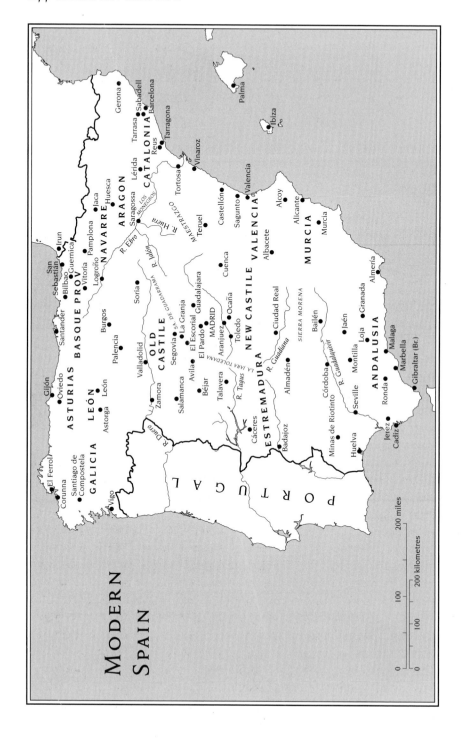

MODERN SPAIN

that it was their self-imposed duty to maintain; they were also concerned at the possible restructuring of an army bloated by officers that would lead to mass redundancies. For many of these conservative strata of society, democracy was not only against their interests, it was anti-Spain. Only on their fringes, however, were there plans at such an early moment to overthrow the Republic by military force.

Reform from above. The provisional government of the new Republic gathered together representatives of the broad consensus of political opinion that had overseen the end of the monarchy and the Restoration state. They ranged from socialists to left republicans, such as the liberal intellectual Manuel Azaña, and to conservative, Catholic republicans, such as the first premier, Niceto Alcalá Zamora. The two overriding objectives they set themselves were to transform a corrupt and unrepresentative political system into a pluralist democracy and to carry out from above a programme of reforms to modernize Spanish society. The first raft of legislation passed by the government focused on labour relations and aimed at improving immediately the appalling conditions of rural and industrial workers. These measures were received by the landowners in particular as a challenge to their power and wealth. As minister of war, Azaña set out to bring the armed forces under the Republic's control and turn them into a modern and purely professional institution. His reforms, generous though they were to officers agreeing to retire, enraged others, many of whom felt poorly recompensed for their arduous service in the Moroccan war.

The Republic's aims were clearly stated in the new constitution of December 1931, drafted when Azaña succeeded Alcalá Zamora as prime minister. It abolished the unrepresentative Senate and established a unicameral parliament. The electoral laws were reformed to ensure the practice of democracy and women were given the right to vote and stand for parliament. A range of civil liberties was promulgated, including a progressive divorce law, and the right to landed private property was made dependent on public good. Like its social legislation, the more controversial articles of the new constitution also hit at the established order. They separated church and state, limited the church's wealth, and withdrew its control over education. At a stroke, therefore, the church was transformed from one of the official expressions of Spain's identity into a mere voluntary association. 'Spain', Azaña declared incautiously, 'is no longer Catholic.' The government's dissolution of the Jesuit order, justified by the latter's sole allegiance to the Vatican, was part of a determined effort to make all of Spain's institutions accountable to the state, ensuring thereby that the government had the necessary tools to modernize society. These laicizing measures, however, infuriated the church hierarchy and further alienated it from the new state.

Obstacles to reform. The most immediate problem facing the new Republic was that it had to operate in the context of a worldwide recession. It was indeed this economic depression that had helped to create the Republic, but it also made it difficult to carry through social and labour reforms without a redistribution of wealth to which the elites in Spain were fiercely opposed. Beholden to orthodox financial policies, Azaña's government was unwilling to transform the meagre tax system (the highest rate of which was 4 per cent), which had remained essentially unchanged since the days of the nineteenth-century *Moderados*. The search to finance reforms was made even more difficult by the budget deficit inherited from the Primo de Rivera dictatorship. The drought of the winter of 1930–1, which had badly affected the harvest and increased the hardship of the poor in the rural south, had made this redistribution an even more urgent task. Yet the Law of Agrarian Reform, intended to remedy the crisis in the countryside, was a half-hearted and underfinanced measure.

A deeper underlying problem was that the Spanish state had a weak hold on society. The process of modernization in Spain had been highly uneven, concentrated mainly in the north, north-east, and the Levant, with the result that in the more backward areas the traditional elites still exercised considerable power. The new Republican state had to mediate between a wide range of contradictory social and political forces, none of which held the balance of power in the Cortes. In several senses, therefore, the crisis in Spain was a regional variant of a crisis that had rocked most of Europe since the First World War in which three opposing projects for the reconstruction of the post-war state—liberal democracy, fascism, and revolutionary socialism—had vied for hegemony.

The Republic's social base was especially fragmented. The professional middle classes were relatively small in number and they and the landless labourers, industrial workers, and, potentially at least, the rural tenants and small proprietors represented a range of different and sometimes conflicting interests. All these social groups had to be drawn together and mobilized by the Republic if it was to challenge the powerful elites and their constituents and carry through its programme of reform. But the Republic found itself almost immediately at odds with sections of its own supporters.

One of the major problems in this respect was law and order. The expectations awakened by the advent of the Republic, reflected by the rise in union membership from just over a quarter of a million at the end of 1930 to over 1 million a year and a half later, gave rise to a wave of strikes and land occupations. Impatient at the slow pace of reform and spurred on by the desperate conditions of rural labourers, the anarchists staged abortive uprisings. An insurrection in January 1932 in Catalonia brought libertarian communism to the Llobregat valley for four days. Having neglected to reform the forces of law and order, the Republic found itself responsible for the bloody suppression of these uprisings by a Civil Guard used to shooting down protestors. A year later, the massacre by the Civil Guard of twenty-one labourers and members of their families in a village near Cadiz would help to bring down the Azaña government.

Divisions within the Republic. The political groups supporting the Republic were also divided. They ranged from conservative republicans who wished to modernize Spanish capitalist society, to anarchists who sought to overthrow it. At the centre of this spectrum stood small parties representing centre and left republicans (amongst whom were Catalan republicans seeking autonomy), whose social base was mainly middle class. Further to the left lay the Socialist party—the largest party in parliament and the only nationwide organization in Spain—as well as the still tiny Communist party, and anti-Stalinist communists. The first fissure in the coalition government of republicans and socialists was provoked by the reform of the church. It led to the resignation of the two more conservative members of the government, the premier himself, Alcalá Zamora (who agreed to become president shortly after), and the minister of the interior, Miguel Maura.

There were also sharp divisions amongst the left and even within the Socialist party itself about strategy. The anarchists regarded the bourgeois state as the oppressor of the working class and the Cortes as a mere 'brothel'. Agendas among the socialists ranged from reform to revolution. These discrepancies were often articulated in an atmosphere of tension and rhetorical excess. The relative absence of a culture of consensus and dialogue among parties supporting the Republic was partly the result of the lack of experience of parliamentary democracy, after decades of clientelist politics and almost eight years of dictatorship. It also derived from the intensity of the social and economic problems, which, in the south above all, required immediate solution.

The response of the right. These tensions were exacerbated by the response of the right to the new democracy. A minority, the so-called 'catastrophists', turned to conspiring to overthrow the Republic; in September 1932 General José Sanjurjo staged an abortive and slipshod coup. The bulk of the right, self-named the 'accidentalists', accepted the Republic in order to work within it to restore the privileged position of the church and prevent a shift in the balance of social and economic power (though amongst them a tiny Christian-Democratic wing supported the idea of social reform). A coalition of the right, the Spanish Confederation of Autonomous Right-Wing Groups, or CEDA, was formed in February 1933 under the leadership of a staunchly Catholic lawyer, José María Gil Robles. At the core of the new coalition was Acción Popular, a party formed a year previously and backed by the clergy and the landed oligarchy. Its base was a network of supporters built by the church and the landholders amongst the peasantry in small provincial towns throughout the more economically backward areas of Spain. Making little secret of its desire for an authoritarian and corporatist solution to the crisis in Spain, the new coalition set out to create a mass party and win the elections in defence of the 'persecuted church'.

The right was also able to exert extreme economic pressure on Azaña's government. The industrial and financial bourgeoisie, the bulk of whom supported the right, reacted to the Republic's social legislation by exporting capital abroad, causing the value of the peseta to fall on the world markets. The rural supporters of the right, believing that the agrarian reform of the Republic threatened their property, organized to resist legislation whose purpose was both to improve the wages and conditions of labourers and reduce unemployment.

The evasion of social reforms and the CEDA's blocking of legislation by filibustering in parliament widened the divisions among the Republic's supporters. They also deepened the distrust of parliamentary democracy amongst the left. In the summer of 1933 the leader of the Socialist Union and minister of labour, Francisco Largo Caballero, disillusioned with the experience of co-operation with bourgeois reformists, withdrew his support from the government. Keen to maintain the backing of his more radical rank and file, he declared: 'Today, I am convinced that to accomplish socialist aims in a bourgeois democracy is impossible.' The growing polarization in the country led the president, Alcalá Zamora, to withdraw his support from the Azaña coalition of socialists and republicans, thereby bringing to an end almost two and a half years of reformist attempts to modernize Spain. For all its failures, the first government of the Republic had carried out a range of modernizing reforms. A new, more democratic constitution was in place, education had been wrested from the church, new schools had been built, and the Catalans had been awarded a statute of autonomy.

The government of the right. Riven by contradictions, the socialists and republicans failed to campaign on a joint ticket in the elections of November 1933. Because of the workings of the electoral law, the socialists in particular, lost an inordinate number of seats. The CEDA became the largest party in the new parliament and gave its backing to a minority government of the right-wing Radical Republicans, on which it exercised heavy pressure. Accordingly, the new government began to repeal the progressive legislation of the reformist regime of 1931–3.

In the autumn of 1934 the CEDA entered the government, placing three representatives in the crucial ministries of Justice, Agriculture, and Labour. The announcement sparked off an insurrectionary general strike planned and backed by all the organizations of the left against what they perceived as the coming of fascism in Spain. The action was poorly organized in most of the country except in the Basque Country and most notably in Asturias, where the miners, the most militant group of the Spanish labour movement, joined with all sections of the left to form a united front, the Workers' Alliance. For two weeks workers fought an army stiffened by the Spanish Foreign Legion and Moroccan mercenaries. In Catalonia, at the same time, Catalan republican nationalists had taken advantage of the general strike briefly to set up an autonomous government. The crushing of the revolt and the brutal reprisals against the Asturian workers rebounded against the government.

The defeat of the October revolution, as it came to be called on the left, led to the wholesale imprisonment of labour leaders and the decapitation of the left organizations. Even the ex-premier Manuel Azaña was put on trial and jailed for over a month, despite the fact that he had not taken part in the uprising. CEDA representatives entered the government and began to pressurize their Radical colleagues for a further erosion of Republican legislation. Gil Robles joined a new cabinet in May 1935 as minister of war and proceded to purge the army of officers sympathetic to the Republic, while he placed prospective military conspirators, such as General Francisco Franco, into key positions. It is clear from both its press and its speeches that the CEDA was seeking to impose an authoritarian government in Spain by gaining a majority in the Cortes.

The Popular Front. The Radical-CEDA coalition, however, began to wobble towards the end of 1935 as the Radicals were undermined by corruption scandals. Anxious to protect the Republic from any further encroachment by the CEDA, Alcalá Zamora decided to call for fresh elections. The old electoral alliance of socialists and reformist republicans was painstakingly rebuilt, after protracted negotiations led by Manuel Azaña and the moderate socialist leader and ex-minister of the Republic, Indalecio Prieto. Out of these talks emerged the Popular Front, an exclusively electoral pact signed in January 1936 by almost all the organizations of the left except the anarchist labour confederation, the CNT. The CNT's members, on the other hand, now voted *en masse* for the Popular Front in order to secure the release of militants who had been jailed after the October 1934 uprising.

The heady rhetoric of the electoral campaign at the beginning of 1936 encouraged the sense that Spain was divided into two antagonistic blocs. Largo Caballero declared that if the right won, 'we must of necessity move to civil war'. Gil Robles's propaganda was unequivocally divisive: 'For God and Country; to conquer or to die.' In the February elections the Popular Front emerged as outright victors, although the number of votes it received was only slightly more than that of the right, whose support had grown. The map of electoral results drew a familiar picture. The strongholds of the left were in the cities, in the industrial areas of Spain, and in the south and south-west where agrarian unemployment and the demand for a break-up of the great latifundia were at their most acute. The Popular Front also gained majorities in many areas of Galicia, where the poorest peasants were concentrated, and in Catalonia and the Basque Country, where the urban and industrial vote was strengthened by the Popular Front's support for regional autonomy.

The right, on the other hand, was overwhelmingly backed in the central regions of Spain, in that great swathe of wheat-producing areas dotted with towns, where the landowners, smallholders, townsfolk, and priests alike shared a common fear and hatred of the left as harbingers of Bolshevism. The right was by now politically divided. The electoral results discredited the CEDA strategy of gaining a parliamentary majority in order to reverse the reforms of the first government of the Republic. The victory of the Popular Front also strengthened the demand for a military coup to overthrow democracy and impose an authoritarian state. The CEDA found itself outflanked on the right by two new political formations influenced by European fascism. The most important of these was National Block, led by the authoritarian right-wing monarchist José

Calvo Sotelo, for whom democracy was 'the supreme inanity'. Calvo openly appealed to the army to overthrow the Republic in order to install a Catholic, authoritarian regime. A smaller but even more vociferous party on the right, the fascist Falange, had been created in 1933 by the dictator's son, José Antonio Primo de Rivera. Much given to fascist lyricism, the Falange declaimed 'our place is in the open air watching our weapons with the stars shining above us'. Faced by this competition, the youth organization of the CEDA adopted many of the trappings of fascism—mass rallies, salutes, flags, and the celebration of the *Führerprinzip* around the figure of Gil Robles. The CEDA leader's electoral strategy faced bankruptcy as his supporters increasingly moved towards military solutions. The strategy of an uprising against the Republic was also backed by the oldest of the right-wing formations in Spain, the Traditionalists or Carlists, who had risen on countless occasions in the past against a liberal monarchy and the Republic of 1873, in a fruitless attempt to impose a discarded and authoritarian dynasty. They and the monarchists had already approached Mussolini to gain Italian support for an uprising.

The new government, led once again by Azaña, was made up solely of the centre and left republicans, because the radical wing of the socialists led by Largo Caballero was no longer willing to collaborate in a 'bourgeois' government. Largo's increasingly revolutionary rhetoric caused an open breach with the Prieto wing of the socialists. Azaña was deeply concerned to keep the process of reform off the streets and in parliament. The most acute problem was, as before, in the southern countryside, where unemployment had worsened. The government's reforms were outdistanced by the action of landless labourers under the direction of the socialist landworkers' federation, which proceeded to occupy over half a million hectares of land. A wave of strikes broke out in the industrial areas to restore the wage levels and conditions lost after the October revolution. The strike activity was marked by a more radical, if not revolutionary determination because of the relative failure of the first reformist government of 1931–3.

More than the strikes and the unrest in the countryside, the climate of crisis that began to invade Spain was the result of attempts by the right to destabilize the Republic through civil disorder. Clashes in the streets of the cities between right and left multiplied in the spring of 1936 amidst an escalating rhetoric of mutual recrimination. The long-fostered preparations by the military to stage a coup were sharpened. The government, aware of these plans, moved generals they suspected were plotters to distant outposts. Franco, who had not yet decided whether to join the

A photograph by the American Robert Capa showing Republican militiamen and Assault Guards setting out in August 1936 to defend Madrid. It captures the brimming self-confidence of the defenders of the Republic in the early days of the Civil War that they could repel the right-wing uprising by popular mobilization.

conspiracy, was posted to the most remote command, the Canaries. Among the conspirators, his continuing hesitation earned him the nickname of 'Miss Canary Islands'. The assassination of Calvo Sotelo on 13 July provided a convenient detonator for the coup. On 17 July, in the mistaken belief that the Republic could easily be overthrown, the Spanish Army of Africa rose in Morocco and was followed the next day by garrisons throughout Spain. The failure of the military coup led to a protracted and bloody civil war.

The Civil War

The areas that fell to the insurgents largely replicated the voting pattern of the 1936 elections. The centre and north-west and parts of the south of Spain were taken over by the rebels after heavy fighting in some of the cities, where workers put up fierce resistance with few arms. The Republic held most of the northern coast (although it was cut off from the rest of the Republican-controlled areas) and all of the east and centre-east (including the capital, Madrid) and part of the southern coast. The Republic survived the attempted coup above all because of the spontaneous resistance by workers armed with improvised weapons. More cities could have been saved had the government and their local representatives been prepared to arm the civilian supporters of the Republic. Their reluctance to do so indicated that their fear of revolution was as great, if not greater, than their apprehension of counter-revolution.

The map of civil war loyalties, however, did not necessarily correspond to the allegiances of individuals or social groups. In those cities that fell to the rebels through military action or deceit, huge numbers of Republican supporters found themselves on the wrong side. But there were also many individuals who were torn between the two sides or who had no strong feelings towards one or the other, and whose allegiance was determined by where they found themselves on the outbreak of the war. When families were split in this way, fratricidal war was waged literally. The poet Antonio Machado was in Madrid at the outbreak of the Civil War, and, as a staunch supporter of the Republican cause, signed a declaration, along with other intellectuals, in support of the government and the people, 'who, with exemplary heroism, are fighting for their liberties'. His brother and fellow poet Manuel Machado was in Burgos when the city fell to the insurgents on the day of the uprising. He joined the team of intellectuals, led by Franco's brother-in-law Ramón Serrano Suñer, who were employed throughout the Civil War in creating propaganda for the insurgent cause. Several of his poems were dedicated to the leaders of the revolt against the Republic.

The issues of war. On each side, the war was fought over different but interrelated issues. Within the insurgent side a wide range of political agendas coexisted, from the defence of the traditional order to fascist 'modernity'. In the absence of commonly defined objectives as to the shape of the regime that would replace the Republic, the rebels united around a few basic principles: the restoration of the role of the Catholic church, the defence of territorial integrity against the supposedly separatist ambitions of Catalans and Basques, the imposition of order over 'chaos', the return to the hegemony of the elites and the destruction of democracy, which, in the words of one prelate, was 'godless'. The unifying force among the insurgents was Catholicism. The defence of the faith was a duty to God and to Spain. According to the Bishop of Salamanca in his pastoral address of 30 September entitled 'The Two Cities', the conflict was part of a global struggle. 'On the soil of Spain a bloody conflict is being waged between two conceptions of life, two forces preparing for universal conflict in every country of the earth... Communists and Anarchists are sons of Cain, fratricides, assassins of those who cultivate virtue.' The war, he went on, 'takes the external form of a civil war, but in reality it is a Crusade'. Religion and nationalism became intertwined, seen as the defence of religion against the Antichrist, the defence of the true Spain against the anti-Spain of liberals and communists, behind whom lay a conspiracy of the historic enemies: Marxists, Jews, and freemasons.

The Republican side was fighting for objectives that were not always compatible with each other: for the defence of liberal democracy and modernity; for pluralism; for the redistribution of land and an immediate improvement in the living standards of workers, peasants, and rural labourers; for the recognition of the language and culture of the historic regions and the award to them of self-government; for social revolution; and, on an international level, for the defence of democracy against the spread of fascism. To add to these potential divisions, the polarization that had taken place during the Republic among its supporters, fuelled by its relative failure to overcome the obstruction of the right, had given rise to a false dichotomy between war and revolution. The anarchist leader, Federica Montseny, exclaimed: 'We have died for the democrats too often.'

The proponents of the primacy of revolution over war, the anarchists, the dissident communists, and some of the left socialists, could point to the wholehearted response to the coup of thousands of workers and labourers. In the 'spontaneous revolution' of the summer of 1936, militias sprang up and halted the advancing rebels, workers took over factories, shops, and transport, and rural labourers seized the landed estates of the gentry and divided them up into collectives. Without this revolution, according to the CNT, the war could not be won. In the first exuberant moments of the aftermath of the coup in many of those areas where the insurgents were defeated, it seemed that the power of the people was unstoppable. Such was the confidence inspired by this revolutionary atmosphere that discipline and organization at the various fronts grew lax. A moderate socialist leader claimed that, despite the 'vehement passion' with which workers were fighting the war, they also maintained 'trade union conditions over rates and hours'.

For those such as republicans, reformist socialists, and communists, victory could only be achieved by constructing a strong central government and by harnessing the revolutionary energies released by the attempted coup to the task of forging a centralized popular army to confront the professional army of the enemy. But more was at stake, they believed. The Republic had a broader base than workers and landless labourers. Maintaining or gaining the support of the middle classes and small proprietors, among others, required the moderation of social demands. Beyond the frontier the potential allies of the Republic, France and Britain, needed to be reassured that it was under the control of liberal democracy so that the government could count on their support.

The European Powers. International support became an immediate priority for the rebels also. The key to their success was the Moroccan-based Army of Africa, battle-hardened Spanish soldiers and Moroccan mercenaries, which had crushed the October revolution of 1934. But the army could not be shipped across the Straits of Gibraltar because most of the Spanish navy had supported the Republic, either because their officers were loyal or because the pro-Republican ratings mutinied. Conscious that they could not win without external aid, the Nationalists sought the help of Mussolini and Hitler. The Italian dictator instinctively identified with the insurgents' cause, but before giving them military aid he was careful to consider the potential reactions of the French and British governments. Correctly surmising that both were unenthusiastic towards the Republic, if not actually hostile, as in the British case, he provided bombers to airlift the Army of Africa to the mainland of Spain and then began a further and massive programme of military aid to the rebels, including a total of 100,000 regular Italian troops.

Hitler also calculated that the risk of alarming the Allies was smaller than the advantage that could be gained from winning an ally in the strategically crucial area of the eastern Mediterranean, on Gibraltar's doorstep. He and his generals also welcomed the opportunity to test out new weapons and techniques of war. So German transport planes were also sent to Morocco to help in the airlift, followed by further aid in weapons and crack troops.

The British foreign policy of appeasement at the time was defined by a determination to avoid another European conflagration and by a hope that German expansionist ambitions could be diverted towards the Soviet Union. The Civil War was seen by the Conservative cabinet of Stanley Baldwin as a spark that might set off a wider war, so priority was given to attempting to confine the Spanish conflict to the peninsula. This meant turning a blind eye to the intervention of Germany and Italy. Among British conservatives there was little sympathy for the Republic, whose reforms were reputed to threaten extensive British commercial interests in Spain, if revolution did not wholly sweep them away.

The French Popular Front government joined the British in adopting a policy of non-intervention. Though sympathetic to the Republic, the premier Léon Blum was concerned to maintain the strategic support of the British in the face of threats to European peace. He was also keen to avoid exacerbating political tensions within France, where the Civil War was exciting opinion on the right and the left. The neutrality of the British and French governments and the diplomatic isolationism of the United States meant that the Spanish state was deprived of the right to buy arms from its fellow democracies. It was forced consequently to turn to the private arms market, where its purchasing agents found themselves in an unfamiliar world of crooks and sharks. The Soviet Union soon promised material support. However, Stalin was also concerned to maintain good relations with Britain and France because of the threat of war with Germany and was therefore opposed to the social revolution that seemed to be engulfing the Republican areas of Spain.

The efforts of British and French governments to contain the Spanish Civil War as a local conflict seemed to be rewarded when the European powers subscribed to a Non-Intervention Agreement in August 1936 and approved the creation of a London-based committee to monitor its implementation. However, neither Germany nor Italy respected the Agreement and both continued to pour military aid into the zones held by the Nationalists. Portugal, under the dictatorship of Salazar, also provided logistical support to the military insurgents. The failure of France and Britain to respond to this blatant violation of non-intervention led Stalin to change his mind, because a rapid Nationalist victory would strengthen fascism in Europe and further threaten the Soviet Union. So Soviet military aid, paid for later at inflated prices with much of Spain's gold reserves, began to arrive in the Republican-held areas in mid-October, just in time to stiffen the defence of Madrid against a violent offensive by the insurgents.

The atrocities of war. By then rebel units, including the Army of Africa, had begun to converge on the capital from the north and the south. They had been operating on several fronts, in Andalusia and Extremadura in the south, in the Basque Country and Asturias in the north, and on the Aragon front in the north-east. Indeed, the battlefront stretched across most of Spain. As they advanced, they had massacred thousands of captured Republican soldiers, government officials, and known Republican supporters, trade-unionists, and freemasons, men and women, following a deliberate policy of sowing terror to overcome resistance. The atrocities were particularly savage in the south, where class conflict had been severe. In Granada the working-class districts were shelled and right-wing squads were given a free hand to kill Republican sympathizers. The poet Federico García Lorca, a special object of their hatred for his homosexuality and his celebration of gypsy culture, was abducted and murdered.

Atrocities had also taken place behind Republican lines, mainly in the first few weeks after the uprising when public order briefly collapsed. Over 4,000 priests, more than 2,600 monks and nuns, and thirteen bishops were murdered; churches were looted or burnt down and the mummified bodies of nuns exposed to public gaze. The main target of popular wrath was the church, because it was an easily accessible symbol of a repressive order and because the ecclesiastical hierarchy had sided with the rebels. But there was a crucial difference between the atrocities committed by each side. Neither the Republican authorities nor the political parties on the left sanctioned reprisals. Indeed, they condemned such violence and soon restored democratic order in the Republican zone. The savage repression perpetrated on the Nationalist side, on the other hand, was an official, systematic, and calculated strategy of dissuasion aimed at eliminating the 'enemies' of Spain.

The battle for Madrid. As the two rebel armies approached Madrid, the Army of Africa commanded by Franco moved eastwards to capture the historic city of Toledo, where a small number of insurgents were besieged by Republican militiamen in the fortress, the Alcázar. The two-week delay of the assault on Madrid gave time for Republican forces to prepare for the defence of the capital. It was then that the first units of the international anti-fascist volunteers, the International Brigades, arrived under the auspices of the Comintern. The Civil War had become the stirring symbol for the left in Europe and elsewhere of the struggle to halt fascism. To the English poet Cecil Day Lewis, it was a 'battle between light and darkness'.

It has been suggested that Franco's decision to divert troops from Madrid in order to stage a strategically unimportant but spectacular victory in Toledo was part of his campaign to promote himself as undisputed leader of the Nationalists. A few days after the uprising, the rebel generals had set up a Junta in the city of Burgos and on 21 September chose Franco as commander-in-chief, after the nominal chief of the rising, José Sanjurjo, had been killed in an air accident. The relief of the Alcázar certainly became the most enduring symbol of the insurgent cause and the assertion of Franco's supremacy.

The advance of the rebel armies in the early autumn of 1936 and the popular power in the streets of Republican-controlled cities had forced significant changes to the make-up of the Republican government. A solely republican cabinet had given way on 5 September to one which better represented the balance of power on the Republican side, headed by the socialist union leader Largo Caballero and made up of left republicans, socialists, and communists. Two months later, when the rebel units had already entered the suburbs of Madrid, four members of the anarcho-syndicalist union, the CNT, joined the government, breaking with the CNT's traditional rejection of participation in bourgeois politics. After their initial chaotic efforts, the Republican defence forces had also been reorganized to meet the challenge of a well-armed and largely professional enemy. Loyal officers and units of the army and the myriad militias and committees that had sprung up in the first weeks of the war began to be merged into a single force, the Popular Army. Attached to the new units were political commissars, whose main duty would be to instil discipline in the troops.

The battle for Madrid was one of the most bitter of the Civil War. Stationed in the suburbs of the city, the rebel artillery fired constant salvoes into the centre while planes bombed the streets and buildings unmolested, killing many civilians. The vast majority of the Madrid population responded according to the city's old insurrectionary traditions, digging trenches, helping the wounded, and moving supplies, while the Madrid metalworkers refurbished used cartridges to renew the short supply of ammunition. It was the combination of popular support and the commitment of the troops that ensured the successful defence of the capital. All the fighting units of the Popular Army in Madrid, including the anarchists and the communists, played a role in its defence, and the morale of its citizens was raised by the presence of the International Brigades.

Civil war within the Civil War. Soviet aid indirectly helped to consolidate the growing power of the Spanish Communist Party on the Republican side, given the Republic's international isolation. The communists were also gaining support from middle-class backers of the Republic because of their insistence on law and order and their political moderation. Their reputation was boosted by their role in the defence of Madrid, after the government had decided to move to Valencia in the belief that the capital was about to fall.

The rise of the Communist party's influence brought the underlying tensions of the Republic to the surface. The Republican state was determined to bring order to the chaos in food supplies and labour relations caused by dual power on the streets and in the factories of Barcelona. Its pursuit of this objective led in May 1937 to a small-scale civil war in Barcelona, a social war between two opposing constituencies of the Republic. After several days of street-fighting, the anarchists decided to lay down their arms in favour of the war effort against the rebels.

The balance of power in the Republican camp now shifted decidedly to the proponents of the centralized state capable of mounting an effective war effort. The communists continued to persecute their internal enemies. The leader of the POUM, regarded by the communists as Trotskyite, Andreu Nin, was abducted by Soviet secret police, tortured, and killed. The Catalan autonomous government, the Generalitat, set up in 1931, was stripped of its control of public order and military affairs in Catalonia. The clash ended with the ousting of Largo Caballero as premier and the formation on 18 May of a new cabinet under the leadership of the reformist socialist, Juan Negrín.

The new premier's close association with the Communist party throughout the remainder of the Civil War has given rise to accusations that he was its stooge. In fact, although he disapproved of their sectarianism, Negrín had little option but to work closely with the communists because they shared a common strategy for the war effort. Moreover, the Communist party was the only well-organized and disciplined party on the Republican side. Negrín and his party, like that of the communists, were convinced that the Republic's affairs—war, law and order, the economy—had to be brought under the full control of a reconstructed and centralized state. They were all sure that the Republic had to be based on a broad class alliance to preserve the loyalty of the middle classes. Equally important, this agenda was the only one they thought could persuade Britain and France to come to their senses and help the Republic. The aid required was not only military but also economic, as the Republic began to face severe shortages in industrial inputs and essential

An international photomontage poster in support of the Republic showing a victim of the Guernica bombing. More than any other incident in the Civil War, the bombing of Guernica by the German Condor Legion aroused international anger. It was the first time in history that a city had been destroyed by aerial bombardment. The poster and the famous painting by Picasso did much to spread the news of the Nationalists' brutality, despite their attempts to deny the bombing.

supplies. Franco held the wheat-producing regions, so the Republic had to rely on 'Dr Negrín's resistance pills'—lentils—to feed its overcrowded cities filled with refugees. During the war, some 2,500 people died of malnutrition. In the rearguard, hunger led to demoralization.

The battle-front. On the war front, Republican forces were slowly being driven back. Nationalist troops, with the aid of the Italians, had been mopping up Republican forces in the south. An offensive by the Nationalist army in the north, backed by the German Condor Legion which was trying out blitzkrieg techniques for the first time, was pushing back the defences of the Basque Country. In an attempt to break the stalemate around Madrid, Franco and the Italian commander-in-chief had agreed at the beginning of March 1937 on a pincer attack on Republican defences from the south-west and the north-east. The Italian offensive towards Guadalajara in the south-west had run into difficulties owing to bitter cold and snow and to the tenacity of the Republican defence. Unable to mobilize back-up transport and troops or use their aircraft, the Italians had been defeated by Republican forces, amongst which the Italian volunteers of the Garibaldi Batallion of the International Brigades had played an important role.

The Guadalajara victory, however, had done little to reverse the fortunes of the Republic. In the north the German Condor Legion, acting with the knowledge of the Spanish high command, had dropped a rain of high-explosives and incendiary bombs on the historic capital of the Basque Country, Guernica, in April 1937. It was a target of dubious strategic value but one whose destruction was a devastating blow to the morale of the Basques. In June Bilbao fell, and in August, Santander. By the end of October the north had fallen to the insurgents, who thereby acquired not only the ports and the industry but also the reserves of iron ore and coal that had been vital to the embargo-ridden Republican war effort.

The Republican high command attempted several initially successful diversionary tactics: in July they had punched a hole through enemy lines west of Madrid, but their forces were too weak to follow it through; the second push, on the Aragon front, came to a halt through poor communications and continued political divisions within the Popular Army, exacerbated by the communists' drive to destroy the local grip of the anarchists; the third, in December 1937 in mountainous southern Aragon, led to the capture of the town of Teruel in bitterly cold conditions, but

A Robert Capa photograph of Republican troops in Teruel during their counter-offensive in Aragon in the winter of 1937–8. The attack on Teruel was a desperate attempt by the Popular Army to break the Nationalist lines and hinder their advance on Madrid. The battle was fought in appalling conditions. During the campaign the lowest temperature of the century was recorded and many soldiers died of cold.

Republican troops were driven back in January by the power of the Nationalists' artillery, tanks, and air-force.

Backed by overwhelming superiority in the air and in artillery, the rebels launched an offensive in March 1938 through Aragon and south-west Catalonia and then down the Ebro valley. They reached the sea in mid-April, cutting the remaining Republican territory in two. Their attempts to advance from there towards Valencia, where the government was based, were slowed down by the tenacious resistance of Republican forces. Though it might have been possible to launch a more decisive offensive against Catalonia, Franco was happier to follow a cautious military strategy. A last and imaginatively conceived diversionary offensive was launched by the Republic in July. Troops crossed the Ebro at night and drove the enemy back forty kilometres. Once again, the Republican army was unable to follow up an early breakthrough. The Nationalists deployed their superior military power, and after three months of the bloodiest engagement of the whole war, the Popular Army was forced to retreat.

The Negrín government clung on grimly in the hope that the looming threat of a new world war in Europe might persuade France and Britain to secure the Republic as an ally. The Anglo-Italian Treaty of April 1938 and the Munich Agreement of 29 September, however, merely sanctioned further British connivance at the violation in Spain of the Non-Intervention Agreement. In a fruitless attempt to broker peace talks, Negrín ordered the withdrawal of the International Brigades in October, and on 15 November they marched through the streets in an emotional farewell to the people of Spain.

The end of the war. In the final stage of the Civil War, the Nationalist army advanced into Catalonia, sowing panic and death by aerial bombing and strafing the civilian population. On 26 January 1939 their troops marched into an almost empty Barcelona, whose streets 'were littered with paper, torn-up party and union membership cards'. The president, Manuel Azaña, fled to France and then resigned from his post. In the zone still held by the Republicans, a block of territory in the centre-east, Negrín, backed by the communists, called for continued resistance. But Madrid-based socialist, anarchist, and republican leaders, convinced of the hopelessness of the situation and hostile to the communists, launched a new civil war within the war and unsuccessfully sued for peace with Franco. Their action precipitated the collapse of a demoralized and starving civilian front. When the Nationalists set off on their final offensive, they encountered little resistance. On 27 March they entered Madrid, and three days later the war came to an end.

Of all the causes of the defeat, the most important was the superiority of the Nationalist army over the Popular Army. It is true that the technical resources on both sides of the war were not the most modern; according to Álvarez del Vayo, minister of foreign affairs in two governments of the Republic, it had been a 'colonial war'. Yet Franco's armed forces had better weapons, they had experienced battle units, and preserved from the outset the military discipline of a regular army under a single command. The Popular Army, on the other hand, had to be forged out of politically divided fighting units inherited from the militias of the early days, some of which were reluctant to lose their independence. An anarchist slogan read 'Militiamen, yes, soldiers, no!' Republican fronts collapsed because of lack of co-ordination or through political division. Sometimes they gave way because the ammunition ran out or the weapons were not good enough. Unlike the Nationalists' *mando único*, central command remained elusive. On several occasions reliable regiments were let down by weak units on their flanks. In the bitterness of defeat, the general who planned the Republican offensives, Vicente Rojo, blamed the political infighting in the rearguard for the victory of the enemy. While the Nationalists were united under a single banner, the so-called National Movement, the Republicans had fought small-scale civil wars in their rearguard.

The Republic's defeat was ensured by the failure of the democracies of France and Britain to come to its aid. British Conservatives, in particular, had been hostile towards the Republic because they saw it as a communist Trojan Horse. On the other hand, they were sympathetic towards the rebels because they appeared to offer a better guarantee of British investments in Spain. Both Britain and France had failed to grasp the seriousness of the Nazi and fascist threat to European democracy. Their support of non-intervention forced the Republic to seek arms in the murky world of the private market, where they were obliged to pay astronomical prices and were often cheated. Non-intervention also made shipments of essential Soviet supplies difficult. British and French readiness to leave a fellow-democracy defenceless merely strengthened the confidence of their future enemies and enabled them to prepare for the new world war by testing their new military technology in real battle. It also delivered a potential ally into Axis hands that might threaten Gibraltar, one of the most strategically vital military points of the British Empire and the Mediterranean. Millions of Spaniards paid for the Allies' mistake with incalculable suffering.

The Franco Dictatorship

The new Nationalist state that replaced the Republic at the end of the Civil War was forged during the conflict itself. In April 1937 all the political parties supporting the rebellion had been united into a single state party, the National Movement. Franco became the personification of the new regime, enjoying absolute authority both as chief of state and head of government granted by his fellow generals in September 1936. His power rested on three institutions, the church, the army, and the Falange, but within the regime there existed an unofficial pluralism of 'families' representing the different political tendencies that had joined the uprising—the original Falangists, Carlists, Catholic conservatives, and monarchists. Beyond them lay the diverse social forces that had backed the uprising. In addition to a common religious, nationalist, and anti-democratic ideology, what welded these contradictory interests together was the so-called 'pact of blood', a bond forged during the violence of the Civil War and the bloody repression practised or sanctioned by all in its aftermath.

The Francoist state was essentially a conservative and authoritarian regime. Its totalitarian tendencies, represented by the Falange, were displayed in the pageantry of the state in the early years, when it appeared the Axis would win the world war. They were kept on a leash, however, by the church, the generals, and the monarchists. Towards the end of the war the Falange's power as a mass party was effectively emasculated. They felt compensated to some extent by their continued control over the compulsory social organizations of the regime, the state syndical system modelled on Italian corporatism, and the youth and women's organizations. Franco's own ideology was deeply conservative but it was subordinate to the perpetuation of his own power. He maintained control by repeatedly shifting the balance of influence within the regime according to internal and external pressures, and he continued to command loyalty by allowing the self-enrichment of his elites through the institutions of the state.

The victorious regime was consolidated by a prolongation of the civil war by other means. Despite its espousal of Christian values, the new state showed no forgiveness for the defeated. 'Spaniards, alert', the state radio announced on the day of victory: 'Peace is not a comfortable and cowardly repose in the face of History. The blood of those who fell for the Fatherland does not allow for forgetfulness, sterility, or treachery. Spaniards, alert, Spain is still at war against all internal and external enemies.' The repression carried out in the Nationalist rearguard was institutionalized in a series of laws aimed not just at the political supporters of the Republic but also at class and regional identities. The Law of Political Responsibilities, issued in February 1939 shortly after the Nationalist troops marched into Barcelona, declared 'serious passivity' towards the Republic to be a crime, and it was made retroactive to 1934. The definition of crime itself was broadened so as to enable the prosecution of trade-union activities carried out during the Republic.

The overt objective of the repression was to rid Spain of the systems and ideologies that had 'corrupted' her 'true identity'. Among these were democracy, atheism, and, at least in the early years of the regime, capitalism as a liberal market system. The beginning of the process of Spain's corruption was located in the eighteenth-century Enlightenment. The most immediate enemies were the communists, Jews, and freemasons who had been feeding off the decaying body of Spain. The true Spain was to be sought in the imperial and hierarchical traditions of the Catholic Kings. Her health lay in a mythologized Castilian countryside, while the city was seen as the source of her sickness. Combining the language of religion and medicine, the new regime sought the spiritual disinfection of Spain. The means to achieve this end were mass executions, imprisonment, redemption through penal labour, and the inculcation of the regime's values through education, psychological programming, and media propaganda.

It would be hard to exaggerate the consequent suffering of millions of Spaniards. Apart from the immediate effects for Republican supporters of defeat and repression—exile, imprisonment, execution (according to cautious Foreign Office estimates, some 10,000 people were executed in the first five months after the Civil War), most families in the early years of the Francoist regime suffered semi-starvation, disease, and exploitation. For all those who did not share the aims of the new regime, life was claustrophobic; without freedom of expression, their beliefs, and—in Galicia, the Basque Country, and Catalonia—their own language, were confined to private spaces. In public, they had to give the fascist salute and make sense of the official slogan 'For the Empire towards God'. Language became a tool of the victors. Even footballing terms were renamed to eliminate words with foreign derivations.

Autarky. The Francoist cure for a 'sick' economy was withdrawal from the world market, the creation of import substitution industries, and state intervention to supplement the weakness of private capital. The motor of the economy was to be the brutal exploitation of a tamed labour force. The autarky thus adopted was modelled on that of European fascism and reflected the admiration felt by Franco and his Falangist supporters for Nazi Germany and Fascist Italy. Although Spain remained officially neutral during the Second World War, close links were maintained between the Francoist regime and the fascist dictatorships from the beginning of the conflict. Franco and his advisors, led by his brother-in-law Ramón Serrano Suñer, first as minister of the interior and then as foreign secretary, attempted to negotiate Spain's entry into the war on the Axis side. For Hitler, however, Spain was of peripheral interest to the German war effort; moreover, the price Franco was demanding for her participation, the award of French Morocco, was, Hitler believed, more than Spain's contribution was worth. An awkward meeting between the two on the French–Spanish border at Hendaye on 23 October 1940 resulted in a formal undertaking by Spain to join the war, but no date was specified when

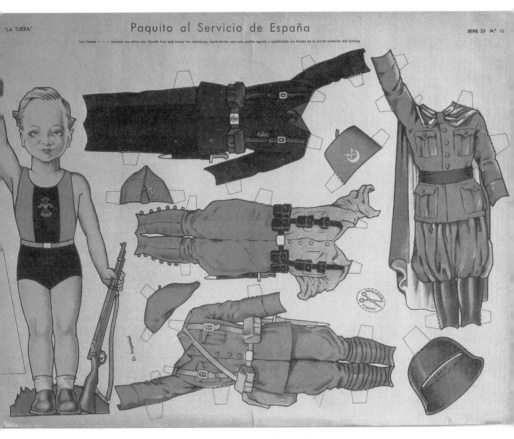

'Paquito in the Service of Spain'. A Francoist cut-out for children (Paquito was a common name amongst children and was Franco's nickname). The state made strenuous efforts to indoctrinate children in the martial and ultra-nationalist values of the regime, encouraging them to see Franco as the personification of these values.

she would do so. Hitler later complained to Mussolini about his meeting with Franco (whom he subsequently called 'that fat little sergeant'): 'Rather than go through that again, I would prefer to have three or four teeth taken out.' Franco, for his part, was not impressed by Hitler, whom he found 'a stage actor'. In the meantime, flouting its official policy of non-belligerence, the Francoist regime recruited a volunteer force, the Blue Division, to fight for Germany on the Russian front.

In the wake of the Allied invasion of North Africa in November 1942, Franco began to hedge his bets, assuring the Allies of Spain's friendship while continuing to provide material support to Germany. On the eve of peace in April 1945 Franco announced a series of cosmetic reforms, including a Charter of Rights for Spaniards, aimed at persuading the Allies of his democratic credentials. Spain was henceforth described as a

Catholic and organic democracy. A corporative parliament, the Cortes, was set up, based not on universal suffrage, but on the 'natural organs of society', and later a Law of Succession was promulgated defining the regime as a monarchy without a monarch, with Franco as regent. The survival of his regime in the post-war world order, however, derived above all from the growing tensions of the incipient Cold War, encouraging the West to tolerate Spain under Franco. Despite the efforts of the exiled monarchist and Republican opposition, international disapproval of the Franco regime was reduced to a token gesture, the diplomatic boycott of Spain agreed by the United Nations in December 1945.

Spain's self-imposed economic isolation was abandoned when it became clear by the late 1940s that autarky had failed. In comparison to countries experiencing rapid industrial growth thanks in part to the Marshall Aid denied to the Spanish, Spain's economic situation had not improved significantly. Inflation was rising steeply and the balance of payments had plunged into a chronic deficit. The crisis of the late 1940s obliged the regime to modify its policy of autarky. Franco reshuffled his cabinet to permit a timid liberalization of the economy. Diplomatic isolation also came to an end in 1953. In that year the Vatican signed a concordat with Spain, and the United States, keen to extend its Cold War defences, signed a pact with the regime allowing for the creation of US military bases in Spain in exchange for financial aid amounting over six years to some $625 million. Two years later, the UN voted to readmit Spain.

Economic liberalization. Despite its semi-liberalization, the Spanish economy was still in trouble in the mid-1950s. The balance-of-payments deficit had doubled and record inflation was eating into the value of wages, which were as little as 35 per cent of their pre-Civil War level. The first wave of illegal strikes swept across Spain. A new generation of university students was also beginning to mobilize against the state from within the official student association previously dominated by the Falange. Within the regime itself, the first stirrings of opposition took place. Cracks appeared in the church's formerly ardent support, and tensions were growing between the Falange and the military, many of whom were monarchists disappointed by Franco's refusal to install a monarch in the person of Don Juan, son of Alfonso XIII. Against his will, Franco was persuaded in 1957 to sack his ministers and appoint a new cabinet with more pliant Falangists and an economic team made up of neo-liberal technocrats linked to the Catholic lay organization, the Opus Dei.

The technocrats' objective was to dismantle the 'orthopedic apparatus' of autarky and open up the economy to the boom of the West without political, cultural, or social liberalization. It was driven by the belief that economic growth and an accompanying rise in living standards would be sufficient to sustain the regime. In doing so, the regime's 'legitimacy of origin' based on victory in the Civil War would be replaced by the 'legitimacy of exercise', the provision of prosperity. A reluctant Franco was forced to accept the technocrats' Stabilization Plan of 1959, which turned the peseta into a convertible currency, thereby cutting its value by half. It also reduced public expenditure, and opened the gates to foreign investment. The Plan had a radical effect on a hitherto protected economy. After a brief recession, it began to enjoy higher rates of growth than any other country in the West, for a while more than twice that of the European Community. Once a mainly agrarian economy only partially integrated into Europe, Spain became part of the industrialized, urban, and consumer society of the West by the early 1970s.

The engine of this growth was the economic boom of the western economy. Foreign investment was attracted to Spain by her potential for expansion, by government subsidies, and by low labour costs. The rise in living standards in Europe and a cheap peseta in Spain drew increasing numbers of tourists. Four years after the Plan was put into effect, their number had increased from 4 million to 14 million, and earnings from tourism had risen from $129 million to $919 million. The restructuring of the economy also led to the emigration of one-and-a-quarter million Spaniards to Europe between 1960 and 1973. The money they sent to their families in Spain in the same period amounted to some $5,000 million. Foreign investment, tourism, and emigrant remittances helped to balance the deficit in Spain's balance of payments resulting from economic growth.

Apologists for the regime attributed the boom of the Spanish economy to the *dirigisme* of the technocrats. In reality, much of the economic growth in Spain was unplanned. Despite attempts to reduce regional disparities, economic growth was concentrated in areas where industry had traditionally been located, the Madrid region, Catalonia, Valencia, and the Basque Country. While foreign firms came to play an increasing role in capital formation, the Spanish tradition of state patronage and protection through nepotism and shared ideology became an instinctive practice in the Franco regime, favouring the development of inefficient domestic monopolies.

Economic growth transformed Spanish society. Contrary to the regime's exaltation of rural life, the countryside was emptied of its inhabitants. Rural exodus was accompanied by a massive and largely unplanned growth of cities characterized by speculation, overcrowding, and a lack of urban infrastructure. Yet there were considerable improvements in health, nutrition, and education. Modernization also changed Spain's occupational structure. From a largely agrarian society, Spain became dominated by the industry and service sectors. The size of the professional middle class burgeoned. The speed of Spain's insertion into the consumer market can be illustrated by the rise in the number of television sets. In 1960 only 1 per cent of households had a television; nine years later 62 per cent owned a set.

The ensuing transformation of culture clashed with the archaic values of the regime. Franco had feared the effect of 'breezes from foreign shores corrupting the purity of our environment'. However, the cultural contradictions that accompanied modernization were largely domestic in origin. A remarkable example of these was the metamorphosis of the church. From the most ardent defender of the regime, the church became an outspoken critic from within, spurred on not just by the change in world Catholicism after the Second Vatican Council but also by the radicalization of its lay organizations and urban priests. In 1971 the church voted to ask forgiveness from the Spanish people for its role in the Civil War, and in 1973 the bishops asked for the separation of the church and the state. To Franco, this was a 'stab in the back'.

Protest and opposition. Modernization also bred protest. The vertical, authoritarian syndicates of the regime were increasingly out of tune with the needs of a mobile, educated, and pluralist society. As a result, social and cultural protests adopted a more political character. Of these, the greatest challenge came from the labour movement that had never ceased, even in the 1940s, to stage strikes in protest against the desperate conditions of workers. The wave of stoppages that swept through Spain from 1962 was in part the result of the transformation of production. The reluctant introduction by the regime of collective bargaining in 1958 undermined the legitimacy of its vertical industrial relations model, because it led to the growth of democratic structures on the shop-floor and in offices. The clandestine organization that emerged in workplaces throughout Spain was the Workers' Commissions, dominated by militants of the Communist party. Labour protest overflowed into the surrounding neighbourhoods and workplaces in the form of solidarity

movements. It also influenced other agitations such as the neighbourhood associations. In the process the ideals of citizenship and democracy
were fostered.

After the 1950s the regime faced a new challenge from students and intellectuals. Spanish universities changed from elite to mass institutions in
which violent protests were staged against the lack of democracy in the
official union and the poor conditions of university life. These culminated
in the declaration in 1969 of a state of emergency throughout the country. The repression launched by the regime against the protesting students
evoked widespread solidarity, since the students came overwhelmingly
from middle-class families.

The regime soon had to face a resurgent regional nationalism. By the
1960s regional rights in Catalonia and the Basque Country had become
the focus of the widespread demand for democracy. Catalanism in particular was seen as a modernizing and democratic project linked to
European models, as opposed to the archaic and repressive nationalism of
the Franco regime. On the fringes of Basque nationalism, on the other
hand, there was a more xenophobic ideology. Heavy migration into the
region had intensified the insecurity and exclusivism that lay at the origin
of the movement. Regional protest in the Basque Country took violent
shape with the creation of the terrorist organization ETA in 1959.
Between 1968 and 1975, when ETA was at its most active, forty-seven
people associated with the regime and its repressive apparatus were
assassinated. ETA became a symbol of resistance against the Franco
regime. The Burgos trial of ETA members and sympathizers in 1970
generated a widespread movement of solidarity in Spain, and throughout
Europe.

Out of the agitation of the 1960s a new political opposition emerged.
In contrast to the socialists and anarchists, whose clandestine organization had been largely destroyed by repression (though the socialists, in
particular, retained much residual support in a number of regions, such
as Asturias), the communists succeeded in engaging with the new grievances generated by modernization. Having renounced the guerrilla struggle of the 1940s, the party adopted the policy of National Reconciliation;
a broad political alliance led by the Communist party would direct Spain
on to the path of democracy. Alongside them, new and more radical organizations emerged, closely linked to the revolutionary left in Europe.
Despite its considerable growth and influence, however, the political opposition in the 1960s and early 1970s failed to unite around a common
programme which could embody a viable alternative to the regime, be-

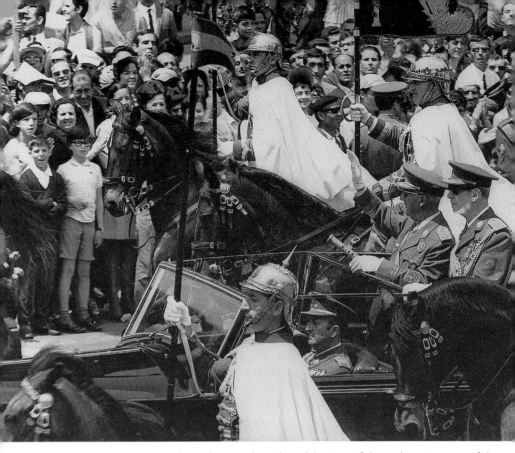

An ageing Franco salutes the crowds in the celebration of the 30th anniversary of the Nationalist victory. A few days later, Franco announced he would be succeeded by Prince Juan Carlos, the son of the Pretender to the throne, Don Juan. By now Franco played little part in decision-making. Under heavy medication for Parkinson's disease, he delegated almost all decisions to his ministers and in particular to the Vice-President, Admiral Carrero Blanco.

cause it was split by the Cold War divisions and by different agendas for political change in Spain.

The decline of the regime. For the regime, modernization without democracy turned out to be an insuperable contradiction. Though it hoped the Spanish economic 'miracle' would bolster its legitimacy, the demands thrown up by socio-economic and cultural change could not easily be reconciled with the structures of the dictatorship. The attempt to win the acquiescence of the population through bread and circuses was only partially successful. Real Madrid became the football team most closely associated with the regime, and the success of the bullfighter El Cordobés led the state to transmit one of his bullfights on 1 May, in the hope that demonstrators could be enticed to stay at home. There were few apologists for the dictatorship amongst artists, writers, and film directors. Creative artists sought oblique, metaphorical means of expressing their dissatisfaction with social and political life in Spain in order to escape censorship. The film *Spirit of the Beehive*, by Victor Érice, portrayed a depressed, listless village, under the surface of which, as beneath the lid of a beehive, a dynamic and restless society was growing.

As part of an effort to renew its image, the regime carried out a superficial refurbishment of its institutions. A Law of Associations was passed in 1964 allowing regime families to set up opinion groups; these were restricted since Franco believed they would degenerate into political parties. A press law was issued in 1966 removing prior censorship. Yet any further liberalization was blocked by the regime's fundamentalists, the so-called 'immobilists'. The essentially reactionary nature of the state was confirmed by the Organic Law of the following year. The nomination in 1969 of Prince Juan Carlos, son of the Pretender to the throne, as heir to Franco and future king of Spain did nothing to resolve these contradictions.

One of Franco's most repetitive self-justifications was that he had brought peace to a society at war with itself. If it still had any purchase, this claim was undermined by the increasing social and political agitation of the early 1970s. The most dramatic expression of that protest was the assassination by ETA at the end of 1973 of Franco's right-hand man and prime minister, Admiral Carrero Blanco. The explosive charge laid by ETA across the path of Carrero's car in the centre of Madrid was so powerful that the limousine was thrown over the top of a high-rise block, prompting the opposition to nickname him Spain's first astronaut. Unable and largely unwilling to liberalize because of internal splits, the regime turned increasingly to martial law and state brutality, such as the execution in 1975 of five anti-Francoist terrorists. Mounting protest, added to the economic recession induced by the oil crisis in 1973, further weakened the regime's legitimacy in the last two years of Franco's rule. His illness and death in November 1975 dissolved the only glue that had held the regime together in its last years.

The Transition to Democracy

Juan Carlos succeeded Franco as head of state and was crowned two days after the dictator's death. Although he had to tread warily for fear of arousing the diehard supporters of the regime, the king was committed to the democratization of Spain. The example of his brother-in-law, King

Constantine of Greece, whose collaboration with military dictatorship had led to the downfall of the Greek monarchy, cannot have been far from his mind. Juan Carlos's inner circle of like-minded advisors included Adolfo Suárez, previously director of state television and radio and, at the time, vice-secretary of the National Movement. In July 1976 the king successfully manoeuvred to get Suárez nominated to replace the old Francoist prime minister, Carlos Arias Navarro. Suárez's past record helped to keep the 'immobilists' off their guard, but it did not initially please those seeking change.

The new prime minister had to navigate between the shoals of the diehard Francoists (nicknamed 'the bunker' by the opposition after Hitler's last stand) and the popular mobilization for reform. But the difficult voyage towards democracy was helped by the moderation of the political opposition, who agreed to subordinate social reform to the achievement of political change, in part because they had failed to turn the mainly localized and issue-driven social protest into political action on a national scale. It had also been facilitated by the work over several years of a group of Catholic reformists closely linked to the Francoist establishment, the so-called *tácitos*. Unofficial negotiations, involving promises and much cajoling, were skilfully carried out with both the opposition and the Francoists by Suárez and his team, who possessed a crucial advantage in controlling the state media.

Democratic reform. A year after Franco's death, the prime minister managed to persuade the unrepresentative Francoist parliamentarians into approving a Law for Political Reform which effectively entailed their own collective suicide and brought democracy to Spain by establishing universal suffrage. In the following referendum, over 94 per cent of voters approved of the bill. In preparation for the elections of June 1977, new parties of the right and centre were created around groups and personalities with little political base to contest the long-established organizations of the left that had emerged from exile and clandestinity. Suárez formed the Union of the Democratic Centre, which went on to win the elections with over a third of the votes, while the Socialists emerged as a close second.

True to the prevailing climate of moderation among the main parties, a new constitution was approved in 1978 after lengthy and intense negotiations to achieve a compromise. Its overriding objective was to allow for pluralism where for decades only one ideology and culture had been possible. Contentious issues, such as abortion, were left for future elab-

A theatrical Lt. Col. Tejero of the Civil Guard as he briefly held the Spanish parliament hostage in 1981. Tejero's storming of the Spanish parliament on 23 February was part of yet another attempted coup against the new democracy by the intransigent Francoist 'bunker'. The king's intervention during the night as commander-in-chief of the armed forces did much to help stymie the coup and few officers joined the action. By the morning Tejero and his men had surrendered.

oration. Where there were disagreements over fundamental questions, the wording was deliberately ambiguous; for example, the 'indissoluble unity' and 'territorial integrity' of Spain was difficult to reconcile with the right to autonomy of all 'nationalities and regions' within Spain. But the constitution was clear on the main outline of the new democracy: a bicameral parliament, a powerful executive, a non-confessional state, and the recognition of the rights of regional nationalism. In the referendum of December 1978 the constitution was approved by 88 per cent of voters.

Three years after his death, Franco's regime had been dismantled and replaced by a modern pluralist democracy based on universal suffrage. It was a remarkable achievement and became a model for transitions to democracy in Eastern Europe and elsewhere. The ease and speed of change in Spain, however, was due to the modernity of Spanish society as much as to the efforts of politicians. Equally important was the widespread popular mobilization for democracy and social reform that created the unavoidable necessity for radical political change. Nevertheless, the thoroughness of institutional change was not extended to the army, whose officers largely opposed the dismantling of the Francoist state and became the rallying-point for reaction. The 'rattle of sabres', a legacy of the dictatorship, would weigh heavily on the new democracy.

The New Democracy

One of the most vexatious problems facing the new state was the persistence of Basque terrorism through the actions of a new generation of militants. During the transition, Basque nationalists had continued to be treated with the same brutality by the forces of law and order under the new minister of the interior, an ex-Francoist bureaucrat. The historic party of Basque nationalism, the Partido Nacionalista Vasco, had come out into the open to participate in the new democracy. But a fundamentalist core of militants continued along the path of violence, on the dubious grounds that democracy and the devolution of power were as damaging for Basque nationhood as the old dictatorship.

Police brutality was part of the wider problem of the traditional, repressive instincts of the forces of law and order, the military, and the intelligence services. While well-known torturers, such as the police chief of the Barcelona suburb of Terrassa, had been comfortably pensioned off, there was no proper reform of these state structures, part of the price for the transition exacted by the right. Within the military, plots were afoot to overthrow the democracy. A planned coup was foiled in 1978. On 23 February 1981 a detachment of the Civil Guard led by Colonel Tejero stormed parliament and held MPs hostage while the tanks rolled out in Valencia and troops began to be mobilized in Brunete. Only prompt action in defence of democracy by the king, as commander-in-chief of the armed forces, persuaded other military conspirators to withdraw from the action.

Felipe González on a campaign poster on the eve of his election as Prime Minister in 1982. There was a huge swing in votes in favour of the Left and in particular the Socialists. Felipe (as he came to be known popularly) and his colleagues carried the hopes of millions of Spaniards for a radical transformation of Spanish politics and society, after the structures of the new democracy had been laid by the Suárez government of 1977–82.

The Socialists in power. The widespread indignation caused by the attempted coup and the gradual disintegration of the disparate elements that made up Suárez's party of the transition led to the spectacular victory of the Socialist party, the PSOE, in the elections of 1982. The PSOE held power, with steadily diminishing electoral support, for the next fourteen years. For all its subsequent failures, the Socialist government oversaw the consolidation of Spanish democracy, the full establishment of regional autonomy, the incorporation of Spain into NATO and the European Community, and the introduction of a range of crucial social reforms. Not without bitter internal conflict and splits, the PSOE's ideology had changed from Marxism to social democracy and, once in power, to economic liberalism under the leadership of Felipe González. After a severe crisis, the economy experienced growth and inflation was cut by 50 per cent, but unemployment reached a record level of almost 23 per cent.

In the 1990s the PSOE government faced two major problems. Revelations were beginning to be made by independent judges and the media about corruption within the party. The most damaging allegations concerned attempts by senior PSOE officials to raise funds for political campaigns by setting up a holding company to carry out fictitious consultancy. At an individual level, some members of the government and MPs were accused of using public office for their own or their family's enrichment. Sleaze, in the form of commissions, backhanders, nepotism, and jobs for the boys, had been a common feature of Spanish political and financial life under Franco and could be found amongst many parties and in business circles. It was particularly damaging to the socialists, who had built their reputation on honesty.

Another scandal that badly hit the PSOE was the revelation that under their rule the secret police had set up a state terrorist squad in the 1980s to kidnap and murder ETA suspects in France. Questions were raised as to how much the Socialist leadership knew or even approved of their activities. In 1998 the ex-interior minister, Rafael Barrionuevo, and his junior minister in charge of state security, Rafael Vera, were sentenced to prison for their part in the affair. Recent allegations concerned the secret police's illegal phone-tapping of statesmen, including the king.

The Socialists' loss of popularity, added to the effects of the semi-recession of 1992–3, resulted in a haemorrhage of votes. The consequence was that in the wake of the 1993 election they were forced to form a pact with the Catalan conservative party, Convergència I Unió (CiU) under Jordi Pujol, in order to form a minority government. The withdrawal of Pujol's support in 1995 led to fresh elections in March 1996. Contrary to expectations that the conservative national party, the Popular Party (PP), would make a clean sweep, the socialist voters denied it an absolute majority. As a result the PP was also forced to make a pact with the regional parties in order to form a government, the first overtly conservative government in Spain since the Franco regime.

The conservatives in power. Committed programatically to rein in the process of devolution, the PP found itself conceding more than any other party had to the nationalists of the Basque Country and Catalonia in order simply to stay in power. The new government, however, rapidly disabused the fear, on which the Socialists had played in the electoral campaign, that the PP's victory signalled a return of Francoism by the back door. The prime minister José María Aznar's team showed in office that, unlike traditional Spanish conservatives, they were neo-liberal modernizers. Their programme included privatization, minimization of state intervention, and the reform of the welfare state. Although the cabinet was drawn from close-knit groups linked by family, property, and business rooted in Francoism, it embodied a renovated Spanish conservatism that respected the basic rules of the democratic constitution.

Profiting from the economic reforms of their Socialist predecessors and the generous funds of the EU, the PP steered the Spanish economy towards convergence with the European Union criteria for monetary union. Though unemployment in Spain remained among the highest in Europe, inflation and the public-sector borrowing requirement were progressively reduced, while new hi-tech and service industries increasingly replaced the old manufacturing sector. The PP government also set out to stimulate the mobility of labour by deregulating the complex labour laws inherited from the bargain struck with the trade unions during the transition to democracy. The withdrawal of state subsidies and the deregulation of the labour market, however, provoked acute social strains.

Benefiting from continued economic growth in the late nineties, the PP won an absolute majority in the general elections of March 2000, leaving the party free to pursue its policies in government without the need for prior bargaining with the Catalan conservatives. The electoral results indicated that the PP was more successful than the PSOE in mobilizing the votes of a new generation who knew and cared little about the old politics of the transition. The Socialists, unable to inspire confidence with a hastily improvised pact with the ex-Communist left, lost almost 3 million votes. The result deepened the PSOE's internal crisis. Its membership still divided, the party was left without a strong national leadership and a coherent political strategy.

The pre-eminent domestic problem facing the Spanish government was the continuing violence perpetrated by ETA in search of Basque independence. The terrorists' campaign of murder and kidnapping aroused mass protests in 1997 among the Basque population and throughout Spain. Such was the level of popular mobilization against ETA that it seemed the organization had dug itself into a hole. Towards the end of that year the leadership of its unofficial political wing, Herri Batasuna (Unity of the People), was jailed for propagating a video in its electoral campaign that sought to justify the use of violence in the pursuit of political ends. Out of the popular outcry in the Basque Country arose the Estella or Lizarra Pact in the autumn of 1998, a nationalist front bringing together the Basque democratic parties and Herri Batasuna. Its aim was to seek an end to the spiral of violence and the beginning of negotiations with the government over Basque nationalist demands. ETA's declaration of a ceasefire in October 1998 raised hopes that its leaders, like successive generations of ETA militants before them, had renounced violence.

Two major obstacles lay in the path of peace. The issue which both radical and moderate nationalists wished to put at the core of any negotiations with the government was the Basques' right to self-determination, a right that no Spanish government has ever contemplated. Complicating this issue further was the status of Navarre and the French Basque region. The radical nationalists, unlike the moderates, continued to demand the integration of these regions into a new Basque state as part of any process of self-determination. By signing the pact with the political wing of ETA, the Basque nationalist parties hoped that they had provided the terrorist organization with a landing strip into democracy. Instead ETA's leaders used the pact to ratchet up their demands on the nationalist parties for independence. Fourteen months after the ceasefire, ETA returned to violence, blowing up a Spanish officer in Madrid and, in early 2000, murdering a Socialist deputy and his police guard, both of them Basques.

Radical Basque nationalism has shown a surprising degree of resilience. Although Herri Batasuna received less than 12 per cent of votes in the Basque Country in the national elections of 1996 and refused to stand in March 2000, the movement of which it is part has created a social and cultural base through its campaigns over unemployment, drugs, ecology, and other social issues. It has been particularly successful amongst Basque youth, from which ETA recruits many of its militants.

One million people protest in Madrid in February 1996 against the assassination by ETA of a Spanish judge. Mass demonstrations had once been held in support of the Basque terrorist organization when it had been part of the struggle for democracy against the Francoist Dictatorship. ETA's continued use of terrorism against the new democracy in pursuit of independence has mobilized the protest of millions of Spaniards from all political persuasions.

These activities are so woven into daily life in the Basque Country, and so many Basques are connected to them through family or friends or empathy for the ultimate aims of radical Basque nationalism, that no simple line can be drawn between the Basque Nationalist Party and ETA. At the same time, ETA's persisting ability to intimidate Basque citizens and extract a 'revolutionary tax' from local businesses by threatening violence continues to thwart attempts by the national and regional authorities to isolate the organization.

Conclusion. The vertiginous changes in Spain since the forging of democracy have not been painless. Spaniards, gratefully or unwillingly, learnt to forget about the past because historical amnesia was an unarticulated price of democratic change. The euphoria experienced by the opponents of the dictatorship during the early part of the transition gave way to disenchantment when the results seemed so meagre compared to their hopes. The high level of politicization gave way to increasing passivity and lack of solidarity. But Spain is a culturally vibrant society with a flexible and sophisticated political structure. The state of the autonomies was devised to placate both regional nationalism and the centralist right; for the leaders of the historic communities, the concession of autonomy to all regions (including some newly invented ones) was tantamount to 'coffee for everyone'. But the historic communities have always kept several steps ahead of the other regions in the continuing process of devolution. The armed forces have been successfully restructured. Now integrated in NATO and the WEU, and equipped with modern weaponry and decent salaries for officers, they no longer pose a threat to the democratic state.

For all the rhetoric of politicians and the press, Spain is now a tolerant, inclusive, and pluralist society. Spaniards from all regions have shown their determination to seek coexistence by mobilizing *en masse* against terrorism. Not all the ghosts of the past have been laid to rest, however. The price of the transition to democracy was that the Francoists have not had to answer for their destruction of democracy and their forty-year persecution of its defenders. A minority of elderly nostalgics continue quietly to celebrate the myths of the Nationalist movement. The learnt reflex of silence about the past among old Republican supporters has meant that many younger people know little about their family's history in the 1930s, and many betray little curiosity about the recent past. The Dictator has slid into oblivion in the space of one generation. On the other hand, for the older generations the hatreds of former times can persist under the surface of the new democracy. An old man gone slightly mad has just died in a village in north-eastern Spain. Since the early 1940s he had lived the life of a recluse in his flea-ridden shack because he had fought for the Republic while many of the other villagers had welcomed the Francoists. Since that time they had hardly exchanged a word. In the new Spain, reconciliation with the past remains unfinished business.

FURTHER READING

1. Prehistoric and Roman Spain

J. de Alarcão, *Roman Portugal* (Warminster, 1988).
A. Arribas, *The Iberians* (London, 1963).
M. E. Aubet, *Phoenicians and the West: Politics, Colonies, and Trade* (Cambridge, 1993).
B. Cunliffe and S. J. Keay (eds.), *Social Complexity and the Development of Towns in Iberia* (London, 1995).
L. A. Curchin, *Roman Spain: Conquest and Assimilation* (London, 1991).
Ma. C. Fernández Castro, *Iberia in Prehistory* (Oxford, 1995).
R. J. Harrison, *Spain at the Dawn of History* (London, 1988).
S. J. Keay, *Roman Spain* (London, 1988).
J. Lazenby, *Hannibal's War* (Warminster, 1978).
J. S. Richardson, *Hispaniae: Spain and the Development of Roman Imperialism* (Cambridge, 1986).
J. S. Richardson, *The Romans in Spain* (Oxford, 1996).
P. O. Spann, *Sertorius and the Legacy of Sulla* (Fayetteville, 1987).

2. Visigothic Spain

Roger Collins, *Law, Culture and Regionalism in Early Medieval Spain* (Aldershot, 1992).
——*Early Medieval Spain: Unity in Diversity, 400–1000* (2nd edn., London, 1995).
A. T. Fear (trans.), *Lives of the Visigothic Fathers* (Liverpool, 1997)
Alberto Ferreiro, *The Visigoths in Gaul and Spain, AD 418–711: A Bibliography* (Leiden, 1988).
Edward James (ed.), *Visigothic Spain: New Approaches* (Oxford, 1980).
P. D. King, *Law and Society in the Visigothic Kingdom* (Cambridge, 1972).
E. A. Thompson, *The Goths in Spain* (Oxford, 1969).
Kenneth Baxter Wolf (trans.), *Conquerors and Chroniclers of Early Medieval Spain* (Liverpool, 1990).

3. The Early Middle Ages

GENERAL

T. N. Bisson, *The Medieval Crown of Aragon: A Short History* (Oxford, 1986).
Roger Collins, *Early Medieval Spain: Unity in Diversity, 400–1000* (2nd edn., London, 1995).
Richard Fletcher, *The Quest for El Cid* (London, 1989).
——*Moorish Spain* (London, 1992).
Hugh Kennedy, *Muslim Spain and Portugal: A Political History of al-Andalus* (London, 1996).
Peter Linehan, *History and the Historians of Medieval Spain* (Oxford, 1993).

D. W. Lomax, *The Reconquest of Spain* (London, 1978).
Angus MacKay, *Spain in the Middle Ages: From Frontier to Empire, 1000–1500* (London, 1977).

SOURCES

Christians and Moors in Spain, 3 vols. (Warminster, 1988–92): a collection of original sources in translation: vols. 1 and 2 are edited by Colin Smith, vol. 3 by Charles Melville and Ahmad Ubaydli.
John P. O'Neill (editor-in-chief), *The Art of Medieval Spain AD 500–1200* (New York, 1993).

4. The Late Middle Ages

Y. Baer, *A History of the Jews in Christian Spain*, 2 vols. (Philadelphia, 1966).
R. Highfield (ed.), *Spain in the Fifteenth Century, 1369–1516* (London, 1972).
J. N. Hillgarth, *The Spanish Kingdoms, 1250–1516*, 2 vols., vol. 1 (Oxford, 1976), vol. 2 (Oxford, 1978).
G. Jackson, *The Making of Medieval Spain* (London, 1972).
A. Mackay, *Spain in the Middle Ages: From Frontier to Empire, 1000–1500* (London, 1977).
J. F. O'Callaghan, *A History of Medieval Spain* (London, 1975).
W. Montgomery Watt, *A History of Islamic Spain* (Edinburgh, 1965).

5. The Improbable Empire

J. S. Amelang, *Honored Citizens of Barcelona: Patrician Culture and Class Relations, 1490–1714* (Princeton, 1986).
Jonathan Brown, *Images and Ideas in Seventeenth-Century Spanish Painting* (Princeton, 1978).
William Christian, Jr., *Local Religion in Sixteenth-Century Spain* (Princeton, 1981).
A. Domínguez Ortiz, *The Golden Age of Spain, 1516–1659* (London, 1971).
John H. Elliott, *The Count-duke of Olivares: The Statesman in an Age of Decline* (New Haven and London, 1986).
——*Spain and its World, 1500–1700: Selected Essays* (New Haven, 1989).
M. Fernández Alvarez, *Charles V* (London, 1975).
David C. Goodman, *Power and Penury: Government, Technology and Science in Philip II's Spain* (Cambridge, 1988).
Stephen Haliczer, *The Comuneros of Castile: The Forging of a Revolution, 1475–1521* (Madison, 1981).
Richard L. Kagan, *Students and Society in Early Modern Spain* (Baltimore, 1974).
——and Geoffrey Parker (eds.), *Spain, Europe and the Atlantic World: Essays in Honour of John H. Elliott* (Cambridge, 1995).
Henry Kamen, *Spain in the Later Seventeenth Century, 1665–1700* (London and New York, 1980).
——*The Phoenix and the Flame: Catalonia and the Counter-Reformation* (New York, 1993).
——*Philip II* (London, 1997).
George Kubler and M. Soria, *Art and Architecture in Spain and Portugal and their American Dominions, 1500–1800* (London, 1979).
Peggy K. Liss, *Isabel the Queen* (Oxford and New York, 1992).

Geoffrey Parker, *The Army of Flanders and the Spanish Road, 1567–1659* (Cambridge, 1972).
——*Philip II* (Chicago, 1995).
Carla R. Phillips, *Six Galleons for the King of Spain: Imperial Defense in the Early Seventeenth Century* (Baltimore, 1986).
R. A. Stradling, *Philip IV and the Government of Spain, 1621–65* (Cambridge, 1988).
I. A. A. Thompson, *War and Society in Habsburg Spain* (Aldershot, 1992).

6. Vicissitudes of a World Power

Jonathan Brown and J. Elliott, *A Palace For a King. The Buen Retiro and the Court of Philip IV* (New Haven, 1980).
Henry Kamen, *Spain 1469–1714. A Society of Conflict* (London, 1991).
——*Philip of Spain* (New Haven, 1997).
Geoffrey Parker, *The Army of Flanders and the Spanish Road 1567–1659* (Cambridge, 1972).
R. Stradling, *Europe and the Decline of Spain. A Study of the Spanish System 1580–1720* (London, 1981).

7. Flow and Ebb

William J. Callahan, *Church, Politics, and Society in Spain, 1750–1874* (Cambridge, Mass., and London, 1984).
John F. Coverdale, *The Basque Phase of Spain's First Carlist War* (Princeton, 1984).
Charles J. Esdaile, *The Spanish Army in the Peninsular War* (Manchester, 1988).
Nigel Glendinning, *A Literary History of Spain: The Eighteenth Century* (London and New York, 1972).
Richard Herr, *The Eighteenth-Century Revolution in Spain* (Princeton, 1958).
——*An Historical Essay on Modern Spain* (Berkeley, 1974)
Douglas Hilt, *The Troubled Trinity: Godoy and the Spanish Monarchs* (Tuscaloosa and London, 1987).
Anthony H. Hull, *Goya: Man Among Kings* (New York, London, and Lanham, Md., 1987).
Henry Kamen, *The War of Succession in Spain, 1700–15* (London, 1969).
Gabriel H. Lovett, *Napoleon and the Birth of Modern Spain*, 2 vols. (New York, 1965).
John Lynch, *Bourbon Spain, 1700–1808* (Oxford, 1989).
Joseph Townsend, *A Journey Through Spain in the Years 1786 and 1787*, 3 vols. (London, 1791).

8. Liberalism and Reaction

Sebastian Balfour, *The End of the Spanish Empire* (Oxford, 1997).
S. Ben-Ami, *Fascism from Above: The Dictatorship of Primo de Rivera* (Oxford, 1983).
Carolyn P. Boyd, *Praetorian Politics in Liberal Spain* (Chapel Hill, 1979).
Gerald Brenan, *The Spanish Labyrinth* (Cambridge, 1936).
Raymond Carr, *Spain, 1808–1975* (Oxford, 1982).
Daniel Conversi, *The Basques, the Catalans and Spain* (London, 1997).
C. A. M. Hennessy, *The Federal Republic in Spain* (Oxford, 1962).
Robert Hughes, *Barcelona* (New York, 1992).
G. H. Meaker, *The Revolutionary Left in Spain, 1914–1923* (Stanford, 1974).

David Ringrose, *Spain, Europe and the Spanish Miracle, 1700–1900* (Cambridge 1996).

Adrian Shubert, *A Social History of Modern Spain* (London, 1990).

Joan Connelly Ullman, *The Tragic Week: A Study of Anticlericalism in Spain, 1875–1912* (Cambridge, Mass., 1968).

9. Spain from 1931 to the Present

Sebastian Balfour, *Dictatorship, Workers and the City* (Oxford, 1989).

——and Paul Preston (eds.), *Spain and the Great Powers in the Twentieth Century* (London, 1999).

Raymond Carr and Juan Pablo Fusi, *Spain: Dictatorship to Democracy* (2nd edn., London, 1981).

Helen Graham, *Socialism and War: The Spanish Socialist Party in Power and Crisis, 1936–39* (Cambridge, 1991).

——and Jo Labanyi (eds.), *Spanish Cultural Studies: An Introduction: The Struggle for Modernity* (Oxford, 1995).

Paul Heywood, *The Government and Politics of Spain* (London, 1995).

John Hooper, *The New Spaniards* (Harmondsworth, 1995).

Stanley G. Payne, *The Franco Regime, 1936–1975* (Madison, Wisc., 1987).

Paul Preston, *The Coming of the Spanish Civil War: Reform, Reaction and Revolution in the Second Republic* (2nd edn., London, 1994).

——*Franco: A Biography* (London, 1993).

——*The Spanish Civil War* (London, 1986).

——*The Triumph of Democracy in Spain* (London, 1986).

CHRONOLOGY

c.16,000 BC	Magdalenian cave painting in Cantabria—the Old Stone Age
c.10,000 BC	Levantine cave painting—the Middle Stone Age
c.3,800 BC	Megalithic buildings found in the peninsula
c.2,600 BC	Copper-using cultures flourish in Almería and the Tagus Valley
c.800 BC	Foundation of Cadiz by Phoenician settlers
c.700–500 BC	'Tartessian' Culture flourishes in the south of Spain
c.575 BC	Foundation of Ampurias by Greek settlers from Marseilles
c.535 BC	Battle of Alalia closes the Western Mediterranean to the Greeks
237 BC	Beginnings of Barcid (Carthaginian) Empire in Spain
228 BC	Foundation of Cartagena by Hasdrubal
218 BC	Outbreak of Second Punic War. Hannibal invades Italy from Spain, Roman troops invade Spain
211 BC	Arrival of Scipio Africanus in Spain
206 BC	End of Carthaginian rule in Spain
197 BC	Two Roman provinces created in the peninsula
147–137 BC	Viriathus' resistance to Roman rule in Lusitania
133 BC	Fall of Numantia
123 BC	Balearic Islands annexed to Spain
80–73 BC	Sertorius carries on a Roman Civil War in Spain
c.60 BC	The orator, 'the Elder Seneca', born at Córdoba
45 BC	Caesar finally secures his rule at the Battle of Munda, probably near Bailén
c.27 BC	The Emperor Augustus divides the Iberian peninsula into three provinces
19 BC	Lucius Cornelius Balbus of Cadiz, nephew of Caesar's confidant and banker, is awarded a triumph for victories in Africa. He is the first non-Italian to receive this, Rome's highest military award. Conquest of Cantabria by Agrippa, bringing all the peninsula under Roman rule
c.4 BC	The philosopher 'the Younger Seneca', born in Córdoba
AD 39	The poet Lucan born at Córdoba
c.40	The poet Martial born in Calatayud
53	The future Emperor Trajan (98–117) born in Italica, near Seville
70s	Vespasian grants 'Latin Status' to the Iberian provinces Quintilian of Calahorra appointed professor of rhetoric at Rome
76	The future Emperor Hadrian (117–38) born in Italica, near Seville
171–3	Moorish raids on Andalusia

260–70	Spain forms part of the breakaway 'Gallic Empire'
c.284	The Emperor Diocletian divides the peninsula into five provinces, to one of which Mauretania Tingitana in Africa is annexed
348	The poet Prudentius born
407	Spain taken by the pretender Constantine III
409	Invasions of Alans, Sueves, and Vandals into Spain mark the end of overall Roman authority in the peninsula
c.415–17	Orosius of Braga writes his *Anti-Pagan History*
417–18	Visigoths under Wallia (416–19) campaign for Rome in Spain, and eliminate the Alans and Siling Vandals; the Visigoths are then recalled to Gaul
418–29	The Hasding Vandals dominate southern Spain, before invading North Africa
430–56	The Sueves control all of the Peninsula other than the north-east, with Mérida as their capital
456	The Visigoths under Theoderic II (453–66) invade Spain in alliance with Rome and overthrow the Suevic kingdom. Most of the south and centre of the Peninsula is added to their Gallic kingdom
466–84	Reign of the Visigothic king Euric, who completes the conquest of Roman Spain
494, 497	Reports of Visigoths settling in Spain
506	Alaric II (484–507) issues the *Breviary*, an edited and supplemented version of the Roman law code of Theodosius II
507	Battle of Vouillé: the Franks overthrow the Visigothic kingdom in Gaul
511	Frankish attacks on the Visigothic kingdom in Spain and south-west France lead to its being taken over by the Ostrogothic king Theoderic (493–526)
531–48	The rule of Theudis, last Ostrogothic king in Spain. This is followed by a period of weak royal rule by short-lived Visigothic kings
551	Revolt of Athanagild (551–68) against Agila (549–54) leads to intervention by the Emperor Justinian I (527–65) and the establishment of an imperial enclave along the south-east coast
569–86	The reign of Leovigild, marked by reimposition of royal authority and the beginning of the reconquest of the Byzantine enclave
579–83	Revolt of Hermenigild (d. 584): an independent kingdom is established briefly in the south, until crushed by Leovigild
585	Leovigild's conquest of the vestigial Suevic kingdom in Galicia
587	Conversion of Reccared (586–601) to Catholicism
589	Third Council of Toledo formalizes the conversion of the Visigoths from Arianism to Catholicism
599/600–36	Isidore, bishop of Seville, the leading intellectual luminary in the early seventh century

624	Expulsion of Byzantines from Spain by Suinthila (621–31)
633	Fourth Council of Toledo under Sisenand (631–6) initiates a series of great kingdom-wide ecclesiastical councils
654	Promulgation of the law code of King Reccesuinth (649–72), known as the *Forum Iudicum*
673	Revolt of Paul against Wamba (672–80), described in the *Historia Wambae* of Julian, bishop of Toledo (680–90)
681	Issue of revised and augmented version of the *Forum Iudicum* by Ervig (680–7), with substantial legislation against the Jews
694	The enslavement of most of the Jews in Spain ordered by Egica (687–702)
710	Death of Wittiza (694–710), followed by civil war
711	Arab invasion, leading to the defeat of Roderic (710–11). A small kingdom survives in the north-east under Achila (710–13)
711–18	Conquest of Visigothic kingdom by Islamic armies
718	Battle of Covadonga
720	Arab conquest of the Visigothic kingdom of Ardo (713–20), centred on Narbonne
756	Foundation of the Umayyad amirate of Córdoba by 'Abd al-Rahman I
778	Defeat of the Franks at Roncesvalles; death of Roland
801	Capture of Barcelona by Louis the Pious, son of Charlemagne
818–842	Discovery of the alleged body of St James at Compostela
866–910	Reign of Alfonso III in the Asturias
929	'Abd al-Rahman III proclaimed first caliph of Córdoba
c.967	Gerbert of Aurillac studying in Catalonia
981–1002	The vizir al-Mansur (Almanzor) in power at Córdoba
c.1020	Striking of gold coin resumed at Barcelona
1031	Deposition of the last caliph: beginning of the period of the Taifa states
c.1055–60	Ibn Hazm composing his *Kitab al-Fisal* or 'Book of Sects'
c.1060	Ferdinand I of León-Castile initiates annual payments of gold to Cluny
c.1067	Cardinal Hugh Candidus undertakes first papal legatine visit to Spain
1070	Foundation of Marrakesh symbolizes Almoravid expansion into northern Morocco
1080	Abrogation of the so-called Mozarabic liturgy in León-Castile
1085	Conquest of Toledo by Alfonso VI of León-Castile
1086	Almoravid invasion: defeat of Alfonso VI at Sagrajas
1086–1124	Bernard of Sédirac archbishop of Toledo
1094–9	Rodrigo Díaz, *El Cid*, ruling in Valencia
1118	Conquest of Saragossa by Alfonso I *el Batallador* of Aragon
1137	Dynastic union of kingdom of Aragon and county of Barcelona

1140	Afonso I Henriques declares himself king of Portugal
1142	Peter the Venerable, abbot of Cluny, commissions the translation of the Koran into Latin
1147	Conquest of Lisbon by Afonso Henriques and of Almería by Alfonso VII
1148	Beginnings of Almohad intervention in al-Andalus
1169–84	Ibn Rushd (Averroes) *qadi* or religious judge in Córdoba and Seville
1170	Foundation of the military order of Santiago
1173	Completion of the Almohad conquest of al-Andalus
1188	First record of the attendance of urban delegates at a meeting of the royal court (at León)
1212	Battle of Las Navas de Tolosa
1229–35	Conquest of the Balearic Islands by James I of Aragon
1238	Conquest of Valencia by James I
1248	Conquest of Seville by Ferdinand III of Castile
c.1250	Introduction of the Merino sheep to Spain
c.1250	Poems by Gonzalo de Berceo
1258	Treaty of Corbeil between James I of Aragon and Louis IX of France
1264	Mudejar rebellions in Andalusia and Murcia
c.1270	The Real Concejo de la Mesta
1282	Conquest of Sicily by Peter III of Aragon
1287	Privilegio de la Union
1292	Conquest of Tarifa
1309	Siege of Algeciras
1332	Birth of the chronicler and chancellor of Castile, Pedro López de Ayala (d. 1407)
1337	Beginning of the Hundred Years War
1340	Alfonso IX of Castile defeats the Muslims at the Battle of Salado
1343	Peter IV of Aragon annexes the Balearic Islands
1348	The Black Death
c.1350	*The Book of Good Love* (*Libro de Buen Amor*) by Juan Ruiz, archpriest of Hita
1350	The accession of Peter the Cruel is followed by the beginnings of Trastamaran opposition and propaganda
1367	Peter the Cruel and the Black Prince defeat the Trastámarans at the Battle of Nájera
1368	Treaty of Toledo between Henry II of Castile and France
1369	Henry II kills his half-brother, Peter the Cruel, at Montiel
1371	John of Gaunt, duke of Lancaster, marries Peter the Cruel's daughter, Constance, and assumes the title of king of Castile
1378	The Great Schism
1385	John I of Castile defeated by the Portuguese at the Battle of Aljubar-rota

1386	Lancastrian army disembarks at La Coruña, but the invasion of Castile subsequently ends in failure
1388–9	Treaties with Lancaster and the Portuguese; end of the Spanish phase of the Hundred Years War and of the Lancastrian claims to the Spanish throne
1391	Anti-Jewish feeling sparks off a wave of pogroms in the towns of the Iberian peninsula
1412	The Compromise of Caspe: the regent of Castile, Ferdinand of Antequera, becomes king of Aragon
1442–3	Alfonso V of Aragon gains control of Naples
1445	John II of Castile and Alvaro de Luna defeat their enemies at the Battle of Olmedo
1465	The effigy of Henry IV of Castile deposed at the Farce of Avila; civil wars in Castile
1469	The marriage of Ferdinand and Isabella
1473	Massacre of *conversos* in Andalusian towns; printing begins in Spain
1478	Setting up of the Inquisition
1479	Union of Castile and Aragon
1492	Conquest of Granada; expulsion of the Jews; Columbus discovers America
1516	Succession of Charles of Ghent to the throne of Spain; known as Charles I in Spain and later in Europe as the emperor Charles V, he was the first ruler of the Habsburg dynasty
1521	Capture by Hernando Cortés of the Aztec city of Tenochtitlan after a long siege
1556	Philip II succeeds to the throne of Spain after the abdication of his father Charles V; he had already been governing the country since 1543
1567	Arrival in Brussels of the duke of Alba, at the head of a Spanish army, to initiate a repression that triggered the Dutch revolt
1571	Victory of the combined Christian fleet, under the command of Don Juan of Austria, over the main Turkish fleet at Lepanto
1580	Occupation of Portugal by the army of Philip II
1588	Debacle of the Spanish Armada sent against England
1598	Death of Philip II, succession to the throne of son Philip III
1609	Signing of the Twelve Years Truce with the Dutch rebels; in the same decade peace was also made with England and France
1618	Political crisis in Bohemia initiates the Thirty Years War in Europe
1621	Death of Philip III and succession of Philip IV; expiry the same year of the Truce with the Dutch
1625	Recapture by Spanish forces from the Dutch, of the city of Bahia in Brazil and of Breda in the Netherlands
1639	Decisive defeat of Spanish fleet at the Battle of the Downs in the Channel

1648	Treaty of Westphalia brings the Thirty Years War to an end, and confirms the independence of the Dutch Republic
1659	Treaty of the Pyrenees agrees peace between France and Spain and the cession of northern Catalonia to France
1665	Death of Philip IV and accession of the sickly Charles II, creating the problem of the future succession to the Spanish throne
1700	Death of Charles II (Habsburg), after naming the grandson of Louis XIV of France as his heir. Reign of Philip V (Bourbon)
1702–13	War of the Spanish Succession. The Grand Alliance of England, the Dutch Republic, Austria, and Portugal declares war on France and Spain supporting the Archduke Charles of Austria for the throne of Spain ('Charles III')
1704	The English and Dutch fleet captures Gibraltar
1707	Philip V revokes the *fueros* of the kingdoms of Aragon and Valencia
1713	Treaty of Utrecht and Treaty of Rastadt (1714) end the War of the Spanish Succession. Philip V recognized as king of Spain. Spain cedes Spanish Netherlands and territories in Italy to Austria, Gibraltar and Menorca to Great Britain, Sicily to Savoy
1716	The Decree of Nueva Planta replaces the government of Catalonia with authorities subservient to Madrid. The Castilian language to be used in administration of justice
1724	Philip V abdicates; reign of his son Louis I. Philip assumes throne again upon Louis's death
1726–39	Benito Jerónimo Feijóo, *Teatro crítico universal*, 9 vols., introduces the critical spirit of the Enlightenment to Spanish readers
1728	Royal Guipuzcoan Company of Caracas founded, breaks monopoly of Cadiz and Seville over trade with American colonies
1739–41	The 'War of Jenkin's Ear' between Spain and Great Britain
1740–8	War of the Austrian Succession, Spain allied with France against Austria
1746	Reign of Ferdinand VI
1749–56	Cadaster of the marquis of La Ensenada, detailed survey of real property and incomes in the provinces of Castile
1759	Reign of Charles III
1762	War with Great Britain (Seven Years War), Spain allied with France through the Family Pact. Spain loses Florida to Britain, gains Louisiana from France
1765	Freedom of grain trade, end of price-controls on grains, inspired by Campomanes
1766	'*Motín* (riot) of Esquilache' in Madrid protests urban reforms and high price of bread. Bread riots follow in other places
1767	Model agricultural colonies of Sierra Morena established with Pablo de Olavide as superintendent. Feb., decree of expulsion of the Jesuits from Spain and its empire

1777	José Moñino, count of Floridablanca, named first secretary of state, effectively becomes the head of government for the remainder of Charles III's reign
1778	Royal *reglamento* opens twelve Spanish ports to free trade with empire in America (except Mexico). Nov., the Inquisition convicts Pablo de Olavide of heresy before a select group of observers
1779–83	Spain participates in War of American Independence against Great Britain. Spain obtains Florida and Menorca from Britain
1781–7	*El Censor*, satirical enlightened periodical of Luis Cañuelo
1788	Reign of Charles IV
1789	Publication of Cadalso, *Cartas marruecas*, written in early 1770s, a satire of Spanish manners and institutions modelled on Montesquieu's *Lettres persanes*. April, Francisco Goya named a painter of the royal chamber
1792	Charles IV replaces Floridablanca with the count of Aranda as first secretary of state to improve relations with France. Nov., Manuel Godoy, duke of La Alcudia, named first secretary of state at age 25, is suspected of being Queen María Luisa's lover
1793–5	War with the Republic of France, loss of Santo Domingo to France
1795	The Economic Society of Madrid publishes the *Informe en el expediente de ley agraria* written by Jovellanos. It recommends ending restrictions on the free exchange of property, an indictment of family entails and ecclesiastical mortmain. Sept., Godoy named the Prince of the Peace
1796–1802	War against Great Britain in alliance with the Republic of France. British blockade devastates Spain's trade with its empire and Europe
1798	Royal decrees order the sale of properties of religious foundations and charitable institutions, proceeds to be used to amortize the depreciated royal notes (*vales reales*). Beginning of extensive disentail of Spanish church properties
1804–8	In alliance with France under Napoleon, Spain renews hostilities with Great Britain. Trade with the empire in America again suffers
1805	Battle of Trafalgar. The British navy under Lord Nelson destroys the combined fleets of France and Spain near Cadiz
1806	Leandro Fernández de Moratín, *El sí de las niñas*, the masterpiece of Spanish neoclassical comedy, a criticism of the subjection of women in marriage and society
1808	Abdication of Charles IV after two nights of rioting in Aranjuez. Reign of Ferdinand VII. Violent anti-French riot in Madrid on 2 May crushed by French troops, traditionally considered to mark the beginning of the Spanish rising against Napoleon. At Bayonne, Charles IV and Ferdinand VII cede their right to the throne of Spain to the Emperor Napoleon, who soon confers it on his brother Joseph. Sept., delegates of the Provincial Juntas formed to fight for the rights of Ferdinand VII come together at Aranjuez to create the Supreme Central Junta to rule in Ferdinand's name

1810	Having fled from Seville to Cadiz before the French armies, the Central Junta turns its authority over to a Regency. News of the change prompts moves to reject Spanish authority in Argentina, Venezuela, and Mexico. Sept., opening of the General and Extraordinary Cortes at Cadiz
1812	After much discussion, the Cortes in Cadiz under the leadership of the liberals, proclaim the constitution of a parliamentary monarchy for Spain
1813	The Cortes of Cadiz decree the abolition of the Inquisition. French forces under King Joseph are defeated at Vitoria by the combined British, Portuguese, and Spanish forces under the duke of Wellington. Joseph flees to France
1814	Ferdinand VII at Valencia during his return to Spain declares the convocation of the Cortes illegal and annuls their legislation, including the constitution
1820	Major (soon promoted to General) Rafael de Riego proclaims the constitution of 1812 at Cabezas de San Juan. March, Ferdinand VII takes an oath to the Constitution
1823	The French army 'Hundred Thousand Sons of Saint Louis' invades Spain to rescue Ferdinand VII from 'imprisonment' by the constitutional regime
1827	Rising of the *Agraviados* in Catalonia in favour of royal absolutism and restoration of the Inquisition, a precursor of Carlism
1830	Ferdinand VII publishes the Pragmatic Sanction of 1789 re-establishing the right of female succession to the throne. Oct., birth of Isabella, daughter of Ferdinand VII. His brother, the Infante Carlos, will reject validity of the Pragmatic Sanction
1833	Death of Ferdinand VII, opening the conflict between Isabella (II) and Don Carlos ('Carlos V') for the throne. Isabella is declared queen, with her mother María Cristina as regent
1833–9	The first Carlist War against Isabella II and her supporters, who form the Progressives and Moderate parties. *El Vapor*, the first steam-powered factory in Barcelona
1835	Juan Mendizábel, the 'Jupiter of the Progressives', becomes prime minister. Sale of church lands, abolition of aristocratic entail and guilds to create a market economy
1840–3	Regency of General Espartero. Progressives in power. María Cristina and the Moderates exiled in France. Progressives fall into factions
1843–54	A *pronunciamiento* of Moderate generals and Progressive dissidents led by General Narváez establishes Moderates in power based on their constitution of 1845. Administrative reforms on French models. Concordat with Vatican, 1851
1854–6	General O'Donnell stages a *pronunciamiento* which establishes the Progressive *biennio* under General Espartero. Economic liberal legislation makes possible the boom of the 1860s; railway network laid down.

Democratic constitution invalidated by the rise of O'Donnell and the retirement of Espartero

1858–63   O'Donnell as prime minister forms the Liberal Union to 'unite the liberal family'. It disintegrates

1862–8   Queen Isabella and her court faction commit political suicide by excluding the Progressives from power and exiling the Liberal Unionist generals

1866   The boom collapses

1868   'The Glorious Revolution' result of a *pronunciamiento* staged by 'September Coalition' of Liberal Unionists, Progressives, and Democrats

1869   Constitution establishes a constitutional monarchy with universal male suffrage and religious toleration. September Coalition disintegrates

1873   King Amadeo abdicates. First Republic and Cantonalist revolt of provincial Federal Republicans

1870s   Rapid expansion of iron ore exports and exploitation of copper pyrites by British companies

1874   *Pronunciamiento* of Brigadier Martínez Campos restores Alfonso XII

1876   Constitution of 1876, which lasts until 1923

1879   Foundation of Socialist party by Pablo Iglesias

1884   Leopoldo Alas publishes *La Regenta*

1885   Establishment of the *turno pacífico* by which Liberal and Conservative parties alternate in power through elections managed by the minister of the interior and local bosses (*caciques*). Sagasta as Liberal prime minister (1885–90) establishes universal male suffrage

1886   Benitez Peréz Galdós, *Fortunata y Jacinta*

1892   Bases of Manresa demands Home Rule for Catalonia

1898   'The Disaster'. Defeat by the United States and loss of Cuba, Puerto Rico, and the Philippines. In reaction, the emergence of regenerationism and criticism of the Restoration society and political structure

1906   Liberals give extensive powers to the army. Formation of Solitaritat Catalana; wins 41 seats

1907–9   Conservative statements; Antonio Maura attempts his 'revolution from above'

1909   The convent burnings and street riots of the Tragic Week in Barcelona. Maura dismissed by Alfonso XIII and replaced by liberal Moret. Collapse of *turno pacífico*. Party system begins to fragment

1910–11   Foundation of the anarchist-syndicalist union, the CNT

1912   Spain receives protectorate in Morocco

1917   A year of pseudo-revolutions: Catalan Assembly; a general strike of CNT and UGT; the formation of the *Juntas de Defensa* of bureaucratic soldiers

1919–23   The social war of strikes and lockouts. Gang fighting in Barcelona

1921	José Ortega y Gasset publishes *Invertebrate Spain*. Attacks on 'old politics' in *El Sol*
1923	Coup of Primo de Rivera abolishes the constitution of 1876; Primo is accepted by Alfonso XIII as a military dictator
1924	Formation of the National Union
1927	National Assembly opens
1929	Rebellion of Sánchez Guerra
1930	Primo de Rivera abandons power
1931	Municipal elections record majorities for the Republican-Socialist coalition in the large cities. Alfonso XIII abdicates. The Second Republic proclaimed. The Generalitat of Catalonia created
1932	General Sanjurjo stages an abortive coup
1933	The Falange created by José Antonio Primo de Rivera. The right wins the general elections
1934	CEDA enters the government. Insurrection in Asturias and Catalonia. The Spanish Army of Africa crushes the Asturian miners
1935	Gil Robles made minister of war
1936	16 Feb., Popular Front wins the general election. 10 May, Azaña becomes President of the Republic. 13 July, assassination of Calvo Sotelo, leader of the hard right. 17–18 July, military uprising in Morocco spreads to Spain. 4 Sept., Largo Caballero forms a government with participation of the CNT. Non-Intervention Committee starts work in London. Nov., Nationalist advance on Madrid. 8 Nov., International Brigades arrive on Madrid Front
1937	18 April, unification of the Falange and Traditionalists under leadership of General Franco. 26 April, bombardment of Guernica. 3 May, street fighting in Barcelona between the CNT, the POUM, and the Communists. 17 May, Negrín replaces Largo Caballero as Prime Minister. 18 June, fall of Bilbao and collapse of Northern Front
1938	Feb., Franco recaptures Teruel, and the beginning of the Aragon offensive which cuts Republican zone in half. July, the last Republican offensive on the Ebro
1939	26 Jan., Nationalists enter Barcelona. 1 April, Civil War ends with victory of Nationalists. Period of autarky and fierce repression of supporters of the Popular Front
1940	Spain declares non-belligerency in the Second World War. Franco and Hitler meet in Hendaye on 23 November
1941	The Blue Division recruited to fight on the Russian front
1945	Franco promulgates the Charter of the Spaniards
1946	The UN agrees on a diplomatic boycott of Spain
1951	Timid liberalization of the economy begins
1953	Spain signs a Concordat with the Vatican and a military base pact with the USA
1955	Spain readmitted to the UN

1956	First serious student troubles
1957	Franco forms a new cabinet with Opus Dei technocrats committed to economic liberalization
1959	Stabilization Plan announced. ETA created. From the early 1960s, the economic, social, and cultural transformation of Spain
1962	Labour stoppages throughout Spain. The Workers' Commissions appear
1963	Spanish intellectuals protest against labour repression
1964	Law of Associations announced
1966	The Press Law and the Organic Law of State promulgated
1969	Prince Juan Carlos officially designated as successor to Franco. State of Emergency after students' and workers' protest throughout Spain
1970	Trial of ETA militants in Burgos. Spain signs a Preferential Trade Agreement with the EEC
1973	Prime Minister Carrero Blanco assassinated. Arias Navarro appointed in his place. Economic recession brings Spain's economic boom to a halt
1975	Execution of five anti-Francoist militants. Franco dies. Juan Carlos crowned king of Spain
1976	Adolfo Suárez forms government. The transition to democracy begins. The Political Reform Act closes down the Francoist parliament and legalizes parties
1977	The Spanish Communist Party legalized. Democratic elections for a constituent parliament. UCD government formed
1978	The new democratic Constitution approved overwhelmingly in a referendum
1979–80	Catalonia and the Basque Country gain autonomy and hold regional elections
1981	Parliament held hostage during an abortive military coup
1982	Spain joins NATO. PSOE wins the elections with a large majority and Felipe González becomes president. The consolidation of the new democracy begins
1986	Spain joins the EC and NATO membership is approved in a referendum
1989	Felipe González becomes president of the EC. Spain joins the European Monetary System
1993	PSOE loses its absolute majority in the elections and forms a new government with the support of the Catalan conservative party, CiU
1996	In the elections, the conservative Popular Party wins a majority of votes and forms a government with the support of CiU, PNV, and Coalición Canarias. José María Aznar becomes president
1997	Spain joins the EMU. Mass protests against continued terrorism in the Basque Country. The leadership of Herri Batasuna jailed

1998	Mesa de Estella created. Ex-ministers Barrionuevo and Vera jailed for approving state terrorism against ETA
1999	Spain joins NATO military action against Serbia
	ETA breaks cease-fire
2000	Popular Party wins election with overall majority

ILLUSTRATION SOURCES

The editor and publishers wish to thank the following for their kind permission to reproduce the illustrations on the following pages:

14   La Consejería de Cultura de la Junta de Andalucía/Museo de Cadiz

19   Archivo Fotográfico. Museo Arqueológico Nacional, Madrid

21   Deutsches Archäologisches Institut, Madrid, photo: P. Witte (R-19-74-9)

29   Paisajes Españoles S.A.

30   Espasa Calpe S.A.

33   Prof. Mauricio Pastor Muñoz

36   © Museu Monográfico de Conimbriga. Photo: Mário de Oliveira

43   Hirmer Fotoarchiv

45   Deutsches Archäologisches Institut, Madrid, photo: P. Witte (R-159-75-3)

48   Main picture: Real Academia de la Historia, Madrid, Inset: Isabel Velázquez Soriano 'Las Pizarras Visigodas' Murcia 1989

51   Fitzwilliam Museum, Cambridge

52   Bibliothèque nationale de France (Ms Latin 13396 fol IV)

56   Institut Amatller d'Art Hispànic

59   Hirmer Fotoarchiv

67   Espasa Calpe S.A.

68   Hirmer Fotoarchiv

72   © Photo RMN. Photo: Hervé Lewandowski

74   Institut Amatller d'Art Hispànic/ Archivo Corona Aragon

79   Oronoz

85   Institut Amatller d'Art Hispànic

88   Bibliothèque nationale de France

94-95 V&A Picture Library

96-97 Institut Amatller d'Art Hispànic

101 © Patrimonio Nacional/Institut Amatller d'Art Hispànic

102 Getty Research Institute, Research Library, Wim Swaan Photograph

Collection, 96.P.21

105 Institut Amatller d'Art Hispànic

109 Rights Reserved © Museo Nacional del Prado, Madrid

112 Institut Amatller d'Art Hispànic/ Archivo Municipal, Burgos

114 Institut Amatller d'Art Hispànic

118 Institut Amatller d'Art Hispànic

125 © Patrimonio Nacional/Institut Amatller d'Art Hispànic

128-129 Bildarchiv, Österreichische National Bibliothek, Vienna

130 Spanish Tourist Office

137 Dumbarton Oaks House Collection, Washington, DC

138 Rights Reserved © Museo Nacional del Prado, Madrid

141 © Patrimonio Nacional/Institut Amatller d'Art Hispànic

147 Institut Amatller d'Art Hispànic

148-9 ©Patrimonio Nacional/Institut Amatller d'Art Hispànic

153 Institut Amatller d'Art Hispànic/Bib. Nacional, Madrid

157 Lauros-Giraudon

159 Courtesy of The Hispanic Society of America, New York

160 Institut Amatller d'Art Hispànic

163 National Maritime Museum, Greenwich, London

165 The Syndics of Cambridge University Library (Eytzinger 'De Leone Belgico' 1585)

168-9 Rights Reserved © Museo Nacional del Prado, Madrid

171 Rights Reserved © Museo Nacional del Prado, Madrid

175 © Patrimonio Nacional/Institut

INDEX

Abacus 71
Abbasids 64
'Abd al-Rahman III, Caliph 65, 70–1
'Abd Allah ibn Buluggin 73, 78
Abdibaal 16
abortion 274
Abu Yaqub, emir 100
'accidentalists' 248
Acción Popular 248
Achaea 34
Achila II, king 61
Acuña, Martín Vásquez de 115
Adrianople, battle of 41
Aelian: *On the Ways of Animals* 34
Aemilius Paullus 25
aero engines 237
afforestation 214
Afonso Heriques, king of Portugal 80, 82
afrancesados 197
Africa 50, 63, 64, 93, 162, 200
Agar valley 12
Agaric culture 12
Agila, king 50, 51
agrarian reform 193–4, 209, 243, 248, 250, 251
  law of 246
Agreda, Sor María de 144
Agricola 27
agriculture 3–4, 65, 69–70, 95, 98, 178, 179, 181, 183, 184, 187, 193, 204, 207, 216, 224, 233, 237, 238, 239, 242, 246, 247
Agriculture, Ministry of 249
Agrippa 15, 24, 31
Agüelles, Augustín 198
Aix-la-Chapelle, Peace of (1668) 170
Alalia, battle of (*c.* 535 BC) 13
al-Andalus 64, 65, 66, 70, 71–3, 78–9, 84, 87
Alans 37, 39, 41, 42
Alaric II, king 44, 57, 58
Alba, duke of 155, 161–2
Albacete 16
Alcantara 65
  bridge 32
Alcobaça 80
Alexandria 96
Alfonso II, king of Asturias (791–842) 66–8
Alfonso III, king of Asturias (866–910) 66–8, 75

Alfonso III, king of Aragon (1285–91) 102
Alfonso V, king of Aragon (1416–58) 110–11
Alfonso VI, king of Léon-Castile (1065–1109) 73, 75, 77–8, 87
Alfonso VII, king of Léon-Castile (1126–57) 77, 79, 80, 84
Alfonso VIII, king of Castile (1158–1214) 80, 82
Alfonso X, king of Castile (*el Sabio*) (1252–84) 95, 98–9 100, 115
Alfonso XI, king of Castile (1312–50) 99, 103–4
Alfonso XII, king 223, 225
Alfonso XIII, king 220, 226, 233, 235, 236, 238, 240, 242
Algarve 12, 16, 80, 82, 83
Algeciras 28, 92, 103, 104
Algiers 152
al-Hakem, Caliph 65
Alicante 16, 18
Aliseda, Caceres 15
aljamas 105
Aljubarrota, battle of 106
Almería 3, 12, 79, 84, 103
Almansa 174
Almanzor, vizir 71, 76
Almohads 78–9
Almoravids 78–9, 83, 89
al-Muqtadir, ruler of Saragossa 73
Alps 20
Alpujarras 8
alquerías 98
Altamira cave paintings 11
Altamira, R. 224
Altos Hornos de Vizcaya 236
Álvarez, Fray Antonio Baltasar 140
Alvarez del Vayo, Julio 263
Alvaro de Luna 111
Amadeo of Savoy, king 220
Amalaric, king 45
ambergris 65
America 5, 9, 93, 143, 153–6, 164, 166, 170, 173, 174, 179, 180, 181, 182, 184–6, 187–8, 192, 198, 200, 203–4, 219
  silver 117, 144–5, 158
  War of Independence 175, 192–3
  see also United States
Amiens, Treaty of 192

Amigos del País 180, 194
Ampurias 20, 31
anarchists 230–2, 247, 250, 254, 258, 259,
    261, 263, 271
Andalusia 1, 3, 4, 12, 16, 20, 25, 27, 31, 32, 79,
    80, 82, 83, 92, 98, 106, 113, 123, 170,
    182, 183, 186–7, 194, 197, 198, 204, 209,
    216, 220, 231, 232, 237, 240, 257
Anglo-Italian Treaty (April 1938) 263
Annunciation 107, 110
Antequera 107
    tombs 12
anticlericalism 205, 226, 231, 232, 233
anti-Semitism 106
Antonio, prior of Crato 162
Apostólicos 204
Appian 26
Aquitaine 42
'Arabic' numerals 71
Arabs, Arab culture 29, 49, 55, 56, 58, 60,
    61–2, 63, 99, 104
Aragon (*Corona de Aragón*) 6–7, 69, 77, 78,
    80, 83, 84, 87, 93, 95, 96, 98, 100–2,
    103, 107–11, 120, 121, 122, 124, 152–3,
    166, 170, 173, 174, 176, 177, 205, 261–2
    'Aragonese party' 111
    Cortes 103, 176
    Council of 156, 176
Aragonese Union 102
Arana, Sabino de 229
Aranda, Count of 179, 187, 191, 194
Aranjuez 179, 197
    motín of 195–6
arbitristas 164, 167, 170, 172, 180
architecture 123, 126, 130, 181, 217, 238
    French 77
    Islamic 64
    military 65–6
    Mozarabic influence 71
    rural 4
    Roman 31–2, 46
    Visigothic 45–6
Ardo, king 61
Arganthonius 15, 17
Argentina 200
Argericus, abbot 71
Arianism 49–50, 51, 53
Aristotle 86, 127
Armada (1588) 144, 164
'arms' and 'letters' 115
arms market, private 256, 264
army 135–6, 145, 155, 156–8, 162, 165, 174,
    197–8, 200, 201, 202–3, 214, 219, 220–1,
    225, 228, 231, 235–6, 237, 240, 242,
    243–5, 249, 251–2, 255, 257, 262, 263,
    265, 268, 275, 276, 282
Army of Africa 252, 255, 257
art 11–12, 33, 71, 85, 87, 97, 100, 114, 115, 116,
    117, 124, 139, 146, 149, 181–2, 190, 217,
    238, 273
Arthurian legends 97
Artois, province of 170
Asia 165
asiento 174
association, freedom of 223
Astarte 16
Astorga 44, 77
astronomy 65, 86, 180
Asturias 4, 11, 33, 66–7, 68, 69, 198, 229,
    249, 257, 271
Atahualpa 153
Athanagild, king 50, 51
atheism 243, 265
Athenaeum, Madrid 217
Atlantic ocean 95, 156, 166, 199
Augustine, St 37
Augustinians 77
Augustus 31
Aurelius Clemens Prudentius 37
Austria 173–4
Austrian Succession, war of 174
Averroes (Ibn Rushd) 86
Avienus 35
Avila 49, 134
    'Farce of' 111–13
Ayala, Pedro López de 91
Azaña, Manuel 226, 233, 245, 246, 247, 248,
    249, 250, 251, 263
Azcárate, Gumersindo de 226
Aznar, José María 279
Aztecs 128, 153–4

Baalyaton 16
Baebelo mine 20
Baetica 31, 34, 41
Baghdad 65
Bahia, Brazil 166
Bailén 27, 197
Balbus of Cadiz 28
Baldwin, Stanley 256
Balearic Islands 27, 83, 95
Balfour, Arthur 217
Balts 41, 45
banks, banking 214, 215, 216, 217, 236, 237,
    238
Barcelona 41, 45, 61, 83–4, 87, 98, 103, 106,
    131, 132, 133, 146, 147, 167, 174, 184, 188,
    196, 203, 209, 226, 228, 230, 231, 234,
    235, 236, 237, 238, 263, 265
    civil war (1937) 259

Cortes 102
Counts of 73–5
'Fever of Gold' 236
opera house 238
Barcids 18–20
Baroja, Pió 2, 225, 229
Barrionuevo, Rafael 278
Basques, Basque provinces 3, 4, 7, 12, 64, 69, 76, 176, 181, 184, 186, 189, 192, 198, 203–4, 205, 215–16, 232, 236–7, 238, 249, 250, 257, 261, 266, 269, 279–81
nationalism 7, 225, 228–9, 254, 271, 276, 279–81
Basque Nationalist Party 280, 281
Bayonne 96, 105, 196
Baza 17–18
Beata of Piedrahita 93
Beatriz, Queen 106
Bécquer, Gustavo Adolfo 217
Bede: *Ecclesiastical History of the English People* 54
Belgida 26
Belo 32
Benamarin 93
Benguela 143
Benidorm 65
Bentham, Jeremy 211
Berbers 39, 61, 62, 63, 64, 78
Berengaria, Queen 86
Bernard of Sédirac 76
bigamy 135
Bilbao 5, 87, 207, 215, 225, 229, 232, 236, 237, 238, 261
Bilbilis (Calatayud) 13
Black Legend 1, 231
Black Sea 84
Blake, Robert 167
Blanco, Admiral Carrero 6
Blastophoenicians 20
'Block of the Left' 233
Blue Division 267
Blum, Léon 256
Bohemia 165
Bokhara 65
Bolívar, Simón 200
Bolshevism 231, 240, 250
Bonaparte, Joseph 196–7, 198, 199–200
Bonaparte, Napoleon 145, 173, 175, 192, 194–6, 197–8, 199, 201
Bordeaux 96
Borrow, George 8
The Bible in Spain 216
botany 65, 180
Bougie 96
Bourbons 7, 174, 177, 179, 187, 199, 203, 219, 227
Bourgneuf, Bay of 106
braceros 4, 231
Braga 37, 69
brandy trade 5
Braudel, Fernand 161
Braulio, bishop of Saragossa 49
Brazil 143, 165, 166, 195
Breda 166
Brenan, Gerald 5–6, 8, 231
The Spanish Labyrinth 5
Bretons 98
Brihuega 174
Britain 8, 24, 27, 31, 34, 122, 173, 174, 175, 178, 187, 192, 197, 199, 202, 204, 215–16, 217, 223, 239, 255–6, 259, 263–4
Act of Union 176
navy 192, 194
see also England
broadcasting 9, 265, 274
Brunete 276
Brussels 162
Buenos Aires 162, 198
Bulgar, Count 55
Buñuel, Luis 219
Burgos 11, 69, 77, 98, 130, 131, 132, 253, 258, 271
Burke, Edmund 9
Byzantines 50–3, 57, 60

Cabriada, Juan de 171
Cáceres 49
caciques, caciquismo 66, 223, 224, 228, 233
Cadalso, José de: *Cartas marruecas* 188–9
cadaster of La Ensenada 177–8
Cadiz 13, 17, 18, 28, 34, 35, 81, 92, 161, 166, 184, 186, 192, 194, 197, 198, 199, 200, 201, 202–3, 204, 247
Cortes 200
Caesar 24, 27–31, 39
Calagurris (Calahorra) 34, 37
Caliphate 6
calligraphy 65
Calvo Sotelo, José 250–1, 252
Cambó, Francesc 227–8
Cambodia 145
Campillo y Cossío, José del 180
Campomanes, Pedro Rodríguez de 179, 180, 181, 182, 184, 187, 189, 191, 194
Canada 175
cañadas reales 98
Canal of Isabella II 213
Canalejas, José 233–4, 240
Canary Islands 152, 252
cancionero poets 111

Cánovas de Castillo, Antonio 217, 220–1, 223–4, 231
Cantabria 11, 24, 31, 64, 132, 134
Cantabrian mountains 4, 66
Cantigas de Santa María 100
Cañuelo, Luis 189
Capitoline Triad 23
car manufacture 237
Caracas 198
Carande, Ramón 158
Carcassonne 44
Cardeña 69
Caribbean 153, 154
Carlists 4, 205–7, 208, 214, 220, 225, 228, 229, 236, 239, 251, 264
Carlos María Isidro, Don, first Carlist pretender 204, 205
Carmona 20
Carolingian dynasty 66, 75
Carrero Blanco, Admiral 273
Cartagena 18, 20, 23, 50, 51, 81
Carteia 28
Cartesian logic 180
Carthaginians 17, 18, 20–4, 26
Casa de Contratación 184
Casas, Ramón 230
Caspe, Compromise of (1412) 107
Castelar, Emilio 172, 218, 223
Castellón 11
Castile 3–7, 66, 69, 80, 81–3, 87, 91, 92–3, 95, 96, 97, 98, 103, 104–5, 106, 107, 110, 119, 120, 121, 122, 124, 126, 127, 128–9, 131, 133, 143, 144–5, 146, 152–6, 158–9, 162, 167, 170, 173, 174, 176–7, 178, 179, 186–7, 194, 199, 200, 203, 216, 231, 232, 233, 237, 266
  Cortes 106, 176
  Council of 176–7, 179, 180, 187, 196
  Council of Finance 156
Castro, house of 82
castros 32
Catalan Action 228
Catalan Company 184
Catalan revolt (1640) 7
Catalanism 227–8, 229, 238, 242, 271, 279
Catalans 7, 8, 98
Catalonia 3, 5, 7, 9, 13, 17, 44, 66, 69–70, 71, 75, 77, 83, 84, 96, 102, 110, 120, 133, 146–7, 148, 150, 166, 167, 170, 174, 176, 184, 186, 187–8, 192, 198, 201, 203, 204, 205, 216, 231, 234, 237, 238, 240, 242, 247, 249, 250, 262, 263, 266, 269, 278, 279, 282
  Cortes 103, 176
  Generalitat 103, 259

nationalism 225, 226, 227–8, 229, 254, 271
'catastrophists' 248
Cateau-Cambrésis, Treaty of (1559) 158, 161
Catherine of Lancaster 106, 107
Catholic Action 232
Catholic church, Catholicism 2, 4, 6, 50, 51, 53, 63, 92–3, 99, 113, 114, 133, 136–9, 140, 162, 177–80, 183, 199, 204, 208–9, 211, 214, 219, 221, 225, 229, 231, 232–3, 238, 243, 245–6, 247, 248, 251, 253–4, 257, 264, 265, 268, 270, 274
  growth of religious orders 232, 233
  'Social Catholicism' 232
'Catholic Kings' 6, 9, 113, 140, 266
Cato, Elder 24, 25
cave paintings 11–12
CEDA (*Confederación de Derechas Autónomas*) 248, 249, 250–1
Cela, Camilo José 8
Celanova 71
  monastery 75
Celtiberian Belli 25–6
Celtiberians 13, 26, 27
  Termestines 31, 32
Celts 12–13, 15, 17, 20, 32
Censor, El (journal) 189
censorship 191, 197, 273
Centcelles 36–7
Cerignola, battle of 143
Cervantes Saavedra, Miguel de 143, 161
  Don Quixote 2, 8, 127, 134, 189
Ceuta 96
Chambers of Commerce 224
Charlemagne 66
Charles II, king 150–1, 170–1, 173
Charles III, king 173, 175, 177, 179–80, 181–3, 184, 187, 189, 192, 193, 198
Charles IV, king 173, 174, 188, 189–93, 194–6, 197, 199, 201, 204
Charles V, Emperor 119, 123, 124, 131, 132, 133, 154–5, 156, 158–9, 161, 174
Charles of Valois 102
Charter of Rights (1945) 267
Chaucer, Geoffrey 92
chemicals 237
Chile 200
China 145
Chindasuinth, king 57–8
Chintila, king 49
chivalry, cult of 126–7
chocolate 184
cholera 236
Christian Democrats 248
Christian, William Jr 134
Christians, Christianity 6, 35–7, 42, 49–50,

51, 58, 60, 63–5, 66, 69, 70, 71, 73, 75,
  76–81, 83, 84–7, 92–3, 95–8, 103–4,
  106, 113, 126, 132–9, 142, 181, 265
  see also Reconquest
Chronicle of Fredegar 55, 57
Cicero 28
Cienfuegos, Nicasio de 189
cinema 9, 239, 273
Cines 89
Cisneros, Cardinal 142
Cistercians 77, 80
city status 131
Ciudad Real 127, 132
civil disorder 251–2, 253, 257
Civil Guard 211, 231, 247, 276
civil liberties 245
civil war (1833–9) 205
Civil War (1936–9) 8, 9, 253–64, 265, 269,
  270, 282
  atrocities 257
  battle for Madrid 257–8
  battle-front 257, 261–3
  civil war within 258–61
  European powers 255–6
  final stages 263–4
  issues of war 253–5
  prolongation of 265
Claret, Father 232
Clarín (Leopold Alas) 225
  La Regenta 225
Claudius, Emperor 32
Clement XI, pope 178
Clement XIII, pope 179–80
climate 3, 4, 86, 194, 239, 246
Clodius Albinus 34
Cluny, monastery 76
Cluniac monks 76
CNT (*Confederación Nacional del Trabjo*) 231,
  234, 242, 250, 254, 258
coal 5, 215, 229, 237, 261
Code of Theodosius (*The Breviary*) 58
Coimbra 77
coins, coinage 28, 35, 50, 56, 57, 61, 69, 73,
  83, 99, 177
Colaeus 15
Colbert, Jean-Baptiste 180
Cold War 268, 272
collective bargaining 270
Columbus, Christopher 93, 122–3, 153, 156,
  174
Columella 34
Comillas, marquis of 229, 232
Comintern 257
Communion 134–5
communism, communists 247, 254, 255, 258,

259, 261, 264, 265, 271
  anti-Stalinist 247
Communist Party 247, 259, 270, 271, 279
Company of Jesus 200
Comuneros, revolt of 154, 179
Concordat (1851) 211
Condé, Prince de (Duke of Enghien) 166
Conquistadores 28
conscription 209
Conservative party 223–4, 233–4, 235, 242
conservatism 264, 265, 279–80
Constables of Castile 131
Constans, Emperor 37
Constantine, Emperor 36
Constantine, king of Greece 273–4
Constantine III, king 37
Constantinople 50, 60
Constitution 235, 236, 249
  1812: 201–3, 219
  1834: 205
  1845: 211
  1856: 214
  1869: 219, 220, 221
  1876: 223, 232
  1931: 245
  1978: 274–5, 279
consumerism 242, 269, 270
Contreras, Alonso de 136
Convergencia I Unió (CiU) 278
conversos 105–6, 113
convivencia 93
copper 12, 34, 186, 215
Córdoba 6, 28, 31, 33–4, 35, 36, 50, 51, 61, 64,
  65–6, 69, 70, 71, 79, 85, 87, 96, 98, 106,
  183
  mosque 64
Cortes 7, 81, 100–1, 103, 111, 176, 198–201,
  202–3, 204, 205, 211, 214, 233, 236, 246,
  247, 249, 268
  Constituent 220
  Pragmatic Sanction 204
Cortés, Hernando 128, 153–4
Cortés, Juan Donoso 211–12
Costa, Joaquín 224, 240
cotton 186, 188, 192, 216
Council of State 176–7
Council of Trent (1565) 135
Counter-Reformation 114, 136
Court of Chancellery 132
Covadonga 68–9
Covarrubias 70
Cromwell, Oliver 167
Crónica Profética ('Prophetic Chronicle') 69
crucifixion 113–14
crusades 77, 81, 116

Cuba 166, 184, 203, 216, 224
  war 219
cubism 238
Czech nationalism 227

Dagobert I, king 57
Dalmau Gallery 238
Dama de Baza 16, 17–18
Dama de Elche 16, 17–18
dams 241
Dartmouth 106
Dato, Eduardo 240
Day Lewis, Cecil 257
de la Mota family 131
de la Rosa, Francisco Martinez 201
Delibes, Miguel 9
democracy, 20th-century 265, 268, 271,
  273–82
  and conservatism 279–80
  new democracy 276–80
  reform 274–6
  and socialism 278–9
  transition to 273–6
Democratic party 209–10, 213, 214, 215, 216,
  218, 220, 223
deputies of the commons 182–3
desengaño 167
Desiderius of Vienne, Bishop 49
Deza, Lope de 167
dictatorship 236, 256
  under Franco 264–73
Diocletian 35
Diodorus Siculus 18, 20
Diputació 103
Disaster (1898) 224–5
divorce 245
Domènach i Montaner, Lluis 238
Dominicans 134, 154
Domitian 34
Don Carlos (son of Philip II) 140
Don Juan, Count of Barcelona (son of Alfonso
  XIII) 235, 268, 278
Doria, Admiral Andrea 155
Douglas, Sir James 92
Downs, Battle of the (1639) 166
Drake, Sir Francis 164
drugs 280
'dual economy' 2, 216
Duero valley 31, 63–4, 69, 70, 123
Dutch United Provinces 166

Eastern Europe 237, 275
Ebro valley 20, 25, 32, 34, 44, 61, 63, 66, 77,
  83, 262
Ecija 143

ecology 280
Economic Society of Madrid 181, 193
economics, economists 180, 181, 189, 241–2
economy 158–9, 167, 182, 183–8, 192–4,
  204, 209, 216, 224, 234, 236–7, 239–40,
  246, 259–61, 266, 268–70, 272, 273,
  278 279; see also taxation
Edict of the Expulsion of the Jews 113
education and learning 27, 47, 49, 86–7, 99,
  117, 124, 127, 142, 155, 171–2, 179, 180–1,
  201, 211, 218–19, 224, 226, 232, 233, 240,
  243, 249, 266, 270; see also universities
Egica, king 55, 60–1
Egypt 65
Ejea, Cortes of 100
El Carambolo burial site 16
Elche 18
El Cid 189
El Cordobés 272
electricity 236, 237
El Greco 139
Elice 18
Elizabeth I, queen 164
Emerita Augusta (Mérida) 42
emigration, 1960–73 269
Emma, Abbess 69–70
Emporion (Ampurias) 13
Encubierto (the Hidden One) 92–3
England 3, 62, 75, 81, 82–3, 96, 99, 105, 106,
  129, 140, 145, 156, 161, 162, 164, 166,
  167, 176, 216
  armada against 144, 164
  'Great Rebellion' 146
Enlightenment 2, 172, 180, 181, 183, 193, 232,
  265
Ensor, James 238
epidemics, plagues 145–50, 166, 167, 194,
  203, 236, 266
epistemology 180
Equestrian order 35
Erasmus 142, 155
Érice, Victor 273
Ervig, king 60
eschatological expectations 92–3
Escorial 123, 124, 139, 140
Espartero, Baldomero 207, 208, 211, 213, 214,
  217
Esquilache, marquis of 179
estates 4, 35, 47, 81, 82, 126, 150, 216, 231,
  254
Estella (Lizarra) Pact 280
Estelle, Diego de 139
Estoria de España 99
Estremadura 3, 4, 15, 31, 82, 183 257
ETA 7, 229, 271, 273, 278, 279–81

Burgos trial (1970) 271
Etruscans 13
Eugenius II, bishop of Toledo 54
Euric, king 38, 44, 58, 61
Europe 9, 38, 41, 53, 75, 93, 105–6, 116, 135, 143, 155, 165–6, 167, 170, 171, 173–4, 176, 180, 183, 201, 203–4, 215, 216, 217, 225, 234, 236, 238, 242, 246, 250, 256, 257, 262, 264, 269, 271
    Northern 1, 5, 12
European Community 9, 269, 278
European Revolution (1848) 211
Euzkadi 7, 9, 229
evangelism 132, 134–6, 139, 142
Evora, Portugal 28
Exaltados 201–2, 203
excusado 178
exequator 178

Falange, Falangists 120, 251, 264–5, 266, 268
Family Pact 175, 192
famine, starvation 132, 150, 179, 194, 203, 236, 261, 266
fascism 249, 251, 253, 254, 256, 257, 264, 266
Federal Republicans 228
Feijóo, Benito Jerónimo:
    Cartus eruditas 180
    Teatro crítico universal 180
Ferdinand I, king of Portugal 106
Ferdinand I, king of Léon-Castile (1037–65) 75, 77
Ferdinand III, king of Castile (1217–52) 80–1, 84, 86, 87, 96, 98
Ferdinand IV, king of Castile (1295–1312) 103
Ferdinand (the Catholic), king of Aragon and of Castile 6, 91, 113, 117–21, 123–4, 126–7, 129, 131, 132–3, 152, 155, 174, 178
Ferdinand VI, king 173, 175, 177, 180
Ferdinand VII, king 173, 194–7, 198, 200–3, 204
Ferdinand of Antequera, king of Aragon (1412–16) 107–10
    order of the Jar and the Griffin 107, 110
    coronation 107–10
Fez 93
First Republic (1873) 220–1, 251
fiscales 176–7
Flanders 82, 131, 162, 164, 165, 166, 167
Flemings 156, 162
Floréz Estrada, Alvaro: *Course of Economic Policy* 209
Florida 175
flour mills 236
football 239, 266, 272
Ford, Richard 1, 3, 5, 11, 121, 216

Handbook for Travellers in Spain 1
Foreign Office 266
Forum Iudicum ('Judge's Book') 47
France 8, 17, 20, 42, 57, 62, 66, 71, 75, 76–7, 81, 82, 87, 96, 98, 100, 105, 106, 117, 123, 145, 146, 150, 151, 152, 155, 156, 162, 166–7, 170, 173–6, 177, 179–80, 184, 186, 187, 192, 194–7, 199–200, 202–3, 211, 217, 229, 238, 239, 255–6, 259, 263–4, 278
    air force 237
    navy 175
    Revolution 173, 191, 192, 193, 200, 203
francesa ('French writing') 76
Franche-Comté, province of 170
Franciscans 134, 142
Franco, General Francisco 1, 2, 7, 9, 120, 215, 240, 241, 249, 251–2, 257–8, 261, 262, 263, 264–73, 274, 278; *see also* Franco dictatorship
Franco dictatorship 264–73, 274, 275, 281, 282
    autarky 266–8
    decline of regime 272–3
    economic liberalization 268–70
    executions under 266
    protest and opposition 270–2
Franks 44–5, 54–6, 57, 61, 66
free trade 2, 185–6, 187, 203, 209, 214, 216, 227
freemasonry 200, 201, 219, 232, 254, 257, 265
French Basque region 280
Fronde 167
fruit trade 5, 187, 216, 237
fueros (customary laws) 6–7, 58, 82, 84, 85, 99, 176, 177, 205

Galba 26
Galdós, Benito Pérez 225
    O'Donnell 214
Galera 16
Galicia 3, 4, 8, 9, 42, 51, 66, 69, 71, 75, 89, 98, 123, 135, 170, 186, 189, 216, 237, 238, 250, 266
Gallaecia (Galicia) 42, 44
Gallic Empire 35
Games, Díez de: *El Victorial* 106
García, Count 70
Gargoris, king 17
garum 34
gas 236
Gascony 96, 99
Gaudí, Antoni 238
Gaul 17, 20, 24, 27, 34, 37, 42–4, 64

Gazeta 194
Gelmírez, Diego, Archbishop 76
General Historia 99
Generalitat 103
'generation of 1898' 225
Genoa 83–4, 96, 98, 123, 155, 158
Gerald of Beauvais 77
Gerbert of Aurillac 71, 86
Germany 98, 154–5, 156, 158, 166, 230, 255–6, 266, 267
  Condor Legion 261
Geronia 106
Gerontius 37
Geryon, king 17
Gibraltar 8, 11, 32, 103, 104, 174, 175, 204, 255, 264
  Straits 61, 64, 77, 78, 255
Gil Robles, José María 248, 249, 250, 251
Gladstone, William Ewart 217
glass 186, 238
God 92–3, 100, 104, 108, 122, 132, 134, 136–9, 142, 145, 166, 194, 254
Godoy, Manuel, Prince of the Peace 191–2, 193, 194–7, 199
gold 16, 34, 57, 58–9, 64, 73–5, 76, 83, 108, 154, 170
Góngora, Luis de 127
  Lazarillo de Tormes 127
González, Felipe 278
Gormaz, castle of 656
governments, multiple 235
Goya, Francisco 181–2, 188, 217
Gracchuris 25
grain trade 184, 186, 187
Gran Dama Oferente 18
Granada 1, 16, 63, 73, 80, 84, 93, 97, 103, 113, 120, 124, 126, 132, 133, 152, 161, 178, 257
  Alhambra palace 97
Granada, Luis de 139
Grau, Perpiña 241–2
Gravesend 106
Greece 11, 12, 73, 84, 274
Greek artefacts, trade in 13
Greeks 13, 15, 18
Gregory, St 134
Gregory of Tours: *Ten Books of Histories* 54
Guadalajara 46, 126, 261
Guadalquivir valley 15, 16, 23, 25, 32, 34, 50, 64
Güell dynasty 236
Guernica 260, 261
Guerra, Sánchez 242
Gundemar, king 55
Guzmán, house of 82
Guzmán, Leonor de 104

gypsy culture 257

Habsburg monarchy 7, 39, 123, 153, 154, 155, 172, 173, 174, 176, 180, 198, 203
Hadad 16
Hadrian 34
Hamilcar Barca 18, 20
Hannibal 20
Hasdrubal 18–20
Hasta Regia 25
Hastings 106
Hawkins, John 164
health 270
Hebrew culture 99
Hendaye 266
Henry II, king (Henry Trastámara) of Castile (1369–79) 105–6
Henry III, king of Castile (1390–1406) 106–7
Henry IV, king of Castile (1454–74) 111–13
Heraclius, Emperor 60
Hercules, temple of (Cadiz) 28
Hermann of Carinthia 86
Hermenegild, king 51–3
Herodotus 15, 17
Herri Batasuna (Unity of the People) 279–80
Hezekiah 140
Hildebrandine reform of Papacy 76
Hispania 87
Hispania Citerior (Hispania Tarraconensis) 23–4, 25, 27, 31, 34, 35, 38, 44
Hispania Ulterior 23–4, 25–6, 27, 28
Hispaniola 154, 167, 170
Hispano–Suiza 237
historiography 65
Hita 104
Hitler, Adolf 255, 266–7
Holy Alliance 200, 202, 204
Holy League 139
Holy Roman Empire 99, 154
Holy Week 149
Homo antecessor 11
Honorius 37–8
Honorius I, pope 49
Hosius, Bishop 36
Houses of the People 230
Huelva 15, 16, 215
huertas 3, 89, 95
Huesca 27
humanism 111, 122, 142, 155, 180
Hundred Years War 93, 105, 106
hunting 182
hybridae 28

Ibáñez, Blasco 242
'Iber' , river 20

Iberians 12–13, 15, 16, 17–18, 20, 21, 23, 27, 28–31
sculpture 17–18
Ibiza 95
Ibn Hazm: *Kitab al-Fisal* ('Book of Sects') 86
Ibn Khaldun 78
Iglesias, Pablo 229, 230, 232, 238
Ildefonsus, bishop of Toledo 54
Iliturgi 25
imagism 239
Imilce of Castulo 20
Immaculate Conception 232
'immobilists' 273, 274
imperator 68
Incas 153
India 15, 24, 65
Indians, American 154
Indies 165, 167–70, 178, 187
Council of 177
see also West Indies
Indortes 20
industry, industrialization 4, 5, 8, 215–16, 225, 229, 236–8, 242, 243, 247, 270
Innocent III, pope 81
Innocent IV, pope 95
Inquisition 2, 113, 132–3, 135, 143, 171, 179, 180, 187, 197, 199, 200, 201, 204, 231
Institute of Free Education 219
insurrection (1520) 131
intelligence services 276
intermarriage 126
International Brigades 257, 258, 263
Garibaldi Batallion 261
Iran 65
Iranzo, Miguel Lucas de 91
Iraq 65
Ireland 3, 164, 184, 227, 237
Iriarte, Tomás de 189
iron, iron ore 5, 186, 215, 229, 236–7, 238, 261
irrigation 241
Isabel Farnese of Parma 174
Isabella, queen 6, 91, 113, 117–21, 123–4, 126–7, 129 132–3, 152, 155, 174, 178
Isabella II, queen 204, 205, 207–8, 214–15, 223
Isidore, bishop of Seville 53–5, 56, 57, 92
Etymologies 53–4
Hispana 54
History of the Goths, Sueves, and Vandals 54
Isle of Wight 106
Italica 23, 24
Italy 3, 20, 23, 27, 32, 34, 42, 73, 83–4, 98, 110, 111, 131, 152, 155, 156, 158, 161, 165, 167, 174, 179, 202, 230, 236, 239, 251,

255–6, 261, 265, 266
Council of 156
Iudila, king 55
Iuvencus 37
ivory 15, 65
Izquierda Unida (United Left) 280

Jaca 77, 106
'Jacobins' 7, 206
Jaén 4, 18, 91
Jalón valley 26
Jamaica 148
James I, king of Aragon (1213–76) 89, 95–6, 100
Llibre dels feyts ('Book of Deeds') 83, 85, 95
James II, king of Aragon (1291–1327) 103
James the Greater, St 75–6, 78
Jansenists 178–9, 189, 198, 199
Japan 8, 134
Játiva 95
Jehosophat 140
'Jenkin's Ear, war of' 174
Jerez 5, 98
Jerónimo, bishop 76
Jerusalem 78, 92–3, 113–14, 122–3
Jesuits 120, 134, 136, 178–80, 200, 201, 232, 245–6
Jesus Christ 100, 113, 133, 134, 225, 232
jewellery 16
Jews, Judaism 2, 60, 63–4, 71, 84–5, 87 93, 98, 104, 105–6, 113, 123, 127, 132, 208, 254, 265
Joanna I, Queen Mother 119
Joanna II of Naples 110
John I, king of Castile (1379–90) 106
John II, king of Castile (1406–54) 107, 111
John II, king of Aragon (1458–79) 111
John of Biclar 46
John of Gaunt, duke of Lancaster 106
John of the Cross, St 139
Dark Night of the Soul 136
José, Don Juan (of Austria) 150, 171–2
Josiah 140
journalism 189, 217, 218, 224
Jovellanos, Gaspar Melchior de 189, 191, 193, 197, 198
Informe en el expediente de ley agraria 193
Juan Carlos, king 273–4, 276
Juan Manuel: *Libro de los enxemplos del Conde Lucanor et de Patronio* 104
Juana, 'la Beltraneja' (Henry IV's putative daughter) 113
Julian, Bishop of Toledo 54, 59–60
History of Wamba 55, 59
Junius Gallio 34

juntas 209
Juntas de Defensa (Committee of Defence) 235
jury system 220
Justice, Ministry of 249
Justin 17
Justinian I, emperor 50

Knights Templar 78, 80, 82
Koran 84, 86
Krause, Karl 218–19

Labour, Ministry of 249
labour relations 245, 259
La Coruña 106
La Ensenada, marquis of 177–8, 186
La Granja 181
La Guardia 113–14
La Luisiana 184
La Mancha 12, 82, 183
landed private property 245
language 11, 12–13, 44, 63, 254, 266
  Arabic 65, 83, 87
  Basque 12, 87, 228–9, 266
  Castilian 87, 99, 176
  Catalan 87, 227, 228, 266
  Celtiberian 32
  Galaico-Portuguese 87, 99
  Iberian 12, 28
  Latin 28, 32, 33, 38, 86, 99
Lara, house of 82
Largo Caballero, Francisco 242, 248, 250,
  251, 258, 259
Laristan 143
La Rochelle 106
Las Casas, Bartolomé de 154
Lascuta, Tower of 25
Las Mesas 140
Las Navas de Tolosa 80
Lateran Council, Fourth (1215) 81
law 28, 31, 47, 49, 58, 60, 61, 68, 76, 81, 85,
  99, 104, 121, 176, 180, 199, 201, 214,
  216, 217, 220, 226, 228, 243, 245, 249,
  265; *see also fueros*
law and order 247, 259, 276
Law of Associations 273
Law of Jurisdictions 228
Law for Political Reform 274
Law of Political Responsibilities (1939) 265
Law of Succession 268
Leander, bishop of Seville 53
lentils 261
Leo XIII, pope 225
Léon 31, 66, 68, 69, 70, 71, 75, 77, 81, 87, 131
Léon, Fray Luis de 139
Léon-Castile 73, 75, 76, 78, 79, 80

Leonor (sister of Alfonso X) 99
Leovigild, king 46, 50–3, 58
Lepanto, battle of (1571) 155, 161
Lérida 106
Lerma, duke of 145
Lerroux, Alejandro 226, 228
Leulingham, truce of 106
Levant 32, 209, 216, 220, 231, 237, 246
Levantine cave paintings 11–12
Lewes 106
Lex Visigothorum ('The Law of the Visigoths')
  (*Fuero Juzgo*) 58, 60, 68
'Liberal Conquests' 220
Liberal Unionists 207, 214–15, 220
liberalism 1–2, 4, 7, 193, 204, 205–10, 213–14,
  227, 232, 233, 236, 239–40, 245, 265,
  268–70, 273, 278
Liberals and Liberal parties 198–201, 203,
  223, 233–4, 235
Lisbon 80, 162
literacy 16, 49, 201, 207, 223, 239
literary societies 217
literature 49, 53–6, 66–8, 75, 83–7, 95, 99,
  104, 115, 127, 136, 140, 142, 145, 149,
  164, 167, 170, 172,180–1,188–9, 194,
  217, 224–5, 228, 229, 239, 242, 273; *see
  also* poetry
Liuva II, king 55
Livy 17
Lliga 228
Llobregat valley 247
local government 182–3
Logroño 77, 106
Lombardy 96
London 204, 208, 256
López dynasty 236
Lorca, Federico García 219, 257
Los Millares 12
Louis XIV, king of France 167, 170, 173, 176,
  182
Louis XVI, king of France 191, 192
Louis XVIII, king of France 202
Louisiana 175
Lucan 34
Lucius Piso 31, 32
Lucullus 24
Luddites 216
Lugo 77
Luna, Saragossa 16
Lusitani 25, 26, 27
Lusitania, province of 31, 41–2
Luther, Martin 2, 100, 140, 142
Lyceum Theatre, Barcelona 231

Machado, Antonio 225, 253

Machado, Manuel 253
Machiavelli, Niccolò 122, 129
Macia, Colonel Francesc 228
Macrobius 17
Madinat al-Zahra, palace complex 64
Madrid 7, 8, 124, 126, 131, 136, 143, 145, 150,
    154, 164, 165, 179, 180, 181, 184, 188,
    189, 192, 194, 195–6, 197, 199, 200, 203,
    211, 213, 217, 219, 220, 226, 227, 228,
    229, 236, 238, 239, 253, 256, 257–8, 259,
    261, 263, 269, 273
  Economic Society 181, 193
  Museo Arqueológico Nacional 58
  Palace 181
Magdalenian culture 11
Maghrib 64, 80, 82
Magnus Maximus, emperor 37
maketos 229
malae consuetudines ('evil customs') 70
Malaya 5
male suffrage 203, 209, 214, 220, 223
mali usatici ('evil usages') 70
Mallorca 95, 106, 110, 167
Malta 84
  siege (1565) 161
Manchester 216
Mancomunidad 228
Manila 126
manos muertas (ecclesiastical mortmain) 184
Manrique, Gómez 115
Manrique, Jorge: Coplas por la muerte de su padre
    115
Marbella 5
Marcabrun: Lavador 77
Marcus Aurelius 34
María (wife of Alfonso XI) 104
María Cristina, Queen Regent 204, 205,
    207–8, 211
María de Molina 103
María Luisa, queen 191–2, 194, 196
Maria Teresa, Infanta 167
Mariana of Neuburg 170
Marie Louise of Orléans 170
marine turbines 237
Marineus 38
Marinids 92, 98, 100, 104
marriage 135
Marseilles 13, 20
Marshall aid 268
Martial 13, 34
martial law 273
Martin I, king 107
Martin of Braga, bishop 51
Martin of Tours, St 37
Marxism 229, 254, 278

Mary Queen of Scots 164
Mary, Virgin 99, 100, 104, 107, 108, 133, 134,
    136
masía 3
Master of Avis, king of Portugal 106
Maternus Cynegius 37
mathematics 65, 71, 86
Maura, Antonio 217, 233–4
Maura, Miguel 247
Mauretania 32, 34
Mauretania Tingitana 35
Maximus ('Emperor of the Spains') 37–8, 41
Mayáns, Gregorio 180
mayorazgos (entails) 184, 193, 201
medicine 65, 85, 172, 180, 266
Medina del Campo fair, Castile 5
Medina Sidonia, duke of 164
Mediterranean sea, region 95, 106, 110, 143,
    155, 156, 158, 161, 162, 187, 255, 264
megaliths 12
Melqart (Punic god) 28
Mena, Juan de: Laberinto de Fortuna 111
Mendizábel, Juan 208
Mendoza Iñigo Lopez de, marquis of
    Santillana 115
Mendoza palaces, Guadalajara 126
Menéndez y Pelayo, Marcelino 232
Menorca 95, 174, 175
Mérida 31, 46, 50
meseta 3, 4, 216
Mesta 82, 98, 184
metallurgy 236–7, 239
metalworking 16, 65, 190, 258
Mexico 186, 214
  creoles 203
Michoacán 126
military coup, attempted (1981) 276, 278
mineral resources 5, 215–16
mining 12, 20, 34, 216, 229, 249
Miró, Joan 238
missionaries 232
Moderados 201, 203, 204, 246
Moderate party 207–8, 209, 210–12, 239–40
modernism 239
modernization, 20th-century 236–9, 246,
    247, 248–9, 270, 272
monarchists, 20th-century 264, 265, 268
Monçao, truce of 106
Moñino, José, count of Floridablanca 187,
    191, 197
Mons Mariana 34
Montesquieu, Charles de 180, 181
Montiel 105
Montsény, Federica 254
Moors 1, 2, 3, 6, 107, 110, 115, 123, 127, 132–3

Moratín, Leandro Fernández de 194
Moret, Segismundo 233
Moriscos 161
Morocco 78, 84, 93, 100, 104, 249, 252, 255, 266
   war 235–6, 241, 245
Morris, William 238
Motilla culture 12
motín of Esquilache 179, 182, 184
Mozarabs 71
Mudejars 83, 84–5, 95–6, 98
Mulva 32
Munda 27
Munich Agreement 263
Muniga (Mulva) 32
Münster 166
Murcia 3
Murciélago (the Bat) 92
Murillo, Bravo 212–13
music 65, 228, 238
Muslims, Islamic rule 1, 58, 61, 63–73, 77–80, 82, 83, 84–7, 92, 93, 95–8, 100, 103–4, 107, 152, 161, 162, 178
   bureaucratic state 65–6
   conversion 64–5
   court culture 65
   morerías (settlements) 98
Mussolini, Benito 251, 255, 267
Mycenaeans 12
mysticism 136–9

Nájera 105
Naples 131, 152, 166, 170, 174, 196
Narbonne 42, 44, 61
Narváez, Ramon María 207, 211–12, 217
National Assembly 241
National Block 250–1
National Catholic Agrarian Confederation 233
National Militia 208, 211
National Movement 264, 274, 278
National Political Union 240
National Reconciliation 271
nationalism, nationalists 6, 7, 120, 207, 215–16, 250–1, 254–8, 261–2, 263–4, 265
   regional 271, 275, 279–80, 281, 282
NATO 278, 282
Navarre 66, 71, 73, 76, 80, 99, 111, 120, 176, 198, 231, 233, 280
   annexation (1512) 152
Navarro, Carlos Arias 274
navy, naval operations 106, 117, 155, 156, 158, 161, 164, 177, 255
Nazis 264, 266

Neanderthals 11
Negrín, Juan 259–61, 263
neighbourhood associations 271
Nero, Emperor 34
Netherlands 131, 143, 145, 148, 155, 158, 161–7, 170, 173–4
'neutral' state 233
Nin, Andreu 259
new aristocracy, 19th-century 217
New Castile 8
'New David' 92
Nicolson, Harold 235
Nijmegen, Peace of (1678) 170
Non-Intervention Agreement (Aug. 1936) 256, 263
Normans 76–7
North Africa 12, 20, 35, 42, 60, 61, 92, 98, 152, 158, 188, 267
North Sea 164
Nueva Planta (1716) 176
Numantia 26–7, 189
nutrition 270

October revolution (1934) 249, 250, 251, 255
O'Donnell, Leopoldo 207, 213–14
oil crisis (1973) 273
Old Testament 15, 37, 79, 140
Olite, Navarre 46
Olivade, Pablo de 6, 7, 180, 183, 187, 189
Olivares, Count of 7, 146, 150, 166
olive cultivation 4
olive oil 15, 34, 35, 96, 186, 187
Olmedo, battle of 111
Oña, Pedro de 134
opera 238
Opus Dei 268
Oran 152
Orense family 131
Organic Law (1967) 273
'orientalizing period' of prehistory 16
Ortega y Casset, José 225, 226, 239
Ortiz, Alonso 122
Osca 27
Osnabrück 166
Ostrogoths 44–5, 50
Ottoman empire 161
Ottonian dynasty 75
Oviedo 66–8, 87, 180, 196

'pact of blood' 365
Palace of Music 238
Palafox, Juan de 170
Palestine 77, 95
Pamplona 27, 71, 77, 89
Papacy 76

Papal States 179
paper 124
parias (tribute payments) 73, 97
Paris 1, 204, 217, 238
   revolution (1830) 204
Partido Nacionalista Vasco 276
Pasamonte, Jerónimo de 136
patria chica 8, 133
patronato universal 178
Paul, Count 55, 59
Paul, St 34, 36
Paulus Orosius: *Anti-Pagan History* 37
Pavia, General 220
Pelayo, king 189
penal labour 266
peninsulares 219
Périgord 76
Perpignan 106, 152
Peru 154
peseta, devaluation of 248, 269
Peter I, king of Castile (1350–69)('the Cruel')
   104–6
Peter III, king of Aragon (1276–85) 100–2
Peter the Venerable: *The Abominable Heresy or
   Sect of the Saracens* 86
Philip II, king 7, 123, 124, 127, 129, 131, 133,
   134, 140–2, 143, 145, 155, 156–9, 161,
   162–5, 167
Philip III, king 124, 133, 145, 164
Philip IV, king 7, 123, 124, 143, 144, 149, 150,
   156, 166
Philip V, king 171, 173–4, 176–7, 178, 180,
   181, 184, 204
Philippines 134, 143, 162, 203, 224
philosophy, philosophers 86, 171, 180, 189,
   212, 218, 223, 225, 226, 229
Phocaeans 13, 18
Phoenicians 13–16, 17, 28
phone-tapping 278
physics 180
Pi y Margall, Francisco 220
Picasso, Pablo 230, 238
pilgrims 75, 77, 232
Piquer, Andrés 180
Pisa 96
Pissarro, Camille 238
Pius IX, pope 211
Pizarro, Francisco 153–4
Pla de Nadal 46–7
Pliny 34
Plymouth 106
PNV (Basque nationalist party) 229
Poema de Mio Cid 77
poetry, poets 54, 65, 77, 99, 100, 104, 111,
   115, 127, 132, 136, 139, 189, 229, 253, 257

police brutality 276
Polybius 23
Pompaelo (Pamplona) 27
Pompey 27
Ponce de Léon, Don Rodrigo 92
Popular Army 258, 261, 262, 263
Popular Front 250–2
Popular Party 279–80
population 98, 131, 132, 180, 183–4, 186, 236,
   238, 242
porcelain 186
Portland cement 236
Portsmouth 106
Portugal 25, 31, 39, 41–2, 66, 69, 70, 76, 78,
   80, 82, 83, 96, 104, 106, 113, 121, 124,
   143, 148, 150, 156, 162, 166, 170, 173,
   179, 180, 194–5, 197, 199, 202, 256
Post Office 208
postal services 155
Potosí mines 158
POUM (*Partido Obrero de Unificación Marxista*)
   259
Pozo Moro, tomb of 16
Prat de la Riba, Enric 227–8
Premonstratensians 77
press 189, 191, 197, 199, 201, 217–18, 235,
   239
   freedom 218, 223, 240
   law (1966) 273
pretendientes 208
Prieto, Indalecio 229, 242, 250, 251
Prim, Juan 207, 214–15, 220
Primo de Rivera, General Miguel 236, 240–1,
   242, 246, 251
printing 124
Priscillian of Avila 37
privatization 279
privilegio de la Unim (1287) 102
Procopius 47
Progressive party 207–11, 213–15, 216, 220,
   223, 236
pronunciamentos 201, 207–8, 209, 211, 213,
   215, 220, 223, 236, 242
propaganda 266
prostitution 232
protectionism 2
Protestants, Protestantism 1, 7, 8, 99, 136–9,
   140–2, 162, 178, 218–19, 243
Proust, Marcel 239
PSOE (*Partido Socialista Obrero Español*)
   229–30, 242, 247, 278–9
   corruption 278
   and secret police 278
psychological programming 266
Publius Cornelius Scipio (Scipio Africanus)

21–3
pueblo 8
Puerta de Sevilla, Carmona 20
Puerto Rico 203, 216, 224
Pujol, Jordi 278
Punic communities, Punic influence 13–15,
    16, 18, 20, 23, 28
Punic Wars:
    First 18
    Second 20, 23
Pyrenees 12, 23, 27, 39, 44, 54, 61, 66, 69, 75,
    152, 181, 192, 194, 197
    Peace of (1659) 167
pyrite resources 215

Qart Hadasht (New Carthage) 18
Quevedo, Francisco de 170
Quintana, Manuel 189, 194, 198
Quintilian 34
quinto 158
Quintus Fulvius Nobilior 26
Quintus Sertorius 27

racism 229
Radical-CEDA coalition 250
Radical Republicans 226, 249, 250
railways 5, 214, 215–16, 217, 234, 236, 237
Ramiro II, king 71
Ramón Berenguer I, count 73
ranching 82, 87
Rastatt, Treaty of 174
Real Madrid 272
Reccared, king 46, 53, 55, 57, 60
Reccared II, king 56
Reccesuinth, king 47, 57–9
    and *Lex Visigothorum* 58, 60
Reccopolis 46
Rechiarius, king 42–4
Rechila, king 42
Reconquest (*Reconquista*) 1, 3, 6, 63, 66, 78,
    81, 87, 91–2, 93, 98, 104, 115, 152
redistribution:
    of land 254
    of wealth 245
Reformation 99, 100, 139, 140, 142, 143
Reformist Republican party 226
regenerationism 224–5, 232, 241
regidores 182, 199
regional autonomy 243, 249, 250, 254, 278,
    281
Regoyes, Dario de 238
reguli (petty kings) 17
religion:
    'official' 139–42
    'popular' 132–6

remensa movements 110
repartimiento 98
Republican party 209, 218, 220, 223, 225,
    226, 233
republican revival, republicanism 225–6, 228,
    229, 230, 243–52, 253, 254, 255, 256,
    257, 259–64, 266, 268
Reshef 16
reparto 4
Restoration 220–1, 223, 225, 228, 232, 233,
    245
retraimiento 214
Revolution (1854) 213–14, 221
Revolution (Sept. 1868) 215, 219–21, 223
revolution over war, primacy of 254–5
Rhode (Rosas) 13
Riego, Rafael de 200–1, 203
Rijswijk, Peace of (1697) 170
Rilke, Rainer Maria 2
Rio Guadalete 13
Rio Tinto valley 15
Ripoll, monastery 71
Ritz Hotel, Madrid 238
Rizo, Juan Pablo Mártir 129
roads 5, 27, 123, 183, 186, 214, 238, 241
Robert of Ketton 86
Robert the Bruce 92, 93
Rocroi, battle of 143
Roderic, king 61
Rodrigo, Archbishop 81
Rodrigo Díaz (El Cid) 73, 89
Rojas, Juan de 132
Rojo, General Vicente 264
Romanones, count of 221
Romans, Roman Empire 6, 18–21, 23–38,
    39–44, 46, 49, 54, 60, 61, 64, 65, 81, 87,
    99, 146
    arms and armour 24
    building projects 31–2
    calendar 25
    and Christianity 35–7
    and civic life 32–3, 35
    coloniae 31, 32
    commerce 34
    end of rule, legacies 37–8
    hospitalitas 42
    'peripheral imperialism' 24–5
    provinciae 23–4
    provincial bureaucracy 35
    'Romanization' 28–33
    villas and estates 35
Romantic movement 2, 8, 217
Rome 34, 41, 57, 93, 131
Ronda 32, 65
Rosendo, Bishop 71

Rousseau, Jean Jacques 2, 180
Royal Guipuzcoan Company of Caracas 184
Ruiz, Juan: *Libro de Buen Amor* 104
rural exodus, 1960s 4, 270
Ruskin, John 216
Russia 267
Rye 106

Sabadell 237
Sabora 32
Sacred Heart of Jesus, cult of 232
Sagasta, Práxedes Mateo 223
Sagrajas 78
Sagunto (Saguntum) 13, 20, 220
Sahagún, monastery 75
Sahara desert 64
St Ives 106
St Quentin, battle of (1557) 155
Salado, battle of 104
Salado, river 104
Salamanca 20, 47, 49, 76
    University 38, 89, 117–19, 189
Salamanca, bishop of 254
Salamanca, José de 217
Salazar, Oliveira 256
Salic Law 204
Salisbury, marquis of 217
Samos, monastery 71
Sancho IV, king of Navarre (1054–76) 73
Sancho IV, king of Castile (1284–95) 99, 100
San Juan de Baños, church 47, 58
San Juan de las Abadesas, nunnery 69–70
San Julián de los Prados (Santullano), church
    of 68
Sanjurjo, General José 248, 258
San Miguel, General 210
San Salvador de Valdediós, church of 68
Santander 261
San Vicente del Realejo, Tenerife 133
Santa Cruz, marquis of 164
Santiago de Compostela 75–6, 77, 89, 115
Santillana 134
Santo Domingo 192
Santo Niño de la Guardia 113–14
Saragossa 16, 53, 61, 66, 73, 77, 196
    Cortes of 102
Sardinia 84, 110, 174
Savoy 174
science 71, 86, 99, 117, 132, 171, 180, 181
Scipio Aemilianus 26
Scipio, Gnaeus Cornelius 20–3, 31, 38
Scotland 92, 176
Sculpture 17–18, 33, 65, 117–19, 123, 124
Sebastian, king of Portugal 162
Second Republic (1931–6) 7, 225, 226, 233,

242, 243–52, 253, 254, 255, 257, 259–64
    divisions within Republic 247
    government of the right 249
    obstacles to reform 246–7
    Popular Front 250–2
    reform from above 245–6
    response of the right 248–9
    secret police 278
Segeda 25–6
Segovia 32, 120, 129–30, 181
*Semanario de agricultura y artes dirigido a los
    parrocos* 194
Semanario erudito (journal) 190
Seneca the Elder 34
Seneca the Younger 34
señoríos 199, 200
Septimania 44, 55, 57, 59
Septimius Severus 35
Serge, Victor 231
Serrano, General Francisco 219–20
Serrano Suñer, Ramón 253, 266
settlement of land 3–4, 31, 69–70, 183
Seven Years War 175
Seville 15, 16, 28, 50, 51, 53, 61, 69, 82, 83,
    84–5, 87, 96, 98, 106, 131, 136, 167, 180,
    183, 184, 189, 196, 202
    Hospital de la Caridad 149
    Libro de Repartimiento 84
    University 180
sex 135, 136, 217
sherry trade 5, 216
shipping, maritime enterprise 5, 80, 84, 87,
    95, 96, 143, 156, 184–6, 192, 236
shipyards 236–7
Sicily 84, 93, 96, 100, 110, 166, 174, 186, 196
Sierra Morena 4, 15, 16, 23, 34, 183
Siete Partidas (law code) 99
Siglo de Oro (Golden Age) 5, 6, 115, 116–17
Siguenza 115
silk 71, 183, 186
Silos, monastery 75
Silvela, Francisco 224, 225
silver 15, 20, 23, 34, 59, 108, 117, 144–5, 148,
    154
Simancus 71
Sisbert, bishop of Toledo 55, 61
Sisebut, king 49, 55, 56, 60
Sisenand, king 57, 58
slaves 64, 154, 174
Smith, Adam 193, 209, 211
smuggling 174, 203–4
socialism, socialists 229–31, 245, 247, 248–9,
    250, 251, 254–5, 258, 263, 271, 274,
    278–9
Socialist Union 248

Sol, El 240
soledades 132
Soler, Miguel Cayetano 193
Solidaritat Catalan 228
solidarity movements 270–1
Soria 26
Soto, Hernando de 155
Sotomayor, Valladares de 189
South America 200
Southampton 106
Soviet Union 256, 258–9, 264
Spanish Foreign Legion 249
Spanish March 66, 71, 75
Spanish Succession, War of 173–4, 176, 178, 204
Spinola, General 166
Spirit of the Beehive (film) 273
Stabilization Plan (1959) 269
Stalin, Josef 256
'State of the Autonomies' 7
Strabo 16
strikes 229–30, 231, 234, 240, 247, 249, 251, 268, 270
student unrest 242, 268, 271
Suárez, Adolfo 274, 278
Sueves 37, 39, 42–4, 51
Suinthila, king 56–7
Suniefred, king 55
Supreme Court Junta 197–8
Supreme Junta of State 187, 191
surrealism 239
symbolism 239
syndicalism 231, 265
Syria 16, 18, 64, 77

tacitos 274
Tacitus 39
Tagus valley 12, 32, 64, 82
taifa states 6, 73, 78, 83, 89
  'Second Taifas' 79
Talavera 26
Tangier 96
Tanit 16, 18
Tarifa 100, 104
tariffs 239
Tarraco (Tarragona) 21
Tarragona 36, 37, 38, 77
'Tarshish' 15
Tarsus 15
Tartessian culture, 'Tartessos' 15–17
taxation 35, 41, 42, 81, 98, 103, 124, 131, 143–4, 149, 150, 155, 158, 177, 192, 209, 211, 239–40, 242, 245, 280
Teba de Ardales, battle of 92
Tejero, Colonel 275, 276

television ownership 270
Tenerife 133
Tenochtitlán 154
tercias reales 178
Teresa of Avila, St 134, 136, 139
tertulia 9
Terrasa 237
Teruel 261
textiles 5, 65, 71, 82, 183, 186, 187–8, 216, 236, 239
Thames, river 106
theatre 189
Theoderic II, king 42–4
Theodosius I (the Great) 37, 41
Theudis, general (later king) 45, 47, 48
Theudiscius, king 50
Theron, king 17
Thirty Years War 143, 145, 165–6, 176
Thomas of Villanueva, St 139
Tiberius Sempronius Gracchus 25, 27
Timbuktu 64
Titian (Tiziano Vecellio) 182
  Spain coming to the Aid of Religion 139
Titus Didius 26–7
Toledo 32, 50, 58, 61, 77, 81, 87, 113–14, 122, 123, 126, 135, 257–8
  Alcazar 257–8
  Fourth Council 54, 60
  Second Council 50
  see of 54
  synod (580) 53
  Third Council 50, 53, 55
Toletum (Toledo) 32
Tomar 80
Torrero, Father Diego Muñoz 198
torture 276
tourism 9, 76, 205, 269
trade unions 229–30, 232, 243, 247, 255, 257, 258, 265, 279
  military 235
Traditionalists 251
Trafalgar, battle of 194
'Tragic Week' (1909) 226, 233
Trajan 34
trams 238
Trebizond 84
Tridentine clerical elite 133, 225
Tromp, admiral 166
Trotskyites 259
Tujibid family 66
Tulga, king 56, 57
Tunis 84, 93, 96, 158, 161
Turdetanians 16–17, 24
Turks 139, 143, 155, 158, 161
turno pacífico 223, 233, 235

UGT (*Union General de Trabajadores*) 229–30, 234, 242
Ullastret, Catalonia 17
'Umar ibn Hafsun 65
Umayyad dynasty 64, 65
Unamuno, Miguel de 229, 242
unemployment 278, 279, 280
Union of the Democratic Centre 274
United Nations 268
United States 24, 219, 224, 256, 268
    bases in Spain 268
Universal Exhibition (Barcelona, 1888) 238
universal suffrage 274, 275
universities 117, 127, 155, 179, 180, 187, 189, 211, 232, 268, 271
University of Duesto, Bilbao 232
Urban II, pope 76, 77
Urgel 71
Urraca 70
Utrecht, Treaty of (1713) 174
Uztáriz, Gerónimo de 180

Vaccaei 24
Valdés, Juan Meléndez 189
Valdes Leal, Juan de 149
Valencia 3, 5, 7, 32, 46, 53, 76, 83, 87 89, 95, 102, 103, 106, 110, 131, 167, 171, 174, 176, 180, 186, 189, 196, 200, 226, 235, 241, 242, 259, 262, 269, 276
    Cortes 103
Valens, emperor 41
Valera, Diego de 127
vales reales 193, 194
válidos 124
Valladolid 98, 124, 131–2, 145
    tableaux (1428) 111
Vandals 37, 39, 41, 42, 50
    Hasding 42
    Siling 42
van Wyngaerde, Anton 129
Vatican 268
    Council, Second 270
Velasco family 130
Velasco, Don Fernando de 127
Velázquez, Diego 143, 182
    The Lances 166
Venezuela 184
Venice 83, 132, 161
'Venus, Hill of' 26
Vera, Rafael 278
Verdaguer, Jacint 229
Versailles 181, 187
Vespasian, emperor 28, 32, 34
Vicar of the Spains 35
Vicent, Father 232

Vienna 158, 173
Vigo 238
Vikings 76
Vilar, Pierre 5
Virgil 37
Viriathus 26
Visigoths 6, 38, 39, 41, 42–62, 63, 64, 65, 66–7, 77, 87
    and Arianism 49–50, 53
    building 46
    and Hispano–Romans 53
    and Jews 60
    legislative activity 58, 60
    literacy 49
    liturgical crowns 58–9
    rural life 46–9
    script 76
    slate documents 47–9
    unstable monarchy 50 ff.
    urban contraction 46
Vitoria 197, 200
Volciani 17
Voltaire 2, 180
Vouillé, battle of (507) 44

Wagner, Richard 238
Wales 215
Wamba, king 55, 59–60
Ward, Bernardo 180
water-sellers 217
welfare state, reform of 279
Wellington, Duke of 9
Westphalia, Treaty of 167
West Indies 184, 194
WEU (Western European Union) 282
wheat 154, 186, 250, 261
White Legend 2
William of Nassau, Prince of Orange 162, 164
Winchelsea 106
wine 15, 24, 186, 187, 189
Witteric, king 55
Wittiza, king 61
women :
    in employment 238–9
    voting rights 245
women's organizations 265
wool trade 5, 24, 82–3, 183, 186, 237
Workers' Alliance 249
workers' associations 209, 229, 251; *see also* trade unions
Workers' Commissions 270
World War I 143, 230, 231, 234, 237, 246
World War II 263, 264, 265, 266–7

xenodochia 46

yellow fever 194, 203
Young, Arthur 188
youth organizations 265
yunteros 4

Zacatecas mines 158
Zamora, Niceto Aicalá 245, 247, 248, 250
Zorita de los Canes 46
Zurburán, Francisco de 143